The Handbook of
CHINESE
HOROSCOPES

ALSO BY THEODORA LAU

Best-Loved Chinese Proverbs

The Handbook of
CHINESE
HOROSCOPES
Third Edition

Theodora Lau

Calligraphy by Kenneth Lau

HarperPerennial
A Division of HarperCollinsPublishers

HarperCollins books may be purchased for educational, business, or sales promotional use. For information please write: Special Markets Department, HarperCollins Publishers, Inc., 10 East 53rd Street, New York, NY 10022.

FIRST EDITION

Designed by Caitlin Daniels

Library of Congress Cataloging-in-Publication Data

Lau, Theodora.
    The handbook of Chinese horoscopes / Theodora Lau ; calligraphy by Kenneth Lau. —3rd ed.
      p.   cm.
    ISBN: 0-06-273370-2 (pbk.)
    1. Astrology, Chinese. I. Title.
BF1714.C5L38 1995
133.5—dc20   95-21524

98 99 00 01 RRD 20 19 18 17 16 15 14 13 12 11

For Jonathan, Michele & Laura

Contents

Introduction: The Animal That Hides in Your Heart

The Origin and Nature of the Lunar Signs

The Chinese lunar calendar originated with the Emperor Huang Ti, who introduced the first cycle in 2637 B.C., the 6lst year of his reign. A complete cycle of 60 lunar years is made up of five twelve-year cycles. The seventy-eighth sixty-year cycle, the one we are currently in, started February 2, 1984 and will bring us into the next millenium, ending in the year 2044.

The appointment of an animal sign to each of the twelve years is attributed to a legend about the Lord Buddha, who had summoned all the animals to come bid him farewell before he departed the Earth. Only twelve showed up and, as a token of his appreciation, he named a year for each animal in the order of its arrival. First came the Rat, then the Ox, the Tiger, Rabbit, Dragon, Snake, Horse, Sheep, Monkey, Rooster, Dog and, finally, the Boar. The animal that rules the year of your birth is said to exercise a profound influence over your life. Hence, the Chinese have coined the saying, "This is the animal that hides in your heart."

There is also a secondary animal that hides in your heart—your ascendant sign. In the lunar calendar, the day begins at 11 P.M. and the twenty-four hours are divided into twelve sections of two hours each. Each section is again ruled by one of the animal signs (see Table 5). As in Western solar astrology, the sign which rules the time of birth is the ascendant and helps shape the personality. This birth hour influence can be very strong. For example, an aggressive Sheep person may prove to have been born between 3 and 5 A.M., in the hours governed by the Tiger; on the other hand an uncharacteristically quiet Rat person was probably born between 9 and 11 A.M., the hours ruled by the introverted Snake.

During the complete sixty-year cycle, each of the animal signs (also referred to as the twelve Earth Branches) is combined with the five main elements: Metal, Water, Wood, Fire and Earth (see Table 2). These five elements are further divided into active and passive sides (or stems). The active side is identified as positive—yang, or male; the passive—yin, or female. The Rat, Tiger, Dragon, Horse, Monkey and Dog (the odd-numbered signs) belong to the positive yang. The Ox, Rabbit, Snake, Sheep, Rooster and Boar (the even-numbered signs) are negative yin (see Table 4).[1]

Besides the element assigned to a year, which changes continuously (see Table 2), each of the twelve Lunar Earth Branches has a fixed element and season (see Table 4).

The only element missing from Chinese astrology that is featured in the Western horoscopes is: AIR. However, the Air element is prominently utilized in the Chinese art of Feng Shui[2] and is loosely referred to as the "Feng" or Wind. Air is universally described by the Chinese as "Ch'i" or the lifeforce.

The ideal natal chart based on Chinese horoscopes should contain all the elements. For example, let us say a person was born in the year of the Fire Rat, 1936. The element of that year is Fire and the Rat sign has Water as its fixed element. Our subject was born in the month of the Tiger (see Table 7) whose fixed element is Wood. Finally, the time of birth was between 5 P.M. to 7 P.M., the hours of the Rooster whose fixed element is Metal. Since the Earth element is automatically generated by the four others, this native's elements are considered to be "complete or balanced."

Element deficiencies in the natal chart should be remedied. In China, the usual way to do this was to compose a name for the child which contained the character of the missing element. So, if the Metal

---

[1]In this context, "negative" does not mean bad or undesirable. The positive yang and negative yin forces both have good and bad aspects. A person born under a positive sign will be more effective if he proceeds in an active way. It would be "negative" (in the pejorative sense) for him to proceed passively. Similarly, a person born under a negative sign is at his best behaving in a passive or nonaggressive manner. The first is compelled to be a doer and innovator; the second excels as a thinker and negotiator. Generally, yang people are more spontaneous, yin people more reflective and intuitive.

[2]For more on this subject, please read Theodora Lau's upcoming book on Feng Shui, entitled *Harmony of the Forces*.

element was missing, the child would have the Gold character in his or her name. Likewise, if the Water element was missing, adding the character for lake, rain, clouds, would incorporate Water into the child's life composition. Characters for trees, plants and flowers symbolize the addition of the Wood element. Characters for flames, the sun or burning do the same for Fire. For more on the elements and how they affect the natal chart, see "Understanding the Five Elements" p. xxix, and also the sections on the elements in the chapters on animal signs.

The division of the sixty-year cycle into five smaller twelve-year cycles is also significant. Twelve was the age when childhood was considered over, since adolescence begins with the teens years. Someone who had completed two twelve year cycles was usually married and a parent. At thirty-six and forty-eight, most people were, respectively raising a family and preparing for the third generation. In the context of the Chinese lunar cycles, the charming Western custom of naming children after grandparents is more meaningful than we realize. If the grandparent is sixty years older than his or her namesake, then the lunar calendar will have come full cycle—both persons will have been born under the same animal sign and under the influence of the same element of the year. In China and Japan, one's sixtieth birthday was a very special event and celebrated with as many family members as possible. If a family had four generations under one roof or at a banquet, it was considered a great blessing.

It is interesting to note that countries are formed under lunar signs as well—and their activities, choice of allies and form of government will display qualities common to their lunar birth sign. China, for example, was formed anew in 1949, the year of the Ox. True to form, she has progressed largely through her own hard work and the dedication of her people. China will have different fortunes in a given year than, say, France, 1958 (the 5th Republic), a Dog; or Canada, 1867 (British North American Act), a Rabbit; or colorful Hong Kong, born in 1842 (the Treaty of Nanking), a Tiger. Japan and Germany were formed anew in 1945 under the industrious Rooster, and Israel was born in 1948, the year of the innovative and progressive Rat. And is it a coincidence that America, born 1776, the year of the Monkey, is renowned for her inventiveness, communications skills and leadership in commerce?

While the Soviet Union was born following the communist revolution of 1917, the year of the Fire Snake, it was reborn as the Russian Federation in December of 1991, the year of the Sheep. Will the new Russia be more conciliatory and peace-loving? Only time can tell. However, it is noteworthy to point out that Mikhail Gorbachev was also born in the year of the Sheep, exactly 60 years earlier. Boris Yeltsin, on the other hand, was born in the Year of the Horse. As you read the chapter on the Horse, you will find that Yeltsin has displayed many of this sign's qualities—both the positive and the negative!

HOW TO USE THIS BOOK

To get the most out of this book, you must study not only the animal of the year in which you were born (see Table 2), but several other factors as well: your ascendant—the lunar sign that rules the hour of your birth (see Table 5); the Western sun sign corresponding to your moon sign (see Table 7); the element of your birth year (see Table 2) as well as your sign's fixed element (see Table 4); and the animal that rules the month of your birth (see Table 7). By integrating all these factors and assessing their effects, you should discover—if you don't already know—the person you truly are. And, by analyzing the horoscopes of others, you may discover the people they truly are as well.

Beside being able to understand your total self, you may be able to predict the course and nature of your personal and professional relationships in any given year. The knowledge gained by analyzing your horoscope may also shed light on why you dislike certain people, while with others you have an almost instant rapport.

The section in each chapter on how a particular sign fares over different years, as well as the marriage combinations and the compatibility tables, serve as a general guide only. The assumption in these sections is that we are dealing with pure or strongly dominant lunar signs. For instance, a Snake born during the hours of the Snake is a "pure" sign. However, a Dragon born during the hours of the Rabbit will usually maintain his more "dominant" Dragon characteristics. On the other hand, a Sheep born during the hours of the Tiger may display the "stronger" Tiger traits of his ascendant sign and could be compatible with a Dog, which would not normally be the case according to the compatibility tables.

That is why when consulting the marriage combinations and compatibility tables, you should keep in mind other factors in the horoscope that may affect the relationship. For instance, most people display a strong affinity for persons born under their ascendant, even if that sign is the most incompatible with their own birth sign. Thus, a Boar lady born during the hours of the Snake may get along extremely well with Snake persons, even though the compatibility chart shows that a Snake is the worst possible partner for a Boar.

When a person is born during the hours of the sign most incompatible with his birth sign, it is often very difficult (even for experienced fortune readers) to predict what traits are most likely to come to the fore. Take, for instance, a Rooster born during the hours of the Rabbit. He may turn out to be an extremely shy Rooster secretly harboring grand designs and lofty ambitions, or a loquacious one who is shrewd, diplomatic and strictly noncommittal in spite of all the noise he makes. Needless to say, such persons are usually complicated in nature and volatile in temperament. A sure way to determine which sign dominates such a person is to observe the lunar signs of the people he prefers to work with or is attracted to. He will probably be drawn to persons with a close affinity to his ascendant, even if they do not match his birth sign.

Although persons with conflicting ascendants and birth or month signs do experience more inner conflict and possess a great many opposing traits, it is my observation that such people often turn out to be excellent mediators and intermediaries. This is because they understand how opposite sides think and work and so, consequently, they make the best go-betweens. Such persons excel in bridging the differences between signs which otherwise could not get along together. The world would be a poorer place without these invaluable middle men!

Basically, Chinese lunar horoscopes depict a kaleidoscope of relationships which are based on the interaction among signs or combinations with the highest likelihood of success. Working out variations with high affinity or the least possibility of discord has proven effective for the matchmakers who were indispensable in Chinese society. Success was considered synonymous with good or workable relationships. Everyone had to have "guan xi" or special relationships in order to get things done.

In other words, who you know or have good relations with is more important than what you know. It is relationships that open doors for us. Relationships bring us in contact with people who can effect changes in our lives or make us part of a bigger, better team. Relationships foster synergy and symbiotic relationships. Relationships help us manage the unmanageable. Relationships bring the unreachable within our grasp and foster ties that were previously impossible. Relationships are influence. It may sound simplistic, but in the end, everything boils down to good, working, harmonious relationships. Society cannot exist without them. In the final analysis, we are all social animals.

Modern society has created all kinds of new names for relationships. Business management calls them "networking". Connecting with the right parties is the major aim. The link-up of a network or networks is essential to making it in today's corporate world. We are all encouraged to send emissaries to feel out the competition or to get some feedback on the likes and dislikes of others before making any move. Lobbying is a way of life in the American Congress. When relations break down, we resort to arbitrators to work out our differences before it is too late. Whether we are busy mending broken fences of friendship, building new communications bridges, making new connections to other networks or simply expanding our sphere of influence, we are employing the basic principles of trying to establish good relationships.

The knowledge acquired in this book should help you to both make and maintain good relationships. It may enable you to dismiss the occasional crankiness of your Dog boss, and deal with the changeable and capricious mind of a Horse client, the domineering but expansive ways of a Dragon friend or the serene but skeptical attitude of a Snake.

You may be surprised to find that your local handyman, who is capable of fixing everything, was indeed born in the year of the dexterous Monkey, and that your slow, sure and conservative banker just happens to belong to the year of the reliable Ox. Again, you may be more patient with that annoying associate who is always the first to complain and cry wolf, when you discover he was born in the year of the Sheep. And you may laugh to learn that the business colleague who wears such atrocious ties was born in the year of the flamboyant Rooster.

Perhaps after reading this book, you may believe enough to listen to the wise counsel of the Snake, look for sympathy from the gentle Sheep, go along with the clever schemes of the Monkey, have fun with the ever-youthful and carefree Horse, rely on the Rabbit's good taste and unerring diplomacy, or depend on the strength of the indomitable Dragon. You may get your way by humoring the critical Rooster, reasoning with the fair-minded Dog, joining forces with the optimistic Tiger, or bargaining with the indefatigable, cost-conscious Rat. It's up to you to use the knowledge gained to make life easier and more productive for yourself and others.

As a final note, I'd like to point out that although the Western calendar, which is based on the movements of the sun, is more consistent and easier to follow, the East's lunar calendar is more accurate in registering the changes in the seasons and the growth of all life in the universe.[3] Chinese farmers originally used the calendar as an almanac for selecting the most favorable days of each year to sow and reap their crops. And, long before modern science developed ways to forecast the weather, the Chinese relied heavily on the horoscope to predict their rains. (This holds true even at the present time.) Gradually, over the years the calendar began to be consulted for such things as the most auspicious days to visit the barber, start building a home, get married and, of course, to figure out when to hold the numerous Chinese festivals. An authentic lunar calendar contains all the Do's and Don't's for each day of the year, down to the most favorable and unfavorable hours of each day. This complete calendar-almanac is still published yearly in Hong Kong and Taiwan. It requires a special technical knowledge to interpret it, but no self-respecting fortune teller would be found without it.

I have written this book based on my own research and empirical observations and theories. Chinese horoscopes have endured through countless generations. They are made up of an amalgamation of popular beliefs, legends and mythology, as well as the factual material contained in the lunar almanac.

I hope my interpretations and explanations will serve to bring you new insights into a subject rich in self-analysis, understanding of others, and acknowledgement of the value of compromise and cooperation in relationships.

I would like to take this opportunity to express my deep appreciation to the thousands of readers around the globe, from Alaska to Zimbabwe, who have written or spoken to me over the last fifteen years. Their questions, requests, suggestions, corrections and even arguments about this fascinating subject have been an endless source of inspiration to me. This valuable interaction has helped me more than they can imagine. I am grateful for all their comments, as I could not have learned or grown without them.

To my readers, past and present, I dedicate this new edition.

TABLES AND CHARTS

1. THE LUNAR SIGNS FROM 1900 TO 2007

Rat	1900	1912	1924	1936	1948	1960	1972	1984	1996
Ox	1901	1913	1925	1937	1949	1961	1973	1985	1997
Tiger	1902	1914	1926	1938	1950	1962	1974	1986	1998
Rabbit	1903	1915	1927	1939	1951	1963	1975	1987	1999
Dragon	1904	1916	1928	1940	1952	1964	1976	1988	2000
Snake	1905	1917	1929	1941	1953	1965	1977	1989	2001[1]
Horse	1906	1918	1930	1942	1954	1966	1978	1990	2002
Sheep	1907	1919	1931	1943	1955	1967	1979	1991	2003
Monkey	1908	1920	1932	1944	1956	1968	1980	1992	2004
Rooster	1909	1921	1933	1945	1957	1969	1981	1993	2005
Dog	1910	1922	1934	1946	1958	1970	1982	1994	2006
Boar	1911	1923	1935	1947	1959	1971	1983	1995	2007

2. THE EXACT LUNAR YEARS FROM 1900 TO 2007[2]

Sign	Exact Solar Dates	Element
Rat	January 31, 1900 to February 18, 1901	Metal (+)
Ox	February 19, 1901 to February 7, 1902	Metal (-)
Tiger	February 8, 1902 to January 28, 1903	Water (+)
Rabbit	January 29,1903 to February 15, 1904	Water (-)
Dragon	February 16, 1904 to February 3, 1905	Wood (+)
Snake	February 4, 1905 to January 24, 1906	Wood (-)
Horse	January 25, 1906 to February 12, 1907	Fire (+)
Sheep	February 13, 1907 to February 1, 1908	Fire (-)
Monkey	February 2, 1908 to January 21, 1909	Earth (+)
Rooster	January 22, 1909 to February 9, 1910	Earth (-)
Dog	February 10, 1910 to January 29, 1911	Metal (+)
Boar	January 30, 1911 to February 17, 1912	Metal (-)

[1] 21st century starts in the cusp of the Dragon and Snake years. Note: Please check your exact birth date against the more detailed listing that follows, since the years overlap between the Solar and Lunar calendars.

[2] Year Texts taken from the Chinese Ten Thousand Years (Perpetual) Lunar Calendar.

Rat	February 18, 1912 to February 5, 1913	Water (+)
Ox	February 6, 1913 to January 25, 1914	Water (-)
Tiger	January 26, 1914 to February 13, 1915	Wood (+)
Rabbit	February 14,1915 to February 2, 1916	Wood (-)
Dragon	February 3, 1916 to January 22, 1917	Fire (+)
Snake	January 23, 1917 to February 10, 1918	Fire (-)
Horse	February 11, 1918 to January 31, 1919	Earth (+)
Sheep	February 1, 1919 to February 19, 1920	Earth (-)
Monkey	February 20, 1920 to February 7, 1921	Metal (+)
Rooster	February 8, 1921 to January 27, 1922	Metal (-)
Dog	January 28, 1922 to February 15, 1923	Water (+)
Boar	February 16, 1923 to February 4, 1924	Water (-)
Rat	February 5, 1924 to January 24, 1925	Wood (+)
Ox	January 25, 1925 to February 12, 1926	Wood (-)
Tiger	February 13, 1926 to February 1, 1927	Fire (+)
Rabbit	February 2,1927 to January 22, 1928	Fire (-)
Dragon	January 23, 1928 to February 9, 1929	Earth (+)
Snake	February 10, 1929 to January 29, 1930	Earth (-)
Horse	January 30, 1930 to February 16, 1931	Metal (+)
Sheep	February 17, 1931 to February 5, 1932	Metal (-)
Monkey	February 6, 1932 to January 25, 1933	Water (+)
Rooster	January 26, 1933 to February 13, 1934	Water (-)
Dog	February 14, 1934 to February 3, 1935	Wood (+) *Wayne*
Boar	February 4, 1935 to January 23, 1936	Wood (-)
Rat	January 24, 1936 to February 10, 1937	Fire (+)
Ox	February 11, 1937 to January 30, 1938	Fire (-)
Tiger	January 31, 1938 to February 18, 1939	Earth (+)
Rabbit	February 19,1939 to February 7, 1940	Earth (-)
Dragon	February 8, 1940 to January 26, 1941	Metal (+)
Snake	January 27, 1941 to February 14, 1942	Metal (-)
Horse	February 15, 1942 to February 4, 1943	Water (+)
Sheep	February 5, 1943 to January 24, 1944	Water (-)
Monkey	January 25, 1944 to February 12, 1945	Wood (+)

May 16 1940

Rooster	February 13, 1945 to February 1, 1946	Wood (-)
Dog	February 2, 1946 to January 21, 1947	Fire (+)
Boar	January 22, 1947 to February 9, 1948	Fire (-)

Rat	February 10, 1948 to January 28, 1949	Earth (+)
Ox	January 29, 1949 to February 16, 1950	Earth (-)
Tiger	February 17, 1950 to February 5, 1951	Metal (+)
Rabbit	February 6, 1951 to January 26, 1952	Metal (-)
Dragon	January 27, 1952 to February 13, 1953	Water (+)
Snake	February 14, 1953 to February 2, 1954	Water (-)
Horse	February 3, 1954 to January 23, 1955	Wood (+)
Sheep	January 24, 1955 to February 11, 1956	Wood (-)
Monkey	February 12, 1956 to January 30, 1957	Fire (+)
Rooster	January 31, 1957 to February 17, 1958	Fire (-)
Dog	February 18, 1958 to February 7, 1959	Earth (+)
Boar	February 8, 1959 to January 27, 1960	Earth (-)

Rat	January 28, 1960 to February 14, 1961	Metal (+)
Ox	February 15, 1961 to February 4, 1962	Metal (-)
Tiger	February 5, 1962 to January 24, 1963	Water (+)
Rabbit	January 25, 1963 to February 12, 1964	Water (-)
Dragon	February 13, 1964 to February 1, 1965	Wood (+)
Snake	February 2, 1965 to January 20, 1966	Wood (-)
Horse	January 21, 1966 to February 8, 1967	Fire (+)
Sheep	February 9, 1967 to January 29, 1968	Fire (-)
Monkey	January 30, 1968 to February 16, 1969	Earth (+)
Rooster	February 17, 1969 to February 5, 1970	Earth (-)
Dog	February 6, 1970 to January 26, 1971	Metal (+)
Boar	January 27, 1971 to February 15, 1972	Metal (-)

Rat	February 16, 1972 to February 2, 1973	Water (+)
Ox	February 3, 1973 to January 22, 1974	Water (-)
Tiger	January 23, 1974 to February 10, 1975	Wood (+)
Rabbit	February 11, 1975 to January 30, 1976	Wood (-)
Dragon	January 31, 1976 to February 17, 1977	Fire (+)

Snake	February 18, 1977 to February 6, 1978	Fire (-)
Horse	February 7, 1978 to January 27, 1979	Earth (+)
Sheep	January 28, 1979 to February 15, 1980	Earth (-)
Monkey	February 16, 1980 to February 7, 1981	Metal (+)
Rooster	February 5, 1981 to January 24, 1982	Metal (-)
Dog	January 25, 1982 to February 12, 1983	Water (+)
Boar	February 13, 1983 to February 1, 1984	Water (-)

Rat	February 2, 1984 to January 19, 1985	Wood (+)
Ox	February 20, 1985 to February 8, 1986	Wood (-)
Tiger	February 9, 1986 to January 28, 1987	Fire (+)
Rabbit	January 29,1987 to February 16, 1988	Fire (-)
Dragon	February 17, 1988 to February 5, 1989	Earth (+)
Snake	February 6, 1989 to January 26, 1990	Earth (-)
Horse	January 27, 1990 to February 14, 1991	Metal (+)
Sheep	February 15, 1991 to February 3, 1992	Metal (-)
Monkey	February 4, 1992 to January 22, 1993	Water (+)
Rooster	January 23, 1993 to February 9, 1994	Water (-)
Dog	February 10, 1994 to January 30, 1995	Wood (+)
Boar	January 31, 1995 to February 18, 1996	Wood(-)

Rat	February 19, 1996 to February 6, 1997	Fire (+)
Ox	February 7, 1997 to January 27, 1998	Fire (-)
Tiger	January 28, 1998 to February 15, 1999	Earth (+)
Rabbit	February 16,1999 to February 4, 2000	Earth (-)
Dragon	February 5, 2000 to January 23, 2001	Metal (+)
Snake	January 24, 2001 to February 11, 2002	Metal (-)
Horse	February 12, 2002 to January 31, 2003	Water (+)
Sheep	February 1, 2003 to January 21, 2004	Water (-)
Monkey	January 22, 2004 to February 8, 2005	Wood (+)
Rooster	February 9, 2005 to January 28, 2006	Wood (-)
Dog	January 29, 2006 to February 17, 2007	Fire (+)
Boar	February 18, 2007 to February 6, 2008	Fire (-)

3. THE INTERACTION OF THE FIVE ELEMENTS

NORTH

WATER = WINTER
guards the kidney
controls the Fire element

WEST

METAL=AUTUMN
guards the lungs
controls Wood

CENTER

EARTH
guards the spleen
controls Water

EAST

WOOD=SPRING
guards the liver
controls Earth

SOUTH

FIRE=SUMMER
guards the heart
controls Metal

4. THE ANIMAL SIGNS AND THEIR FIXED ELEMENTS,[1] SEASONS AND STEMS

Stem	Sign	North (Winter)	East (Spring)	South (Summer)	West (Autumn)
-	Boar	Water			
+	Rat	Water			
-	Ox	Water			
+	Tiger		Wood		
-	Rabbit		Wood		
+	Dragon		Wood		
-	Snake			Fire	
+	Horse			Fire	
-	Sheep			Fire	
+	Monkey				Metal
-	Rooster				Metal
+	Dog				Metal

5. ASCENDANTS: THE TWELVE ANIMAL SIGNS AND THEIR HOURS

11 P.M. to 1 A.M.	Hours ruled by the Rat
1 A.M. to 3 A.M.	Hours ruled by the Ox
3 A.M. to 5 A.M.	Hours ruled by the Tiger
5 A.M. to 7 A.M.	Hours ruled by the Rabbit
7 A.M. to 9 A.M.	Hours ruled by the Dragon
9 A.M. to 11 A.M.	Hours ruled by the Snake
11 A.M. to 1 P.M.	Hours ruled by the Horse
1 P.M. to 3 P.M.	Hours ruled by the Sheep
3 P.M. to 5 P.M.	Hours ruled by the Monkey
5 P.M. to 7 P.M.	Hours ruled by the Rooster
7 P.M. to 9 P.M.	Hours ruled by the Dog
9 P.M. to 11 P.M.	Hours ruled by the Boar

[1]The Earth element is not present in the chart as it is reasoned that Earth is symbolically composed of the four other elements and therefore cannot be appointed to any one of the twelve lunar signs. Some Chinese astrologers take one representative from each of the other elements, the Ox from Water, the Dragon from Wood, the Sheep from Fire and the Dog from Metal and appoint Earth as their secondary element. Other fortune readers insist that the presence of all the four other elements in one's natal chart creates the missing Earth element.

6. THE MONTHS OF THE LUNAR SIGNS AND THEIR MATCHING SOLAR ASTROLOGICAL SIGNS

Have you ever wondered why Western astrological signs fall on odd days of the month instead of simply on the 1st or 30th? Looking into the lunar calendar, I found that it is divided into twenty-four sections which were originally used as a guide for agriculture. In matching the closest dates of these twenty-four sections or stems with the Western calendar, one finds that they coincide with the twelve astrological signs of the West. The twelve animal signs are also assigned a month in this calendar, so we can readily match Eastern lunar signs with Western solar signs.

The twelve animal signs or Earth Branches are also each assigned a month of their own in the lunar calendar. Thus, we can match a Western zodiac sign with its Eastern counterpart by the months each occupy.

LUNAR SIGN	SOLAR SIGN	CORRESPONDING DATES
1st Rat =	Sagittarius	22nd November–21st December
2nd Ox =	Capricorn	22nd December–20th January
3rd Tiger =	Aquarius	21st January–19th February
4th Rabbit=	Pisces	20th February–20th March
5th Dragon =	Aries	21st March–19th April
6th Snake =	Taurus	20th April–20th May
7th Horse =	Gemini	21st May–21st June
8th Sheep =	Cancer	22nd June–21st July
9th Monkey =	Leo	22nd July–21st August
10th Rooster =	Virgo	22nd August–22nd September
11th Dog =	Libra	23rd September–22nd October
12th Boar =	Scorpio	23rd October–21st November

7. LONG AND SHORT LUNAR YEARS AND THE INFLUENCE OF THE LI CHUN

"Short" lunar years are made up of 12 months of 29 days.

"Long" lunar years or "leap" years have 13 months of 29 days each.

Because the lunar month is shorter than the solar month by one day each month, every 29 months, an extra month is added to that year to create a lunar leap year.

The first day of Spring in the Gregorian calendar is termed the Li Chun, the "eyes of Spring" in the Lunar Almanac. When Chinese New Year comes before the Li Chun, it is said the year has seen the first day of Spring. If the lunar year begins after the first day of Spring and terminates before the next Li Chun on the following year, then such a year is said to be a "blind" year. Often, a lunar year may begin after the first day of Spring on the Solar Calendar, which is usually on the 4th or 5th of February, but it could catch up on the following year and end after the first day of Spring, giving it the symbolic "eyes" of Spring, which is considered by the Chinese as a sort of hindsight and, better than no sight at all. To be truly "blind", a year must miss the first day of Spring at both its beginning and at its end. Blind years are generally not auspicious for getting married or starting a business.

1. Example of a year with double "eyes" of Spring:
Wood Boar = January 31, 1995 to February 18, 1996. This is a lunar leap year and sees February 4th (the first day of Spring) once in 1995 and again in 1996.
2. Example of a year with "eyes" of Spring at the end of the year.
Fire Rat = February 19, 1996 to February 6, 1997
3. Example of a blind year with no first day of Spring:
Fire Ox = February 7, 1997 to January 27, 1998

Special Section

UNDERSTANDING THE FIVE ELEMENTS

A fundamental part of Oriental philosophy is the interrelationship and interaction among the five basic elements of which the universe is composed: metal, water, wood, fire and earth. Each of these is divided into Conducive and Controlling relationships. These elements are interdependent. Each is controlled by another while contributing to the existence of a different element. See Table 3.

CONDUCIVE RELATIONSHIPS

From Metal we get Water

Metal is usually represented by the Chinese symbol for gold, but in this context metal indicates a vessel or container for holding liquids, so we can say that metal traps water. In another sense, metal is the only element that will change into a liquid when heated to a high temperature. And when it resolidifies, the metal is in a much purer state.

From Water we get Wood

Water here means the rain or dew that makes plant life flourish, producing wood in the process. Wood is dependent on water for life and growth.

From Wood we get Fire

Fire cannot exist by itself but is produced by burning wood. Also, fire is generated by rubbing together two pieces of wood.

From Fire we get Earth

Symbolically, fire reduces everything to ashes, which become part of the earth again and will serve to nourish life.

From Earth we get Metal

All metal has to be extracted from the earth in which it resides.

CONTROLLING RELATIONSHIPS

Metal is controlled by Fire

Metal can only be melted and forged into something useful by the application of great heat.

Fire is controlled by Water

Nothing will put out a fire as quickly as water.

Water is controlled by Earth

Earth directs the flow of water. We dig canals to irrigate fields and build dikes to keep out water. Earth absorbs water as well as contains it.

Earth is controlled by Wood

Trees and their roots hold the soil together and draw nourishment from the earth. Without the helpful presence of wood, the Earth would erode or dissipate.

Wood is controlled by Metal

Even the largest tree can be felled by the metal blade of an axe. Metal cuts wood into useful pieces. We need metal to prune a tree's dead branches and help wood rejuvenate.

According to this philosophy, no one element can be called the strongest or the weakest. Like the yin and yang, they are forever interdependent and always equal in strength. They are eternally joined in the chain of life that brings about their existence. There is no power or struggle for dominance. Each has its own place and function.

Even in the human body, these five elements maintain their reciprocal relationships. In Chinese medicine and acupuncture, the elements rule the five major organs of the body. Metal is linked to the lungs, Fire controls the heart, Water is associated with the kidneys, Earth rules the spleen and pancreas, and Wood is identified with the liver.

So when a Chinese doctor, herbalist or acupuncturist treats an illness, he has to keep these interrelations in mind. For example, when the Earth (pancreas) is affected, the Metal (lungs) are weakened, too. If the Water (kidney) malfunctions, then it cannot produce its counterpart, Wood. And, consequently, the Wood organ, the liver, will begin to deteriorate.

METAL ELEMENT

Its color is white, season is autumn, weather is dry; it is associated with the sense of hearing and its body organ is the lung.

Positive Metal is the yang or active part; it can be identified as a sword which can cause bodily harm or a surgeon's knife which must cut to heal.

Negative Metal is the yin or passive side; it can be represented by a cooking pot, metal container, gong or musical instrument, jewelry, work of art, or any rounded metallic shape that is neither pointed nor sharp like a weapon is.

People born in a year controlled by the Metal element will be as rigid and resolute in expression as their particular signs permit. They are guided by strong feelings and will pursue their objectives with intensity and little hesitation. Sustained by their convictions, they are capable of prolonged effort to get what they want. They are very success-oriented and determined.

These persons are not easily swayed or influenced to change a course once they have decided on it, even by hardships, drawbacks and initial failures. Whatever constancy and perseverance their native lunar signs contain will be greatly enhanced by the Metal element. But they do have trouble letting go when situations become unfeasible and can be unreasonably stubborn about their fixations.

They prefer to handle their problems alone and will not appreciate interference or unsolicited assistance. They map out their own destinies, clear their own paths and set their own goals without outside help.

Although they may appear inflexible and coldly self-reliant, persons ruled by Metal can conduct electricity; their strong impulses and generative powers will be felt by everyone they come in contact with, thereby bringing about the changes and transformation they desire.

They have strong monetary and accumulative instincts and will use these traits to insist on having their own way. Often, they are unbending and opinionated and will break off a good relationship because others do not heed their wishes or conform to their will.

WATER ELEMENT

Its color is blue, season is winter, weather is cold; it is associated with the sense of sight and its body organ is the kidney.

Positive Water is a wave or moving current while negative Water is still or ebbing. Active or yang water pushes forward relentlessly and is a fearsome force to be reckoned with. Negative Water is the gentle rain or dew that nurtures and seeps into the soil. The positive can destroy, the negative nourishes.

People born in a year dominated by the Water element have a better than average ability to communicate and to advance their ideas by influencing the thoughts of others. Other people's minds are their vessels and help carry their creative ideas into positive action. They are basically ruled by sympathetic vibrations and convey their feelings and emotions to the best degree that their native animal sign will permit.

They have a knack for noticing things that will become important and can accurately gauge future potentials. They set things into the orbit they desire by prodding others and utilizing their talents and resources. However, they know how to be unobtrusive in their persistence and will never make others feel they are being imposed upon. In this manner, like their element, Water, they will be able to wear away the strongest rocks of opposition by their silent but unceasing efforts. Because these people would rather infiltrate than dominate, they will know how, when and whom to approach about any given subject. They have the talent for making people desire what they desire, thus achieving their goals in a sure but indirect way. They like to propel instead of compel others into motion.

Because of their awareness and flexibility, they are fluid like their element. In their negative states, such people tend to be too conciliatory and will take the easiest route open to them. At their worst, they will be inconstant and passive and lean too much on others for support. Thus, they sabotage their basic abilities. To succeed, they must be more assertive and use their immense power of persuasion to turn their plans into reality. Others would be wise to be guided by their intuitions.

WOOD ELEMENT

Its color is green, season is spring, weather is windy; it is associated with the sense of smell and its body organ is the liver.

The positive stem of Wood is the fir tree and the negative, the bamboo. Firs and pines are green all year round while the passive, delicate and graceful bamboo is dormant in the winter but still very pliable and adaptable, with a surprising resilience and strength. Positive Wood is also symbolized by live branches, negative Wood by the lumber used to build things. Seeds are considered negative; flowers are positive. Each stem dominates one end of the life cycle of constant growth and renewal.

People born under the auspices of a Wood year value their ethics; they have high morals and a good deal of self-confidence. They know the intrinsic value of things and their interests are wide and varied. Expansive and cooperative by nature, they will like to do things on a grand scale. Wood natives possess executive personalities because they can apportion and separate matters into the correct categories and work orders. Their progressiveness and generosity enable them to take on large projects, long-term or sizable developments or prolonged scientific studies—definitely not one-man ventures.

They have the ability to convince others to join forces with them. They branch out rapidly and diversify into as many fields as possible, being people who advocate constant growth and renewal. They know how to share whatever rewards they reap by these collective efforts with all who justly deserve a piece of the corporate pie. Their innate goodwill and compassionate understanding of how others think and operate will enable them to rise to fortunate positions. Wood personalities will find support and finances whenever and wherever they need them, because others will have faith in their ability to turn information and ideas into profit.

Their chief shortcoming is a tendency to bite off more than they can chew and thereby push things to the breaking point. Often, they may not be able to finish what they start if they spread their resources too thin. At such times, their plans could turn sour or they may drift from one project to another without achieving any satisfactory results.

FIRE ELEMENT

Its color is red, season is summer, weather is hot; it is associated with the sense of touch and its body organ is the heart.

The positive or active stem of this element is the forest fire or lava flow spewing from a volcanic eruption; the negative or passive stem is the fire from a stove used for cooking or the flame of a lamp giving beneficial light. The active side is spontaneous and hard to control. The passive fire is easily directed to serve our needs. However, it is wise to remember that there is a very small difference between the two. A (passive) lamp that is tipped over can easily become a (positive) forest fire. There is always the need to maintain that delicate balance in the yin and yang of every element.

Persons born in a year ruled by the Fire element will display above-average qualities of leadership; they are decisive and sure of themselves. Having the natural capacity to motivate people and bring ideas to fruition, Fire people tend to be more positive and aggressive than others of their particular sign. Hence, we can say that a Fire Horse is more aggressive than a Water Horse. Loving adventure and innovation, Fire personalities readily adopt bright new ideas and try to dominate others with their creativeness and originality. They do not fear risks and like to keep on the move and pioneer new trails. Danger may even excite them. The higher the stakes, the more motivated they are.

They are the doers—given to dynamic action and speech. However, they must keep a tight rein on their emotions as their forceful ambitions may make them inconsiderate and impatient when their wishes are not gratified quickly. The more a Fire person tries to achieve his ends by force or violence, the more he will encounter opposition and danger.

If a Fire person learns to hear others out before leaping into action and is able to sympathize with the views of fellow workers, he has the prerequisites to be a winner of the highest caliber. No one can exceed the Fire persons' intense drive but they must learn to curb their impulsiveness. Often, they are too outspoken for their own good. They only realize that a little courtesy and diplomacy go a long way when it is too late.

Like the element of their year, Fire, they constantly draw others to their warmth and brilliance and they will benefit all those who seek their company. But Fire persons can also turn destructive when they are angry and can cause irreparable damage when they fail to control or direct their energies properly.

EARTH ELEMENT

Its color is yellow, season is end of summer, weather is humid; it is associated with the sense of taste and its body organ is the spleen.

A hill or mountain is the positive side of the Earth element, a valley the passive or negative aspect. Raised ground is aggressive while depressions in the landscape and lower areas bring the opposite result. One journey, the positive, is uphill; the other, the passive, is downward. Hills are useful as lookout points but are subject to the fury of the winds and weather. The valleys or other lower areas are suitable for raising crops because they are protected and water can accumulate in them to nourish plant life.

People born under signs influenced by the Earth element are more concerned with functional and practical aspirations. They have excellent deductive powers and prefer solid and reliable pursuits. Blessed with foresight and a talent for organization, they are effective planners and administrators. They will put whatever available resources they have to optimum use and are wise and prudent in financial affairs. Intelligent and objective, they can direct others toward realizing attainable and well-plotted goals.

Earth personalities are generally enterprising in a serious and methodical manner; they can organize and manage businesses that require a firm hand. These are the managers who build and reinforce the foundations of industry, commerce and government. Rarely excitable, such people will always verify their findings and will demand sound reasons for everything they do. While they may move slowly, they proceed toward good and lasting results.

Earth persons like to keep things in perspective and are conservative by nature. They will seldom exaggerate their findings, calculations or expectations. They will give you the true undiluted picture of any situation with no retouching, modifications or frills. When they are negative, their most common shortcomings will be their lack of imagination, overprotectiveness and pessimistic outlook. However, they can be expected to shoulder their responsibilities admirably and discipline themselves. These dependable and solid citizens are the pillars of the community.

THE INFLUENCE OF THE MOON'S FOUR PHASES

Man's relationship with the moon has always been a profound and intimate one, much more so than his relationship with the sun. The sun, with its brilliance, was revered, but since it shone without fail every day, no assurances were needed that it would rise again on the morrow.

But the mystical moon held mankind in the sway of her magic and beauty. Her dark face and moods could plague humanity with doubts and foreboding, while her shimmering light brought enchantment, happiness and romance. Gradually, it became clear that the moon's influence was large and multifaceted and touched every aspect of life and the environment.

Humankind slowly learned to recognize the moon's many faces and interpret her signs. As her movements and their significance began to be better understood, man found he could benefit immensely by following her rhythm and guidance. It is no accident that a woman's natural cycle of reproduction also coincides with the length of the lunar month. Based on these observations, many thousands of years ago, the lunar horoscope was born.

In following a lunar month, the rule to remember is: a new moon heralds in a new lunar month. The monthly cycle reaches its peak on the 15th day of the lunar month, with the full moon dominating the night sky. It is a spectacle hard to ignore and has awed human beings since the dawn of recorded history.

The four weeks that comprise the twenty-nine and a half days of each lunar month mark the four phases of the moon. The first week starts with the new moon, and lasts for seven and a half days. The second moon phase makes up the first quarter, which reaches its peak a day before the full moon (the fifteenth lunar day of the month), which starts the third week of the lunar month. The fourth week

begins with the last quarter on the twenty-second and a half day—
and this fourth and last phase of seven and a half days brings the lunar
month to an end.

The Chinese believe that the four phases of the moon, like the
four seasons that make up the year, have their own special functions
and significance.

Major modern medical studies now show that body rhythm is an
important factor that must be taken into consideration when pre-
scribing drugs or chemotherapy. The time of day medication or treatment is administered is crucial to having fewer side effects such as
nausea, upset stomachs, cold sores, pain or numbness. Furthermore,
the body, when treated in synchrony with its circadian cycle, responds
better to treatment. Cancer drugs and chemotherapy deliver a
stronger punch when introduced into the body at times when the
malignant cells are reproducing and the normal body functions are at
their ebb, such as when we are asleep.

Chinese doctors and herbalists have always been aware of the
body's own clock and have prescribed herbs and treatment to be
taken at specific times. They went even further by scheduling medical
treatment according to the moon's phases. Surgery of any kind
(including tooth extractions) was usually done after the full moon,
preferably during the last quarter, as bleeding would be considerably
less and the wound would heal faster if the moon was in decline.
Cutting one's hair was recommended during the first phase of the
moon as it would promote further hair growth in somewhat the same
way that pruning branches encourages a tree's renewal. Medications
used to regulate a woman's menstrual cycle also had to be taken after
the full moon and in the evenings to get the best results. Farmers, too,
relied on the moon phases (on which the *Farmer's Almanac* is based),
to plan the planting and harvesting times of their crops.

THE NEW MOON

Symbolizes birth, renewal, sowing and awakening.
lst lunar phase—from the lst day to the 7 1/2th day.
Season is spring
Direction is east
Element is Wood
Rules the lunar signs of Tiger, Rabbit, Dragon

This first phase represents a young and vibrant spring in which birth, growth and beginnings are emphasized. It is an excellent time to put seed into the ground, to start new ventures or open a business. People born during the first week of the lunar month are the spring people—equipped with lively, innovative minds, free spirits and a love for new ideas and adventure. They are generally impressionable, inventive and outgoing, but also impulsive and restless by nature.

 ## THE FIRST QUARTER

Symbolizes potency, maturity, full growth or complete development.
2nd lunar phase—from the 7 1/2th to the 15th day.
Season is summer
Direction is south
Element is Fire
Rules the lunar signs Snake, Horse, Sheep

This second phase is identified with summer and denotes both mental and physical maturity since it ends at the peak of the lunar month. This is a prime time to transplant seedlings and to fertilize the soil to promote lush growth. The moon's continuing ascent favors aggressive and forceful action. Summer or first-quarter people will likewise be strong-minded, as they are competent fighters and capable doers. Full of potent energy, they are the leaders of the cycle.

THE FULL MOON

Symbolizes organization, harvest, collection and storage.
3rd lunar phase—from the 15th to the 22 1/2th day.
Season is autumn
Direction is west
Element is Metal
Rules the lunar signs Monkey, Rooster, Dog

The third phase, commencing with the full moon, has a great affinity for autumn or fall. This is a time to harvest ripened fruit and grain, mend broken fences, cut wood and preserve food for winter and consolidate one's resources after the harvest. The moon begins her descent after the fifteenth day. Autumn natives will like to organize, restore order, resolve problems and settle disputes with intelligence and calm reason. Theirs is the phase of the harvester and collector.

 ## THE LAST QUARTER

Symbolizes completion, conclusion, hibernation and rest.
4th lunar phase—from the 22 1/2/th to the 29th day.
Season is winter
Direction is north
Element is Water
Rules the lunar signs Boar, Rat, Ox

During this fourth week, the lunar month is in its winter, and this is generally the time to settle debts, close a business or finish up a project. The waning moon is also conducive to the slaughter of livestock, extraction of teeth, pruning of plants, etc. It is also believed that operations performed during this period will result in less bleeding. Winter people born during the 7 1/2 days of the last phase are the thinkers, keepers of confidences and makers of analytical decisions. Like potent roots that lie asleep in the earth beneath a blanket of winter snow, they will conserve their energy and burst forth with new life when the time is right.

1

The First Sign
of the Lunar Cycle

The Rat

I am the self-proclaimed acquisitor.
I am a link yet I function as
   a complete unit.
I aim at encompassing heights
   and strike my target,
   sure and steady.
Life is one joyous journey for me.
Each search must end with a new quest.
I am progress, exploration and insight.
I am the womb of activity.

I AM THE RAT.

Lunar Years of the Rat in the Western Calendar	Elements
31 January 1900 to 18 February 1901	Metal
18 Febraury 1912 to 5 Febraury 1913	Water
5 February 1924 to 23 January 1925	Wood
24 January 1936 to 10 February 1937	Fire
10 February 1948 to 28 January 1949	Earth
28 January 1960 to 14 February 1961	Metal
15 February 1972 to 2 February 1973	Water
2 February 1984 to 19 February 1985	Wood
19 February 1996 to 6 February 1997	Fire

If you were born on the day before the start of the lunar year of the Rat, e.g., 27th January 1960, your animal sign is the one before the Rat, the Boar, the twelfth lunar sign.

If you were born on the day after the last day of lunar year of the Rat, e.g., 15th February l961, then your sign is the one after Rat, the Ox, the second lunar sign.

The sign of the Rat rules the two-hour segment of the day from 11 P.M. to 1 A.M. This period of time closes the day at midnight as well as heralds in a new day. Persons born during this two-hour segment are said to have the Rat sign as their ascendant and will display many of the characteristics peculiar to this sign and have great affinity for persons born under this sign.

The direction appointed to the Rat is directly north; its season is winter and its principle month, December. The Rat corresponds to the Western astrological sign of Sagittarius which rules winter from November 22nd to December 21st. Water is its fixed element and the Rat has a positive stem or is considered a yang or male sign.

THE RAT PERSONALITY

The charm and innovative personality of the Rat is legendary. He did not become the first sign of the cycle without good reason. I have woven a tale about how this might have come to pass. According to my story, when the Lord Buddha gave out the summons for all the animals to come to him before he departed the Earth, he entrusted the rat with the mission to get the word around. It is entirely possible that the Rooster was also chosen to announce the same message and both did their utmost to reach as many of their fellow beasts as possible. The Rooster worked days and did most of its crowing during the sunlight hours while the Rat worked during the night. In its intense diligence to round up as many animals as possible, the Rooster was delayed and the 10th animal to arrive. After the Rooster came the Dog and lastly, the Boar.

One can imagine the Rat rushing about with the good news. He went from place to place, encouraging all the other animals to meet the Buddha at the appointed time and place. However, being the resourceful and practical animal that it is, the Rat decided to save energy by asking for a ride from other animals since it was tired from running about conveying the Great Sage's invitation. And, he certainly did not want to be late.

Knowing the Horse was the swiftest of the lot, the Rat tried to get a free ride from it. But the temperamental Horse would have none of it. Fiercely independent and proud, the Horse decided that no one could tell it what to do and when to do it. There was plenty of time to trot to the appointment when it was ready. It told the Rat to get a ride somewhere else. From that time on, the Rat and the Horse never got along. The Rat thought the Horse was selfish and thoughtless while the Horse felt that the clever Rat was too manipulative and demanding.

Nonetheless, the Rat was too intelligent to be discouraged for long and used its wits again. This time it approached the sturdy and kind-hearted Ox who was more than happy to carry the little Rat on its back. Furthermore, the dutiful Ox was early for the appointment and therefore the first animal to arrive on the scene. But, when the Lord Buddha said he was going to honor the Ox by naming it the first sign of the lunar cycle, the Rat jumped down from the Ox's back and claimed that privilege. The Ox did not oppose the Rat as it felt the Rat had done more than its fair share by bringing the news to all the animals. So the Buddha justly conferred the esteemed first place and leadership of the lunar cycle to the crafty Rat. This was how the Rat got its free ride and also got to be number one.

The Rat can be forthright, inquisitive and intrusive but always in such a disarmingly honest way that we find ourselves at a disadvantage. It is in business that this sign really excels. I remember seeing a young man in the streets of London one summer promoting some security or time-saving gadget. He presented quite a novel image of himself and his wares, but above all else, everyone noticed the T-shirt he had on. It read: "Be Alert! England needs Lerts!" That sense of humor combined with keen business acumen summarizes the Rat's inborn entreprenuerial sense. Yes, the Rat is always alert to any opportunity for making money.

Remarkably easy to get along with, hard working and thrifty, he will be generous only to those he is inordinately fond of, so if you get an expensive gift from him, you know he holds you in high esteem. Yet, in spite of his penny-pinching ways, the Rat will never be found wanting for admirers as he emits such fantastic appeal.

On the surface, some Rats may appear reserved, even placid, but they are never as quiet as they may seem. Something is always going on inside that sharp mind. Actually, the Rat is easily agitated but able to maintain self-control, which explains why he is so popular and has such a multitude of friends.

The Rat person is usually a bright, fun-loving and sociable character. Occasionally, you may come across a supercritical or grouchy, fault-finding one. But on the whole, he enjoys parties and other large gatherings. He will endeavor to join exclusive clubs and as a rule can be found in a close circle of friends or fellow conspirators. He is very outgoing and likes getting involved. How else is he going to be in the thick of things and amass all that information he has about everyone?

The Rat really cherishes his friends, associates and family relations; at times he gets hopelessly tangled in other people's affairs because he cannot easily rid himself of strong emotional attachments once he makes them. His capacity to love can only be overruled by his shrewdness and love of money.

A Rat boss may demonstrate great concern about whether his employees are getting enough exercise or eating a balanced diet. In his heart, he sincerely cares about their welfare; he will visit them when they are sick and make their problems his problems. Yet when it comes to giving them that well-deserved raise, he will hedge and be a little stingy. A lot of arm twisting and collective bargaining is needed when it comes to parting a Rat from his money.

The Rat lady may continually amaze you by being a model of frugality. She is forever distributing old clothes, recycling toys, buying or selling secondhand items, and stretching meals, leftovers and the budget until the family could scream. However, she may not care to apply these same penny-pinching standards when dealing with her precious offspring. If her children know how to get around her, she will find it hard to deny them anything. Rat people are rarely tightwads where their loved ones are concerned. Strange how every time a Rat mother cuts a cake, her child will get the largest slice, no matter whose birthday it is. Rat females are also voted most likely to recycle a Christmas gift, which gives new meaning to the saying: What goes around, comes around.

Rats are by nature decidedly clannish. Maybe there is some truth about safety in numbers. The Rat never worries about having another mouth to feed and will allow his relatives, in-laws and friends to stick around his house and live off him. Why? Because the crafty Rat will always find something for them to do to earn their keep. Laggards, professional bums and freeloaders will all get put to work swiftly in his household. Charity has its limits. Trust the efficient and practical Rat.

The Rat native keeps his own secrets well but he can be an expert at weeding other people's gardens. He has few qualms about using vital confidential information or capitalizing on the mistakes of others. Trust him to investigate stock tips and follow through on privileged information. What do you mean, insider trading? That couldn't possibly apply to him. After all, one certainly cannot expect the Rat to ignore opportunity's knock, especially when his ear is glued to the door so much of the time! A wink, a nod, or the tiniest move of an eyebrow is all you need to signal the Rat that something's afoot. He will track it all the way to its source.

As much as the Rat likes to camouflage or hide his feelings, one can always tell when he is upset. He becomes edgy, curt and impertinent. Some may even become absolute nags. Inefficiency, idleness, waste and tardiness go against his active and industrious nature and cause him to harp at the subject of his displeasure until things are done right. The Rat loves to run the show and everyone and everything had better look sharp under his stewardship.

On his negative side, the Rat person loves to gossip, criticize, compare, carp and bargain—endlessly and usually over unimportant issues. Maybe he enjoys doing so just for the fun of it. Debates stimulate him and he is never lacking an opinion or an intricately reasoned argument. He often buys things he does not really need just because he can get a good deal and is easily taken in by bargains. It's his inborn accumulative urge. Mementos, souvenirs and hoards of sentimental junk will be found tucked away in his room and in his heart. He also tends to be the neighborhood busybody, though more often than not, his intentions are good. The solicitous Rat is always ready to share money-saving tips, recipes, fire sale specials, free samples, advice about discount store outlets and where to go to get the most for least. If you are planning a garage sale, the Rat is the best ally to have around. The one problem may be that he will cart all your junk over to his home and try to find uses for it. They don't call such people "pack rats" for nothing.

It is not surprising that the Rat is reputed to be an excellent writer. He makes it a point to know practically everything about everyone in town. He keeps tabs, has an uncanny eye for detail, a good memory and is incredibly inquisitive. The Rat loves to investigate. A reporter par excellence, he is good at keeping records and is always in on the latest news.

The native of this year will be successful in whatever he chooses to do because the Rat will adapt himself to the situation at hand. He has the ability to cope with difficulties and is at his best during a crisis. Levelheaded and alert, he possesses keen intuition and foresight. Adversity merely serves to sharpen his wits as he is always busy cooking up some scheme. One can't blame him, he just thrives on challenges.

There is no need to worry about the Rat's safety as he always checks out the back door before entering. This is in case he has to make a quick or untimely exit from the scene. Self-preservation is high on his list of priorities and he usually finds the path with the least repercussions. If you want to get out of trouble fast, follow the Rat's course. He has a built-in alarm system and a defense mechanism that rarely fails.

His stumbling block is overambition. He tries to do too much too soon and as a result scatters his energies. If he can avoid doing this and persevere in finishing what he's started, a person of this sign will end up wealthy, which is just as well, as the Rat loves money!

Despite the Rat's inborn ability to sense danger, he often has great difficulty relying on his own sound judgment because he simply cannot pass up bargains and so-called "great deals." Alas, he ends up falling into the proverbial trap. He will have no problems in life if he can only conquer his greed and quit while he is ahead. In his lifetime, the covetous Rat has to suffer at least one large financial blow before he learns that avarice does not pay. However, it is most unlikely to find a poor Rat native, and if you do, well, with his resourcefulness, you can bet he will not remain poor for long. It would be totally out of character for him not to have a nest egg hidden away somewhere.

Being the true sentimentalist of the Chinese cycle, the Rat is not only deeply attached to his children but to his elders as well. Parents with children born in this year can be sure they will be well-regarded and cared for by them. Unlike the Dragon child, who may demand perfection of his parents, the Rat child will have infinite trust in his parents, cater to their needs and overlook their shortcomings. Many Rats go into the medical profession, just so that they can provide health care for their parents. They will be willing to have their parents live with them in their old age. Rats also make excellent doctors, nurses and pharmacists.

Aside from doting on their children and husbands, the Rat mother revels in being a superb homemaker. She will help her husband's career development as if she were his campaign manager, drive the children to piano, ballet and violin lessons, and take on so much social activity one's head would spin. A husband belonging to this sign, on the other hand, can be found helping out with household chores and spending his free time in the nest he provides for his family.

The time of the day he was born plays an important role in the Rat's way of life. Needless to say, one born in the evening will have a more hectic and strenuous life (night Rats scurry around constantly in search of food) than his brother Rat born during the quiet of the day.

The Rat person will be attracted to people of the Ox sign, whom he finds strong, reliable and appreciative of the devotion he has to offer. Equally compatible with the Rat will be the mighty Dragon people. Likewise, the Rat finds the Snake attractive and intelligent, and may make a suitable alliance with him. Power and brilliance captivates the Rat, and that is why he will always fall for the irresistible Monkey born. He admires the clever Monkey's way of doing things and the Monkey will be overjoyed to find the Rat on his own cunning wavelength. Tiger, Dog, Boar or another Rat will have no trouble teaming up with a Rat.

The Rat will come into conflict with persons born under the Horse sign. The Horse is just too independent and changeable to please the clannish Rat. The two could never team up well and find harmony. It would also be unwise for the Rat to marry the Rooster. The Rooster, being the intrepid dreamer, will exasperate the practical Rat no end. Their constant arguments and fault-finding union will bear little fruit. A marriage with the Sheep is similarly questionable; the indulgent Sheep may squander the Rat's hard-earned savings and fail to appreciate the Rat's practical and frugal ways.

THE RAT CHILD

A child born in the year of the Rat will be sweet and loving. Outwardly, he may be shy, but inwardly he is fiercely competitive. Often, he resorts to crying to get more attention and usually clings to one or two people with whom he identifies. Although he has a charming disposition, he tends to be possessive of parents and friends and jealous of attention given to others.

He will talk early. He likes to eat (mention of his favorite foods always makes him light up) and he takes an early interest in cooking and other household chores. Because he is so affectionate and demonstrative, he will not like being left alone. He will enjoy group play, can concentrate on detailed work and will make friends easily. You can depend on him to keep things tidy or at least know where his possessions are.

The Rat child will start to show his calculating nature early in life. He will insist on getting the bigger half of the apple, and exactly the same number of cookies as his sibling (preferably more, but under no circumstances less). It will be hard to cheat him. He learns fast and never misses a trick. He takes regular stock of his possessions—so don't try to give away any of his old toys thinking he won't miss them. Then again, if you consult him about donating his old toys or clothes, be prepared for a struggle as the little Rat won't part with anything easily.

With younger children, the Rat child will tend to be motherly; at his worst, he will boss them around mercilessly. Given the proper encouragement, he will be ambitious in school. An avid reader, he will learn the importance of the written word early and be able to express himself well. Many of the world's greatest writers and historians were born in the year of the Rat.

THE FIVE DIFFERENT RATS

METAL RAT—1900, 1960

This type of Rat is most likely to be idealistic in thought, vivid in speech and actions and intensely emotional. He may cover up his feelings by presenting himself as a cheerful, generous and outgoing person. In reality, he is easily moved to jealousy, anger, selfishness and possessiveness. His outlook is based on what his senses can appreciate. He loves money but will not hoard it and won't mind spending if he can get good value and quality. He knows how to invest wisely. He will not be as romantic and sentimental as the Rats of other elements but could be sensual and moralistic at the same time.

He likes to impress people and his home will be as splendidly decorated as he can afford. He loves drama and pageantry and has classic, expensive tastes. He will probably be athletically inclined. If he curbs his domineering tendencies, he will succeed in making himself known and liked by all the right people. Here is a Rat who will advance himself by getting into influential circles.

WATER RAT—1912, 1972

More concerned with mental exercise and the intricacies of the thinking process, this Rat's insight is excellent, allowing him to relate well to people of all levels. He will be respected and able to promote his talents because of his accommodating and understanding nature. Traditional and conservative, he prefers to swim with the current rather than fight it. Still, he is calculating and shrewd. A person born under this combination will manifest all the qualities needed to wield influence in areas important to him. He is instinctively aware of other people's likes and dislikes and knows how to please those in a position to help him. However, he may not be too discriminating and tend to confide in anyone who cares to listen. This might sometimes get him into trouble.

Drawn to the written word and the acquisition of knowledge, the Water Rat is adept at putting his thoughts on paper and will work to further his own education throughout his life.

WOOD RAT—1924, 1984

Progressive, success-oriented and amicable, this Rat will try to explore everything and find good use for almost anything he comes across. Expansive and very comprehensive in outlook, the Wood Rat is a corporate soul who knows how to make the system work for him. He is farsighted and always concerned with finding out the whys and the wherefors. Although he is egotistic, he makes himself agreeable and is quite thoughtful of others because he seeks universal admiration and approval.

Yet he has his principles and knows what he wants. He has strict priorities, but can be flexible in order to achieve his aims. One reason the Wood Rat works so hard is because he loves security and worries constantly about his future.

Outwardly, this person exudes confidence and know-how and is probably professional in manner. He is a good talker and can promote ideas objectively and manage projects capably. Here is someone who will have little difficulty in drumming up support for his ventures.

FIRE RAT—1936, 1996

This chivalrous and dynamic Rat loves getting involved in all sorts of activities and never tires of embarking on new campaigns for justice and a better deal. He loves travel and fashionable clothes and is open and aggressive by nature. He can also be the most generous of the Rats.

Although he is energetic and idealistic, he tends not to be very diplomatic, and at times may be too blunt to win the support he requires. Because he is not very disciplined, he will follow the dictates of his heart more often than those of his head. As much as he is devoted to his home and family, he may still take off whenever he feels too hemmed in. He needs lots of room and attention to soothe his oversized ego. An independent and very, very competitive Rat, he will not be content to maintain a simple middle-of-the-road existence. If he is too impatient for success, his fortunes may change often and quite drastically.

EARTH RAT—1948, 2008

The Earth Rat matures early; for him, happiness and contentment are found in order, discipline and, above all, security. He will strive to develop his positive traits and be recognized for his talents. He is realistic and not at all given to flashy dreams and expectations. He likes to maintain good relations with everyone and prefers to work in one place or job where he will have loyal friends for a long time. He can zero in on one subject at a time and is thorough in his work. On the darker side, he can be too achievement-oriented, self-righteous and impatient with others, especially if he is in a rush to get things done exactly to his specifications.

This person cares a great deal for his reputation and public image, but is warm and protective toward those he loves. He has high material expectations and is always comparing his degree of success with his contemporaries. At times, he becomes overpractical and stingy with his money. This is a Rat who does not like to gamble and rarely takes chances. He sticks to proven rules and modes of operation and expects those who work with him to do exactly the same. As a result, his fortunes will increase slowly but surely.

COMPATIBILITY AND CONFLICT CHARTS
FOR THE RAT

The Rat is part of the First Triangle of Affinity, a group of positive people identified as DOERS. The Rat, the Dragon and the Monkey are performance- and progress-oriented signs adept at handling matters with initiative and innovation. Self-starters, they prefer to initiate action, clear their paths of uncertainty and hesitation and forge ahead. Restless and short-tempered when hindered or forced to be unoccupied, they are full of dynamic energy and ambition. This trio is the melting pot of ideas. They can team up beautifully because they possess a common way of doing things and will appreciate each other's method of thinking.

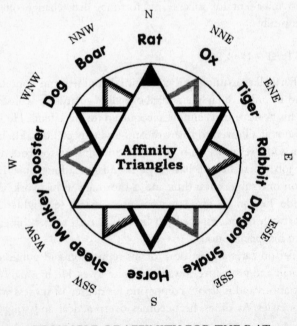

TRIANGLE OF AFFINITY FOR THE RAT

The Rat will encounter his most serious personality clashes with someone born in the year of the Horse. Anyone whose ascendant is of the Horse will also be likely to come into conflict with the Rat. In the Circle of Conflict, the Rat and Horse are 180 degrees apart and thus total opposites. The Rat's direction or compass point is directly north, the Horse's directly south. The Rat represents winter, the Horse, summer. The Rat's natural element is Water, which puts out its opposite, Fire, which is the Horse's natural element.

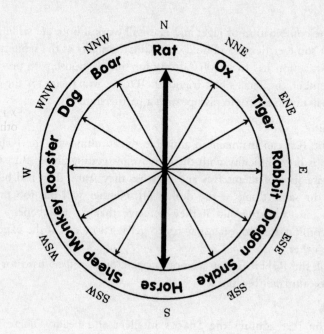

CIRCLE OF CONFLICT

Aside from the super-compatible Dragon and Monkey, and the super-incompatible Horse, the other nine signs are compatible with the Rat to varying degrees.

Rat

The Rat works well with its own sign. Two Rats will make a good team if they have a common goal. However, they are competitive and should try not to take things too personally. This combination is compatible to a certain degree.

Ox

A union with the Ox will work out well. The Ox has need of the Rat's expertise, while the Rat will appreciate the stable and devoted Ox. A nice partnership as both will take their roles to heart and work for the common good. Besides, the shy Ox will not try to upstage the Rat.

Tiger

The combination of Tiger and Rat will work if both are willing to accept some criticism and hold on to their tempers at the same time. The attraction has to be very strong for this relationship to prosper. Remember, the Tiger's best friend, the Horse, won't care for the Rat and will no doubt try to disrupt such a partnership.

Rabbit

The Rat can maintain an amicable relationship with the Rabbit. There is little difficulty with these two signs getting along. But since both are sure of themselves and of what they want, they had better want the same thing or the deal is off. Neither will put too much effort into a partnership if they perceive that no real benefits are forthcoming. Instead, each may try to get what he can at the expense of the other.

Still, the Rabbit is such a smooth operator, it will be hard for the Rat to outmaneuver him.

Snake

The Rat admires the Snake's intellect and beauty. These two signs know how to cooperate to make a relationship work. The Rat is willing to make commitments if the Snake is not too intense and demanding. With mutual respect and understanding, such a partnership will be successful to a good degree.

Sheep

The Rat has little sympathy for the frivolous ways of the Sheep. They do not have a lot in common. The Rat saves every penny; the

Sheep spends, borrows, and indulges every whim. The aggressive Rat enjoys hard work and challenges; the creative Sheep wants to be pampered and protected. Such different outlooks will generate animosity on both sides. However, if a Sheep is born during the hours of the Rat or if a Rat is born during the hours of the Sheep, the two signs may be able to establish a good rapport.

Rooster

There will be difficulties in communications, as these two signs seem to test each other's patience. The Rooster likes to criticize while the Rat can be just as picky and argumentative. In such a competitive and fault-finding atmosphere, nothing lasting or special can develop. If they can work through friends to defuse potential clashes, their chances for a successful relationship will be better.

Dog

The Dog is friendly but pragmatic. The Rat has great respect for the Dog, who will not contest the Rat in any struggle for dominance as he has different priorities. Both know their limits and territories. They do not have any serious differences in outlook and will work together as a team when necessary. However, should the Rat clash with a Horse or Tiger, the Dog will not be on the Rat's side since most Dogs will be on the side of the Horse and Tiger every time.

Boar

A moderately happy and workable partnership. The Boar will respond generously to the Rat's need for commitment. The crafty Rat brings intuition and an ability for self-preservation into such a union, two things that a Boar will find invaluable. The Rat will also discover that luck always favors the good-hearted Pig. Both will benefit from their association and come out feeling like winners.

THE RAT AND HIS ASCENDANTS

We all have a shadow that follows us throughout life. Sometimes it grows bigger than life and at other times it shrinks until it disappears into the soles of our feet. Sometimes it walks tall before us and on other occasions it lags behind like a sulking friend. In Chinese horoscopes, this constant partner, manifested or not, is our ascendant, the animal sign that rules the hour of our birth and becomes a comrade in our journey through life. We may view it as friend or foe or even a little of both. It surfaces when we least expect and shows a better or worse side of our nature. We can often be confounded by the way we listen to our "other self" as well as feel resentful of the significant influence it can exert on us. Actually, a personality has many rings around the centered "self." Each ring can have a different size, texture and aura. When all these factors combine, they bring forth the unique individual that the person truly is. Hence, a Dragon with an ascendant that is not compatible, like the Dog, has perhaps a more difficult inner struggle than say a Snake born during the hours of the Snake. The double intensity of the Snake person will be easily understood by horoscope readers while the more intricate Dragon/Dog may exhibit the contrary Dog and Dragon traits to varying degrees. There are many voices within each person. But, in the end, only the individual determines which course he will follow, which choices he will make.

The time of birth used to determine the ascendant is always the local time in the place of birth.

If you were born between:

11 P.M. and 1 A.M. = The Hours of the Rat

You are a supercharming, very intuitive and, at times, a conceited person. Besides being an excellent writer, reporter or lawyer, you are openly inquisitive and love the limelight. You are quick to learn new things, agile and superior in mental pursuits and can also be demanding and domineering. You are renowned for your spicy wit and dry sense of humor. Try not to be so possessive and critical.

1 A.M. and 3 A.M. = The Hours of the Ox

You have a serious nature and favor the slow, sure ways of the Ox. You will still have the Rat's appealing personality but your gambling instincts will be curtailed by the Ox's caution. You may be dominated by the Ox's love of home and duty and be less adventurous than other Rats. Nonetheless, you are strong-minded and cannot be easily deterred from what you want. With the Ox's fortitude and the Rat's intuition, you should go far.

3 A.M. and 5 A.M. = The Hours of the Tiger

The Tiger is an aggressive ascendant. Added to your normally acquisitive nature, you will be an overachiever. You find it hard to be satisfied with anything you have and will always strive for better and more. With the Tiger roaring in you, however, you will find it hard to hold on to your money. You are more generous than other Rats and more colorful, too. A natural performer, you will love being on stage or in films.

5 A.M. and 7 A.M. = The Hours of the Rabbit

A soft-spoken and docile person with impeccable taste, you could inherit the Rabbit's taste for diplomacy and be known for your astuteness and business acumen. You may be calculating and ambitious, but with your beautiful Rabbit manner, they will never know—until it's too late.

7 A.M. and 9 A.M. = The Hours of the Dragon

Having the Dragon as your ascendant will be a blessing. You will be big-hearted and magnanimous—sometimes against your better judgment. You will give someone a large loan and then regret it almost immediately. But the Dragon's expansive nature could curb your covetous ways. People are drawn to your leadership abilities. The Dragon's luck combined with your money-making talents will bring you the attention and success you crave.

9 A.M. and 11 A.M. = The Hours of the Snake

The Snake ascendant gives you immense sex appeal. You will have hordes of admirers. But the Snake could make you secretive and introspective. You are charming, intelligent and inscrutable where your emotions are concerned. It will be hard for others to read you. It has to do with that Snake mystique. You love your privacy and will not explain your motives to anyone. They will have to accept you the way you are.

11 A.M. and 1 P.M. = The Hours of the Horse

You are a dashing but daring Rat who tends to take unnecessary risks. The fun-loving ways of the Horse may also make your love life turbulent. Financially, you tend to ride high on a wave of success or be on the brink of bankruptcy. You must learn to rein in the passion of the impulsive Horse within you and take the middle of the road.

1 P.M. and 3 P.M. = The Hours of the Sheep

You have a very loving nature, compliments of the Sheep ascendant, but you may be oversentimental and easily discouraged by criticism. The Sheep brings good taste and refinement to your life, and you will be gifted with a keen eye for making good investments in the arts. Both your natural sign and ascendant are opportunistic, but at different ends of the spectrum. It's hard to imagine you not getting your way. You can talk or cry your way out of every tough situation.

3.P.M. and 5 P.M. = The Hours of the Monkey

What an enterprising combination! Your Monkey ascendant in you will help you find every trick in the book while the Rat sign won't hesitate to use it. With the Monkey's influence, you are less sentimental and more inventive and creative. This is the sign of a problem solver and natural showman who will never accept No for an answer.

5 P.M. and 7 P.M. = The Hours of the Rooster

The perfection-loving Rooster will make you even more capable and alert. Nothing will escape your eagle eye. However, while the Rat in you may be saving money for that rainy day, the Rooster side has grand designs on how to spend it. You can redeem yourself by applying all your admirable qualities to running a business with other people's money. Overconfidence will be your main stumbling block.

7 P.M. and 9 P.M. = The Hours of the Dog

Under the Dog's influence, you will be fair-minded and unprejudiced but your basic craving for wealth and power could gnaw away at the Dog's noble conscience. You may be forever in a struggle between doing the right thing or the profitable thing. This combination could make you a writer of some authority or a journalist/philosopher with an acid pen. People may fear your sharp tongue, too. There's no shutting you up when you want to make a point.

9 P.M. and 11 P.M. = The Hours of the Boar

Your Rat personality will hate carrying the Boar's scruples around. What a burden. It makes you hesitant to take advantage of potentially profitable situations. You could end up a popular do-gooder who is taken advantage of. But then, everyone will envy you for your large circle of friends and extensive influence. You will truly be surrounded by love.

HOW THE RAT FARES IN THE LUNAR CYCLE

1. The Year of the Rat 1996

The year of the Rat brings prosperity to the Rat born. He can look forward to a promotion or other advancement in his career. The Rat will find it a busy year in which he will have to earn whatever he receives. His schedule will be hectic, he will have too much to do and not enough time to do it. Aside from unexpected achievements and monetary gains, the Rat should take care of his health as small illnesses, loss of property and accidents worry him and may hamper his overall progress.

2. The Year of the Ox 1997

A fairly good and stable year for the Rat. His gains will not be substantial but he will enjoy them. There will be happiness and contentment on the homefront. In his work, the Rat may find more stress and responsibility than usual but, being a team player, he will readily shoulder his load and possibly benefit from the good fortunes of the group. On the whole, the Rat will meet his challenges with a cheerful and positive attitude.

3. The Year of the Tiger 1998

A moderate year for the Rat, as it will be unsafe for speculation of any kind and the Rat will have to be on guard against taking risks. He may become involved in misunderstandings that force him to act against his better judgment. It would be wise for him to seek counsel before making any major decisions and to get second and third opinions before coming to any conclusions. This is not the time for the Rat to act alone or be aggressive. He will feel lonely or sad and may be required to travel more than usual. A time for him to listen to the advice of others and maybe even take a back seat.

4. The Year of the Rabbit 1999

A calm and quiet year, during which the Rat will acquire new and valuable business or career contacts—and we all know how good he is at networking. His popularity is on the rise and he will move in new or better circles. Secret dreams and aspirations can be realized if he plays his cards right and finds the right sponsor or mentor. Working behind the scenes will be more useful to the Rat than open opposition at this time.

5. The Year of the Dragon 2000

A very good year for the Rat person, and an excellent time for his business and romantic prospects as smooth sailing is assured under the auspices of the lucky Dragon. However, the Rat should not be overconfident; some rain will certainly fall during the Dragon's year. Although the Rat will receive recognition for his achievements, he must be wary of newfound friends who want to involve him in dangerous ventures. Now is also the time to put away something for that rainy day.

6. The Year of the Snake 2001

This year brings mixed fortunes for the Rat who must be extra cautious with investments and important decisions. An illness or loss of money will cast some gloom on his home. His family and friends will make enormous demands on his time. His efforts may go unrewarded and he may feel unappreciated especially if his expectations are too high. If he perseveres, his luck will take a turn for the better by the end of the year; he will be able to recoup his losses and see his efforts pay off. The Rat has an immense faith in himself, so he will end the Snake's year with a positive outlook.

7. The Year of the Horse 2002

A difficult and unpredictable time is in store for the Rat. He must be very conservative in assessing his prospects as the Horse forces him to entertain lavishly, waste money or become tangled in lawsuits. Most of his problems may not be of his own making, but he has to deal with them anyway. This is definitely a time for the Rat to display his fortitude and act with grace under pressure. He may incur large debts or have to guarantee the loans of others. He should be forewarned that any loan made this year may not be repaid. Irritating delays will plague him and even love affairs may not turn out well.

8. The Year of the Sheep 2003

The Rat's finances make a recovery this year and there are some achievements career-wise, as there will be little or no resistance to his plans or efforts. Along with the many changes in his lifestyle, he may be able to discover and take advantage of previously unseen opportunities. Romantically, it will be an especially vulnerable time when the Rat seeks love, approval and emotional support.

9. The Year of the Monkey 2004

A fruitful year for the Rat as he enjoys the Monkey's company immensely. There will be no problems he cannot handle in the home or business front. He receives good news, recognition and unexpected bounty from unlikely sources. This is an excellent time for the Rat to build upon friendships, partnerships and new romantic relationships. But it is not a time to give any long term commitments since, in the heat of his optimism, the Rat may make promises he cannot fulfill. Overall, the sociable, hard-working and thrifty Rat will marvel at the innovation and excitement the year of the Monkey brings.

10. The Year of the Rooster 2005

Activity, celebrations and complications await the Rat during the hectic year of the Rooster. New jobs, responsibilities and even marriages in the family keep him on his toes. Everything will seem to be ahead of schedule as the Rooster is an ultra-punctual perfectionist and a taskmaster. The Rat thrives on challenges but even he will be exhausted by the energetic Rooster year. The Rat should take care to slow down; he does not have to take advantage of every opportunity that comes his way. He should pick only the most promising and pass up the rest. If he tries to do everything, he will be exhausted from overwork, and accidents and painful mistakes could occur.

11. The Year of the Dog 2006

A less pleasurable year for the Rat person, who may have to compromise on many issues and take on projects he does not really like. Although he feels oppressed by his many obligations, he diligently fulfills them. He may be unable to influence the events in his life and derives no benefit from his efforts. Still, he does find support and happiness in his family and close circle of friends. He is preoccupied with unsettled issues that should work themselves out. It is, however, a time for the Rat to be patient and prudent.

12. The Year of the Boar 2007

Not too much progress is made in business or investments during the reign of the Pig. The happy-go-lucky Boar does not fret about finances nor plan too far ahead. A time for the Rat to consolidate his position. Friends and relatives make excessive demands on the Rat's time and bank account. His reserves are spent foolishly and the gains he anticipated may not materialize. A time for him to make alliances and join forces with others to achieve his goals. There is plenty of goodwill in the year of the Boar, and the Rat can certainly make it work for him.

WHEN MOON SIGNS MEET SUN SIGNS

In my interpretation of Chinese Horoscopes, the Rat is not linked with the first Western astrological sun sign, Aries. Instead, I pair the Rat with its counterpart based on the month and season of the Rat, which are December and winter. This makes the most sense as the lunar month of December (also called the Twelfth Moon or the Twelfth Earth Branch) is supposed to parallel the sun sign, Sagittarius, the Archer. I envision the Eastern and Western horoscope cycles as two large wheels, each with twelve spokes. To correctly juxtapose these cycles, we must find the matching notch that will join them together. Once the Rat and Sagittarius are paired as the first signs, the other eleven fall into place. Please see the Twenty-Four Segments of the Lunar Almanac. All the dates correspond with the twelve Western solar signs.

If you are born in the year of the Rat under the Western sign of

Sagittarius: 22nd November to 21st December
The Sagittarian Rat = Fire + Positive Water

A serendipitous dancer—the Sagittarian Rat is sleek and speedy with the Archer's aim and the Rat's opportunistic insight. Sagittarius is Jupiter's bold and proud child and the Rat exudes charm and brilliance. This personality will be accommodating and cheerful. He possesses great joie de vivre coupled with a strong hold on reality. He is a clever judge of situations. Blessed with great presence of mind, he will not flounder when faced with a crisis. A person of this combination loves to be in the thick of company. However, the Sagittarian Rat can be brutally frank when angered or if he decides to speak his mind.

If you are born in the year of the Rat under the Western sign of

Capricorn: 22nd December to 20th January
The Capricorn Rat = Earth + Positive Water

Sociable, steady, resourceful. A consummate hoarder, he labels, catalogs, and takes stock of possessions endlessly. Don't laugh—come rainy weather, he may have cornered all the umbrellas on the market, and you will have to depend on him. The Capricorn Rat is wise and careful, and less mobile and adventurous than other Rats. Faithful and dependable, he likes to form permanent relationships. With the secure Capricorn inside him, this Rat is less likely to take chances or gamble. Whatever else he is, you can be sure this fellow believes in being insured.

If you are born in the year of the Rat under the Western sign of

Aquarius: 21st January to 19th February
The Aquarian Rat = Air + Positive Water

A match that could produce a bubbling or a babbling brook. Positive and versatile, this aerated water personality is crystal clear in expressing himself and needs variety and freedom in every aspect of his life. The Aquarian Rat is less acquisitive and values his personal relationships more than his financial ones. Impatient and at times audacious, he can be defiant when challenged. Armed with sharp perception and gifted with enticing charm, he can usually convince others to dance to his tune. He makes amends for his uneven moods by giving his allegiance to good causes and serving others without expecting rewards. This is not a person who carries a grudge.

If you are born in the year of the Rat under the Western sign of

Pisces: 20th February to 20th March
The Pisces Rat = Water + Positive Water

A pleasing double water personality; as Pisces is melodious and psychic and the Rat well-versed in taking care of his family and interests. A person who combines these two signs will always be able to demonstrate his creativity, even if he is shy and not desirous of facing the public. He could be a prolific writer because of the Fish's deep appreciation of human emotions and the written word. The natural aggressive and selfish tendencies of the clannish Rat are subdued to a fair degree, leaving a less charged individual with peaceful inclinations. This person will value home and security before all else. Meditative, resourceful, sensitive but productive, the Pisces Rat will get straight A's for deportment.

If you are born in the year of the Rat under the Western sign of

Aries: 21st March to 19th April
The Aries Rat = Fire + Positive Water

A person with typical Aries fearlessness tempered by the Rat's craft and immense charm. A magnificently headstrong but likable, progressive personality. Self-assured and always in full control of situations, he will plunge into a busy and involved existence, with a tendency to being somewhat rushed and too goal-oriented. Well-read and boldly inquisitive, the Aries Rat mixes and mingles freely in all circles because of his vibrant love of the limelight.

If you are born in the year of the Rat under the Western sign of

Taurus: 20th April to 20th May
The Taurean Rat = Earth + Positive Water

Here, enterprise and activity blend with a love of security. The Taurean Rat is practical and companionable. He keeps up with changing times and has strong literary leanings. Money is very important to this type of person and his realistic soul teaches him early in life not to bank on anyone but himself. The Rat is amenable and clever at arranging beneficial compromises, while the Bull is not curiosity prone or given to misadventures, especially monetary ones. A person born with this combination could write or talk his way out of trouble, but he won't like to waste his money on legal fees. William Shakespeare was a Taurean Rat.

If you are born in the year of the Rat under the Western sign of

Gemini: 21st May to 21st June
The Gemini Rat = Air + Positive Water

A tremendously energetic combination. Both signs have an unmistakable flair for words and hence this personality could be an indefatigable talker or writer, or both. But the Rat is careful where the Twins are carefree. The result is this person tends to give his attention to too many different projects without being selective and, in the end, accomplishes less than he should. No doubt, the Gemini Rat is innovative and exciting to have around, but his interests may change too quickly to be relied on.

If you are born in the year of the Rat under the Western sign of

Cancer: 22nd June to 21st July
Cancerian Rat = Water + Positive Water

A deeply intuitive and secretive personality. The Cancerian Rat is a veritable well of emotions. The Rat's outgoing personality here could enliven and lessen the Moonchild's strong inhibitions or shyness. In this combination, we find a person not easily lead astray by impractical aspirations. Things have to be tried and found true before the

Cancerian Rat gives his trust. He is relaxed only in familiar surroundings. Both solar and lunar signs are concerned with domestic affairs, and this personality desires a close-knit family life in addition to accumulating wealth and material possessions.

If you are born in the year of the Rat under the Western sign of

Leo: 22nd July to 21st August
The Leo Rat = Fire + Positive Water

The perceptive Rat is a strong believer in getting real value for money. The Lion checks the Rat's avarice and makes this personality less calculating. The Leo Rat is aristocratic, impetuous and involved in everything. Daring and proud, he loves his freedom but can be relied upon to lead, a trustworthy person who will not neglect important details or the financial aspects of matters. Leonine integrity coupled with the Rat's presence of mind and sagacity result in a person who is magnetic, appealing and has a lively sense of humor.

If you are born in the year of the Rat under the Western sign of

Virgo: 22nd August to 22nd September
The Virgo Rat = Earth + Positive Water

These two active signs make up a superindustrious soul with a natural aptitude for investigation. The pure-minded Virgo will be made more jovial and delightful by the Rat. This person is bound to be an inquisitive perfectionist who will explore every option before making a move. The Virgo Rat will be an ingenious and studious soul with limitless capabilities if he learns how to hold his critical tongue.

If you are born in the year of the Rat under the Western sign of

Libra: 23rd September to 22nd October
The Libra Rat = Air + Positive Water

An exciting personality, bubbling like soda water with life and laughter. The balanced scales of Libra love society and harmonious relations as does the Rat—both signs are born charmers. The Libra Rat is bound to be very flexible and understanding. Yet a person born under this combination will not lose the Rat's love of economy or Libra's knack for joint ventures. Because of these qualities, he will possess a sharp eye for beauty matched by a keen nose for bargains.

If you are born in the year of the Rat under the Western sign of

Scorpio: 23rd October to 21st November
The Scorpio Rat = Water + Positive Water

A scheming, intense and fantastically effective Rat. The Rat is competitive by nature and here Scorpio will stengthen his willpower and possessiveness. Efficiency is at top level here. Hardworking and productive, this personality is as powerful as a waterfall and will generate tremendous support wherever he goes. Being a double water combination, the Scorpio Rat is silent and deep. If he had the power, he would not hesitate to strike out at his adversaries with the use of his pen. While he is a good writer, he is an even better critic.

THE SEASONS OF THE RAT

SPRING

As I mentioned earlier, Rats born in the evening are more alert, active and hardworking than those born during the day. When a Rat is born in the spring, he or she will lead an exciting existence. Just as spring awakens us from the long sleep of winter, spring Rats will show above average involvement, curiosity and creativity. Like eager-beaver go-getters, these people are self-starters and do not need to be told twice how to do something. Forever enchanted by the new, the fastest and the best things or way to do things, the lively spring Rat is abreast of the latest news and trends. Quick and agile, both physically and mentally, persons of the Rat year born in this season possess ample wit and humor and will liven up any party.

SUMMER

The summer Rat born during the day will enjoy a comfortable existence. Food is plentiful and he will not be in need. Feeling warm and indolent, he will not have to work too hard to have a good life. The long summer nights spent in full granaries are his to enjoy and explore. If he stays close to his family and home, he need never fear danger or want.

A rat born in the summer during the night, however, must work harder and be more aggressive than his brother rat born during the day. His cumulative urge is greater. He is not satisfied with what he has—he feels the need to expand and invest. Socially involved and very knowlegeable, the capable summer rat is the catalyst of large-scale ventures that require great planning and expertise.

AUTUMN

The autumn Rat born during the evening will be an excellent organizer. He or she will be virtually indispensable in arranging charity functions, family reunions, banquets, and all sorts of gatherings. Attending to details and mindful of every implication, this is one person who should always be entrusted with long-term planning. He worries not only about the harvest, but also about ensuring its proper storage, away from theft, spoilage and other forces beyond his immediate control.

Similar to the evening Rat, the daytime autumn Rat is less anxious to please. He is likely to be just as qualified as his nighttime sibling but he moves with less urgency and is not as prone to worrying. He will be able to delegate tasks. One who likes to weigh the pros and cons carefully before making commitments, the Rat person of this season is an excellent advisor and meticulous administrator.

WINTER

This is the time for all Rats to snuggle down and enjoy the fruits of their labors. But the Rat is always anxious in winter, the night ones more so than their daytime brethren. Winter should be the time of rest for them but still they venture forth in search of dwindling resources. Hopefully, winter Rats will learn early that they are only safe in the security of their homes and families. They will care a great deal about their education, be well-read and be able writers and communicators. The winter Rat is naturally reflective and intuitive, and will also be sentimental and possessive of those he loves.

FAMOUS PERSONS BORN IN THE YEAR OF THE RAT

Metal
Adlai Stevenson
Lucrezia Borgia

Wood
William Shakespeare
James Baldwin
George Sand
Jimmy Carter
Sidney Poitier
Doris Day
Marlon Brando

Water
James Callaghan
Pope John Paul I

Fire
Charlotte Brontë
Wolfgang A. Mozart
Karim Aga Khan IV
Pablo Casals
Yves St. Laurent
F. W. de Klerk

Earth
Leo Tolstoy
Jules Verne
Maurice Chevalier
Charles, Prince of Wales
Peggy Fleming
V. P. Albert Gore

2

The Second Sign
of the Lunar Cycle

The Ox

Mine is the stabilizing force
    that perpetuates the cycle of life.
I stand immobile against the
    test of adversity,
    resolute and unimpeachable.
I seek to serve integrity,
    to bear the burdens of righteousness.
I abide by the laws of nature
    patiently pushing the wheel of Fate.
Thus, I shall weave my destiny.

I AM THE OX.

Lunar Years of the Ox in the Western Calendar	Elements
19 February 1901 to 7 February 1902	Metal
6 February 1913 to 24 January 1914	Water
25 January 1925 to 12 February 1926	Wood
11 February 1937 to 30 January 1938	Fire
29 January 1949 to 16 February 1950	Earth
15 February 1961 to 4 February 1962	Metal
3 February 1973 to 22 January 1974	Water
20 February 1985 to 8 February 1986	Wood
7 February 1997 to 27 January 1998	Fire

If you were born on the day before the start of the lunar year of the Ox, e.g., 14th February, 1961, your animal sign is the one before the Ox, the Rat, the first lunar sign.

If you were born on the day after the last day of the lunar year of the Ox, e.g., 5th February, 1962, your animal sign is the one after the Ox, the Tiger, the third lunar sign.

The Ox, or Buffalo, rules the two-hour segment of the day between 1 A.M. and 3 A.M. This period of time follows that of the Rat and precedes that of the Tiger hours. Persons born during these two hours are said to have the Ox sign as their ascendant and will display many of the characteristics peculiar to this sign and have great affinity for persons born under the sign of the Ox. Quite possibly, one parent will also belong to the year of the Ox.

The direction appointed to the Ox is north-northwest; its season is winter, and its principle month, January. The Ox corresponds to the Western astrological sign of Sagittarius which rules winter from December 22nd to January 20th. Water is its fixed element and the Ox has a negative stem and is considered a yin or passive sign.

THE OX PERSONALITY

The Ox symbolizes the attainment of prosperity through fortitude and hard work. A person born during this year will be dependable, calm and methodical. A patient and tireless worker, he sticks to routine and conventions. Although he is generally fair-minded and a good listener, it is difficult to persuade him to change his views as he is stubborn and often has strong prejudices.

Still, because of his steady and reliable character, the Ox person will be awarded positions of authority and trust. He will not fall short when duty calls. As a matter of fact, he should be careful not to get totally wrapped up in his responsibilities.

Beneath the Ox's somewhat modest but neat appearance is a resolute and logical mind. His intelligence and dexterity are masked by his reticent and undemonstrative front. Yet, in spite of being basically an introvert, his forceful nature can turn him into a commanding and eloquent speaker when the occasion demands. In times of turmoil his presence of mind, refusal to be intimidated and innate self-confidence will enable him to restore order. He walks with his head held high.

A person born under this particular sign is systematic. He adheres to fixed patterns and has great respect for tradition. In fact, he tends to do exactly what is expected of him and is so predictable that he may be unfairly criticized for a lack of imagination. But the dutiful Ox knows that only through doing things in their proper order can he hope to achieve lasting success. His is the uncluttered mind. You won't find him muddling through life depending on others or his luck to pull him through. What people born under the other signs may accomplish by guile and wit, the Ox will achieve by sheer tenacity and dedication. You can rely on his promises; once he gives his word, he will stick by it. Public opinion means little to him. He will apply himself wholeheartedly to whatever task he is doing and finish the job. The Ox detests loose ends.

When it comes to affairs of the heart, the Ox can be terribly naive. He cannot fully comprehend the entrapments of love, much less employ enticing strategy and other allures to plead his romantic cause. Don't expect lyric poetry and moonlight serenades from him. He just doesn't have the right chemistry for these sort of things. Even his gifts are likely to be strong, durable and unpretentious.

Because they are traditionalists, Ox men and women will also be inclined to long courtships. It takes them time to develop intimate relationships because they are slow to warm up and reveal their true feelings. The Ox man may be a well-educated, distinguished speaker, a well-travelled leader of men, yet he can turn into a fumbling, tongue-tied lad when it comes to wooing his fair maiden.

But if you marry him and place your trust squarely on his shoulders, he will never disappoint you; he will stick by you faithfully. You never need worry about the rent or bills getting paid on time. The Ox likes to get his priorities straight, so don't expect diamonds and caviar unless he can really afford them. Life will always be as comfortable as he can make it and his family will never be in need.

If you have the good fortune to marry an Ox lady, you have picked a no-nonsense type of girl. She is efficient without being fussy and protective without being too dominating. Soft-spoken and confident, she will know what needs to be done and how to do it without wasting time and resources. She tends to take the intiative and you will find her anticipating your wishes with uncanny accuracy. At times, she can be overly concerned about details and punctuality. The Ox hates being late for anything. Like the well-trained girl scout, she is always prepared. She will handle finances well and do more than her fair share of housekeeping. Honest, hard-working and above reproach, she is the ideal wife.

The Ox may not be the life of the party, but he or she is certainly the backbone of society. Persons born under this sign are charitable by nature and make good social workers. The Ox may be the good Samaritan who saved someone and then left without giving his or her name. The Ox will not abandon you in times of trouble. He is around for the good times as well as the bad.

A lot of wonderful things come wrapped in plain brown paper. The Ox is one of them. Don't ever belittle the packaging. He is worth his weight in gold.

Aside from his many sterling qualities, the Ox person is also known to nurture grievances far too long. He has a long and exacting memory and injuries are remembered down to their last detail. The Ox holds grudges for too long. He would be better off if he could lighten up and stop taking life so seriously. Injuries and insults, real or imagined, can be magnified by the Ox person, who tends to be over-sensitive where his pride is concerned.

Whereas other signs such as the Tiger, Rooster or Dragon may complain vehemently when they are upset, and the Sheep and Rabbit will sulk and become morose, the Ox will react by plunging himself into hard work to alleviate his misery and tension. If severely disappointed in love, he may bury himself in his work forever and lead a solitary existence instead of running the risk of ever being humiliated or rejected again.

The Ox will insist on settling his accounts. Debts will be paid to the last decimal point. If he owes you something, he will never forgive himself if he doesn't show his gratitude in a meaningful and tangible way. No profuse but empty phrases of appreciation from him. He considers flowery words and lavish flattery uncouth and beneath his dignity. But won't it come as a surprise when you find out that the gruff fellow who barely managed to mumble a "Thank you," left you something in his will? Well, that's a typical Ox gesture for you. If anyone's actions speak louder than his words, his do.

Beware if you overtax the Ox's legendary patience. When an Ox person does lose his temper, he is really someone to reckon with. It could be a terrifying experience. There will be no reasoning with him: he will act like a bull and attack anyone in his path. The only advisable thing to do is to get out of his way until he cools off. By and large, however, he is seldom given to such a taxing display of temper unless he finds his situation truly unbearable. Most of the time, we find the Ox suffering quietly and bearing his problems without complaints.

At home, the Ox's word is law. He knows how to give orders as well as follow them. And he expects his directives to be carried out to the letter. He has a materialistic outlook on life and although he may be inordinately fond and proud of his family, he demands a lot from them, too. He will use the yardstick of success and personal achievement to measure his love for them. Even though he is not easily moved by emotions, he is a good parent and provider, and is capable of great sacrifices for his family's welfare. When and where it really counts, the Ox person will not let his loved ones down. He has no reason to feel insecure himself as he will likewise be well cared for all his life. Reason dictates that one so valuable should not be left to fend for himself. An Ox person will always be an asset to his firm and family.

The Ox born during the day will be more aggressive and active than the quiet night Ox. Similarly, the winter Ox will have a more trying life and leaner times than the summer Ox. The native of this lunar sign is a down-to-earth type who will follow his head rather than his heart. To win your case, appeal to his reason and intelligence. Make a list of the pros and cons and support every item with pertinent and credible data. Sentiment alone rarely makes the Ox change his mind. He also possesses a strong constitution and does not get sick easily. Proud and uncompromising, the Ox is disdainful of weaknesses in others. If he can learn to cultivate more humor and compassion, he will be much happier.

Likely to be a self-made man, he staunchly believes everyone should pull his own weight—and no hedging about it either. At his worst, the Ox is unapproachable, inflexible and narrow-minded. His lack of tact and consideration for others coupled with a militant view of life could at times make him unsuitable for positions involving public relations and diplomatic maneuvering. However, he is respected and liked for his basic honesty, unpretentiousness and steadfast principles. He inspires loyalty in all his subordinates, and no task is beneath him.

As mentioned earlier, the Ox person is not someone who takes shortcuts. His dignity and integrity will prevent him from resorting to unfair means to achieve his goals. He will dislike asking others for help. As a matter of fact, he is so self-reliant that you may have to beg him to accept any aid.

The Ox has dynastic tendencies. Careful and conscientious, he builds things to last. This sturdiness will extend to his offspring and generations to come even if they are not born under the same sign. His excellent character makes him an empire builder. If he is true to his ideals and follows his superior instincts, he will take all precautions to ensure the prosperity and survival of his lineage.

A natural-born leader and disciplinarian, he can sometimes be too rigid. The Ox will lay down the law and stand for no rebellion in areas under his control. He builds his life around his home, work and country and will always prefer long-term, stable investments. Being a creature of habit, he is no gambler: risks and razor-thin margins unnerve him because they endanger his profound need for security.

Of all the twelve signs, the colorful but somewhat eccentric Rooster will bring sunshine into the Ox's orderly life and make him a splendid partner. Both have high respect for authority, admire efficiency and possess a strong dedication to duty, and these common attributes will unite them successfully. Almost as well suited will be the affectionate Rat or the wise Snake, both of whom will care deeply for the worthy Ox. Dragon, Rabbit, another Ox, Horse, Boar and Monkey will be compatible to a lesser degree.

The Dog may find the Ox too bland and criticize his lack of humor; the Ox himself will not care for the company of the capricious Sheep or the rebellious Tiger native, who in turn will resent his authoritarian ways.

Whatever happens, one can be sure that the success enjoyed by the Ox will have been earned by his own merits. In short, the strong and disciplined Ox does not expect and will not get any free rides in his life. This stalwart fellow will emerge a winner through his own efforts and no one could be more deserving of his victories.

THE OX CHILD

The Ox child will not be a crybaby even if he or she is sickly. This child has the willpower and inner stamina to endure whatever trials life may bring. Usually tough and not very talkative, the Ox child will likely be obedient and attentive. He will follow the examples of his elders without question, be they good or bad. So it is imperative that he learns the difference between right and wrong at a very early age.

A rugged individualist, the Ox child tends to begin speaking late and prefers to settle arguments with his fists instead of his tongue. Stubborn and unyielding when his mind is made up, he can turn the house upside down when he insists on having his own way. He is not a whiner or complainer, but he can be adamant about the few concessions he does demand. One of them will be his privacy. He will know how to be discreet, even secretive, at an early age, and can be trusted to keep confidences.

He won't resent discipline and in fact will welcome your establishing a schedule for him. He may insist that his meals be served at the same time each day, although he will not be particular about food. Regularity is what the Ox thrives on: knowing where everything is and what exactly is expected of him gives him a sense of security. A girl born under this sign will keep her room neat and organized and will establish her own routine without too much supervision.

The Ox youngster enjoys taking charge when mother or teacher is away and is stern and unsympathetic to offenders. He can and usually will give you an unbiased opinion, as he is not easily influenced or taken in by flattery. Instead of bribing him or her, it would be more effective to simply say: "It is an order!" He is not argumentative by nature but you must gain his respect before he will cooperate with you.

The Ox child relishes teaching younger children and will display remarkable patience waiting for what he wants and great perseverance while working for it. Being the strong, silent type, he may not readily reveal his feelings. He can be deeply hurt and no one may even suspect it. Although he always presents a strong, brave front, the Ox can be terribly naive about the realities of life. He needs to be protected in this respect and will rely heavily on moral support from his parents, teachers and family.

At school, he may be an exemplary student as he is not one to lock horns with the authorities. His serious and no-nonsense outlook on life makes him avoid joking or clowning around. He should be encouraged to overcome his natural shyness and develop his sense of humor.

Above all, the Ox child will be responsible and reliable. He will win the respect of his elders as well as his peers. This child could be an outstanding example of both a good leader and follower. With a minimum of guidance, he will take the initiative to perform to the best of his ability and prove his worthiness to himself and all who know him.

THE FIVE DIFFERENT OXEN

METAL OX—1901, 1961

The Metal Ox will have clashes of will with people, even his superiors, who do not agree with his views. He expresses himself clearly, intensely and resolutely: no one can ever accuse him of being vague about what he wants! He will stick to his guns at all costs. When necessary, he can be quite eloquent—and will use his abilities to the full when he wants to forge ahead. He is definitely the "Do or Die" type.

Although he is not affectionate by nature, he may have scholarly inclinations and love classical music and art. He has a strong sense of responsibility and can be relied upon to keep his word, which shouldn't be too difficult as he or she will be a person of few words.

At times, he tends to force issues; he can become a formidable and fanatic one-man army when he is obsessed with succeeding in his objectives. Tough and arrogant, he does not know the word "failure." A person of remarkable stamina, he will require little rest or diversion. He won't mind working around the clock if that is what it takes to get things done. The Metal Ox should guard against being narrow-minded and vengeful when he doesn't get his way.

WATER OX—1913, 1973

This is a more realistic rather than idealistic Ox. Patient, practical and unrelentingly ambitious, he possesses a shrewd mind and a keen sense of values. He puts things to their proper use and makes many notable contributions because he knows how to bide his time and organize his activities.

This Ox will be more reasonable and flexible than other types of Oxen. He is open to suggestion, although he may not approve of change or unconventional methods being introduced into his life. But he will not be too unhappy if asked to bend a little to achieve his goals. He is primarily concerned about improving his status and security and will uphold law and order in everything he undertakes.

He will make his mark by working well with others and can steer his own course without any difficulty, provided he is not too rigid or does not demand too much from others. He can concentrate on more than one goal at a time and can both wear out and wait out the opposition by his methodical calmness, patience and unshakeable determination.

WOOD OX—1925, 1985

This type of Ox is less rigid and reacts faster than other Oxen. As a result, he is likely to be more graceful socially and considerate of other people's feelings. He will be admired for his integrity and ethics. He is fair and impartial although his lunar animal sign draws him toward conservatism. He understands and operates within a fixed social system and will be a much better showman than the Oxen of the other elements.

Given the chance and motivation, he will embrace new and progressive views; he is less stubborn and able to concede to majority rule.

He could climb to great heights, amassing wealth and achieving prominence, if he can succeed in founding and developing sizable industrial outfits. With his strong drive, he can exploit his potential to the maximum. He understands the importance of coexistence and will link his ambitions to a larger order of things. He is capable of teamwork and is likely to be very corporate minded.

FIRE OX—1937, 1997

This Ox is a combustible performer and the type most drawn to power and importance. The Fire element reinforces his native sense of control and determined temperament. As a result, he can be more forceful and proud than the other Oxen, with the exception of the quiet Metal Ox. He is materialistic and may have a superiority complex. Consequently, he tends to eliminate persons or things he considers useless or inappropriate without attempting to see their true worth. He is objective and outspoken and can be harsh to those who dare oppose him.

The Fire element could turn his hard-working nature toward military service. With his militant tendencies, he will not hesitate to wage an all-out war against his opponents. The Fire Ox tends to overestimate his abilities at times and may show a lack of consideration for the feelings of others. Despite all this, he is basically an honest soul and will not take advantage of others if he can avoid it. His family will benefit most from his labors as he will be very protective of his loved ones and will see to it that they are always well provided for. The Fire Ox will never shrink away when duty calls. He will most likely be flying his banner high and leading the charge.

EARTH OX—1949, 2009

This is an enduring although less creative type of Ox who is always faithful to his ideals and principles. He becomes aware of his limitations and imperfections quite early in life. However, he will shine in any career he decides to undertake as he is practical, industrious and prepared to pay the price demanded for success. He contributes his share willingly and will favor practical and worthy endeavors. Security and stability are his two master goals.

Although he may not be sensitive or emotional by nature, he is capable of sincere and lasting affection and will be loyal and steadfast to his loved ones.

He will fight for advancement constantly throughout his life and will endure difficulties and suffering without complaint. Purposeful and determined, this Ox will go far; it will be hard to push him back because he will never surrender captured ground. He may be the slowest but surest of all the Oxen.

COMPATIBILITY AND CONFLICT CHARTS
FOR THE OX

The Ox is part of the Second Triangle of Affinity, which consists of the most purposeful and steadfast signs. The Ox, Snake and Rooster are dutiful and dedicated fighters who strive to reach great heights and conquer by their sheer constancy and unfailing determination. These three are fixed in their views and given to thought and systematic planning. They are the most intellectual signs of the cycle. They rely on their own assessments of facts and figures and give little credence to hearsay evidence. They are most likely to comply with the dictates of their heads rather than their hearts. Slow and sure, they prefer to act independently. They will invariably seek each other out and can marry and intermingle most successfully.

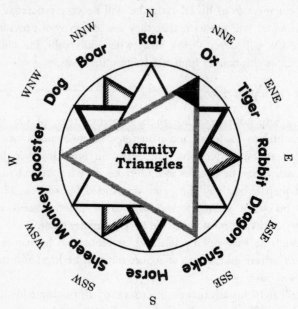

TRIANGLE OF AFFINITY FOR THE OX

The Ox will encounter his most serious personality clashes with people born in the year of the Sheep. Anyone whose ascendant is in the hours of the Sheep will also conflict with the Ox. In the Circle of Conflict, the Ox and the Sheep are 180 degrees apart and thus total opposites. The Ox's direction or compass point is north-northwest, the Sheep's direction is identified as south-southwest. The Ox rules in winter, the Sheep's season is summer. The Ox's fixed element is Water while its opposite, the Sheep's natural element, is Fire.

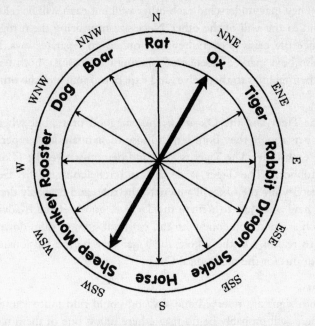

CIRCLE OF CONFLICT

After the most compatible signs, the Snake and the Rooster, and the least compatible partner, the Sheep, the other nine signs are compatible with the Ox to varying degrees.

Rat

The Rat and the Ox born do well in marriage or business relationships. Both are hard workers, family oriented and have a mutual need for security. The Rat tends to nag but that will be tolerated by the patient Ox because he knows that the Rat has his interests at heart. These two could live well and prosper if they keep to their proper roles in the relationship: the Rat will be the more verbal partner, the Ox the good listener and superachiever.

Ox

Ox and Ox make for a lukewarm partnership. There may be areas of common interest but not enough to sustain real in-depth commitment. They may understand each other well but each will be reluctant to bend to the will of the other. Necessity may bring them together but once the crisis is over, they may opt to go separate ways. There may also be a marked absence of communication since both tend to keep their feelings to themselves and expect too much of the other.

Tiger

The Tiger and the Ox are friends in good times, but when the going gets rough, they both tend to lose their infamous tempers and blame each other. The Tiger is loud and demonstrative, the Ox quiet and stubborn. The Tiger is defiant and rebellious in the face of authority, while the Ox will adhere to the rules and probably draw up a few new ones just to irritate the Tiger. A good referee is advisable for such a union, someone who can get both sides to calm down and listen to reason. On the whole, the Tiger may be too passionate and adventurous for the methodical Ox.

Rabbit

Both signs are reserved and shy and could find mutual interests. But there will probably be no magic here unless one of them has the other's sign as an ascendant. The Rabbit is too well-mannered to offend, but he or she may be turned off by the Ox's spartan outlook on life. The Ox will not be attracted by the Hare's love of ease and luxury. Besides, the Rabbit's best friends, the Sheep and the Boar, are not on the same wavelength as the Ox. Compatibility may be strained if the Rabbit has to choose between his friends and the exclusive company of the Ox.

Dragon

A workable relationship as these two powerhouses of energy make a good team. There is mutual respect and understanding. Both can identify and work on their goals with religious zeal and for the common good. These two will have no major struggle for dominance if each keeps his end of the bargain. The Ox will let the Dragon hog the limelight so long as the Dragon pulls his own weight and gives the Ox his just due.

Horse

Relations are moderate or temporary between the Horse and the Ox. Nothing lasting can result unless one has the other's sign as an ascendant. The Horse is mercurial and independent while the Ox has his feet firmly planted on the ground. The Horse uses his intuition and charisma to achieve his goals while the Ox prefers to go by the book. Communication barriers could easily preclude a close relationship between these two signs. The Horse prefers short cuts while the Ox sticks to the proven path.

Monkey

Both signs have mutual reservations about each other and with good reason. The clever and intricate Monkey considers the Ox too slow and unimaginative for his taste. The Ox distrusts the Monkey's schemes and cannot fully comprehend the Monkey's ideas. They would actually make a good team if each were able to appreciate the qualities in the other that he lacks and learn to make use of their differences. The Monkey is most likely to be the brain, the Ox the brawn. If they can work out their differences, their partnership will bear fruit.

Dog

Dog and Ox could do well together if they are moving toward the same goals or in the same circles. Otherwise, they may not have much sympathy or attraction for each other. The Dog is warm, likable and idealistic in general. The Ox is stern, determined and loyal only to his own ideals. They may expect too much from each other and in the end go their separate ways if the chemistry is not right. The congenial Dog may find the Ox too uncompromising unless they both champion the same cause. In a fight for justice or freedom, these two would make a great team.

Boar

The Ox can be compatible with the Boar to a certain degree. There will be no great personality clashes between these two unless the Boar's best friends, the Sheep and the Rabbit, interfere. Then the relationship could cool or die since the Boar will always choose the Sheep and Rabbit over the domineering Ox. Otherwise, the social Boar will get along with the Ox and do his best to keep the peace. While there may be no struggle for dominance here, there may be no lasting bond either.

THE OX AND HIS ASCENDANTS

We all have a shadow that follows us throughout life. Sometimes it grows bigger than life and at other times it shrinks until it disappears into the soles of our feet. Sometimes it walks tall before us and on other occasions it lags behind like a sulking friend. In Chinese horoscopes, this constant partner, manifested or not, is our ascendant, the animal sign that rules the hour of our birth and becomes a comrade in our journey through life. We may view it as friend or foe or even a little of both. It surfaces when we least expect and shows a better or worse side of our nature. We can often be confounded by the way we listen to our "other self" as well as feel resentful of the significant influence it can exert on us. Actually, a personality has many rings around the centered "self." Each ring can have a different size, texture and aura. When all these factors combine, they bring forth the unique individual that the person truly is. Hence, a Dragon with an incompatible ascendant, like the Dog, has perhaps a more difficult inner struggle than say a Snake born during the hours of the Snake. The double intensity of the Snake person will be easily understood by horoscope readers while the more intricate Dragon/Dog may exhibit the contrary Dog and Dragon traits to varying degrees. There are many voices within each person. But, in the end, only the individual determines which course he will follow, which choices he will make.

The time of birth used to determine the ascendant is always the local time in the place of birth.

If you were born between:

11 P.M. and 1 A.M. = The Hours of the Rat

You have a sentimental side to your nature. The Rat's charm softens you and makes you more flexible and communicative. You are more adept with words and in relationships than other Oxen and have a keen sense of humor. Still, you never forget an injury or how to count your pennies. You can be critical and demanding when you set your standards too high. Otherwise, everyone would love to have you for a friend.

1 A.M. and 3 A.M. = The Hours of the Ox

Yours is a double Ox sign or a "pure" sign since you have the same ascendant as birth year. You are gifted with extraordinary stamina, self-control and determination. It would be foolish for anyone to try to outlast or outfight such a combination. Not much can be said for your humor or imagination. Try to lighten up a bit on that discipline—not everyone is out to deliberately break the rules. If you don't overreact when you are in control, people will learn to appreciate your true worth and respect you more.

3 A.M. and 5 A.M. = The Hours of the Tiger

You are a captivating Ox with a lively, dramatic personality that draws people to you. You won't be as soft spoken as other Oxen, or as shy either. Watch out for your explosive temper and don't jump to conclusions without checking everything twice. It will be worth your while to restrain your impulsiveness. With the Tiger's influence, you will need and demand more attention than other Ox natives. Performance is where you excel; you are a natural actor or athlete.

5.A.M. and 7 A.M. = The Hours of the Rabbit

With the Rabbit's influence you will be kind, diplomatic and discreet but like the Ox, you are not likely to change your opinions easily. A creature of habit, you dislike disruptions or unforeseen delays and will seek to establish order and control over your life. You are a refined Ox who will collect art and antiques and appreciate music and the theatre. Usually, you will not become a workaholic with your Rabbit ascendant.

7 A.M. and 9 A.M. = The Hours of the Dragon

You have the strength and power of the Dragon for achieving your ambitions in life. Your main shortcoming will be your opinionated and inflexible Ox character. If you could adapt to changes and accede to the wishes of the majority, you would gain much more. The Dragon's intensity makes you see things only one way: your own. But to succeed, you will need help from different sources. Try to learn to negotiate instead of dictate.

9 A.M. and 11 A.M. = The Hours of the Snake

With the Snake as your ascendant, you will be doubly secretive since the Ox sign is not exactly one to confide in others either. This makes you uncommunicative about your true feelings. Give others a chance to understand you by being more candid and open. Otherwise, you will end up being a loner. You have a deeply religious side to your personality and trust in your beliefs and intuition immensely. More often than not, you will be right to rely on your own judgment. Others will find the hidden mystic side of you intriguing.

11 A.M. and 1 P.M. = The Hours of the Horse

The Horse as your ascendant makes you a happy-go-lucky person. You are open-minded and carefree. The Horse makes you a good dancer, a lover of music and a sharp dresser. But he also makes you change your mind more often than you would like. However, you are one Ox who will like to have variety in your life and enjoy travel and new adventures.

1 P.M. and 3 P.M. = The Hours of the Sheep

You are an artistic Ox with a tender side to your personality. Easily moved by sad news or tragedy, you are generous and trusting and always ready to help the less fortunate. With the Sheep's ascendant, you are receptive to new ideas and have a flair for art. However, with the stable influence of the Ox, you will be business-minded enough to make money out of your talents. The biggest inner struggle you could have is the conflict between the Sheep's lavish, free spending ways and the Ox's love of frugality and simplicity.

3 P.M. and 5 P.M. = The Hours of the Monkey

You will be a shrewd but jovial Ox who will not take your problems too seriously because, with the Monkey's influence, you won't have to. The Monkey brains will always find a way out or invent a solution if there isn't one. The Ox in you strives for discipline and order, while the Monkey part bends the rules to suit his own agenda. People will have to wake up very early to put one over on you.

5 P.M. and 7 P.M. = The Hours of the Rooster

People would describe you as dynamic and dutiful and probably vote for you if you ran for public office. A cross between the soldier and the preacher, you could hold the Bible in one hand and a weapon in the other. What you won't win by rhetoric, you will win by sheer force. Not one to deal lightly with opposition, you may tend to keep fighting even after you have won the battle. Your enemies are the ones who need our sympathy—they won't be able to keep up with you.

7 P.M. and 9 P.M. = The Hours of the Dog

The Dog ascendant brings popularity and happiness to the Ox's rather spartan outlook. You are fair minded and will listen to all sides before making a decision. However, you do tend to favor the underdog and like to champion difficult and hard-to-win causes. The Ox will accept any challenge without flinching and the Dog is loyal to a fault. Everyone would love to have you working for him or at least on his side.

9 P.M. and 11 P.M. = The Hours of the Boar

Although you are still conservative and disciplined, the Boar colors your world with his zest for life and love of material things. You will no doubt like to work hard but you will know how to play hard, too. Good food, fine wine and the company of friends are what you like best. The Boar's generosity combined with the Ox's sincere ability to make strong commitments will produce a dependable and friendly personality who is more than willing to shoulder responsibilities others may find overwhelming.

HOW THE OX FARES IN THE LUNAR CYCLE

1. The Year of the Rat 1996

The year of the Rat brings smooth and prosperous times for the hard-working Ox. Luck will favor his undertakings and his problems will tend to work themselves out if he is not overanxious and does not try too hard. There won't be much need to be overly concerned about finances, although the Ox tends to worry about security more than necessary. The Ox gains recognition for his previous contributions and may assume new positions of importance. At home, there will be many events to be celebrated and to the Ox this is one area that he needs to be secure about. It is a good year to set aside money for a rainy day or lay the foundation of a new business or enterprise that could grow into something substantial.

2. The Year of the Ox 1997

Overall, this will be a good year, although the Ox's plans may suffer delays, and difficulties may crop up unexpectedly. The Ox will work hard this year and there will be many functions on his schedule. It is also an auspicious time for marriage or forming new partnerships. Children and family events will feature largely in the Ox's activities as he devotes time to youngsters, sports or family get-togethers. The problems that beset him are mainly due to forces beyond his control and the negligence of others. The Ox must patiently deal with the demands on his time and attention, and manage some unwanted traveling and entertaining besides.

3. The Year of the Tiger 1998

In this difficult year the Ox must be on guard against opposition from many sources. The good news is that he will be able to overcome or persevere through his hardships. Results and rewards are not immediately evident, so the Ox must not be discouraged when the going gets rough. His patience and tenacity will eventually pay off. This will be the time for him to take stock of his situation and make tough decisions about what he truly wishes to achieve. Unnecessary risks and drastic measures during the reign of the Tiger are not advised. Things will look bleakest just before the sun breaks through the clouds. The Tiger is full of flash and fireworks that, in the end, may not do any real damage.

4. The Year of the Rabbit 1999

On the whole, the Rabbit provides a fair year for the Ox, although there are many loose ends to tie up and other problems to settle. He may lose money on some investments or fail to collect debts. The death of, or separation from, people close to him bring some sorrow and distract him from his work. However, the tranquil atmosphere of the Rabbit's year brings him respite from his many commitments. His progress will be steady and predictable and he does not have much to worry about. This is a good time for him to catch up on the things he really enjoys. Go sailing, fishing, mountain climbing, play golf, or simply take time off.

5. The Year of the Dragon 2000

In this moderate year for the Ox, many changes and unforeseen troubles beset the Ox and keep him as busy as a firefighter in summer. After much effort, his plans will be realized but not without prodding from the Ox's horns. The Dragon's year will be demanding for everyone and the Ox will be no exception. However, the Ox is blessed with extraordinary stamina and a strong sense of purpose. He will also find help with his heavy burden from good friends and influential people who will come to his aid. The Dragon tends to magnify problems as well as prosperity, so the Ox should keep his eyes on his goals and concentrate on his objectives.

6. The Year of the Snake 2001

Good times are predicted this year for the Ox born. He will find it easy to make money. Things are all within his reach this year. Investments and hard work finally pay off and his personal life is alive with romance and new friendships. On the darker side, he may have a misunderstanding with some associate or find out that someone has betrayed his confidence. He could resolve his problems by being open to discussions, otherwise he will invite complications. Hopefully, the wisdom of the Snake this year will help the Ox to seek counsel and not lose his famous temper when things are not working out as he wishes.

7. The Year of the Horse 2002

The fast and unpredictable Horse will provide a rather unsettling time for the methodical and orderly Ox native. One moment he could be on top of the world and the next he will be fighting battles he never anticipated. The Horse is as changeable as the wind and this unnerves the steady, reliable Ox. Financial setbacks and delays make the Ox unable to fulfill his promises or meet his commitments. Stubborn resistance will be useless, and angry reprisals or blind attacks may just make the Ox accident prone during the reign of the Horse. He will do best by biding his time, consolidating his resources and making conservative estimates until the fall. Matters should definitely quiet down by winter.

8. The Year of the Sheep 2003

The Year of the Sheep will not bring much progress for the plans of the Ox although he will receive good news and reviews to boost his self-confidence. He will have no serious illnesses, quarrels, or problems with his love life. His home life will be relatively peaceful, his complaints minor and easily resolved. However, this is not a time to be overoptimistic as the Ox could discover that he did not make the gains he thought he had. He may also make mistakes in calculations he cannot even talk about. The Sheep's year is not a good time to make long-term commitments or to negotiate for the future. This is a time that could bring the normally decisive, action-oriented Ox, indecision and doubt.

9. The Year of the Monkey 2004

In this lucky and prosperous year, the Ox will be sought after by important people and his accomplishments will be recognized. Good tidings at home or on his job await him and he will climb the ladder of success with help from the right people. New ventures and partnerships can be formed under the auspices of the clever Monkey. The Monkey will realize the value of the strong and dutiful Ox and have use for his many talents. The responsible Ox person will find many opportunities in the year of the Monkey.

10. The Year of the Rooster 2005

The Rooster's year shines on the Ox's diligence and his devotion to duty. The Ox will have a moderately happy time with a good deal of fame and success. However, this will be a year to pay attention to details, read the fine print and never second-guess anything. The Rooster watches his pennies, which is fine with the frugal Ox. It will be an easy time for the Ox to organize his life and make long-term plans. Both the Rooster and the Ox have a love for order and discipline, and this year will be predictable enough to suit the Ox's taste. Progress is slow but sure and gains can be measured in terms that the Ox person will accept.

11. The Year of the Dog 2006

The Dog's Year is a watchful and anxious one for the Ox. But although problems loom large this year, they will turn out to be less serious than they originally seemed. Expected complications do not materialize and the Ox's path is clear of obstacles. Still, the year of the Dog will be a guarded time. The Ox's accomplishments will be hard earned and he may be separated from his loved ones and forced to work or travel alone. Yet, the Dog is always fair and the Ox will be justly rewarded for his efforts.

12. The Year of the Boar 2007

A busy time is in store for the Ox native. He will not net much to show for his efforts because he will have to spend more than he earns in the year of the overly generous Pig. However, he should not begrudge this as he will make valuable contacts for later use. He will also enjoy the social interaction and goodwill that abounds during the Boar's reign, though family, work and romantic problems will take up most of his time and keep him more involved than he wants to be. Affairs of the heart may bring disappointments during this year, so it will be wise for the Ox to look before he leaps.

WHEN MOON SIGNS MEET SUN SIGNS

In my interpretation of Chinese horoscopes, the Rat is not linked with the first Western astrological sun sign, Aries. Instead, I pair the Rat with its counterpart based on the month and season of the Rat, which are December and winter. This makes the most sense as the lunar month of December (also called the Twelfth Moon or the Twelfth Earth Branch) is supposed to parallel the Sun sign, Sagittarius, the Archer. I envision the Eastern and Western horoscope cycles as two large wheels, each with twelve spokes. To correctly juxtapose these cycles, we must find the matching notch that will join them together. Once the Rat and Sagittarius are paired as the first signs, the other eleven fall into place. Please see the Twenty-Four Segments of the Lunar Almanac. All the dates correspond with the twelve Western solar signs.

If you are born in the year of the Ox under the Western sign of

Sagittarius: 22nd November to 21st December
The Sagittarian Ox = Fire + Negative Water

The Archer here will utilize the Ox's authority with more finesse and goodwill. The Sagittarian Ox is still heavy-handed, but will make up for his stubborness with his exquisite yet practical taste and manners. A more focused perfectionist, he is realistic but has flair and style. Looking for the good in others and planning how to salvage hopeless situations brings him the most happiness and success. The Ox is a strong helmsman, and the Archer's instincts and showmanship are above par. As a result, the Sagittarian Ox can conduct flawless rescue operations and will probably be an excellent entreprenuer. Noble, altruistic and practical, the Sagittarian Ox loves both wisely and well.

If you are born in the year of the Ox under the Western sign of

Capricorn: 22nd December to 20th January
The Capricorn Ox = Earth + Negative Water

A serious marriage of these two slow but sure signs produces a personality made of granite who will withstand hard times and adversity. His convictions are often inflexible, and his righteousness is overpowering. This harsh but extremely self-sufficient person conceals the lighter side of his nature and wills himself to climb the loftiest cliffs without a word of complaint. Although he may be tender and selfless toward those he loves, he is rarely demonstrative. This spartan subject is simple and deliberate. He knows what he wants and to get it he will be able to bear twice the responsibilities that others find hard even to think about. The Capricorn Ox is sure to reach the peak of any mountain he decides to climb.

If you are born in the year of the Ox under the Western sign of

Aquarius: 21st January to 19th February
The Aquarian Ox = Air + Negative Water

The belligerent qualities of the Buffalo are altered by the cool and airy ways of this Uranian Sign—the Water Bearer. Nonviolent but nonconforming, too, the ebullient Aquarius will teach the stiff Ox that he must sometimes stoop to conquer. The Water Bearer is too intelligent to resort to the brute force Buffalos may employ when they are vengeful. Likewise, this subject will have above average foresight and social graces. He is less predictable than other Oxen and not above defying public opinion by bending the rules to suit himself.

If you are born in the year of the Ox under the Western sign of

Pisces: 20th February to 20th March
The Pisces Ox = Water + Negative Water

Prim and proper, the Piscean Ox will possess a mystical and sweet nature marked by strong inhibitions. Yet people are drawn to him despite his reticence because he exudes a feeling of security and displays the Ox's knack for being able to control his environment. His reserved ways and quiet mannerisms only emphasize his strength and trustworthiness. Solemn, but with Pisces' gourmet tastes, he will also use the Ox's ability to achieve financial stability. As genuine as 24K gold and absolutely honest, the Piscean Ox will still have an ego that bruises easily, partly because of the Fish's sensitivity and partly because the Ox will refuse to tolerate any disrespect.

If you are born in the year of the Ox under the Western sign of

Aries: 21st March to 19th April
The Aries Ox = Fire + Negative Water

Because the Buffalo is slow and sure and the Ram is self-possessed and occasionally arrogant, this will be a temperamental and stubborn personality. Since neither sign is gifted with words, the result could be too much action and strength of will and not enough tolerance. Still, this person does look before he leaps, as both animals here are sure-footed and reluctant to give up territory staked out as theirs. The Aries Ox goes a long way by himself and seldom seeks help or burdens others with his troubles. But, if and when he decides to challenge authority, he can be intolerable.

If you are born in the year of the Ox under the Western sign of

Taurus: 20th April to 20th May
The Taurean Ox = Earth + Negative Water

When dealing with this slow but extremely persistent climber, bear in mind that he has four horns and eight hooves and this amount of armor is enough to overwhelm anyone. The Venus personality of the Bull is sensuous, but both signs here are very definite about who they are and what they want. Orderly, practical and determined, the Taurean Ox can also be dictatorial and obsessed with self-enforced discipline. He expresses himself in plain, down-to-earth language and abhors flattery and fancy talk. When he is aroused, he can suddenly turn into a one-man stampede. And once he sets his mind to something, well, he is about as open to discussion and as movable as the Sphinx.

If you are born in the year of the Ox under the Western sign of

Gemini: 21st May to 21st June
The Gemini Ox = Air + Negative Water

The Gemini virtuoso brings wit and vitality to lighten the Buffalo's stodginess. Yet the Ox's methodical ways should prove a blessing as the Gemini personality will not be so mercurial. He will be able to finish tasks on schedule and will not resist carrying out routine or boring but essential assignments. This responsible soul will be able to both take care of himself and utilize his sound visionary qualities. And this Ox will certainly know how to speak his mind, thanks to his Gemini gift of eloquent speech.

If you are born in the year of the Ox under the Western sign of

Cancer: 22nd June to 21st July
The Cancerian Ox = Water + Negative Water

A person born with this combination will not be half as amiable as he looks. But he will be thoughtful and considerate in spite of behaving like a motherly dictator at times. The Cancerian Ox is not a sacrificial lamb and will create an uproar if his rights are trampled on. Nor will the Buffalo allow the Crab to be overly controlled by his emotions. On the other hand, the Cancerian influence on the Ox will definitely ameliorate some of his dictatorial and dogmatic ways. This person may turn out to be a very good listener who can be firm and understanding at the same time.

If you are born in the year of the Ox under the Western sign of

Leo: 22nd July to 21st August
The Leo Ox = Fire + Negative Water

This will be a warm-hearted yet slightly impersonal character with a dignified appearance. The Leo Ox could also be dramatic and even pompous at times, as the Lion's ego does take up a lot of room. The Buffalo's sternness and uncompromising outlook will only serve to reinforce this sun sign's indomitable will. But the Lion spreads his largesse and radiance onto the otherwise dour Ox, and this person will be far from dull. A respected and commanding personality, the Leo Ox will have the ability to lead effortlessly.

If you are born in the year of the Ox under the Western sign of

Virgo: 22nd August to 22nd September
The Virgo Ox = Earth + Negative Water

The Virgo Ox is shrewd, very careful and in his own mind quite infallible. It does not matter how much formal education this sort of person has had, for he will never stop assimilating knowledge and bettering himself throughout life. He will also hate being in crowded or noisy places as it offends his monastic soul and interferes with his desire for quiet contemplation. Need someone to set down every letter of the law? No one should be better qualified than he. Very strong, deeply religious and systematic to a fault, this combination emphasizes discipline and will never hesitate to take wrongdoers to task.

If you are born in the year of the Ox under the Western sign of

Libra: 23rd September to 22nd October
The Libra Ox = Air + Negative Water

The Libra Ox will not be stubborn or hot tempered, for Venus's child always opts for comfort and compromise. The Buffalo's rigidity is curbed a good deal here, although this personality will not have that strong Libran need to be dependent nor its notorious inability to make up his mind. Cheerful and undemanding of others, this Ox will make friends easily while maintaining high standards for those he chooses to model himself on. An Ox who loves the good life, he won't plan on working too hard without in-between bouts of leisure. Trust the Libra Ox to enjoy the fruits of his labor.

If you are born in the year of the Ox under the Western sign of

Scorpio: 23rd October to 21st November
The Scorpio Ox = Water + Negative Water

This personality is gifted with the Buffalo's armor and the Scorpion's deadly sting. Never doing things by halves and quick to retaliate, he will fearlessly navigate the deep waters this combination represents. Endowed with an inflexible will and a demanding ego, this subject will be an outstanding religious or military leader. Or, he could use all his energies to uphold the law or go against it. Never vague about his desires, he will pursue his dreams with rare intensity. The Scorpio Ox will reach the finish line first because of his innate tenacity and absolute refusal to come second to anyone.

THE SEASONS OF THE OX

SPRING

Oxen born during the day will be more active, hardworking and social than those born in the evening. Because the Ox must toil endlessly in the spring to prepare the soil for the crops, any person born in the spring will have to work hard in life and shoulder a heavy burden of responsibilities. Usually he will be capable and prepared to deal with whatever life shoves his way. A natural leader and innovator, he hates to waste time and is very achievement conscious. Physically and mentally strong, Oxen born in the spring will be noted for their invaluable contributions to society and to their families.

SUMMER

The summer Ox is fattened by the fruits of his own labor and will have a contented life. Grass is plentiful and he will be well cared for as he is the farmer's most valuable asset. The long warm days are still filled with duty and chores but the Ox of summer enjoys a busy life filled with commitments he loves. He has few fears and does not need to prove anything to himself or others. Self-assured and reliable, this Ox will go through life ready and able to pull his own weight. He will love learning and be dedicated to whatever profession he decides to master.

AUTUMN

The autumn Ox values security more than his brothers of the other seasons. He must attend to responsibilities entrusted to him by family and friends and he is usually serious and protective in his outlook. In the fall, the Ox is weighed down by demands on his time and strength. The autumn Ox knows that he must strive harder and longer than others, but he also has great stamina and purpose in life. People will be drawn to him because he knows that only through unselfish service and dedication can he make his mark on the world.

WINTER

The winter Ox knows how to count his blessings and weigh the pros and cons of each situation before making a move. This is the most meditative of all the Oxen. He is cool, deliberate and unhurried. He will bide his time and can outlast his foes by his sheer ability to withstand adversity. In the tranquillity of winter, the Ox draws on his strength to prepare for the work ahead. He will be an introvert who can make up his own mind with little or no outside help. An excellent organizer and analytical person, the winter Ox will have a protected existence, especially if he is born in the evening, when Oxen are sheltered for the night.

FAMOUS PERSONS BORN IN THE YEAR OF THE OX

Metal
Walt Disney
Emperor Hirohito
Eisaku Sato

Wood
Gore Vidal
Sammy Davis Jr.
Peter Sellers
Richard Burton
Margaret Thatcher
Melina Mercouri

Fire
Robert Redford
Vanessa Redgrave
Dustin Hoffman
Boris Spassky

Water
Richard Nixon
Gerald Ford
Archbishop Makarios of Greece
Willy Brandt
Vincent Van Gogh
Carlo Ponti

Earth
Adolf Hitler
Jawaharlal Nehru
Charlie Chaplin

3

The Third Sign
of the Lunar Cycle

The Tiger

I am the delightful Paradox.
All the world is my stage.
I set new trails ablaze,
    I seek the unattainable,
    and try the untried.
I dance to life's music
    in gay abandon.
Come with me on my carousel rides.
See the myriad of colors,
    the flickering lights.
All hail me the unparalleled performer.

I AM THE TIGER.

Lunar Years of the Tiger in the Western Calendar	Elements
8 February 1902 to 28 January 1903	Water
26 January 1914 to 13 February 1915	Wood
13 February 1926 to 1 January 1927	Fire
31 January 1938 to 18 February 1939	Earth
17 February 1950 to 5 February 1951	Metal
5 February 1962 to 24 January 1963	Water
23 January 1974 to 10 February 1975	Wood
9 February 1986 to 28 January 1987	Fire
28 January 1998 to 15 February 1999	Earth

If you were born on the day before the start of the lunar year of the Tiger, e.g., 4th February 1962, your animal sign is the one before the Tiger, the Ox, the second lunar sign.

If you were born on the day after the last day of the lunar year of the Tiger, e.g., 25th January 1963, your animal sign is the one after the Tiger, the Rabbit, the fourth lunar sign.

The Tiger rules the two-hour segment of the day between 3 A.M. and 5 A.M. Persons born during this time are said to have the Tiger as their ascendant and will display many of the characteristics common to this sign and have great affinity for persons born under the sign of the Tiger.

The direction appointed to the Tiger is east–northeast; its season is winter and its principle month, February. The Tiger corresponds to the Western astrological sign of Aquarius, which rules the sky from January 21st to February 19th. Wood is its fixed element and the Tiger has a positive or yang stem.

THE TIGER PERSONALITY

In Eastern culture, the Tiger symbolizes power, passion and daring. A rebellious, colorful and unpredictable character, he commands awe and respect from all quarters. This fearless and fiery fighter is revered as the sign that wards off the three main dangers to a household: fire, thieves and ghosts.

The Tiger is a fortunate person to have around, provided you are prepared for all the activity that comes along with his dynamic personality. The impulsiveness and vivacity of the Tiger person are contagious. His vigor and love of life are stimulating. He will arouse every sort of emotion in people, except indifference. In short, the captivating Tiger loves being the center of attention.

Restless and reckless by nature, the Tiger is always ready for action. However, because of his suspicious and impatient nature, he is prone to vacillate or else to make hasty decisions. He also can't help speaking his mind when he is upset. But, just as he is quick-tempered, he is equally sincere, affectionate and generous. What's more, he has a marvelous sense of humor.

Every Tiger has humanitarian instincts. He loves babies, endangered species, sick or orphaned animals, exotic plants and anything that catches his imagination or attention. He will have many pets to share his home and when he gets involved, his involvement is total. Everything else will have to take second place to the object of his adulation. The Tiger is never halfhearted about his endeavors. He'll always give 100 percent of himself—or even more if he can.

The more sensual types of Tigers usually have a fling at the bohemian life in their youth. Some never grow out of it. Aspiring and adventurous models seeking fame and romance in Paris, budding painters displaying their wares on street corners, amateur bands on the road, one-night-stand rock singers and ambitious actors or writers all working and living on shoestring budgets are more likely to be Tiger children than flower children. This may be because, aside from being the supreme optimist, the Tiger is just not materialistic or security conscious. He trusts his own luck and charisma to see him through and to finally bring him success.

He or she must have one phase in his life in which he acts out his impulses—playing all the fantastic roles others only dream of. This is his time to thumb his nose at what he disapproves of and meet the challenges he has devised for himself: skydiving, deep sea diving, safaris in unchartered wildernesses, or a new commune living off the land. He will lash out at society and scoff at binding traditions. The Tiger must express himself, find his identity and shape his personality, and if rebellion or open defiance of accepted modes of behavior offer him the opportunity to do so, then that's the road he will take. Could one love him any less for these imperfections, if they can be labeled as such? No, nine times out of ten, we find ourselves rooting for him. We may shake our heads at his audacity and gasp at his insane acts of daring, but just the same we never forget to say a silent prayer for him. When we see him succeed, we feel we have experienced a warm personal triumph, too.

When the Tiger is dejected he will need cartloads of sincere, undiluted sympathy. Don't rationalize about who is right and who is wrong. Logic does not appeal much to him. That's beside the point. And don't be stingy about comforting him. He would do twice as much for you if the situation were reversed. He will love to hear your words of wisdom and will hang on to every kind word of advice. But this doesn't mean he will take it. That's his nature, so don't feel hurt. There is a difference, you know. It never pays to be arbitrary with this fellow.

Instead, just hold his hand, pat him gently on the back and wait till he talks himself out, bounces his feelings off of you, and collects the pieces of his shattered ego. Then he will kiss you, hug you and let you leave feeling like you just put Humpty Dumpty back together again.

And, after he packs you off, well, in all probability he will go out and do exactly what he was planning to do in the first place.

No matter how down and out the Tiger is, no matter to what depths of despair and depression he plunges, don't believe for one moment he will ever say die! There will always be a tiny spark left somewhere in that unquenchable spirit of his to rekindle the fire and start him living and loving all over again.

A bit too intense to rely on in times of stress, and not the most objective of leaders, the Tiger is still renowned for his ability to sway a crowd. At his best, he is warm, sensitive and sympathetic. At his worst, he is obstinate, unreasonable and selfish, without even realizing it.

The lady Tiger is the most charming and radiant of hostesses. She can combine home and social life with rare aplomb. Solicitous, vibrant and absolutely disarming, she seems to be a sweet little kitten only because this act gets her good reviews. But don't be misled; she keeps her claws well sharpened in case she needs them.

Fashion-conscious, articulate and liberated, the lady Tiger likes to pamper herself and can spend hours experimenting with new hair-styles, makeup and costumes. Give a ball and she will turn out to stun them every time, though she is the type who constantly laments that she has nothing to wear. In reality, though, she is just as comfortable in blue jeans as with haute couture. She is great with the children, too. She tells lovely stories, mimics and makes fun of herself, flashes her brilliant smile and, most of all, endears them to her forever by bending all the rules in their favor. When she is around, they can have sweets before dinner, double helpings of ice cream for dessert, and stay up late for their favorite TV program. Strange to say, her children are no more spoiled than others and seem to learn well under her guidance. Perhaps this is because, after she shows them how much she cares, she makes sure to enforce all the rules. And when they mind their manners, she is extremely generous with rewards. There will be picnics galore, trips to the zoo and parks and all sorts of spontaneous activities and shopping trips. No wonder she is never without her little troop of loyal followers.

Like the Dragon and the Rooster, the Tiger native has a huge ego. Money, power and fame will mean nothing if his ego is hurt. Thwarted, the Tiger could turn out to be the meanest and pettiest bully you ever came across. He will go to any lengths to get revenge, even bringing down the house with him. Little slights will enrage him, but he may let big issues pass without a murmur. The one thing to remember is that he hates being ignored!

Paradoxically, his two main shortcomings in life will be rashness on the one hand and indecision on the other. If he can learn to take the middle of the road, the Tiger will be a roaring success.

At heart, the Tiger is a romantic. He is playful yet passionate and sentimental all at the same time. It will be quite an experience being in love with or married to one. He or she is also inclined to be over-possessive and quarrelsome when jealous.

The first stage of the Tiger's life will probably be the best. In these formative years, he should be taught to keep a tight rein on the explosive emotions that could be the ruin of him. In his youth and prime, the Tiger will be absorbed by the pursuit of success and the fulfillment of his many dreams. His old age could be calm if he learns to give up the front seat and relax. However, this will be difficult as he will be plagued by bittersweet regrets about the things he did and did not do.

Overall, the Tiger's life will be volatile. It will be filled to the brim with laughter, tears, joy, pain, despair and every conceivable emotion in the book. One thing you should never do is feel sorry for him. He won't need it: he can only love life if he is allowed to live it to the hilt in whatever manner he chooses. The Tiger is the ultimate optimist who will always bounce back for fresh challenges.

The Tiger could make a good life with the honest and good-natured Boar, or Pig, who will complement the Tiger's rash moods and lend him stability and security. The Tiger will also do extremely well with the realistic and practical Dog. The loyal Dog will stick by the Tiger and is capable of not only restraining the Tiger but reasoning with him as well.

The colorful but nevertheless down-to-earth Horse will also make a prime partner for the Tiger. They will share the same zest for life and love of activity. The quick and nimble Horse will sense danger before the headstrong Tiger does, and the Tiger will benefit immensely from the Horse's quick reflexes and common sense.

Persons born in the year of the Rat, Sheep, or Rooster will get along fine with the Tiger, as will another Tiger. The one thing the Tiger should never do is challenge the authority of the Ox native. This is one serious and uncompromising fellow who will take no nonsense from the Tiger. In a confrontation, the Ox could gore the Tiger to death.

Likewise, a union between a Snake and Tiger is ill-advised. The only thing these two have in common is their suspicious nature. But the Snake is quiet, cool and deadly in his misgivings, while the Tiger is loud and accusing. They will not find harmony.

Last, but not least, the Monkey will be the most elusive foe of the Tiger. This quick-witted personality will never tire of teasing the Tiger, who will end up losing his infamous temper and making a fool of himself. The matchless guile of the Monkey may prove too much for the Tiger and, in his dealings with the Monkey, the Tiger could suffer.

THE TIGER CHILD

A Tiger child can be a bundle of joy and a holy terror at the same time. A little live wire who dashes about sparkling with activity, he will throw himself into the thick of things. Even a very quiet one will know exactly where the action is and make a beeline for it.

He is a charming, bright and self-confident chatterbox, and there is no holding him back. His insatiable curiosity and inquisitiveness lead him to pounce at anything that moves, and he will get into all sorts of predicaments. Hyperactive and high strung, he likes romping, screaming and rough play. Tigers are natural athletes, dancers, swimmers, and like to get a lot of exercise. Parents will get enough exercise just keeping up with their Tiger child.

Like the Dragon, he may also bully less aggressive children into submission. But others will still be drawn to him by his affectionate and gregarious character. The Tiger child makes friends easily and is noted for his generosity and happy-go-lucky attitude.

The Tiger child will express his feelings directly. You will have to put up with his strong opinions on how things should be run as he will air his views passionately and without hesitation. He doesn't like anyone to keep secrets from him and he himself is poor at keeping them.

Since he does not bottle up his emotions, you will know immediately when something is troubling him. Just be sure he is given enough outlets to release all that pent-up energy. Once he vents his anger, it dissipates and he is back to his old self.

If the Tiger's assertiveness is unchecked, he could dominate his parents completely and turn into a dreadful brat. He should be taught to hold his temper, listen to reason and understand the value of compromise. But the little rebel won't just take your word for it. He won't be himself if he does not keep testing the boundaries and limits set for him. It will be no mean task making him toe the line. The earlier he realizes who is boss, the better for him and everyone else around.

However, if he is given the proper discipline, coupled with love, warmth and loads of understanding, no other child will respond as spontaneously as the lovable Tiger. Life may not always run smoothly with him around, but it would be dull and empty without him. Having a Tiger child is a reward in itself.

THE FIVE DIFFERENT TIGERS

METAL TIGER—1950, 2010

The Metal Tiger is definitely not a reticent type. He is bound to be active, aggressive and passionate. He may or may not be artistic but he will certainly project a glamorous image and persona that will not go unnoticed. Self-centered and ostentatious, he is a competitive and untiring worker when motivated in the right way.

He approaches his problems in a direct or even a radical way and is never in doubt about what he wants to accomplish. The problem is that he wants too much too soon. He tends to be overoptimistic about expected results.

When Metal is combined with his native lunar sign, it could produce a Tiger who is sudden, unorthodox and drastic in his actions. He is a person who is faithful only to himself and his desires, and doesn't mind stepping on a few toes along the way. Easily stirred by both good and bad influences, this Tiger will tend to act independently, as he hates having to get permission for anything or having his freedom curtailed in any way.

WATER TIGER—1902, 1962

An open-minded Tiger who is always inclined toward new ideas and experiences, the Water Tiger also has a gift for seeing things objectively. The Water element combined with his lunar sign gives him a calmer nature. He is humane, an excellent judge of the truth, and exceptionally perceptive about the feelings of others. His intuition and ability to communicate make him an excellent candidate for public relations or other media work.

This more realistic type of Tiger has his finger on the pulse of the people. He is adept at making deals, seldom makes errors in judgment and is often an engaging speaker. His mental abilities are above par, but like all Tigers, he sometimes wastes precious time procrastinating. Still, he is less temperamental than other Tigers because he can control his impulsiveness and concentrate on long-term endeavors.

WOOD TIGER—1914, 1974

This is a tolerant Tiger who evaluates situations in a practical and impartial light. He is democratic, loves group action and understands the importance of enlisting the cooperation of others in order to advance rapidly. He will attract a great many friends and supporters, as he can mingle with people from all walks of life. The corporate world, however, is his domain.

The Wood element gives him a more even and affable disposition, and his charming, innovative personality is very conducive to group efforts. He is sought after in polite society, and has a talent for bringing different types of people together. However, his loyalty is mostly to himself and, as he is able to look at things in a broad perspective, he is well aware that no one is indispensable.

The Wood Tiger is also inclined to be the least penetrating of the Tigers. He may prefer to merely skim the surface of things, keeping only the semblance of order. Not as fierce or combative as other Tigers, he is a good negotiator. Adept at delegating chores and skillful at commanding and manipulating people into performing their best, he will take on the minimum amount of responsibility possible. He takes his hobbies and leisure time seriously and has many outside interests. As his lunar sign is not blessed with a great deal of self-discipline, he should not embark on more than he can handle. As with all Tigers, it will be hard for him to admit his limitations or readily take any criticism, no matter how constructive or kindly given.

FIRE TIGER—1926, 1986

Because the Fire Tiger finds it difficult to contain his enthusiasm and boundless energy, he is always ready for action. He especially likes going from one place to another experiencing new thrills and discoveries. Transient by nature, he is primarily concerned with the here and now. Because he is so independent and unconventional, his moves are hard to predict. The only thing you can be sure of is that when he acts, he will be dramatic and influential. Fire makes him even more expressive than he already is. This Tiger never fails to impress anyone he is after or to transmit his electric vitality to any project he decides to undertake.

He seeks constant outlets for his nervous energy and channels his ideas into forceful action. At times, he is downright theatrical. Generous to a fault, he will also display more leadership qualities than Tigers of the other elements. To him, everything he does is worthwhile and imperative, so don't try to tell him otherwise. He is thoroughly optimistic and has no use for naysayers. But while he could be on top of the world one day, the next he could be down in the dumps.

Brilliantly imposing, outspoken and sensual the Fire Tiger finds it hard to ever be impersonal about anything in his or her life.

EARTH TIGER—1938, 1998

This Tiger possesses a quieter and more responsible nature. Warm and likable, he will tend to be practical and realistic in what he undertakes. The achievable is what he is after. He will not jump to hasty conclusions or fly off the handle if he suspects somebody is trying to put one over on him. Concerned about others, he can be thoughtful, mature and sensible in outlook.

The Earth element steadies this type of Tiger by giving him a longer attention span, which enables him to work diligently and objectively on important matters without getting restless. Although he may be as brilliant and passionate as other Tigers, he is generally clearheaded and reasonable. He sees issues in their true light and rarely allows his emotions to cloud his vision.

A Tiger apt to form relationships on the basis of usefulness, he is an intellectual and more of a worrier than a daredevil. He applies his knowledge and capabilities to areas that are familiar and which will bring him the greatest reward. At times he can be overly proud, insensitive and callous, especially when he is so wrapped up with his own concerns and cannot relate to anything outside his scope.

The Earth Tiger is the least likely to choose an adventurous lifestyle, no matter what he may like others to believe. He is a realist. First, he will make it to the top, then, when he has proven his genius to the world, he may indulge himself in a radical, scandalous or unconventional way, just to be different or maybe noticed, as all Tigers love to be. Nonetheless, he will always be serious about his work and career. His native element makes him desire status and recognition acquired through his own merits.

COMPATIBILITY AND CONFLICT CHARTS
FOR THE TIGER

The Tiger is part of the Third Triangle of Affinity, a group of action-oriented signs who seek to serve humanity, promote universal understanding and facilitate communication. The Tiger, Horse and Dog are good at making personal contacts and will develop strong bonds with their fellow human beings. This trio relates well to each other and is basically honest, open and motivated by idealism. Unorthodox at times but always honorable in intent, they act more on impulse rather than premeditation and listen to their inner conscience rather than the dictates of convention. They will provide their own counsel and inspire others to action by their high-spirited and aggressive personalities. Extroverted and energetic, defiant in adversity, and relentless foes of injustice, they get along fabulously together.

TRIANGLE OF AFFINITY FOR THE TIGER

The Tiger will encounter the most difficulties with the sign opposite him in the Circle of Conflict. In this case, the Tiger's nemesis is the Monkey. Anyone whose ascendant is in the hours of the Tiger between 3 A.M. and 5 A.M. (birth time) will most likely also be incompatible with the Monkey native. The Tiger's direction or compass point is east-northeast, while the Monkey is across from him at west-southwest. The Tiger rules the winter season while the Monkey is active in the summer and his fixed element, Wood, is also in direct conflict with the Monkey's fixed element of Metal. Tigers and Monkeys are both competitive but in altogether different ways and these two signs are very sore losers. The Tiger has power and daring on his side while the Monkey uses his wits and guile to turn the tables on the Tiger. In their game, there can be no winners, as both will refuse to surrender. They work well or are in agreement only when dealing through experienced go-betweens who are well respected by both parties or if they happen to share a common ascendant.

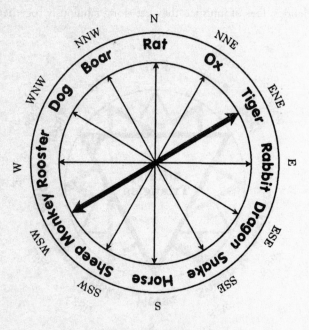

CIRCLE OF CONFLICT

Aside from the totally compatible Horse and Dog, and the totally incompatible Monkey, the other nine signs are compatible with the Tiger to varying degrees.

Rat

Rat and Tiger have few common interests and to a large extent they may not care too much for each other's company unless one has the other's sign as an ascendant. If they have the same goals, they will have a cool to moderate relationship. There may also be many complications as the Rat's best friend is the Monkey and the Tiger's soul mate may be a Horse and neither of these signs is much help when it comes to close friendships.

Ox

Serious clashes of will and intense rivalry could result when Tiger and Ox do not see eye to eye. These two powerful personalities do not take defeat well and hate to accept second prize for anything. Unless they share the same ascendant, such as the Ox having a Tiger's ascendant or the Tiger person having been born during the hours of the Ox, there will be conflict and misunderstanding. Strong tempers, strong wills and a strong need to have their own way contribute to their incompatibility.

Tiger

Two Tigers are compatible to a certain degree. If they have similar backgrounds and relate to the same kinds of people such as Horses and Dog, they will get along fine. Otherwise, they will have reservations about each other and will be easily annoyed by each other's petty habits.

Neither one of them, of course, is willing to change. Their animosities are usually short lived, however, and they can be friends if they can agree never to get mad at the same time. This is easier said than done with unpredictable Tigers.

Rabbit

The lines of communication are not well connected between the Tiger and the Rabbit. The Tiger is too rash for the conservative and peace-loving Rabbit, who is often scandalized by the Tiger's antics and hot temper. They will have sympathy for each other only when their ascendants are in harmony. Otherwise, they will not clash but the diplomatic Rabbit may avoid the aggressive Tiger because he does not share similar interests with the big cat. The Rabbit always watches his tongue, the Tiger, rarely.

Dragon

Moderate success for both signs here since they are both colorful, action-loving personalities who are basically sincere and well intentioned. A shared idealism could unite them into a powerful team capable of bulldozing any opposition with their dynamic ways. Each may constantly struggle for dominance, but if the two of them can share the burdens and define their areas of expertise, they will achieve much together. Mutual respect and cooperation can only follow if they work hard to resolve their differences right from the beginning.

Snake

The Tiger is suspicious of the quiet and introverted Snake and over-reacts when confronted by him. The Snake is not sympathetic to the outspoken Tiger and feels threatened by the jungle cat's often intimidating ways. Their relations range from cold to indifferent unless they share a common ascendant to bind them together. Conflict and misunderstanding arise because these two signs like to come to their own conclusions and, right or wrong, stick to them, especially if anyone dares question them.

Sheep

There will be no outright confrontations or serious rivalry between these two. The Tiger could be protective of the Sheep and the Sheep will give the Tiger lots of sympathy when he needs a good listener. Permanent and lasting relationships result when they share the same ascendant or move in the same circle of friends or work in the same profession. Otherwise, the ties are cordial but not as strong as they may appear. Both these signs could be fair-weather friends and go their separate ways when times get tough.

Rooster

The Tiger and the Rooster are alike in the sense that they are both attracted to controversy and will take on hot issues. They will either be the best of friends or find each other very irritating. And it may depend on something as inconsequential as which day of the week it is. They are both drawn to the limelight and may fight for center stage. The Rooster is the perfectionist who cannot understand how the feisty Tiger can ad lib his way through life and be so popular. The Tiger, on the other hand, thinks the Rooster makes a mountain out of a molehill and will insist on viewing the big picture instead of concentrating on the details as the Rooster prefers to do.

Boar

Theirs will be a successful match. The Tiger and Boar are both outgoing and generous and are secure in each other's company. The honest Boar is forgiving and the Tiger is really not as bad as he likes to pretend. They will find happiness in love and business. The Tiger will provide the ideas; the Boar will find the Tiger captivating and offer his wholehearted support. However, since they both have large appetites and are passionate and impulsive, they need a mitigating influence in their lives or someone to tell them when enough is enough. Self-control is not one of their virtues.

THE TIGER AND HIS ASCENDANTS

We all have a shadow that follows us throughout life. Sometimes it grows bigger than life and at other times it shrinks until it disappears into the soles of our feet. Sometimes it walks tall before us and on other occasions it lags behind like a sulking friend. In Chinese horoscopes, this constant partner, manifested or not, is our ascendant, the animal sign that rules the hour of our birth and becomes a comrade in our journey through life. We may view it as friend or foe or even a little of both. It surfaces when we least expect and shows a better or worse side of our nature. We can often be confounded by the way we listen to our "other self" as well as feel resentful of the significant influence it can exert on us. Actually, a personality has many rings around the centered "self." Each ring can have a different size, texture and aura. When all these factors combine, they bring forth the unique individual that the person truly is. Hence, a Dragon with an incompatible ascendant, like the Dog, has perhaps a more difficult inner struggle than say a Snake born during the hours of the Snake. The double intensity of the Snake person will be easily understood by horoscope readers while the more intricate Dragon/Dog may exhibit the contrary Dog and Dragon traits to varying degrees. There are many voices within each person. But, in the end, only the individual determines which course he will follow, which choices he will make.

The time of birth used to determine the ascendant is always the local time in the place of birth.

If you were born between

11 P.M. and 1 A.M. = The Hours of the Rat

You are a charming hothead of a Tiger with a loving, sentimental side. You can put up with anything except being ignored. Often you will pick a fight just to have the pleasure of making up. Outgoing, impulsive and articulate, you will go far if the Tiger in you allows the Rat ascendant to hold the purse strings and curb your spending.

1 A.M. and 3 A.M. = The Hours of the Ox

You may have the strong will of the Ox and the temperamental nature of the lively Tiger. Hopefully, the Ox brings discipline into your life and you will possess a calmer personality as a result. You like to get things done without too much fuss but can be vocal about your dislikes if you are crossed. Not as dramatic as other Tigers, you are reliable, levelheaded and more predictable.

3 A.M. and 5 A.M. = The Hours of the Tiger

You can be absolutely vivacious, or all teeth and claws when you are angry. Because you are a study in contrasting moods, there is never a dull moment with you. Life is full of excitement and a veritable roller-coaster ride with you at the controls. This is a pure Tiger sign and therefore you will have a double dose of every lovable Tiger characteristic as well as of the negative traits of impulsiveness and indecision.

5 A.M. and 7 A.M. = The Hours of the Rabbit

You will be a serene, quiet, even docile Tiger because of the Rabbit ascendant, but it would be a big mistake for anyone to think that the Tiger fire is quenched. The positive influence of the soft-spoken Hare curbs your impetuousness and impatience. As a result, you make better decisions, know how to be diplomatic and are able to avoid a confrontation when it is not in your best interest. The Rabbit does not enjoy controversy as much as the Tiger does.

7 A.M. and 9 A.M. = The Hours of the Dragon

The dominant Dragon ascendant reinforces your Tiger ego and you tend to be extra competitive. You will try harder and aim higher just to prove to yourself that you are the best. Not one to be outdone, you tend to be easily angered or frustrated when others fail to cooperate with you. You could be a dynamic leader if you were less unpredictable and demanding.

9 A.M. and 11 A.M. = The Hours of the Snake

With the cool wisdom and natural reticence of the Snake ascendant, the Tiger in you will value discretion and be able to hold your tongue. A Tiger who profits from the Snake's intuition and ability to negotiate difficult deals, you will not lose your temper and thereby jeopardize your chances of winning. Your natural Tiger tendencies are muted and you will tend to be more conservative and objective.

11 A.M. and 1 P.M. = The Hours of the Horse

The Horse ascendant makes you more practical and flexible. Your risks will be calculated ones since the Horse is very much in favor of self-preservation and not the daredevil that the Tiger is. However, this combination is composed of two freedom-loving signs who could lack a serious sense of responsibility. You can, however, easily be everyone's best friend as you tend to draw people to you with your magnetic personality.

1 P.M. and 3 P.M. = The Hours of the Sheep

A Tiger who could be artistic and emotional, you may also have the Sheep's tendencies toward jealously and possessiveness. Your talents and innate flair for beauty and art will be recognized. With this combination, you will seek the limelight but also be sought after for your gracious nature and rare abilities. You are a powerful Tiger in Sheep's clothing and not as soft and woolly as you look.

3 P.M. and 5 P.M. = The Hours of the Monkey

Here, Tiger strength and charm meets the Monkey prowess for mental pursuits. If everything is in the right proportion, there is no telling how far you could go. The Monkey ascendant will incline you to use brain instead of brawn to fight the opposition or solve problems. Optimistic and always ready for challenges, you approach life with a positive attitude that wins half the battle. Still, having the most incompatible sign as your ascendant means a constant inner struggle over which side to take.

5 P.M. and 7 P.M. = The Hours of the Rooster

You will have a very colorful and fascinating personality with this combination. The Rooster ascendant gives you focus and a love of order, but in a distinctly unorthodox manner. The troublemaker Tiger meets the troubleshooter Rooster here and your presence in the world will not go unnoticed. A high achiever and mesmerizing performer, you will always insist on being seen and heard. It would be an understatement to say you love to be in control.

7 P.M. and 9 P.M. = The Hours of the Dog

The Dog's inherent love of fair play and common sense will make the Tiger ego more cooperative and easy to deal with. The Tiger's propensity to intimidate instead of negotiate will be toned down by the sensible Dog ascendant and any bullying or colorful tantrums will be discouraged. You will tend to hold strongly democratic views, will never turn from a fight when you feel wronged, and will have a tongue that can be sharper than a razor.

9 P.M. to 11 P.M. = The Hours of the Boar

Vivacious, impulsive and, at times, a bit naive—you tend to attract love and friends like honey attracts bees. The Boar ascendant enhances your love of pleasure and huge appetite for the good things in life. However, both signs in this combination can turn vindictive and destructive under pressure—so it is extra important you guard your emotions and not give in to your desire to get your way at any cost. On the whole, you are extremely giving and helpful, and you'll go out of your way to please family and friends without complaining.

HOW THE TIGER FARES IN THE LUNAR CYCLE

1. The Year of the Rat 1996

The year of the Rat puts restraints on the Tiger's love of action. The Rat favors patience, parsimony and group action, which are not the Tiger's strong points, to say the least. Business and career advancement will be difficult and luck seems to elude the Tiger until after summer. Money could be scarce or withheld from the Tiger, and this makes him frustrated. Progress and success can only be attained by prudence and a conservative approach. Avoid impulsive acts of daring and risk taking. Things could backfire.

2. The Year of the Ox 1997

This will be a mixed year for the Tiger. Misunderstandings and quarrels will stem mainly from stubbornness. The Tiger may be hindered from getting his way by people in authority. This will be a time for him to work around any problems or take an alternative route, definitely not a time for direct confrontation. The Ox will not back down from a collision course with the Tiger and the Tiger could stand to lose more than he can afford. If the Tiger can curb his rebelliousness, his troubles will work themselves out before the year is over. The tough part will be for him to hold on to that temper of his long enough to get what he wants.

3. The Year of the Tiger 1998

A moderately good and happy year for the Tiger. He will be lucky in the sense that others will come to his aid when he needs help or support with his undertakings. Romance and new friendships are on the horizon as he finds people who share his mutual interests and goals. He will suffer no major upheavals but may spend beyond his means or be unable to save any money due to unforeseen expenditures. The Tiger should steer clear of taking risks or making long-term commitments this year as matters tend to be unsettled even though they look rosy.

4. The Year of the Rabbit 1999

A calm and fortuitous year for the Tiger native. Some good news is in store and both romance and business affairs look promising. He will be able to surmount the difficulties in his path as long as he refuses to be drawn into controversy or problems that do not concern him. All in all, he will be content with his achievements this year.

5. The Year of the Dragon 2000

There won't be too much in store for the Tiger this year unless he joins forces with more powerful people. But since this could mean taking a back seat or, worse, coming under the authority of others, he may find it hard to make the adjustment even though it is for his own good. But unless he does, he may find it difficult to raise money or he will make unwise investments on his own. This is no time to go it alone. The Tiger should rally his friends and supporters and network with others instead of criticizing and complaining.

6. The Year of the Snake 2001

This will be a fair year for the Tiger with no large gains or losses in store. His life could be tranquil if he takes care not to get caught up in the affairs of others. His progress will be steady, with only minor health problems and he will not find too many obstacles careerwise. Most of his disappointments will come from persons of the opposite sex. Romantic entanglements tend to get complicated. The Tiger should step back and look at the whole picture to get a clear, objective view before making any decisions. Not a year to be too intense and possessive.

7. The Year of the Horse 2002

An excellent year, as things go smoothly for the Tiger in the year of the Horse. The Horse's quick tempo is more to the liking of the active Tiger and the two signs share a love of challenging work and competition. Love, promotions and recognition will be in store for the Tiger. It will be an easy time for him to make and save money, and he may receive additional income from unexpected sources. This is a time for him to celebrate his good fortune. There will also be good news on the homefront.

8. The Year of the Sheep 2003

This is a good year for the Tiger, on the whole, although difficulties and obstacles will take up more time than expected. Problems at home and tough negotiations or other tensions at work keep him from fully enjoying himself. He should take a vacation even if he cannot afford it or just get away from the thick of things. He needs to cool off and let matters simmer down. Otherwise, he should count his blessings since no great disasters are in store.

9. The Year of the Monkey 2004

Petty irritations and setbacks make the year of the Monkey a difficult one for the Tiger, trying his patience and endurance. He should not voice objections too loudly, make accusations or jump to conclusions. Confrontations could lead to complicated and prolonged lawsuits or disagreements that would have been settled easily if both parties had acted in good faith. If the Tiger does not learn to compromise, he may be forced to. The Monkey is the master gameplayer and if the Tiger does not want to lose, he should refuse to play. A time for the Tiger to seek shelter and wise counsel.

10. The Year of the Rooster 2005

In this moderate and busy year, the Tiger must resist the urge to be overanxious. The Rooster tends to investigate things down to the last detail and still get things done efficiently. The seemingly immense and numerous problems that beset the Tiger this year can be solved as help will come at the last moment from unexpected places or newfound friends. The Tiger should refrain from pushing too hard to get his own way or else he could encounter even more resistance and more delays from the uncompromising Chicken.

11. The Year of the Dog 2006

Although in this year the Tiger is protected from serious danger, he must work hard for his success and will feel tired and unfulfilled from having to assume too much responsibility. Still, the Dog guards the Tiger from controversy as well as from his own inclinations to act on impulse. Luck will continue to help the Tiger as he steers his plans through with the help of influential people who like and support him. However, the Tiger should be careful not to take on more than he can handle.

12. The Year of the Boar 2007

The Tiger will have to curb his free-spending ways and keep a tight rein on the purse strings as the prosperity that comes in the beginning of this year may not stay around for too long. In the reign of the Boar, he must be on guard against high-risk investments and too-good-to-be-true new associates who could take advantage of him. The Boar is the great party giver, but when the party is over, the Tiger may get stuck with the bill. A time for the Tiger to buy insurance and take all precautions necessary.

WHEN MOON SIGNS MEET SUN SIGNS

In my interpretation of Chinese horoscopes, the Rat is not linked with the first Western astrological sun sign, Aries. Instead, I pair the Rat with its counterpart based on the month and season of the Rat, which are December and winter. This makes the most sense as the lunar month of December (also called the Twelfth Moon or the Twelfth Earth Branch) is supposed to parallel the Sun sign, Sagittarius, the Archer. I envision the Eastern and Western horoscope cycles as two large wheels, each with twelve spokes. To correctly juxtapose these cycles, we must find the matching notch that will join them together. Once the Rat and Sagittarius are paired as the first signs, the other eleven fall into place. Please see the Twenty-Four Segments of the Lunar Almanac. All the dates correspond with the twelve Western solar signs.

If you are born in the year of the Tiger under the Western sign of

Sagittarius: 22nd November to 21st December
The Sagittarian Tiger = Fire + Positive Wood

This person is extremely alert and vivacious. As a result, his interpretations of situations are likely to be both swift and accurate. An upright, energetic and expressive combination, the Sagittarian Tiger has few inhibitions. He loves to dispense with formalities and nothing deters him from getting to the heart of the matter once his curiosity is aroused. Fiery wit and colorful manners will typify this person. This Tiger can be argumentative and at times high-handed, however his refinement and intelligence will prevent him from being uncaring or crude.

If you are born in the year of the Tiger under the Western sign of

Capricorn: 22nd December to 20th January
The Capricorn Tiger = Earth + Positive Wood

The result of this combination will be a captivating but less headstrong and impetuous Tiger. No doubt, he or she will still have that strong temper, but Capricorn's influence will see it is properly directed. When linked to the Mountain Goat, the Tiger is not as restless as usual and is inclined to be less of a radical. He does not like sudden changes and can be relied upon to fulfill his promises. This dutiful Tiger can withstand hardships if they help develop his abilities. The Capricorn Tiger will not be entirely led by his heart as are Tigers of more combustible combinations.

If you are born in the year of the Tiger under the Western sign of

Aquarius: 21st January to 19th February
The Aquarian Tiger = Air + Positive Wood

A provocative combination, this Tiger has the courage and grace to carry out his wildest dreams. Transparent and free of guile, he is someone nice to know and love. However, he rarely allows relationships to get too settled or sits still enough for you to study him properly. He gets in and out of predicaments with a paradoxical penchant for puzzles. A publicity lover, the Aquarian Tiger is very communicative and given to cheerfully adjusting regulations to his advantage. Independent and constantly variable, he is ruled by colorful ideals and forever led on by great expectations. His mind and spirit are as free as the wind. It is impossible to ever contain him and one shouldn't even try.

If you are born in the year of the Tiger under the Western sign of

Pisces: 20th February to 20th March
The Pisces Tiger = Water + Positive Wood

The serene, peace-loving Pisces could do wonders for the dramatic Tiger personality. Adaptable but not entirely pliable, the Tiger will take on a calm inner nature, thereby reducing his liveliness to a sparkling yet poetic level. The Piscean Tiger shields his or her claws and uses psychology effectively to gain his or her objectives. The Fish is active and assertive here while the Tiger relaxes and finds less conflict in life. But then, it's never safe to assume that the Big Cat will ever allow himself to be subdued. The Pisces Tiger may purr more than he roars, but he does roar.

If you are born in the year of the Tiger under the Western sign of

Aries: 21st March to 19th April
The Aries Tiger = Fire + Positive Wood

This combination will produce a fiery tempest that will neither wane nor blow itself out. Neither sign in this combination is known for patience or forebearance. Superexciting and magnetic, the Aries Tiger or Tigress will have a life full of exclamation points. It's hard to imagine this personality at rest. A fireball of energy, he could dash about incessantly or suddenly lash out in fretful tantrums if we don't read him right. Restless, innovative and notoriously brave, he is never short of friends or enemies. Sensuous and magnetically attractive, this person is bound for an eventful life because he will make every effort to take center stage.

If you are born in the year of the Tiger under the Western sign of

Taurus: 20th April to 20th May
The Taurean Tiger = Earth + Positive Wood

The otherwise stolid practicality and efficiency of the Bull will be lightened by vivacious feline humor and regality. An endearing and easy-to-relate-to Taurean or an unusually stable and intellectual Tiger, whichever way you want it. He or she is inclined to be rather traditional and conservative in outlook. However, the Taurean reserve may be replaced by the Tiger's natural congeniality here. Firm and methodical about carrying out his goals in life, this person will nonetheless be generous with his time and energy for the right causes.

If you are born in the year of the Tiger under the Western sign of

Gemini: 21st May to 21st June
The Gemini Tiger = Air + Positive Wood

One could almost hear this spontaneous and witty Tiger's laughter cracking the ice at any uneasy gathering. Quick and talkative, he can be an invaluable asset if he does not become temperamental or too outspoken. A person born with this combination is bound to be incessantly on the move and in too much of a hurry most of the time. High-strung and competitive, if he can bring himself to sit down and do some thorough planning before employing his speed and inborn love of activity, he could well be unbeatable.

If you are born in the year of the Tiger under the Western sign of

Cancer: 22nd June to 21st July
The Cancerian Tiger = Water + Positive Wood

This offbeat Crab is full of feline surprises, sparks and ardent love songs. Although all sizzling jealousy and possessiveness up front, he is soft as butter underneath. The Cancerian Tiger is amorous and incorrigibly romantic. An avid party-goer, he is also a great entertainer. Easily carried away by emotions, he can burst into laughter or tears without much provocation. Generally, a person belonging to this combination will be very helpful and considerate because of the Crab's kind-heartedness and the Tiger's lively and optimistic view of life.

If you are born in the year of the Tiger under the Western sign of

Leo: 22nd July to 21st August
The Leo Tiger = Fire + Positive Wood

A fiery personality that can scorch disrespectful onlookers or others who dare to take him for granted, the Leo Tiger is a veritable bundle of roars and claws. He never fails to impress or draw in the crowds. Capable of depth and variety in his emotions, he can be torrid, sulky and magnanimous all in one breath. He tends to act superior, espe-

88 THE TIGER

cially when he is unsure of himself. The Leonine Tiger has very strong
recuperative powers, both mentally and physically. He will never stay
down for long. And when he or she loves, it's all, all the way.

If you are born in the year of the Tiger under the Western sign of

Virgo: 22nd August to 22nd September
The Virgo Tiger = Earth + Positive Wood

The Western Earth element and Eastern Wood element in this
combination work well together. Virgo is reserved and analytical so the
Tiger will be able to keep a close rein on his explosive emotions here.
Hence, the Virgo Tiger will be less spontaneous, but still sparkling—in
a neat, orderly manner. These solar and lunar signs could bridge to
form an exacting but humane soul who is cautious with his choice of
words. With the Tiger's color and daring and Virgo's self-control, this
personality could enjoy the best of both worlds.

If you are born in the year of the Tiger under the Western sign of

Libra: 23rd September to 22nd October
The Libran Tiger = Air + Positive Wood

This will be a fanciful but good-humored Tiger with the enticing
manner of Venus's child, Libra. Both signs tend to procrastinate, so
onlookers may be left sighing anxiously while this subject changes his
mind or fails to sort out his preferences. However, the potent Tiger is
very effective once he does set his mind on something and can be
good-hearted and hard-working to boot. With Libra's graciousness,
this Tiger will stalk his prey with amazing artistry.

If you are born in the year of the Tiger under the Western sign of

Scorpio: 23rd October to 21st November
The Scorpio Tiger = Water + Positive Wood

Full of thrills and skills, the Scorpio Tiger possesses enough sex
appeal and glamor for ten ordinary mortals. Proud and self-confident,
he will undertake ambitious projects with the endurance of the
Scorpion and the optimism of the Tiger. He has strong incendiary

qualities—to the fighting spirit of the Tiger is added the powerful Scorpion intensity. As sure as death and taxes, he will have to take revenge, even if it's only a few playful scratches now and then, to remind you not to take him or her too lightly (as if we would dare).

THE SEASONS OF THE TIGER

SPRING

Tigers born in the spring are playful and optimistic by nature. The noblest and most daring of Tiger people, they throw caution to the wind and pursue their objectives with abandon. Never one to take the middle of the road, this type of Tiger knows what he wants and is not shy about getting it. The toughest lesson the spring Tiger will learn in life is how to conform to society's demands and how to take No for an answer. Prodigiously gifted with superior endurance and an amazing zest for competition, this strong-willed personality will be impossible to ignore. You can either love him or loathe him, but you can never be indifferent to such a character. Tigers born during the day are more likely to be more retiring than their brothers and sisters who prowl by night.

SUMMER

This is a more thoughtful and careful Tiger who is nevertheless given to indecision or sudden moves that make him dangerous and unpredictable at times. But he has reason to be alert and suspicious as his well-being depends on his ability to outsmart the opposition. Big-hearted and helpful, he will never turn his back on his friends or family. He is kind, dependable and protective. People will rally around his leadership. He values his freedom but is sociable and drawn to the limelight. He will bask in the public's adoration and seek center stage whenever there is an opportunity for him to shine.

AUTUMN

A Tiger born in the fall is more apt to question situations and people's motives. Naturally suspicious and wary of anything not to his liking, he tends to have strong opinions and little patience. Self-reliance is his strongest trait as he knows his own inner strength and will always draw from within rather than depend on others. He is a careful, studious and, at times, fastidious personality who needs faithful followers to bring out the best in him. The autumn Tiger is an avid patron of the arts and a discriminating connoisseur. He is also alert to the latest trends and fashions. A nonconformist and rebel at times, he knows how to sway a crowd as well as draw attention to his work, which may be outrageous yet original and exciting.

WINTER

Winter Tigers are the most secure and mature of the lot. They view life pragmatically and are less rebellious. The season calms their roving natures and love of adventure. These Tigers like to stay close to home and to the people they love and trust. Affectionate, passionate and refreshingly outspoken, this type of Tiger knows how to check his aggressive tendencies in order to become part of the team. He is a less assertive and self-centered Tiger who could be a good leader without needing to have total devotion from his followers. Yet, while he presents a competent and optimistic front, he could easily be plagued by the doubts and insecurities that are common to all Tiger personalities.

FAMOUS PERSONS BORN IN THE YEAR
OF THE TIGER

Metal
Charles de Gaulle
Ho Chi Minh
Ludwig van Beethoven
Dwight D. Eisenhower
Princess Anne of Great Britain

Water
Simon Bolívar
Will Geer

Fire

Queen Elizabeth II

Giscard D'Estaing

St. Francis Xavier

Marilyn Monroe

Wood

Alec Guiness

Pierre Balmain

Earth

Karl Marx

Emily Brontë

Isadora Duncan

Diana Rigg

Rudolf Nureyev

4
The Fourth Sign
of the Lunar Cycle

The Rabbit

I am in tune with the
   pulse of the universe.
In my quiet and solitude
   I hear the melodies of the soul.
I float above commonplace
   dissent and decay.
I subdue by my ability to conform.
I color my world
   in delicate pastel hues.
I epitomize harmony and inner peace.

I AM THE RABBIT.

Lunar Years of the Rabbit in the Western Calendar	Elements
29 January 1903 to 15 February 1904	Water
14 February 1915 to 2 February 1916	Wood
2 February 1927 to 22 January 1928	Fire
19 February 1939 to 7 February 1940	Earth
6 February 1951 to 26 January 1952	Metal
25 January 1963 to 12 February 1964	Water
11 February 1974 to 30 January 1976	Wood
29 January 1987 to 16 February 1988	Fire
16 February 1999 to 4 February 2000	Earth

If you were born on the day before the start of the lunar year of the Rabbit, e.g, 24th January 1963, your sign is the one before the Rabbit, the Tiger, the third lunar sign.

If you were born on the day after the last day of the lunar year of the Rabbit, e.g., 13th February 1964, your sign is the one after the Rabbit, the Dragon, the fifth lunar sign.

The Rabbit rules the two-hour period of the day between 5 A.M. and 7 A.M. Persons born during this time are said to have the Rabbit as their ascendant and will display many of the characteristics peculiar to this sign and have great affinity for persons born under this fourth lunar sign.

The direction appointed to the Rabbit is directly east; its season is spring and its month, March. The Hare corresponds to the Western astrological sign of Pisces, which rules from February 20th to March 20th. Wood is its fixed element and it has a yin or negative stem.

In the Vietnamese version of the Chinese Horoscope, the Rabbit is replaced by the Cat. This is an aberration as the Cat was not indigenous to China and was only later imported to Asia from Persia and Egypt via the Silk Route. Besides, the lunar cycle has room for only one feline and that place is taken up by that Big Cat, the Tiger. It is redundant to appoint another "cat" right after the Tiger.

THE RABBIT PERSONALITY

A person born in the year of the Rabbit is considered very fortunate. The Rabbit, or Hare as he is referred to in Chinese mythology, serves as the symbol of longevity and is said to derive his essence from the moon.

When a Western person gazes at the moon, he may tell a child the story of the man in the moon but when a Chinese person looks at the moon, he sees the Moon Hare standing near a rock under a cassia tree holding the Elixir of Immortality in his hands.

During the Chinese mid-autumn festival when the moon is at its loveliest, Chinese children still carry lighted paper lanterns made in the image of a rabbit and climb to the top of hills to observe and admire the immortal Moon Hare underneath his cassia tree.

The Rabbit is the soul of graciousness, good manners, sound counsel, kindness and sensitivity to beauty. His soft-spokenness and graceful, elegant ways embody all the desirable traits of a successful diplomat or statesman. A person born under this sign will lead a tranquil life as he will opt to enjoy a peaceful and congenial environment. He is naturally reserved, artistic and likely to possess good judgment. His thoroughness will also make him a good scholar. He will shine in the fields of law, government and research.

But he is also inclined to be moody; at such times, he appears detached from his environment and indifferent to those close to him. And although the Rabbit may appear outwardly impervious to the opinions of others, inwardly he withers under criticism.

The Rabbit is lucky in business and in all kinds of monetary transactions. Astute at striking bargains, he can always come up with a suitable proposal or an advantageous alternative. His sharp business acumen, coupled with his knack for smooth negotiations, will ensure him a fast rise in any career he chooses.

However, the Rabbit's "rather switch than fight" technique can be deceiving and he can be diabolically cunning when he puts his mind to it. So while a Rabbit person is tender and obliging to his loved ones, he can be superficial and even ruthless in his dealings with outsiders. Suave and self-indulgent, he enjoys his creature comforts and likes to put his own wishes first. It irks him terribly to be inconvenienced for he is a considerate, modest and thoughtful person who would like others to be the same. He sincerely believes it costs people nothing to be nice to each other and he will always make an effort to be civil, even to his own worst enemy. He abhors brawling and any sort of overt animosity or belligerence.

For all his quiet and apparently docile ways, the Rabbit possesses a strong will and an almost narcissistic self-assurance. He pursues his objectives with methodical precision but always in an unobtrusive manner. No one will ever accuse him of being an obvious or thick-skinned person. The well-mannered Rabbit dislikes making a scene. But the special trait that makes the Rabbit person a formidable nego-tiator is his inscrutability. It is difficult if not impossible to know what he is thinking behind that soft blanket of Rabbit niceness.

The Rabbit usually has impeccable manners and discretion. He seldom uses harsh words, foul language or vulgarisms to make a point. There is little need to anyway, as his own techniques are stunningly effective. The Rabbit often assumes a cloak of decency and amiability to undermine his opponents. His credentials are usually flawless or at least in good order. He will wine and dine you and cater to your every whim when he is after something. Then, when you have eaten your fill and are contentedly sipping at the best wine, he will pull out the contract for you to sign. Before you know it, he has cut you off at the knees. He was so deft, you didn't even feel any pain. It was all over with the stroke of a pen. My sympathies are with you, friend. You are just another victim of the incomparable Hare. Now do you under-stand why Bugs Bunny always gets his carrots at the end of those car-toon strips?

The Rabbit may appear a bit slow or overly deliberate at times, but this is due to his inborn sense of caution and discretion. One can be sure he is going to read the fine print before signing any document. Because of his superior ability in assessing people and situations, the Rabbit can afford to be conceited—which, by the way, he is.

The demure Ms. Rabbit is considerate and understanding with her friends: a great person to work, shop or gossip with. She is delightfully warm and witty and her company is always sought after. She has plenty of energy for the things she likes to do and will tirelessly track down antique shops or help plan a friend's wedding to the last detail. But when she feels she has had enough, well, you can expect her to drop whatever she is doing, prop up her dainty feet and go totally limp. That is the philosophical part of the Rabbit. Do you know why she can keep so serene in the midst of all kinds of frantic action? The secret is to know when your batteries need recharging, and no one has a better instinct about this than the Rabbit.

While everyone is killing himself or herself in a mad rush to get somewhere, the Rabbit knows that the world will still be here tomorrow. So, what's the hurry? Why don't you sit down, too? She will probably make you a nice cup of tea and help you forget all about that crazy rat race outside.

In any situation, you can always rely on the Rabbit to be in control of herself. She will notice the license number of the getaway car or remember that the robber wore a special cap and had a small tattoo on the back of his left hand. And, while you are at the police station filing that report, she will calmly recall all the details and help you answer all those irritating questions.

All in all, the Rabbit really knows how to live well. What's more, he or she is more than willing to let others live well, too, so long as they do not harm his or her interests. Not a spoilsport or disciplinarian with an ever-watchful eye, the Rabbit knows when to refrain from criticism. He never likes to embarrass anyone in public when he can settle the score in his own way. He is adept at the art of saving face, both yours and his, and if there is any way he can spare your feelings, he will.

Have no doubt however; the Rabbit makes mental notes of your mistakes or progress. But, if matters are not serious or beyond redemption, he will good-heartedly let you pass. As a result, he is well-liked and popular, makes few enemies and rarely gets into trouble. People respond by being generous to him and letting him pass, too.

No one (except the Sheep) has a more sympathetic ear to lend you than the Rabbit. However, while he is an excellent psychologist and compassionate listener, he will only play the role of a passive advisor. He is, above all, an intellectual, a realist and a pacifist. Do not expect him to go out with all colors flying and do battle for you. That would be asking too much. Let's face it, the Rabbit will never elect to trudge up Mount Calvary with you or volunteer to carry your cross, no matter what great buddies you two claim to be. He'll lend you the money for the lawyer or bail you out of jail if he can afford it, but that's about all. And, if you are getting to be too much of a nuisance or a liability, you can count on his making a quick but graceful exit from your life.

The comely and refined Ms. Rabbit will not be adverse to marrying a good old-fashioned millionaire instead of a handsome but penniless swain. The former will be able to provide her with the advantages and luxuries she demands as necessities. Her man must be powerful enough to protect and support her in style, and sensitive enough to politely disappear when she is in a sullen mood and wishes to remain undisturbed.

When given the choice, the Rabbit will vote for the easy and good life every time. He or she will wear loose comfortable clothing of superb cut and fabric, cashmere sweaters, pure silk blouses and durable linens and tweeds. The clothes, like the manner, will be elegant but understated. Flashy, geometric and loud designs offend the Rabbit's sense of conformity and balance.

While gracious to friends and coworkers, the Rabbit person may be somewhat distant from his own family or simply bored by domestic routine and duties. He or she hates cloying associations. He will shake off encroachments on his privacy and friends who impose without regret. He can be bureaucratic and overly cautious about difficult issues. As he hates binding commitments or overinvolvement, he can also be an expert at passing the buck.

Mr. Rabbit is singularly debonair, possessing charm, grace and courtliness. While he is singing your praises, however, he could also be drinking all your vintage wine. Yes, the Rabbit gravitates toward leisure and the cream of society. On second thought, the cream of society could well consist of poised and genial Hares.

At his best, the Rabbit is admired for his suaveness and intelligence and respected for his sensible advice. At his worst, he is overly sensitive, imaginative, or just acidly indifferent or disinterested. He is allergic to strife and may avoid coming into contact with human suffering or misery, as though it were some highly contagious disease.

The Rabbit is not easy to pin down. He can also resort to repressive and ruthless measures to secure his secrets or his privacy. When the Rabbit person feels threatened, he will hide his anger but his subtle brooding and concealed antagonism can take the form of subversive tactics.

Despite all his positive qualities, a native of this sign will still value himself above all else. When pushed too far, he will discard anything or anyone disrupting the calm of his existence. His beliefs are known to be flexible and he has the knack of playing both sides for insurance. Security could be an obsession to the weaker types of this lunar sign; you rarely find a Rabbit in areas of high risk or volunteering for dangerous missions.

His love of ease coupled with his distaste for conflict may give the Rabbit a reputation for being weak, opportunistic and self-indulgent. Unlike the Dragon, Tiger or Rooster, who enjoy and even thrive on a hearty fight now and then, the Rabbit does not relish combat. He was not born to be a warrior. He is more effective working behind the scenes. Do not be concerned about the Rabbit's well-being. Agile, sagacious and armed with good sense, he will know how to keep out of harm's way. Unlike other signs, who pursue lofty ideals, the Rabbit's main objective in life is simply finding harmony and self-preservation.

The Rabbit year is said to bring peace or at least a respite from conflict or war. Likewise, its practical native will do everything in his power to restore harmony or leave the scene.

The Rabbit person makes a good entertainer and is a wonderful host. Pleasant and warm company, he has a good word to say about everyone. But don't let that fool you. He knows more than he will say. You can easily recognize a Rabbit by his demeanor. He will be your best friend so long as you take care not to ask too much of him.

The well-groomed Rabbit is most compatible with those born in the year of the Sheep. They will share the same good taste and love of material comforts. Equally well suited will be a relationship with the Dog and the honest, big-hearted Boar. The Rat, Dragon, Monkey, Ox, Snake and another Rabbit will make good secondary matches for him. But he will not be able to tolerate the vanity or criticism of the Rooster. He is unimpressed by the dramatics of the Tiger and unappreciative of the quick-tempered and mercurial ways of the Horse.

To sum it up, the Hare simply leaps over obstacles in his path and recovers from calamities with remarkable resilience. No matter how he is tossed, he lands on his feet. He may not be close to his family but will make every effort to provide them with the best of everything. Beneath his soft, vulnerable-looking exterior is an armor of caution and sagacity. In life, the Rabbit will avoid being drawn into conflict unless it affects him directly, at which time he will take the appropriate measures to protect his interests.

There is no great inner struggle in the Rabbit's heart between the forces of good and evil. He believes in his own ability to survive, relies on his own judgment, and as a result is usually at peace with himself. His is the sign most apt to find happiness and contentment.

THE RABBIT CHILD

A child born in the Rabbit's year will have a sweet disposition. Even-tempered and obedient, he will be sensitive to the moods of his parents and act accordingly. He may or may not be talkative, but he won't be rowdy or offensive. He can sit quietly and concentrate on one toy or game at a time. However, this does not mean he is not observing everything out of the corner of his eye. Not much escapes the attention of the Hare's child.

Usually he is a light sleeper and may fret a lot when he is sick. Although he loves being catered to, he will be easy to discipline and should have little trouble fitting in at school. He learns his lessons easily and well. Just because he has better than average manners, it does not mean he can not or will not be argumentative in his own soft-spoken way. He may get his way more often by using this unobtrusive and nonconfrontational method. One who can grasp both sides of an issue quickly, he can debate his point effectively and with intelligence.

At times, it will be difficult to figure out what he wants or really thinks. Adept at masking his feelings, the Rabbit will only say what he knows will please you and thus manuever you over to his way of thinking without your even noticing it.

The Rabbit child will be able to fend for himself and protect his possessions. Remarkably observant, he can calculate his chances of getting his way. Instead of directly resisting rules, the subtle Hare will carefully devise ways around them. In short, this polite little angel is going to bargain for a better deal every time. He is not only aware of his own strengths and weaknesses but those of others as well.

He can take reprimands with a defiant or philosophical sort of indifference. Shrugging off his setbacks, the resilient Rabbit child will patiently start again from square one. Helpful at home, conforming at school and well-tuned to his environment, this child will know his way around people and problems. Rest assured he will be well-liked and accepted everywhere he goes.

THE FIVE DIFFERENT RABBITS

METAL RABBIT—1951

This type of Rabbit could be sturdier physically and mentally than Rabbits belonging to other elements. He will not be as apt to compromise either. He has an unshakeable faith in his own powers of observation and deduction and more often than not he is convinced he has the right answers and solutions to his problems. He can assume responsibility admirably and will display a good deal of creative initiative in his work.

Metal matched with his animal sign will make him preoccupied with his own desires, goals and creative urges. He will be more cunning, but his ambition will be carefully concealed beneath his cool logic and intelligence.

A connoisseur par excellence, he will know how to live well and will savor the good things life has to offer in a refined way. While he may be indifferent to the opinions of others, he is emotionally moved by painting, sculpture, music and other forms of beauty. His basic self-assurance and discerning eye will make him an excellent judge of the arts. He may even become a collector of great distinction, if he has the means, because of his impeccable taste. Whatever career he chooses he will make his mark early as he is naturally a thorough and devoted worker.

But, like all true romantic spirits, this type of Rabbit could be inclined to dark moods, and works well only when he is sufficiently inspired. Ardent in love and with great depth and foresight, he will allow only a handful of people into the inner sanctum of his life because of his many hidden inhibitions.

WATER RABBIT—1903, 1963

A meditative type of Rabbit with a fragile and emotional nature, he cannot bear harassment or any other unpleasantness, such as dissent and bickering. He can be easily influenced because he is so empathetic, able to pick up the thoughts and feelings of others with uncanny accuracy.

This Rabbit will possess an excellent memory and may have the kind of mental power that, without his being aware of it, transmits his ideas to others. Consequently, he attracts the kind of people he relates to and he may be surprised by the many supporters who rally to his defense when he least expects.

However, he is a subjective soul and his perspective gets distorted by the emotional barriers he sets up. He is not very decisive and in many cases could readily come under the sway of others.

At times, his delicate sensitivity makes him dwell too much on the past. Often reminiscing on long-ago injuries and indulging in self-pity, he needs strong associates to help him see the brighter side of life and enjoy himself. In his negative moods, he suspects the motives of those around him, and is uncompromising, secretive and even paranoid. In his positive state, he could rally powerful allies to his aid. He is never without resources or influence so long as he does not carry his neutrality so far that no one will take his side.

WOOD RABBIT—1915, 1975

When Wood is exalted in this lunar sign already governed by Wood, it can produce a generous and especially understanding person who will sometimes be too charitable for his own good. Although he has solid ambitions, he is often intimidated by authority and may choose to ignore mistakes made in his presence in order to maintain the status quo. As a result, others are tempted to take advantage of his sympathetic and permissive nature.

However, this type of Rabbit usually turns out well. He thrives in large corporations or other institutions where he can slowly and diplomatically climb the ladder of success, one rung at a time. Group effort and togetherness appeal to him and offer the kind of security and reasssurance he needs. But, because of his innate desire to belong to a group, he may become a bit too bureaucratic and equivocate when he must make a decision that might offend people or set a precedent in a controversial case. In his refusal to act promptly or take sides, he may end up hurting everyone, including himself. He should be more discriminating and decisive and take the necessary steps to insulate himself from those who prey on his generous nature. As a rule, he is one who is able to bend gracefully without breaking, and will have no trouble fitting in anywhere he chooses.

FIRE RABBIT—1927, 1987

This is definitely a demonstrative, fun loving and affectionate type of Rabbit who has more strength of character than other Rabbits. Although Fire makes him temperamental, he is still able to mask his emotions with charm and diplomacy.

He has an easy and natural personality. People respond positively to his ideas because he expresses them so well. Fire may make him prone to emotional speeches as he can be outspoken in expressing his displeasure. He is more capable of leadership than other Rabbits, but his rule is tempered with moderation and discretion. Despite his outgoing and progressive ways, he will try to avoid direct confrontation with his enemies and will prefer to use subtle plots or deal with go-betweens as natives of his signs are so adept at doing.

This type of Rabbit will have a high level of intuition and even psychic ability. He is intensely aware of changes in his surroundings and easily moved to anger, hurt or disappointment. He could also be terribly neurotic when negative. He requires approval, wholehearted support and inspiration in order to sparkle.

EARTH RABBIT—1939, 1999

A serious and steadfast type of Hare, he has well-defined patterns of thought and is capable of well-calculated moves. He deliberates before giving in to his emotional inclinations. His balanced and rational personality wins him favor in the eyes of his superiors, as does his realistic approach to his goals.

The Earth element makes him more constant and less indulgent, although his constancy will be of a passive sort. His introverted nature causes him to turn inward when beset with problems because he must be in accord with his inner self before he can act. Yet he never hesitates to appropriate whatever resources are available and use them wisely.

A rather materialistic sort of person, the Earth Rabbit's prime concern is his own well being. He could easily be indifferent to the needs of others when they are not in accord with his objectives. Still, he does possess the humility to acknowledge his shortcomings and will strive to overcome them if he can.

COMPATIBILITY AND CONFLICT CHARTS
FOR THE RABBIT

The Rabbit is part of the Fourth and last Triangle of Affinity, a group of the emotionally and artistically guided signs of the Rabbit, Sheep and Boar. These three signs are mainly concerned with their senses and what they can appreciate with them. They are expressive, intuitive, eloquent and talented when it comes to the fine arts, architecture, design and fashion, and innovative computer software. Diplomatic and compassionate, this trio has calmer natures than other lunar signs. Dependent on others for stimulation and leadership, they are flexible because they are sympathetically tuned to the vibrations of their environment. These three signs are drawn toward beauty and the higher aspects of love. They will extol the virtues of peaceful coexistence with their fellow men. No doubt, they will provide each other with excellent company since they share the same basic philosophies.

TRIANGLE OF AFFINITY FOR THE RABBIT

The Rabbit will encounter his most severe personality clashes with someone born in the year of the Rooster. Anyone whose ascendant is in the hours of the Rooster will most likely also come into conflict with the Rabbit native. (Even someone with a strong Rabbit ascendant will not find harmony in the company of Roosters.) In the Circle of Conflict, Rabbit and Rooster just do not see eye to eye. They are worlds apart in their way of thinking because they occupy directly opposite positions on the wheel. The Rabbit's direction or compass point is east while the Rooster's is due west. Spring is the Rabbit's season while the Rooster rules in the fall, and the Rabbit's fixed element is Wood while the Rooster's is Metal. Because Metal cuts Wood, relationships between these two do not last. It would be best for them to deal through intermediaries and mutual friends.

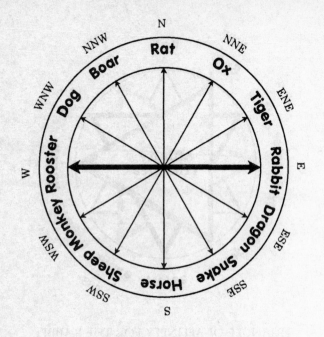

CIRCLE OF CONFLICT

Aside from the Rabbit's most compatible partners, the Sheep and Boar, and his least compatible partner, the Rooster, the other nine signs are compatible with the Rabbit to varying degrees.

Rat

The Rabbit maintains a working relationship with the efficient Rat. There is little difficulty in these two getting along. Both are sure of themselves and what they want but they had better want the same thing or the deal is off! Both tend to be calculating and superficial in situations where there are no real benefits for them. Since the Rabbit is so suave and composed, it would be hard for the charming Rat to outmaneuver him, although he will certainly try.

Ox

Both are reserved and shy. They may show a lukewarm interest, but there is no magic here unless one or the other share the same ascendant. The Rabbit is too polite to openly offend but he may be repelled by the Ox's spartan outlook. The Ox is not attracted to the Hare's love of ease and luxury. Besides, the Rabbit's closest allies, the Sheep and the Boar, are not too fond of the rigid Ox. Compatibility may be strained if interests and friendships are diverse.

Tiger

The lines of communications are not strong between the Rabbit and the Tiger. The Big Cat is too rash for the conservative and peace-loving Rabbit, who is often scandalized by the Tiger's loud and hot temper. They will have sympathy for each other only when their ascendants are in harmony. Otherwise, the diplomatic Rabbit may avoid the aggressive Tiger because of their dissimilar personalities and interests. The Hare always favors discretion; the Tiger, rarely.

Rabbit

Rabbits get along fine with their own kind. Two Rabbits are a study in politeness and quiet diligence since there is mutual understanding and no struggle for dominance. They readily understand the benefits of working together peacefully. However, at times they can be indifferent or aloof when their feelings are hurt. Hopefully, each is considerate enough to give the other room to sulk. Both will work to keep their equilibrium.

Dragon

The Rabbit and the Dragon may have some personality clashes as the Rabbit finds the Dragon domineering at times. But these two signs will strive to settle their differences when they have a common cause or share the same interests. They are not vengeful or petty and will attempt to see matters in a larger perspective. If the Rabbit understands the Dragon's ego, it will be easy for him to manuever things to his advantage.

Snake

The Snake and Rabbit have the wisdom to make a relationship work. How deep that relationship is will depend on how much effort each one is willing to invest. However, there can be no strong bonds or deep attraction unless they share a common ascendant. Otherwise, they will merely tolerate each other to get the job done and achieve their mutual aims.

Horse

The Rabbit may not always appreciate the Horse's quick temper and outspoken ways. Discreet and at times inhibited, the passive Hare may not share the Horse's fiery love of action and danger. When the Horse leads the charge, he cannot count on the Rabbit to follow him. The Rabbit ultimately trusts only his own judgement and will find the Horse too changeable to rely upon.

Monkey

The Rabbit may be attracted to the Monkey's superior intelligence but will find it hard to trust the Monkey completely unless they share a common ascendant. Petty differences and subtle rivalry can cause their relationship to be less than perfect. But the Monkey will work his magic on the Rabbit whenever he needs help and the Rabbit will oblige the Monkey if doing so is to his advantage.

Dog

The Rabbit and the Dog will have a compatible and rewarding union as they can establish trust and understanding with little effort. Both will do their share to make the relationship workable or else they will call a truce and part peacefully. When these two join forces, they will find harmony and happiness as neither of them is overly aggressive or unreasonably demanding.

THE RABBIT AND HIS ASCENDANTS

We all have a shadow that follows us throughout life. Sometimes it grows bigger than life and at other times it shrinks until it disappears into the soles of our feet. Sometimes it walks tall before us and on other occasions it lags behind like a sulking friend. In Chinese horoscopes, this constant partner, manifested or not, is our ascendant, the animal sign that rules the hour of our birth and becomes a comrade in our journey though life. We may view it as friend or foe or even a little of both. It surfaces when we least expect and shows us a better or worse side of our nature. We can often be confounded by the way we listen to our "other self" as well as feel resentful of the influence it can exert on us. Actually, a personality has many rings around the centered "self." Each ring can have a different size, texture and aura. When all these factors combine, they bring forth the unique individual that one truly is. Hence, a Dragon with an incompatible ascendant, such as the Dog, has perhaps a more difficult inner struggle than, say, a Snake born during the hours of the Snake. The double intensity of the Snake person will be easily understood by horoscope readers while the more intricate Dragon/Dog may exhibit the contrary Dog and Dragon traits to varying degrees. There are many voices within each person. But, in the end, only the individual determines which course he will follow, which choices he will make.

The time of birth used to determine the ascendant is always the local time in the place of birth.

If you were born between

11 P.M. and 1 A.M. = The Hours of the Rat
You are affectionate, astute and always well-informed. The Rat ascendant livens up the Rabbit's retiring ways and makes him more involved. A dispenser of good advice and a paragon of proper conduct, you are to be found in a close-knit circle of friends or family relations. Never one to go it alone, you are a good team player and your sound opinions are valued and respected.

1 A.M. and 3 A.M. = The Hours of the Ox
With the Ox as your ally, you will act with more conviction and authority than other Rabbits. You could have a sterner outlook and be more insistent on having your own way. Silence and stubborn resistance may be your weapons of choice. If you learn to be more open and communicative, the Ox's strength and self-control can make you very successful.

3 A.M. to 5 A.M. = The Hours of the Tiger
You can be a colorful, fast-talking, fast-thinking Rabbit, who is quick and always observant. The dramatic Tiger ascendant urges you to be more aggressive while your innate Rabbit good sense will try to maintain dignity and good taste. Both signs in this combination will

land happily on their feet no matter how they are tossed. Hopefully, your Rabbit side will get you to look before you leap and check that impulsive Tiger inside you.

5 A.M. and 7 A.M. = The Hours of the Rabbit

You could be a philosopher extraordinaire, everyone's psychologist, or a wonderful Rabbit sage who contemplates but never takes forceful action because you won't take sides. Yours is a pure Rabbit sign and you tend to magnify the positive and negative qualities of the Hare. You prefer to float above issues and distance yourself from disharmony. If you can bring yourself to make real commitments, your contributions will be greatly appreciated and recognized.

7 A.M. and 9 A.M. = The Hours of the Dragon

You'll be an ambitious and rather tough Rabbit. With the Dragon as your ascendant, you will want to be in charge but won't want to dirty your hands if possible. You will have the ability to convince others to follow your well-devised and commendable plans. The fire of the Dragon gives you the courage and conviction that may not be present in other types of Rabbits. However, you tend to rule by consensus and not by force and will be considerate of the wishes of the majority.

9 A.M. and 11 A.M. = The Hours of the Snake

The Snake could make you an elegant but moody and reflective Hare. Your inborn wisdom inclines you to be self-sufficient and reluctant to solicit advice or confide in others. Extremely sensitive to your surroundings, you tend to be highly artistic, well-informed, social but introverted, and guided strictly by your own intuition. Mystical, religious and intense, you can be an unfathomable enigma to others when your barriers are up.

11 A.M. and 1 P.M. = The Hours of the Horse

The Horse brings fresh breezes into your life, giving you more self-confidence and a happy-go-lucky disposition. Both the Hare and the Horse have winning instincts and tend to follow them without hesitation. The Horse makes you impatient and hot-tempered at times. If the Rabbit can hold the Horse's tongue, there will be fewer problems in relating to others. However, both signs in this combination tend to be self-serving and selfish when they are negative. You must realize that you need the cooperation of others to succeed. To secure it, you must treat their goals as if they were as important as your own.

1 P.M. and 3 P.M. = The Hours of the Sheep

The loving Sheep cajoles the Rabbit toward more sympathy and generosity. Both signs here are highly tuned to beauty, art and the environment. You have many artistic contributions to make with your talents. Your main drawback will be your reluctance to stand up for yourself when necessary. Easily upset and discouraged when others take advantage of your tolerant and peace loving nature, you need strong mentors and administrators to guide you and curb your tendency to spend beyond your means.

3 P.M. and 5 P.M. = The Hours of the Monkey

The Monkey makes you an outgoing and inventive type of Rabbit. Here, your natural intuition and graciousness is colored by the Monkey's love of mischief and innovation. That superior Monkey intelligence may be masked by a calm and collected exterior. People should think twice before matching wits with this combination. Your beautiful Rabbit demeanor is an excellent cover for the Monkey's ingenious plots.

5 P.M. and 7 P.M. = The Hours of the Rooster

Because the Rooster is your direct opposite in the lunar cycle, you will be a study in contrast. In this mixture, your Chicken ascendant could bring out a kind of boldness in you that makes you speak your mind without caring too much about the consequences or what others think of you. With your basic Rabbit sensitivity and sound judgement, you may be well worth listening to. You will also find yourself drawn to persons born under the sign of the Rooster, Snake or Ox. Cautious, analytical and intelligent, you are never in doubt of your abilities.

7 P.M. and 9 P.M. = The Hours of the Dog

With the Dog as your ally and ascendant, you could be a friendly, likable person, concerned about the welfare of others. You are inclined to make serious commitments and will give more of yourself than other Rabbits. The fair-minded but protective Dog teams up with your basic Rabbit sense of purpose and self-preservation for an amazingly stable and trustworthy personality.

9 P.M. and 11 P.M. = The Hours of the Boar

In this combination, your Boar ascendant is most compatible with your native sign and will add texture and bright color to your refined and conformist Rabbit ways. You are drawn to helping the less fortunate and the Pig's generosity makes you volunteer for unrewarding tasks the Hare would normally pass up. You are immensely popular and good-hearted, a great fund-raiser and an eager party goer.

HOW THE RABBIT FARES IN THE LUNAR CYCLE

1. The Year of the Rat 1996

The year of the Rat will provide a quiet and calm time for the peaceful Rabbit. Although progress will be steady, with no big surprises or upsets, the year will not be as fruitful as the Hare would like. No serious opposition is foreseen at work or at home. This is a good time for the Rabbit to make plans for the future, buy property or invest under the auspices of the frugal Rat.

2. The Year of the Ox 1997

The Rabbit faces a rough and rigorous year under the yoke of the rugged Ox. Disappointments, aimless travel, or work without immediate or visible results frustrate the Rabbit. If he lets his worries and anxieties get the better of him, his health may be affected. The best approach for the Rabbit would be to let things settle down by themselves. This will not be a year for the Rabbit to contemplate major changes. Plans take longer to develop than expected, but the Rabbit should bear in mind that though the Ox may be slow, he is always sure.

3. The Year of the Tiger 1998

The year of the Tiger will tend to draw the normally aloof Rabbit into conflicts and controversy. He should take extra care this year of the contracts he signs or promises he makes. Disputes arise from unreasonable demands made on the Hare's time, talents and commitments, especially in monetary or contractual matters. With the coming of cooler weather, his hardships will dissipate and he may make some headway by the end of the year. The year of the Tiger only looks complicated; if the Rabbit perseveres, he will be able to ride out the storm.

4. The Year of the Rabbit 1999

This is a very auspicious year for the Rabbit native. Promotions, career advancement or financial coups may be in store for him. He will reap unexpected benefits, and investments or funds once considered lost could be recovered. Happy tidings and celebrations at home will bring him joy and romance. Projects he has been working on will finally come to fruition. This is definitely a time for the Rabbit to make "hay" while his full Rabbit moon shines on him!

5. The Year of the Dragon 2000

The Rabbit can expect a moderately happy but hectic time at home and in his career under the reign of the illustrious Dragon. Things tend to be mixed or mediocre money-wise. But, on the whole, the Rabbit will still find it easy to be congenial as his overall gains will exceed losses. The Dragon's year also brings powerful friends who will prove very helpful to the Rabbit.

6. The Year of the Snake 2001

The Snake can often be too wrapped up in itself and the Rabbit will find its year unproductive, as not much in the way of tangible results can be obtained. He may have to change direction and rethink his plans to suit others. Difficulties arise from several areas, forcing him to consolidate his position or even to change his residence or job. Unexpected expenses crop up and the Rabbit finds less time to spend with loved ones. Winter brings a peaceful respite to the Rabbit's troubles as he recoups his losses and sorts things out to his liking.

7. The Year of the Horse 2002

A good year is in store for the Rabbit as his luck will come from meeting helpful people who will be happy to work with him or use their influence on his behalf. Although he will experience no big upheavals, the Rabbit will have to do a great deal of work, travel and entertaining just to keep up with the competition. The perceptive Horse is always fast on its feet, but the Rabbit should have no trouble keeping the pace should he want to join the race.

8. The Year of the Sheep 2003

The kindly Sheep brings achievement and easy recognition for the Rabbit during its reign. Plans progress smoothly as the Rabbit finds little opposition to his way of doing things. Love and friendship blossom under the auspices of the romantic Sheep. While the Rabbit will enjoy a prosperous year, he must pay strict attention to detail and not take things for granted or else he may have trouble later on. It would be a good idea for the Rabbit to have others put promises in writing and not rely only on verbal assurances.

9. The Year of the Monkey 2004

The Monkey has many tests in store for the Hare, but it will be a fair year for him provided he is not too optimistic. Contracts and financial deals may meet with unexpected snags or fail to materialize due to the betrayal of trusted friends or allies. His progress is impeded by those who try to take advantage of him or are jealous of his abilities. The Rabbit should triumph if he keeps his wits and calls the bluff of his enemies. He has little to lose in the year of the mischievous Monkey, but he must proceed with caution.

10. The Year of the Rooster 2005

The critical Chicken brings difficult times for the Rabbit, as he finds his money dwindling away and encounters setbacks that could be costly. The best bet for the Rabbit is to merge efforts with others and let them carry him through. The Rooster brings rules and regulations to the fore. He requires that we account for everything in detail, and this is very stressful for the retiring Rabbit. It would be best for the Rabbit to seek modest goals this year and not undertake anything independently.

11. The Year of the Dog 2006

The watchful Dog brings a smooth, protected year for the Rabbit, allowing him to benefit from past favors and to resolve problems that may have overlapped from the year of the Rooster. The refined Rabbit finds time for recreation and the pursuit of his other interests as he encounters no overwhelming problems at home or in romantic affairs. He must, however, refrain from being critical of his superiors and co-workers. Friction could result from his petulant refusal to consider the views of others.

12. The Year of the Boar 2007

Things look brighter than they actually are in the year of the Pig. It will be a mixed time for the Rabbit. The bounty he expects to realize may have to be shared with many. The Boar is indiscriminate in his generosity. Because unexpected difficulties will crop up, the Rabbit must be extra-realistic and take every precaution to protect his interests. He should keep in mind that a bird in his hand is worth two in the bush.

WHEN MOON SIGNS MEET SUN SIGNS

In my interpretation of Chinese horoscopes, the Rat is not linked with the first Western astrological sun sign, Aries. Instead, I pair the Rat with its counterpart based on the month and season of the Rat, which are December and winter. This makes the most sense as the lunar month of December (also called the Twelfth Moon or the Twelfth Earth Branch) is supposed to parallel the sun sign, Sagittarius, the Archer. I envision the Eastern and Western horoscope cycles like two large wheels with twelve spokes each. To correctly juxtapose these cycles, we must find the matching notch that will join them together. Once the Rat and Sagittarius are paired as the first signs, the other eleven fall into place. Please see the Twenty-Four Segments of the Lunar Almanac. All the dates correspond with the twelve Western solar signs.

If you are born in the year of the Rabbit under the Western sign of

Sagittarius: 22nd November to 21st December
The Sagittarian Rabbit = Fire + Negative Wood

This will be a gallivanting Hare, who will enjoy mixing with all colors and creeds. He will also have the ability to understand the incomprehensible—at least he will make every effort to understand his opponents' points of view. Both signs present here have foresight and vision. Open, mild-mannered and perceptive, this Rabbit rarely becomes agitated to the point of losing that splendid composure. A diplomat's dream, he can be calculating and bold without appearing obvious. The Rabbit can certainly make use of the Archer's buoyant spirits and Sagittarius in turn could fare well with the Hare's love of harmony and discretion.

If you are born in the year of the Rabbit under the Western sign of

Capricorn: 22nd December to 20th January
The Capricorn Rabbit = Earth + Negative Wood

As the upholder of society's values, the Capricorn Rabbit is usually blessed with a fortuitous life. While the moralistic Goat in him takes nothing for granted, the sagacious Rabbit will ferret out all the best deals for his own benefit. He will know how to cultivate important friends and invest wisely. The Hare's docility is toughened by sinewy Capricorn resolve. This person will display a passion for sound strategy. He will neither form nor change his opinions readily. Both signs possess a similarly calm disposition. The Rabbit is never above negotiations, while the Goat is a surefooted climber.

If you are born in the year of the Rabbit under the Western sign of

Aquarius: 21st January to 19th February
The Aquarian Rabbit = Air + Negative Wood

An optimistic nature is combined here with an exploring mind. This subject will be neither oversensitive to injury nor quick to anger. The personality formed by these two signs is able to project himself splendidly. He can also facilitate understanding between people through his psychic insight into their character. Both solar and lunar signs here pick up brain waves and vibrations of impending events and decode them expertly. The Aquarian Rabbit has reliable premonitions. However, while the Water Bearer is open-minded and too liberal, the Hare mitigates his impulsiveness as he hesitates to leave familiar settings or trade in his old lamp for a new one. By and large, the Aquarian Rabbit will be more engrossed in the world around him than in his own self.

If you are born in the year of the Rabbit under the Western sign of

Pisces: 20th February to 20th March
The Pisces Rabbit = Water + Negative Wood

Piscean Water nourishes Wood here and produces an imaginative and impressionable personality. The Pisces Rabbit presents a picture of gentility, beautiful ideas and soft words. A poetic soul, dependent on others, he will be ingeniously artistic, clever and even fastidious. Yet, despite his modest and unassuming demeanor, he does not lack foresight or confidence. Actually, his low profile can conceal an observant and astute mind. He will work hard to stabilize his existence and to deflect problems and conflicts away from himself and onto others. Noncommittal in a pleasant and agreeable way, the Pisces Rabbit possesses a certain amount of narcissism and is very concerned about his creature comforts.

If you are born in the year of the Rabbit under the Western sign of

Aries: 21st March to 19th April
The Aries Rabbit = Fire + Negative Wood

This combination will produce a domesticated Ram with the genteel and beguiling calmness of the Hare. He will also possess nerves of steel, always willing to bend in theory yet never quite doing it in actuality. Aries frankness is camouflaged by the Rabbit's carefully chosen words. He is nicer and kinder than most Rams, with slower and more painstaking ways. You can expect him to be solicitous but firm, enthusiastic but given to biding his time. The peaceful but observant Aries Rabbit is assured of getting things done his way in the end.

If you are born in the year of the Rabbit under the Western sign of

Taurus: 20th April to 20th May
The Taurean Rabbit = Earth + Negative Wood

This combination produces a tactful, artistic Bull who will manifest the Rabbit's traits of delicacy and congeniality. Both signs here are well-organized, although the Hare is more keenly observant and placidly disposed than the Bull. The Taurean Rabbit will not seek to impose his will upon others, but rather strive to convince them by his winning graciousness. Failing to win by diplomacy, he can withdraw into a stubborn sullenness that could be dangerous. But, with the help of the Bull's broad shoulders, the Rabbit may be willing to assume heavier responsibilities.

If you are born in the year of the Rabbit under the Western sign of

Gemini: 21st May to 21st June
The Gemini Rabbit = Air + Negative Wood

The mixture of Gemini's cool Air and the Rabbit's fragrant Wood element creates an eloquent and hugely persuasive personality. The spontaneous ways of Mercury's Gemini are here joined to the Hare's subtlety and foresight. A person of this combination will be smart and quickwitted. Both signs are adept at correctly assessing their own potential as well as the probable outcome of a project. The Gemini side discovers worthwhile ventures while the Rabbit devises the most feasible way to profit from them without investing too much labor.

If you are born in the year of the Rabbit under the Western sign of

Cancer: 22nd June to 21st July
The Cancerian Rabbit = Water + Negative Wood

The Rabbit's fixed element of Wood is nourished by the moon's Water sign. The Cancerian Rabbit has a kind nature but may have trouble letting go of things or people. Separation is a traumatic experience and changes are stressful to this person since he thrives on security. He makes few lasting relationships in life and will bare his soul to a precious few. He likes to carefully assess situations from a vantage point located at a safe distance. Although he is blessed with intuition and vision, he tends to concentrate on his own affairs and could be less than compassionate when he must become involved in any controversy. Given to romantic illusions and idyllic dreams, the Cancerian Rabbit should guard against indulging in intense brooding and self-pity when things fail to go his way.

If you are born in the year of the Rabbit under the Western sign of

Leo: 22nd July to 21st August
The Leo Rabbit = Fire + Negative Wood

This will be a proud, majestic Hare with excellent leadership capabilities although he is somewhat self-centered. He will have the charisma to sway the masses and the luck to get him through the trials in his life. This combination links aggressiveness with cool discretion. A person born under these signs will never advocate war openly. While he is not afraid of confrontation, he knows how to use his popularity to achieve his aims. He also has the knack of doing the right thing at the right time. Both the solar and lunar signs take their leisure activities seriously, so this personality may pursue expensive hobbies.

If you are born in the year of the Rabbit under the Western sign of

Virgo: 22nd August to 22nd September
The Virgo Rabbit = Earth + Negative Wood

Virgo's Earth element promotes the Rabbit's growth here because the Rabbit's fixed element is Wood. This combination will produce a virtuous but solitary soul who will do whatever needs to be done with a minimum of fuss. Both the Virgin and the Hare believe in being organized and careful. This person will also be realistic and will enjoy doing everything by the rules. He loves to deliberate in a quiet, factual manner and will approach his problems with cool logic. Tied to Virgo's stability, the Rabbit won't shun commitments if they prove financially rewarding.

If you are born in the year of the Rabbit under the Western sign of

Libra: 23rd September to 22nd October
The Libran Rabbit = Air + Negative Wood

A delightful combination of grace and intelligence; the Libran Hare will have the Rabbit's clarity of thought and excellent appreciation of the arts. Both solar and lunar signs here are good at weighing the pros and cons. Often, however, they want to eat the cake and keep it, too. Despite his immense popularity and ability at forging relationships, this native is twice shy about long-term involvements or being tied down permanently. Not a power grabber or an egotistical person, the Libran Rabbit will be levelheaded and sensible. In spite of his faults, he will always exhibit good taste and gravitate toward the finer things in life.

If you are born in the year of the Rabbit under the Western sign of

Scorpio: 23rd November to 21st December
The Scorpio Rabbit = Water + Negative Wood

A soft-spoken but secretive and recalcitrant personality. Pluto's child is deep while the Hare's soft and seemingly modest appearance provides excellent coverage for the Scorpion's strong emotions. This person disciplines himself admirably but can have a deadly temper and an unforgiving heart when crossed. Still, the Rabbit knows how to preserve his dignity with a feigned acquiescence when it is necessary to keep up appearances. A highly erotic and intense nature hiding beneath a cloak of conformity, the Scorpio Rabbit is sometimes lost between the tugs of Pluto's passion and the Hare's calm intellect and love of harmony.

THE SEASONS OF THE RABBIT

SPRING

Rabbits born in the spring are optimistic and carefree by nature. They have kind dispositions and like to get involved in group action.

Occasionally, they act independently but on the whole they do best in a large circle of friends. The spring Rabbit will pursue an artistic career and be well-informed in areas which interest him. He knows how to position himself strategically to benefit from any revolutionary technologies or future developments. Sociable, intelligent and quick on his feet, the spring Rabbit does not miss a step.

SUMMER

Summer brings love of ease and need for refinement to the Rabbits born in its season. Disharmony and stress is something summer Rabbits will avoid like the plague as they lose their sense of security and balance when there is conflict in the air. These Rabbits know how to negotiate their way out of trouble. They can even retreat from a war front without having to do battle. They will be able to get others to fight for them, and this is probably just as well as Rabbits are not born fighters—they are the peacemakers. People will have need of the summer Rabbit's skills and he will be sought after for his sound advice and ability to communicate.

AUTUMN

Rabbits born in the fall are thoughtful, considerate and cautious in all they say and do. Serene philosophers who always see the whole picture before dispensing advice or making any decisions, they have patience, excellent taste and a good nose for investments, be they real estate, business, modern art or antiques. Autumn children will put their mark on all their achievements as they perform with aplomb and dedication. The autumn Rabbit knows how to bide his time and is adept at manipulating others to do his will. Beneath that calm and indolent exterior, he is both swift and decisive.

WINTER

Inscrutable and at times very calculating, the winter Hare never takes anything for granted. Extremely good at assessing trends and calculating what the public likes, he will make the right call most of the time. A connoisseur and critic par excellence, he is renowned for his flawless logic and love of beauty and the arts. Unlikely to let others influence him, the winter Rabbit largely relies on his own intuition and powers of deduction. He may not pounce on an opportunity as fast as the Tiger does, but then he rarely gets caught in any traps. Sensible and realistic, he does not take on more than he can handle, and as a result will not get in over his head.

FAMOUS PERSONS BORN IN THE YEAR OF THE RABBIT

Metal
Henry Miller
Jomo Kenyatta

Wood
Orson Welles
David Rockefeller
Ingrid Bergman
Johannes Vorster

Earth
Albert Einstein
Josef Stalin
Queen Victoria
David Frost
Ali McGraw

Water
King Olav V of Norway
Dr. Benjamin Spock

Fire
Harry Belafonte
George C. Scott
King Bhumibol of Thailand
Peter Falk

5

The Fifth Sign
of the Lunar Cycle

The Dragon

I am an unquenchable fire,
   the center of all energy,
   the stout heroic heart.
I am truth and light,
   I hold power and glory in my sway.
My presence
   disperses dark clouds.
I have been chosen
   to tame the Fates.

I AM THE DRAGON.

Lunar Year of the Dragon in the Western Calendar	Elements
16 February 1904 to 3 February 1905	Wood
3 February 1916 to 22 February 1917	Fire
23 January 1928 to 9 February 1929	Earth
8 February 1940 to 26 January 1941	Metal
27 January 1952 to 13 February 1953	Water
13 February 1964 to 1 February 1965	Wood
31 January 1976 to 17 February 1977	Fire
17 February 1988 to 5 February 1989	Earth
5 February 2000 to 23 January 2001	Metal

If you were born on the day before the start of the lunar year of the Dragon, e.g., 12th February, 1964, your animal sign is the one before the Dragon, the Rabbit, the fourth lunar sign.

If you were born on the day after the last day of the lunar year of the Dragon, e.g., 2nd February, 1965, your sign is the one after that of the Dragon, the Snake, the sixth lunar sign.

The sign of the Dragon rules the two hour-segment of the day from 7 A.M. to 9 A.M. Persons born during this time are said to have the Dragon as their ascendant and will display many of the characteristics common to this sign and have great affinity for Dragons.

The direction appointed to the Dragon is east-southeast; its season is spring and its principle month, April. The Dragon corresponds to the Western astrological sign of Aries, which rules spring from March 21st to April 19th. Wood is its fixed element and the Dragon is considered a yang or male sign with a positive stem.

THE DRAGON PERSONALITY

The mighty and magnificent Dragon of mythical folklore never ceases to enchant us or stir our imaginations. So it must be said that some of its magical qualities, illusory or not, are contained in those born under its sign.

The Dragon person is magnanimous and full of vitality and strength. To him, life is a blaze of colors, and he is constantly on the go. Egotistical, eccentric, dogmatic, whimsical or terribly demanding and unreasonable, he is still never without a band of admirers. Proud, aristocratic and very direct, the Dragon-born establishes his ideals early in life and demands the same high standards from others that he has set for himself.

In China, the formidable Dragon symbolizes the emperor or male. The indestructible Phoenix is the symbol of the empress or female. Those born in the Dragon year are said to wear the horns of destiny which represent power and duty. A Dragon child will tend to assume burdens and responsibilities even if he or she happens to be the youngest in the family. Often, older Dragon children can bring up their younger siblings with more authority than the parents.

The Dragon is a veritable storehouse of energy. His impetuosity, eagerness and almost religious zeal can blaze like the fabled fire the Dragon emits from its mouth. He has the potential for accomplishing great things, which is fortunate as the Dragon likes to perform on a grand scale. However, unless he contains his enthusiasm, he may burn himself out and end up in a puff of smoke. He is the most likely of the signs to become fanatical over an issue. Whatever the Dragon does, good or bad, he will never fail to make headlines. The Chinese call him the guardian of wealth and power. This is certainly a prosperous sign to belong to. But then again, the Dragon is the sign most prone to megalomania. He just does not take defeat gracefully. The powerful Dragon is difficult to oppose, at times even impossible. He tends to intimidate those who dare challenge him. An angry, spurned Dragon could be like the big bad wolf at your door. He'll huff and he'll puff until he blows your house down.

But the Dragon is likely to be loyal to his loved ones despite his strong temper and dogmatic ways. Whatever differences he or she may have with the family will be forgotten or set aside when they call for help. The Dragon can put aside resentments and come to the rescue promptly. However, his family can also count on a severe lecture from him once the crisis is over. The Dragon seldom minces words. He cites his views as if they were Imperial Edicts. Although he may rave about the virtues of free speech and democracy—don't buy it. He feels himself to be above the law and doesn't always practice what he preaches.

Sometimes being civil, affectionate or honey-tongued can be a terrible strain on the Dragon. He would much rather be rough, rude and utterly inconsiderate when provoked. But don't try to give him the same medicine. Somehow, it just won't work, unless you happen to be another Dragon and decide to do battle. Then we can all sit back and watch magnificent fireworks that will make the 4th of July look like candles on a birthday cake.

In spite of his volcano of emotions, the Dragon is not sentimental, overly sensitive or very romantic. He takes love and adulation for granted: they are his just due. But while he may be stubborn, irrational and overbearing when irked, the Dragon can forgive you the moment he gets over his outburst. And since things are supposed to work both ways, he expects your forgiveness for his errors as well. He may even neglect to apologize at times, which may seem callous, but then the Dragon really has no time to explain himself (he doesn't see the need for it, anyway) or be bothered by grudges or trifles; he just wants to get on with his work.

While the Dragon may be strong and decisive, he is not cunning or manipulative. He shuns easy adaptability and tricky negotiations. When the contest is to be decided on strength alone, the Dragon will conquer hands down. Often, though, he is overconfident, brash and deluded by his wonderful visions and neglects to pay attention to potential upsets or underhanded plots that could overcome him. Instead of sniffing around to nose out what schemes might be brewing, he prefers to plunge right into battle, refusing to retreat even in the face of overwhelming odds. Too proud, he disdains calls for assistance; too sure, he rarely keeps anything in reserve. Too intent on going forward, he forgets to protect his rear and flanks. Too upright, he refuses to lie or compromise. Further, he is unable to decipher information presented indirectly, as in clever innuendoes and insinuations. He also generally fails to spot the evil and subversive intent of his enemies.

To the Dragon person, having a purpose or special mission in life is essential. He must always have a cause to fight for, a goal to reach, a right to wrong. Otherwise, how can he keep that inner fire burning?

Without his pet projects, rallies and other impossible schemes, the Dragon is like a locomotive without fuel. He fizzles out and becomes dull and listless.

The Dragon has the same affinity for success as the Snake, but because he expresses his views more openly and his failures are more likely to involve some form of physical exertion, he is usually spared deep psychological problems. Being a doer, he will take to one-man crusades, lead demonstrations, write letters to the newspapers or collect a million signatures on a petition. This method of belching fire and brimstone effectively rids him of any inner neurosis that could result otherwise.

The Dragon lady is the Grand Dame of the cycle. She will be a suffragette, a believer of equal rights for women. Double standards and discrimination will arouse her wildest passions and greatest anger. What a man can do, she can probably do better. Don't underestimate her. She is determined to beat you at your own game—or die trying. She'll never stand idly by and accept her fate. She is the stuff empires are built on, the matriarch of old. Cross her and the sky will fall.

To tell the truth, the Dragon female is strictly a no-nonsense person. She will show this by the way she dresses. Practical, functional clothes appeal to her most—no frills, flimsy laces, buttons and bows. Clothes that go on and off easily and provide her with maximum comfort and movement will be her choice. She hates unnecessary restrictions and limitations. Actually, she may even secretly prefer a uniform if she has military or institutional inclinations. This way, starched, crisp and superbly efficient, she can pop off to work every day without the bother of having to decide what to wear. Female dragons make excellent teachers and can inspire others to follow their example. Being natural educators and instructors, they are always clear about what they want from others and how things should be done.

The Dragon girl seldom, if ever, over-decorates herself. Her brilliance lies in her mind and this will shine forth without any adornment. Dragons have very high self-esteem and the Dragon female is no exception. She doesn't expect to be treated like royalty (but close to it), she just wants your respect, and she will do everything in her power to get it.

The lady Dragon is totally emancipated and, you might as well know, she never doubts the rightness of her cause, so strong arm tactics will get you nowhere. Resign yourself, she will have the last word.

Despite having faults as numerous as virtues, the luster of the Dragon shines on everyone. He is not petty, nor does he begrudge favors. He may grumble a lot, but he cannot resist helping the needy or coming to the rescue of those in trouble. This may not be because he feels real compassion or even genuine concern; more often than not, the Dragon helps out because he has a profound sense of duty to all.

Somehow, the Dragon will always have a notable contribution to make. You can count on his support, for he will not let you down if he can help it. The Dragon will exhaust all his resources before he admits failure. An extrovert and lover of nature, this person will be an active sportsman, an inveterate traveller and an excellent talker. He has the makings of a supersalesman and he and his band of loyal followers will always be promoting something.

The weather at the time of a Dragon's birth will greatly affect his life. A child born during a storm will lead a tempestuous and hazardous life beset by danger or spectacular experiences. One born on a day when the sea (his ancestral home) and the heavens are calm will have a protected existence and a more amiable nature.

The Dragon native will either marry young or prefer to remain single. He can be happy leading a solitary life, as his work and career will keep him occupied. He will seldom lack friends or admirers to keep him company.

The Dragon is not a spendthrift, but he is not a miser, either. He is generous with money, but never too concerned about his finances unless he happens to have a money-making ascendant like the Rooster or the Rat.

This person is superpositive. Nothing will keep him down for long, and even when he has a bad case of the doldrums, he will snap out of it faster than anyone else. His buoyancy often defies rhyme or reason.

For a sign that never accepts defeat, the Dragon provides his own worst opposition. He will dash headlong into a disastrous situation when he is convinced he is right. Pompous and self-destructive, you say? No, not really. It is just that this person must follow his plans and ideals regardless of the consequences. After all, he was put on earth to raise standards to superlative heights, and the more you try to change his course of action or steer him away from trouble, the more head-strong he may become. He lives up to his reputation for taking the lead even when matters become most unpleasant.

Whatever else, the Dragon will be an open person—you can read him like a book. It is difficult for him to pretend emotions he does not feel. He rarely even bothers to try. He is not secretive either, and cannot keep a confidence for long. Even when he swears not to breathe a word, he will blurt it out when he gets angry and sparks begin to fly. You say he promised to keep it a secret? What secret? How can you bother him with such a trivial thing at a time like this?

His feelings are genuine and always straight from his heart. When he declares he loves you, you can be absolutely sure he is sincere.

Should he belong to the rougher variety of Dragons, he could be very abrasive. His direct, brusque manners and callousness could well antagonize people. But generally speaking, he will inspire action. Things he wants done immediately should be attended to personally, not in writing or over the phone. His presence provides the magnet-ism to swing people over to his way of thinking. He motivates every-one he comes into contact with. He'll need no motivation—he is more than capable of generating his own momentum.

It will never be hard to place your confidence in the truth-loving Dragon. He seldom wavers, cowers or shifts responsibility. He pos-sesses little or no self-doubt. With his natural pioneering spirit, his endeavors will either be stupendous successes or unbelievable exer-cises in futility. He must drive to the very edge of the precipice and take a good look for himself. Just hold your breath, keep your fingers crossed and pray that he has good brakes. Frank Sinatra is a Dragon, and his song, "My Way" concisely sums up how the Dragon ticks.

Of all the animal signs, the Dragon will be attracted most to the irresistible Monkey. The Monkey will similarly be drawn to the Dragon's majesty and they will make an unbeatable team. A

Dragon-Rat union will be an equally winning combination, as the Rat is crafty while the Dragon is strong. They can do great things together. The Dragon will likewise make a good match with the cool and venerable Snake, whose wisdom could check the Dragon's excessiveness.

Tiger, Rooster, Horse, Sheep, Rabbit and Boar will all seek the Dragon out for his beauty and strength. Two Dragons will get along pretty well but the Dragon's relationship with the Ox may be a bit strained by the Ox's similar authoritativeness. Of all the animal signs, perhaps only the Dog will make a miserable partner for the Dragon. The Dragon will come under the close scrutiny of the Dog and the Dog will be too cynical to fall under the Dragon's spell. The Dog could be a pain in the Dragon's rear end as the egalitarian Dog demands equality and justice for all, and when he checks the scales, he may find the Dragon tipping them arbitrarily in his own favor without even realizing. Sometimes the Dragon sees himself as just a little more "equal" than most and this really raises the hackles of our fair-minded Dog.

Above all, it is worth remembering that although the Dragon is dazzling, he is not always deep. Only when he can harness his legendary powers can he perform the miracles he is famous for. He needs people to believe in him!

THE DRAGON CHILD

The high-spirited Dragon child is an innovator. Forceful, fearless and vibrant, nothing will daunt his idealistic outlook on life. He will formulate his own principles early and will need or ask for very little help. Respectful of his elders, he will obey commands precisely.

This intense child needs to anchor his passions to something or someone he considers worthy of his devotion. He will have countless idols—his teachers, his parents or anyone else he regards highly. He is bright, aggressive and independent. Tough and resilient, he can take teasing or shoving around because he is willing and ready to fight for his rights. Outspoken and ambitious, he should be given responsibility in order to keep him occupied and make him feel useful. He could turn the most menial assignment into a task worthy of a medal. However, he should not be allowed to bully less assertive children. His domineering ways must be checked at an early age.

The Dragon child must be made to feel appreciated. He earns his integrity and would honestly prefer that you needed him instead of just loved him. His efforts are always sincere and should be praised, as he will work very hard to please you and gain your respect. Never bruise his ego by laughing at him, even if he goes around performing a simple chore as if it were some intricate ritual or important mission. The Dragon's self-esteem is immeasurable. His dreams of greatness are all real and tangible to him. In life, his emotions will touch soaring heights and unfathomable depths. If he fails at anything, he has to be reassured that the sun will shine again the next day. He judges himself very harshly. Once he realizes his mistake, there will be no need for you to reproach or punish him, as he will be the first to chastise himself and make amends.

If your child is a Dragon, he will want or maybe even demand that you rely on him and will do his best never to disappoint you. This self-reliant youngster will be strong and faithful to his ideals. He was born to lead and excel. The Dragon child needs, above all, for you to be proud of him. He will prove that his parents could not have placed their trust in a more worthy person.

THE FIVE DIFFERENT DRAGONS

METAL DRAGON—1940, 2000

This type could well be the most strong-willed of the Dragons. Honesty and integrity are paramount virtues to him, and although he may be bright, open, and expressive, he is also unbending and critical.

Action-oriented and combative, he will seek out and motivate those on his own intellectual or social level. He has little patience with the lazy and the foolish. Unpliable Metal combined with his natural lunar sign, Wood, will also enable him to intimidate weaker beings into submitting to his will.

He is tremendously intense and will stake his life on his convictions. At his best, he is a magnificent warrior. It is futile to try to convince him that certain things just cannot be done. This type of Dragon will try to exorcise whatever evil he sees in life and could be fanatical regarding his convictions and moral beliefs.

When he is negative, he will have exaggerated views of his own importance. He is a bit short on diplomacy and has the habit of going it alone if others disagree with him or refuse to accept his leadership.

The strong Metal Dragon will rush in where angels fear to tread. He will succeed because he will allow himself no other course of action. He burns his bridges behind him so that he cannot retreat once he goes on the attack.

WATER DRAGON—1952, 2012

This is a less imperious type of Dragon who favors optimum growth and expansion. He can put aside his ego for the good of all and is less selfish and opinionated. An inhibited but progressive person, he tries hard not to be as conspicuous as other power-hungry Dragons. Neither is he going to be labeled as the conciliatory one. He can assume a wait-and-see attitude and his wits are as formidable as his strength of will.

The Water Dragon lives by the to-thine-own-self-be-true philosophy and will not seek revenge on those who choose to go the opposite way. Democratic and liberal minded, he can accept defeat or rejection without bitterness.

Water is calming and beneficial to this lunar sign, enabling him to know how to act wisely and do what is essential for his progress. He is quick and reliable and is capable of marketing his ideas with untiring devotion. He is likely to be successful as a negotiator; he knows when, where and how to apply force.

His main drawback is that he may be like an overoptimistic builder who forgets to reinforce the foundation. By trying to hold on to too much he may lose everything. He must learn to make difficult choices and relinquish whatever is unfeasible or unnecessary. This way, he will be able to devote his energies to fewer but more rewarding endeavors.

WOOD DRAGON—1904, 1964

A creative and magnanimous type of Dragon capable of developing bright new revolutionary concepts. Wood combined with his sign makes him adept at formulating and implenting his ideas and working cooperatively with others, even if he may be a bit condescending on occasion.

Gifted with an exploratory nature, the Wood Dragon loves to look into cause and effect theories; his every action will be guided by sound logic. However, he also has a tendency to overinvestigate subjects or to submit people to endless debate when he is faced with opposition. He is a natural teacher and could be very scholarly in his own offbeat manner.

Nonetheless, this is a generous Dragon who is amenable to taking the middle road, tries to offend as few people as possible, and subtly conceals his domineering ways. The Wood element produces a less fierce and unreasonable variety of Dragon who will compromise when it is to his advantage. Still, as a Dragon, he will ultimately relate everything to his oversized ego and will condescend to change only when sure of the benefits to himself.

Not as vindictive or self-centered as Dragons of the other elements, he will still be outspoken, proud and fearless when challenged.

FIRE DRAGON—1916, 1976

The most righteous, outgoing and competitive of all dragons, the Fire Dragon will expect a lot from everyone. But while he may be demanding and aggressive, he is also blessed with enormous energy and has a lot to offer in return. The trouble is that he may go around with an air of superiority plus authority and make people fear or shy way from him. His leadership qualities are often marred by his desire to be treated like the Messiah. Fire matched with his forceful lunar sign will give him overzealous and dictatorial inclinations. He pushes hard even when there is little resistance.

In reality, he is an open and humane person given to impartiality and uncovering the truth at all costs. His criticisms are objective and he has the power to arouse masses with his vibrant personality. A natural empire builder, he will strive toward the supreme order of things, with himself at the helm, of course.

Because the Fire Dragon is often enveloped by his insatiable personal ambition, he is short-tempered, inconsiderate and unable to tolerate anything less than perfection. He also overgeneralizes or jumps to conclusions, frequently lumping people into categories without allowing for or even perceiving their individual differences.

Nonetheless, here is a performer of the highest degree who could easily be a source of inspiration to his fellow man and a personality who will catch the public eye—when he learns to master his negative traits and communicate more humbly with others.

EARTH DRAGON—1928, 1988

This sociable, executive-type Dragon will have a compulsive drive to control his environment and the people who surround him. As a Dragon he is bound to be autocratic and it would be folly to expect less. However, he will be fair and appreciative of other people's opinions, even if he doesn't agree with them. Earth makes him realistic, stable and, oftentimes, even a bit impersonal.

Although not as severe as the other Dragons, he will still have the basic urge to subjugate others. But he will be reasonable in his approach to problems and his leadership will be less dictatorial. He works incessantly to develop his talents and exploit his resources. One who realizes the value of cooperation, this type of Dragon will seek to work for the good of all. He certainly cannot be accused of being selfish, stingy or petty.

The Earth Dragon's self-control does not mean that he is lacking in initiative. It's just that the Earth element influences him to be unhurried and to keep his aspirations solid and uncluttered.

This aristocratic Dragon is quiet, strong and brave. Given to reflection and organization, his outbursts of temper will be few, nor will he demean himself by arguing with those beneath him when he is angered. However, he will retaliate quickly once his dignity is offended and will demand respect.

COMPATIBILITY AND CONFLICT CHARTS
FOR THE DRAGON

The Dragon is part of the First Triangle of Affinity, a group consisting of positive people identified as DOERS. The Rat, the Dragon and the Monkey are performance- and progress-oriented signs adept at handling matters with initiative and innovation. Self-starters, they prefer to initiate action, clear their paths of uncertainty and hesitation and forge ahead with leadership. Restless and short-tempered when hindered or forced to be unoccupied, they are full of dynamic energy and ambition. This trio is the melting pot of ideas. They can team up beautifully because they possess a common way of doing things and will appreciate each other's method of thinking.

TRIANGLE OF AFFINITY FOR THE DRAGON

The Dragon will have his most serious personality clashes with someone born in the year of the Dog. Anyone whose ascendant is the Dog will also be likely to conflict with the Dragon. In the Circle of Conflict, the Dragon and the Dog are 180 degrees apart. The Dragon faces east while the Dog is oriented to the west. The Dragon is identified with spring while the Dog's season is autumn. Finally, the natural element for the Dragon is Wood while its opposite, Metal, is the Dog's natural element. Since Metal cuts Wood, relationships between these two signs are not always successful.

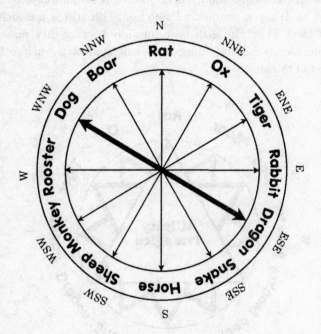

CIRCLE OF CONFLICT

Aside from the most compatible partners, the Rat and the Monkey, and the most incompatible sign, the Dog, the other nine signs are compatible with the Dragon to varying degrees.

Ox

The Dragon and Ox will have a great deal of respect for one another and will be able to cooperate to achieve common goals.

However, the Ox can be uncompromising when pushed too far by the domineering Dragon and will turn out to be a stubborn and unyielding opponent. It would be advisable for both parties to agree upon their exact roles early in their relationship so as to prevent a struggle for power or authority. The Ox is a hard worker so the Dragon will never have cause to complain about the Ox's worthiness.

Tiger

This combination is fated to be moderately successful, but with occasional fireworks. Both signs are easily agitated and can be vocal about their opinions. Clashes of will and misunderstandings may result when they fight for the limelight. The Tiger will not take a backseat but the Dragon wants to do all the driving. Somewhere, somehow they must learn to compromise and resolve their differences. However, both signs are as forgiving as they are colorful, and they quickly resume their friendship after a flare-up.

Rabbit

These two may have many interests in common. The Dragon has great need of the Rabbit's tactfulness and good judgment while the Rabbit admires the Dragon's leadership and power. The Rabbit prefers to work behind the scenes to influence the course of things in an oblique way. He may shy away from the direct and confrontational tactics of a belligerent Dragon on the attack. Yet the Rabbit could do wonders for the Dragon's tarnished image if the Dragon allows him to help.

Dragon

There is not much conflict in a Dragon with Dragon union. Usually they will be fanatical about the same issue or they will not even bother to associate with one another. The danger is that, because this dynamic duo has so much power and steam, they could vent their frustrated zeal on lesser mortals with alarming ferocity. Strong religious beliefs and political causes usually bind this team together.

Snake

The Snake will find the Dragon's courage and affinity for success very attractive and will have no difficulty helping the Dragon achieve their mutual aims. Successful and compatible relationships can be developed since these powerful signs need each other. The Snake can be practical and ruthlessly focused when he is after something, so he will appreciate the Dragon's never-give-up philosophy. Ambition will be the key word in their partnership.

Horse

The partnering of a Dragon and a Horse creates power and speed. There may be some struggle for dominance as the Horse can be impatient and restless under the leadership of the Dragon. But if they have good communication skills, which both usually do, they should be able to iron out their differences and map out respective territories. The independent Horse has a clear perspective and is quick to sense changes blowing in the wind. The Dragon will do well to go along with the Horse's superior instincts and ability to steer clear of trouble.

Sheep

Relationships between the Dragon and Sheep range from cool to acceptable. If the Dragon feels protective toward the peace-loving Sheep and does not make unreasonable demands, matters should work out fine. The Sheep will be more than willing to cooperate and let the brilliant Dragon take command. The Dragon will provide leadership in such a partnership, while the Sheep's creativeness will definitely bloom if the Dragon is able to inspire the sensitive Sheep in non-threatening ways.

Rooster

The Dragon is drawn to the Chicken's expertise and competence while the Rooster is in awe of the Dragon's zeal and enthusiasm. They will strive to find prosperity, success and happiness together. In order to achieve mutual bonds and lasting relationships, both signs must approach the partnership with less expectations and smaller egos. The Rooster can deal with the Dragon's brashness and the thick-skinned Dragon is not afraid of the Chicken's undiluted criticism and need for exactness. The Dragon can fight while the Rooster will perch on its shoulder and definitely supervise. We should pity the opposition.

Boar

The honest and obliging Boar will be happy to be the Dragon's friend and join his fabulous group of faithful followers. There should be no large differences or serious conflicts in such a partnership. Both signs value sincerity and commitment and will work passionately for what they believe in. On the negative side, the Boar may be more lenient and scrupulous than the Dragon cares to be, and the Dragon may be too egotistic and pompous for the sociable Boar, who prefers to make friends instead of vanquish enemies, as the Dragon is fond of doing.

THE DRAGON AND HIS ASCENDANTS

We all have a shadow that follows us throughout life. Sometimes it grows bigger than life and at other times it shrinks until it disappears into the soles of our feet. Sometimes it walks tall before us and on other occasions it lags behind like a sulking friend. In Chinese horoscopes, this constant partner, manifested or not, is our ascendant, the animal sign that rules the hour of our birth and becomes a comrade in our journey though life. We may view it as friend or foe or even a little of both. It surfaces when we least expect and shows a better or worse side of our nature. We can often be confounded by the way we listen to our "other self" as well as feel resentful of the significant influence it can exert on us. Actually, a personality has many rings around the centered "self." Each ring can have a different size, texture and aura. When all these factors combine, they bring forth the unique individual that the person truly is. Hence, a Dragon with an ascendant that is not compatible, like the Dog, has perhaps a more difficult inner struggle than say a Snake born during the hours of the Snake. The double intensity of the Snake person will be easily understood by horoscope readers while the more intricate Dragon/Dog may exhibit the contrary Dog and Dragon traits to varying degrees. There are many voices within each person. But, in the end, only the individual determines which course he will follow, which choices he will make.

The time of birth used to determine the ascendant is always the local time in the place of birth.

If you were born between:

11 P.M. and 1 A.M. = The Hours of the Rat

Your typical Dragon generosity is tempered by the Rat's frugality. The Rat ascendant has a more affectionate and charming nature than the forthright Dragon. A captivating and talkative Dragon, you will be objective and decisive with a certain shrewdness and love of maintaining control of each situation. You know how to get your way without having to resort to Dragon force every time.

1 A.M. and 3 A.M. = The Hours of the Ox

You may tend to be a more cautious, slow-moving Dragon who likes to be sure of what you are doing before acting. Nonetheless, you are still a fire-breathing Dragon and could employ the Buffalo's heavy-handed tactics in dealing with those who dare cross you. The Ox's restraint and reliability, however, may make you more patient and persevering. Dedicated, studious and spirited, you could carry the world on your shoulders if you devote yourself to something you ardently believe in.

3 A.M. and 5 A.M. = The Hours of the Tiger

With the Tiger's wild impulses, you could be motivated for emotional reasons instead of rational ones. The Dragon is always ready to march into battle with all flags flying and the Tiger ascendant is just as idealistic. Big-hearted, helpful and optimistic, you must learn to deal with setbacks and disappointments calmly instead of flying off the handle and blaming those closest to you.

5 A.M. and 7 A.M. = The Hours of the Rabbit

With this ascendant, you possess both strength and diplomacy. You could be a quiet, non-combative Dragon given to reflection and sound thinking. Strong, subtle and intuitive, you will make good use of the Hare's prudence in your actions and be more successful and popular than other Dragons because of your ability to get along with others. You could be the darling of influential society as your advice and views will be valued.

7 A.M. and 9 A.M. = The Hours of the Dragon

This doubly intense combination makes you a "pure" Dragon personality. It will be hard to miss or dismiss you. Possibly the high priest or priestess type, you tend to exact unquestioning devotion and obedience. You could have the charisma to establish a cult of your own or just bask in the adoration of your large fan club. You will have the capacity to give of yourself as much as you receive. Your courage and influence will be felt by all.

9 A.M. and 11 A.M. = The Hours of the Snake

The Snake's finesse and introverted demeanor may mask your Dragon ambition and love of power, and make you a Dragon more apt to plotting your moves and executing plans with calm tenacity. Attractive, witty, elegant and intelligent you will stand out in any crowd. The only things that could hold you back are the Dragon's judgmental and moralistic attitude and that Snake suspiciousness that always lurks in the back of your mind.

11 A.M. to 1 P.M. = The Hours of the Horse

The Horse ascendant makes you happy, carefree and more action-oriented. You like to gamble for high stakes and are skillful and aggressive. When you are negative, you could be a rebellious and stubborn person who is difficult to reason with. But the Dragon's sense of duty and largesse should tone down that temperamental Horse ascendant. Fast and self-assured, you are a quick learner and an athletic, sports-oriented person gifted with above average reflexes. You should have a wonderful life if you can control that Horse temper and impulsiveness.

1 P.M. to 3 P.M. = The Hours of the Sheep

The Sheep ascendant brings modesty and understanding to your Dragon birth sign. Creative, kind and compassionate, you will always seek peaceful solutions to your problems. Sympathetic to others and very cosmopolitan in your outlook, you are one Dragon who can really get things done right without having to resort to brute force. The Sheep makes you lovable and popular, but the Dragon in you won't let people take too much advantage of your generosity.

3 P.M. and 5 P.M. = The Hours of the Monkey

You could be a superstar in your own right with this wonderful combination of problem solver and overachiever. You may appear affable and friendly on the outside, but on the inside you are made of steel and nothing gets past you. Observant, diligent and inventive, you are a Dragon who will make your own rules and have no trouble getting others to support you.

5 P.M. and 7 P.M. = The Hours of the Rooster

With the Rooster crowing at your birth hour, you will be a fearless and active Dragon possessing immeasurable pride and industry. A relentless, hardworking and unconventional character, you will be admired for your resourcefulness and unwavering dedication to your goals. Heaven help those who do not agree with your views. At least there will never be a dull moment in your company.

7 P.M. and 11 P.M. = The Hours of the Dog

The Dog ascendant could make you a very down-to-earth Dragon with practical ideas and an amiable disposition. Loyal, respectable and noble in your intentions, you care deeply for the welfare of everyone you come in contact with. Your battles tend to be more on behalf of your principles than your ambitions or oversized Dragon ego. Helpful, brave and altruistic, you may be the perfect social worker and champion of the masses. However, you could still have a nasty bite when you are angry.

11 P.M. and 1 A.M. = The Hours of the Boar

The Boar ascendant could make you a warm-hearted Dragon who is deeply devoted to working for the benefit of all. Charitable, traditional and even naive and undisciplined at times, you may combine the Pig's appetite for indulgence with the Dragon's devotion to duty. A passionate and commanding personality, you draw people from all walks of life into your great circle of influence and inspire them with your ability to lead.

HOW THE DRAGON FARES IN THE LUNAR CYCLE

1. The Year of the Rat 1996

The year of the Rat brings prosperity for the Dragon, and he will have a lively time with romance and business interests. Although money will flow in, one bad deal may make a serious dent in the Dragon's resources. So while his ally, the Rat, supports ambitious plans, the Dragon should resist get-rich-quick schemes. But no matter what transpires, he will find life relaxing and his overall work performance will be good. No major problems will confront him at home or at work.

2. The Year of the Ox 1997

This will be a fortunate but busy year for the Dragon. Progress will be moderate and the year of the Ox brings many responsibilities for the Dragon. He should consider himself lucky because the numerous disputes and troubles that swirl around him will not affect him directly. A protected time in which he will not be involved in many difficulties. His family life will also be free of interference. The Ox is slow but sure and the Dragon should follow his lead and do things one at a time and not be restless and demanding. Both signs here are "horned" beasts who do not shy away from hard work or dedication to duty.

3. The Year of the Tiger 1998

The year of the Big Cat is a worrying and taxing time. The Dragon's plans are blocked by others and he finds it difficult to achieve desired results without a great deal of argument. He has to choose between embittered camps of opposing views and finds it hard to please everyone. The Tiger's reign is punctuated by excitement and controversy. But if the Dragon knows how to interpret the Tiger's erratic outbursts, he will be able to put things in their proper perspective. If he stays on course, matters will work themselves out and calm will return before the fall. His home life, however, may be disturbed by sad news or the departure of a member.

4. The Year of the Rabbit 1999

Tranquility returns to the Dragon's life in the year of the Rabbit. A fair amount of progress can be expected as the winds of fortune blow on the Dragon's sails again. His home and love life become more settled, although he could experience minor health problems. The Hare year is a reasonable time to make long-term commitments, negotiate new ventures and find influential associates. No financial upsets or bad news await the Dragon in this year.

5. The Year of the Dragon 2000

This will be a very good year for the Dragon native. Numerous benefits are in store and he could gain recognition or make fantastic progress in his work. Success comes easily in his undertakings as this busy and exciting year keeps the Dragon very occupied. However, the Dragon must guard against overconfidence or delusions of grandeur in his year. Taking on more than he can handle or making outrageous promises he cannot keep will catch up with him at a later date, when he will regret his foolish optimism.

6. The Year of the Snake 2001

On the whole, this will be a lucky year for the Dragon's business endeavors. His plans go smoothly although he meets minor opposition or behind the scenes resistance. The Snake's year can be extremely secretive and unpredictable. The Dragon should not take anything for granted or relax his guard in this karmic year. The Snake always settles accounts and never forgives a debt. The illustrious Dragon may encounter some personal or romantic problems because he neglects his home and love life.

7. The Year of the Horse 2002

This will be a year of uncertainty and surprises for the Dragon. The energetic Horse may bring news that will temporarily upset or change the Dragon's life. His problems will tend to work themselves out, however, if he is not too headstrong or aggressive. The year of the Horse is capricious and changes occur quickly with little reason. The Dragon will experience considerable unease as real and imaginary worries beset him. An adventurous and stressful year for the Dragon who, although he loves excitement, may find the lack of commitment in the Horse's year difficult to accept.

8. The Year of the Sheep 2003

The Dragon can only expect moderate progress during the Sheep's year for his financial ventures and career advancement. Unlike the Horse's year, the year of the Sheep is too slow and comfortable for the high-spirited Dragon. People tend to disregard rules and shun responsibility this year and the Dragon will be frustrated by the lack of cooperation from his friends. He will have some health problems but his general family life will be peaceful. However, romance gets complicated in the year of the sentimental Sheep, and the Dragon will have difficulty satisfying those who want more displays of affection or recognition from him. Otherwise, there will be no upheavals or unwelcome changes in his environment.

9. The Year of the Monkey 2004

The arrival of the Monkey means a mixed year for the Dragon. Progress can be foreseen in his career, and financial undertakings may look bountiful but he must not be misled by favorable preliminary results or he could get caught in legal tangles. Broken friendships or romantic quarrels can result if he is too determined to have everything done his way. The Monkey's year is a time for compromises and heeding the advice of others; it favors the tactician who can improvise and solve intricate puzzles without losing his composure. The Dragon must pass certain tests before the Monkey's year will reward him.

10. The Year of the Rooster 2005

This will be a happy and eventful year for the Dragon, with good news, promotions and the recovery of money given up for lost. The Rooster brings new opportunities and possibilities for the Dragon native. His family life is smooth and he is able to recoup previous losses or make new influential friends. However, the Rooster's reign is far from quiet and the Dragon must be prepared to perform well because he will have to shoulder more than his fair share of work. If the Dragon is able to take constructive criticism and accept assistance from others, he will shine just like the resplendent Rooster.

11. The Year of the Dog 2006

The Dog ushers in a difficult time for the Dragon, as unexpected problems arise and well-laid plans go awry. A time in which he must try his best to avoid any confrontation with his enemies or those who do not agree with his views. Because the Dog's year favors the oppressed and disadvantaged, it could pit the Dragon against social issues in a controversy where it may seem he is the oppressor. People could resist the authority and misunderstand the good intentions of the Dragon. The best way for the Dragon to defuse a tense situation would be by removing himself or by dealing through trusted associates.

12. The Year of the Boar 2007

In this year things return to normal for the Dragon and good luck dissipates the dark clouds that hovered over him during the Dog's reign. He could still have mixed results at work or in his financial affairs but there are few major problems. He will have to travel or entertain a good deal more than he may want to, but no troubles are foreseen in his family.

WHEN MOON SIGNS MEET SUN SIGNS

In my interpretation of Chinese horoscopes, the Rat is not linked with the first Western astrological sun sign, Aries. Instead, I pair the Rat with its counterpart based on the month and season of the Rat, which are December and winter. This makes the most sense as the lunar month of December (also called the Twelfth Moon or the Twelfth Earth Branch) is supposed to parallel the sun sign, Sagittarius, the Archer. I envision the Eastern and Western horoscope cycles as two large wheels, each with twelve spokes. To correctly juxtapose these cycles, we must find the matching notch that will join them together. Once the Rat and Sagittarius are paired as the first signs, the other eleven fall into place. Please see the Twenty-Four Segments of the Lunar Almanac. All the dates correspond with the twelve Western solar signs.

If you are born in the year of the Dragon under the Western sign of

Sagittarius: 22nd November to 21st December
The Sagittarian Dragon = Fire + Positive Wood

Pleasant, jovial, warm, forward and somewhat opinionated, the Sagittarian Dragon is swift and faithful and will abide no deception. Both signs here are always ready for action. This masterful and impatient Dragon thrives on involvement and will participate in whatever action abounds. His interests are sure to be numerous and varied. He often offends unintentionally by his pointed speech, but he does so without malice, unaware that the Archer's arrows have struck close to the heart. A noble and unselfish fellow, he shows his true worth when he comes forward to help when no one else will stick up for you. His deeds are more notable than his words.

If you are born in the year of the Dragon under the Western sign of

Capricorn: 22nd December to 20th January
The Capricorn Dragon = Earth + Positive Wood

This combination possesses the sure-footedness of the Mountain Goat and the unquenchable aspirations of the celestial Dragon. Both signs have ample leadership. The resulting personality will be realistic, doubly hard-working and completely self-assured. Exceptionally forceful and commanding, he could almost move mountains by his colossal willpower alone. He spares no one, least of all himself, in his drive to accomplish difficult tasks. The Capricorn Dragon will be more athletic and muscular than cerebral. He loves his privacy, too. Respect that "Do Not Disturb" sign whenever it appears on his door. He really means it!

If you are born in the year of the Dragon under the Western sign of

Aquarius: 21st January to 19th February
The Aquarian Dragon = Air + Positive Wood

The catalytic result of this combination is a person with an uncommon clarity of vision backed by an authoritativeness that is difficult to ignore or challenge. The Aquarian Dragon is forever changing and improving things in highly individualistic and expansive ways. Deceit is anathema to the shining Dragon, while the breezy Aquarian wins distinction for his ability to deal with people and tough situations. This person can be sudden and unorthodox, but never cruel or scheming. Both signs can forgive and forget, although the Dragon is warlike when thwarted, whereas the Water Bearer is more broad-minded and brotherly.

If you are born in the year of the Dragon under the Western sign of

Pisces: 20th February to 20th March
The Piscean Dragon = Water + Positive Wood

This so-amiable looking mortal will possess indomitable willpower. The Dragon's spirit provides ambition and a sense of adventure to the otherwise placid and timid Fish. This subject could act forcefully but with suitable restraint and consideration. Pisces is beneficial to the Dragon here, and although this person may blow hot and cold in one breath when he is unhappy, he rarely finds it necessary to go over-board as Dragons of more fiery matches do. Here, the sun sign's Water nourishes and benefits the moon's Wood, which is the fixed element of the Dragon.

If you are born in the year of the Dragon under the Western sign of

Aries: 21st March to 19th April
The Aries Dragon = Fire + Positive Wood

This bright torch likes to lead the way for anyone in need of his talents. Full of the Dragon's noblesse oblige, it is his birthright to shine. With the Ram's stamina, he will be eternally optimistic, blessed with both a contagious enthusiasm and popular appeal. Yet this over-righteous soul could also be destructively domineering or characterized by imperious self-confidence and reckless courage. He is the all-or-nothing man who marches into battle with flags proudly unfurled. When challenged about his royal rights, the Aries Dragon can be a fearsome beast.

If you are born in the year of the Dragon under the Western sign of

Taurus: 20th April to 20th May
The Taurean Dragon = Earth + Positive Wood

Steady as the beacon of a lighthouse shining through a storm, the mundane-looking Dragon will be endowed with heavenly might and practical, earthbound goals. The normal Taurean predictability will be overshadowed by Dragon dazzle at times, and he will be a bit short of guile and pretense. The Taurean Dragon will be distinctly attractive, although he tends to be an aloof and a somewhat slow mover. He is always honest, fair-minded and performance-conscious, a reliable soul who invests his time and energies wisely and in the right places.

If you are born in the year of the Dragon under the Western sign of

Gemini: 21st May to 21st June
The Gemini Dragon = Air + Positive Wood

The Gemini Dragon will be a hurricane of activity; fast, agile and fearless, he will be noted for his tremendous "do-it-yourself" kind of efficiency. Mercury's child has a sharp and clear mind, while the Dragon never lacks the courage or determination to put his ideas to work. A person of this combination will be a great success if he pays attention to detail, something both these signs tend to dismiss too easily. With the Dragon's leadership and Gemini's ability to relate to people, this personality will acquire a large and respected sphere of influence.

If you are born in the year of the Dragon under the Western sign of

Cancer: 22nd June to 21st July
The Cancerian Dragon = Water + Positive Wood

Here the sensitive charm of the Moonchild and the dignity of the Chinese Dragon are joined in the harmony of Water and Wood. The Cancerian Dragon will not be as militant as other Dragons but will have the quiet and regal bearing of authority. The Dragon is idealistic where the Crab is deep, searching and possessive. Impressions made upon this type of person will be slow but infinitely more permanent. With the Moonchild's cool disposition, this Dragon could be a less keyed-up performer. He will also use the Dragon's strength to develop the acquisitive tendencies of the Crab. Life with him or her could be pleasurable as the Cancerian Dragon is responsive and tolerant.

If you are born in the year of the Dragon under the Western sign of

Leo: 22nd July to 21st August
The Leo Dragon = Fire + Positive Wood

This magnificent, breathtaking personality will loom over everyone, larger than life. He is truly convinced of his right to rule or at least dominate. The Leo Dragon is a commanding performer who will keep his guns loaded all the time. The Lion provides the already bombastic Dragon with more dynamite than he can use, so this personality can be very willful and difficult to manage when others do not yield the right of way. However, he is immensely generous and never holds grudges. When he makes explosive statements, well it's just his way of clearing the air. With a double regal sign, this person is blessed with good fortune. He will always strive to keep his promises and is noble and chivalrous to the less fortunate.

If you are born in the year of the Dragon under the Western sign of

Virgo: 22nd August to 22nd September
The Virgo Dragon = Earth + Positive Wood

Both signs have total confidence in themselves and are inclined to pursue knowledge, although the Virgin is the more realistic and plodding of the two. This person will have a great thirst for learning and perfection. He has to shine and could turn very resentful when opposed. He will not give up easily and sometimes will not give up at all. Both signs in this combination have many sterling qualities and the Virgo Dragon will be admired for his strength of will and character. Yet he is guilty of overdoing things at times and acting with unmitigated zeal in trying to right some wrong, real or imaginary.

If you are born in the year of the Dragon under the Western sign of

Libra: 23rd September to 22nd October
The Libran Dragon = Air + Positive Wood

This will be a congenial, sprightly and lovable soul, not at all fearsome as Dragons go since this combination produces a non-belligerent type of Dragon. The balance is tipped here toward the Dragon's compelling magnetism, yet although the Libran Dragon has a lot of drive, he won't be as dependable as other Dragons. Because both signs in this combination have genuine and sincere personalities, this subject will be endowed with wide-eyed honesty, unintentional frankness and a minimum of inhibitions.

If you are born in the year of the Dragon under the Western sign of

Scorpio: 23rd October to 21st November

The Scorpio Dragon = Water + Positive Wood

With this lusty, plotting Dragon, we have Scorpio's intensity matched with the Dragon's awesome willpower. Both lunar signs here are oversupplied wih strength and commanding magnetism. This combination could be detrimental to the subject's personality if he allows it to lead him to excess. But underneath all that devastating charm, make no mistake, he is as hard as nails, and can be brutally frank about his likes and dislikes. As for the female, one is strongly reminded of that nursery rhyme that goes, "When she was good, she was very, very good, but when she was bad—she was horrid!"

THE SEASONS OF THE DRAGON

SPRING

Dragons born in the spring are very influenced by the weather prevailing at the time of their birth. Spring showers and thunderstorms in the Western hemisphere are unpredictable and sudden and so will be a Dragon born when they occur. Because the Dragon's ancestral home is the sea, unruly waves at the time of birth indicate a tempestuous life, too. The Dragon is also the Lord of the Insects who comes in the spring to awaken them from their long winter's sleep. This way, he brings spring to life with the noisy arrival of his swarming hordes. Spring Dragons are innovators and instigators. How each one goes about announcing his presence depends on the forces evident at the time of his birth.

SUMMER

In China and the rest of the East, summer brings heavy monsoon rains and deadly typhoons. Again, a Dragon born during a violent storm will have a very eventful life. According to Greek legend, Alexander the Great was born during a lightning storm, which the seers saw as a sign that the heavens were announcing the arrival of a great leader. Thunder and lightning are supposed to precede the arrival of the majestic Dragon, so summer Dragons have many leadership qualities and are more aggressive, energetic and egotistic than most. They find it hard or even impossible to do anything halfway. They give 100 percent of themselves to whatever they believe in and their idealism is of the highest order.

AUTUMN

The autumnal Dragon is calmer and less judgmental in outlook. Not as intense as other Dragons but just as strong willed, he knows how to use his strength effectively. Not as easily agitated, he will take on difficult tasks with missionary zeal and will not give up easily. Admirable for his courageous leadership and relentless pursuit of perfection, this steady Dragon could have smooth sailing throughout his life if he is not overly self-sufficient. But Dragons of all seasons tend to be independent and self-reliant to varying degrees. Those born in the evening are less outspoken than their brothers and sisters born during the day, especially those born in the mornings.

WINTER

Dragons born in the cold of winter are quiet but equally demanding and strong willed. They will be persistent in and dedicated to their convictions but when they are opposed, they tend to offer unreasonable and often hostile resistance. Self-contained in their beliefs, they do not change their minds once they have set a course. A veritable storehouse of energy and optimism, the winter Dragon could lead his followers up to the greatest heights or down into the deepest depths, but he will never hesitate or doubt his own abilities. It is this stubborness and power of endurance that will bring him great success and recognition.

FAMOUS PERSONS BORN IN THE YEAR
OF THE DRAGON

Metal
King Constantine II of Greece
Queen Margrethe II of Denmark
John Lennon

Water
Jimmy Connors
St. Joan of Arc
Haile Selassie
Mae West

Fire
Betty Grable
Edward Heath
Frank Sinatra
Yehudi Menuhin
Harold Wilson

Earth
Ernesto "Che" Guevara
Walter Mondale
Shirley Temple Black

Wood
Salvador Dali

6

The Sixth Sign
of the Lunar Cycle

The Snake

Mine is the wisdom of the ages.
I hold the key to the mysteries of life.
Casting my seeds on fertile ground,
    I nurture them with constancy and purpose.
My sights are fixed.
My gaze unchanging.
Unyielding, inexorable and deep,
    I advance with steady, unslacked gait,
    the solid earth beneath me.

I AM THE SNAKE.

Lunar Years of the Snake in the Western Calendar	Elements
4 February 1905 to 24 January 1906	Wood
23 January 1917 to 10 February 1918	Fire
10 February 1929 to 29 January 1930	Earth
27 January 1941 to 14 February 1942	Metal
14 February 1953 to 2 February 1954	Water
2 February 1965 to 20 January 1966	Wood
18 February 1977 to 6 February 1978	Fire
6 February 1989 to 26 January 1990	Earth
24 January 2001 to 11 February 2002	Metal

If you were born on the day before the start of the lunar year of the Snake, e.g., 13th February, 1953, your animal sign is the one before the Snake, the Dragon, the fifth lunar sign.

If you were born on the day after the last day of the lunar year of the Snake, e.g., 3rd February, 1954, your sign is the one after the Snake, the Horse, the seventh lunar sign.

The sign of the Snake rules the two-hour segment of the day between 9 A.M. and 11 A.M. Persons born during these two hours are said to have the Snake sign as their ascendant. They will display many characteristics special to this sign and will have great affinity for persons born under this sign.

The direction appointed to the Snake is south-southeast; its season is spring and its principle month, May. This sixth lunar sign corresponds to the Western astrological sign of Taurus, which rules the sky from the 20th of April to the 20th of May on the solar calendar. The Snake is a feminine or yin sign and it has a negative stem with Fire as its fixed element.

THE SNAKE PERSONALITY

Philosopher, theologian, political wizard, wily financier—the Snake person is the deepest thinker and the enigma of the Chinese cycle. He is endowed with an inborn wisdom; he's a mystic in his own right. Graceful and soft-spoken, he loves good books, food, music and the theater; he will gravitate naturally toward all the finer things in life. The most beautiful women and the most powerful men tend to be born under this sign.

A person of this sign generally relies on his own judgment and does not communicate well with others. He can be deeply religious or psychic, or, on the other hand, totally hedonistic. Either way, he trusts his own instincts rather than any outside advice. More often than not, he will be right!

Like the Dragon, the Snake is a karmic sign. His life ends in triumph or tragedy as his past actions dictate. And although he will deny it, he is very superstitious behind his sophisticated front. People born under other signs may defer payment to the next life (if one so chooses to believe), but the Snake seems destined to pay his dues before he leaves. Perhaps this is also of his own choosing, as a person born under this sign is unusually intense and will seek to settle scores, consciously or unconsciously, in everything he does.

A native of the Snake year is not likely to be bothered by money problems. He is fortunate to have what he needs. Should funds be low, he is extremely well-equipped to remedy the situation. However, a Snake person should not gamble; he will come out poorer in the end. In the event that he does suffer sizable losses, it probably will not happen a second time; the Snake learns fast. He can recoup with amazing speed and as a rule is prudent and shrewd in business. But to a Snake, money is just a means to an end. Snakes are considered ambitious because they strive for control through power and authority. However, a Snake who experiences poverty or extreme deprivation in his youth may never get over it. He could then be fanatical about accumulating wealth and turn into a covetous and miserly person.

By nature, the Snake person is a skeptical being, but, unlike the Tiger, he tends to keep his suspicions to himself. He treasures his privacy and will have many a dark secret locked up within. Elegant in speech, dress and manners, the Snake person dislikes indulging in useless small talk or other frivolities. He can be quite generous with money, but is known to be ruthless when he wants to attain an important objective. He has no qualms about eliminating anyone who stands in his way.

Some Snakes may have a slow or lazy way of speaking but this does not in any way reflect on their speed of deduction or action. It's just that they like to ponder things, to assess and formulate their views properly. Generally, Snakes tend to be very careful about what they say.

It is never safe to draw a line and predict that this is how far a Snake will go. His computer-like brain never stops plotting and he can be viciously unrelenting. Remember, he is one of the most tenacious signs of the Chinese zodiac.

In his relationships with others, he is possessive and very demanding. And yet at the same time, he views his associates with a certain distrust. He will never forgive anyone who breaks a promise. He is also prone to be neurotic, even paranoid, where his pet fears and suspicions are concerned.

When the Snake's anger is roused, his hatred can be limitless. His antagonism is silent and deep-rooted. An icy hostility will express his displeasure instead of a volley of hot words. The more lethal types will like to crush their enemies totally. Time is of no consequence to him. He will wait patiently for years for the opportunity to strike at his foes. There is no predicting the Snake's movements. His mind is calculation itself and he has the staying power to wait until the time is ripe for revenge. For those luckless souls who incur his wrath, self-exile to Siberia may not seem like such a bad prospect.

The Snake lady is the original femme fatale. Her cool, serene and exotic beauty will mesmerize people. She is confident and collected although she oftentimes lolls around, giving the impression of indolence and love of ease. But she is far from slothful and her brain is never at rest.

Despite being finely tuned and high-strung by nature, Snake people of both sexes are characterized by beautiful complexions. The Snake is usually not plagued with pimples or blemishes even when not taking particular care of his or her skin. It seems that tension tends to affect the Snake's digestive and nervous systems more than his epidermis. Underneath their flawless good looks, a good many of these natives succumb to stomach ulcers or nervous breakdowns from containing all that stress internally.

Ms. Snake will opt for well-cut clothes, fluid and classical in design. She loves jewelry and chooses her accessories with care. If she can afford it, she will buy the real thing: diamonds, pearls, emeralds and rubies of the best quality. Besides being beautiful baubles, jewels are an excellent form of investment. No cheap gold plating or imitations for her, please. She is definitely not a peasant and she would rather go without if she cannot have the real thing. You won't find her decked out in worthless junk.

Her standard for a mate will be similarly high. She admires power and the influence money can bring. When she cannot wield it herself, then the next best thing is to marry or merge with it in some way. At any rate, no matter how rich or powerful her man is, she will be his biggest asset once they are married. And if he hasn't yet made the grade but has the potential, the Snake wife will move heaven and earth to make him a success. She will dress the part and play the perfect hostess, while shrewdly pointing out every opportunity along the way. With such guidance, dedication and support, there won't be anywhere for him to go but up.

The philosophical Snake woman is never too concerned about the equality of the sexes. You won't find her agonizing over women's rights. Why should she compete when she feels superior to men in the first place? Capable of holding her tongue, containing her ego and using her talents with finesse and good taste, she knows exactly how to achieve her objectives. A legion of male admirers will fall over one another to carry her suitcases, open doors, and bring gifts and flowers, and she will play her cards in such a way that not one will ever really know how he stands. There is always that mystique and cool ambivalence.

So you can't blame her if she seems a bit puzzled by all the fuss over equal rights for men and women. She has always secretly felt that a person must work with what he has and not waste time lamenting what could have been. Very much a lady who sets her own agenda and makes her own rules, she can be a formidable opponent when challenged and will seek to destroy those who cross her.

Contrary to common belief, Ms. Snake is not always a raving beauty. If you analyze her feature by feature, you will find she has some flaws. Her nose may be too large or her eyes set too close. No, with her it's the total effect that counts. She has her own unique formula and when she puts it all together—it's magic!

See the girl in the striking black number with no jewelry except a diamond brooch pinned strategically on her bosom? Nine out of ten times she will be a Snake. This lady loves expensive perfume, too, another subtle but effective ploy that is part of the game. But she knows how to use such dynamite sparingly. Just a touch here and there. Enough to provide her with that clinging aura that makes her so alluring and irresistible.

All Snakes have a sense of humor. Of course, they may have different brands. Some prefer a dry wit, others are sardonic, scintillating, or, at times, even diabolical. Nonetheless, it's there. The best time to observe this is when he or she is under duress. In a crisis, even when weighed down by enormous troubles, the Snake can crack a joke to lighten the atmosphere.

Orientals sometimes regard the snake as a supernatural creature endowed with a touch of the sinister. This is because it lives a long time and renews itself by shedding its skin for a new one each time the old is outgrown. This particular trait symbolizes its ability to be reborn and to emerge from conflict with restored vigor.

By now, you must have gathered that it is no mean task dealing with the Snake. What makes it even more tricky is the fact that under all that serenity he is always on guard. His outward calm never betrays his true feelings. He possesses the wisdom to plan his moves well in advance. He has willpower and will maintain his position to the bitter end. He can be very evasive and elusive when he chooses, and just when you think you have got a grip on him—he wriggles free. Needless to say, he makes the perfect politician. He can negotiate anything under the sun when he puts his mind to it.

The Chinese believe that Snakes born in the spring and summer will be among the most deadly of the lot. Winter Snakes are quiet and docile, as this is the time they hibernate. A Snake born during a hot day will be happier and more contented than one born during bad weather.

Snake people are passionate lovers; they are also reputed to have roving eyes. Actually, this is a false reputation which they have acquired because they are always sensual about anything they undertake. He or she may exhibit the same fervent, relentless ardor in chasing a much coveted business deal as in winning the affection of a latest heartthrob.

Snake people usually lead dangerous lives—full of excitement and intrigue, especially those Snakes who have an insatiable lust for power and the limelight. Wrapping themselves around the object of their desire, they can squeeze and crush the life out of it. Needless to say, once they attain power, they will not willingly let go.

The best partners for the Snake will be the dependable Ox, the dauntless Rooster or the illustrious Dragon. He could do well by teaming up with the Rat, Rabbit, Sheep and Dog, too.

The Snake should steer clear of the defiant Tiger, who may not appreciate his discerning ways. The impulsive and equally demanding Horse will make only a mediocre match, while the clever Monkey may challenge the Snake with his own brand of cunning. Two Snakes can cohabit peacefully. The Boar and the Snake will not find much in common; the Snake is sleek and sophisticated, the Boar too honest and mundane. They have entirely opposite makeups.

In times of confusion and trouble, the Snake is a pillar of strength because he maintains presence of mind. The Snake can deal with bad news and misfortune with great aplomb. He has a profound sense of responsibility and an unsinkable constancy of purpose. If these are coupled to his natural hypnotic charisma, he can reach the highest realms of power.

THE SNAKE CHILD

The Snake child is a complex personality. Quiet, alert and intelligent, he will possess a serious nature and be inclined to be particular. Being the worrying type, he will assume a pensive outlook on life. He is studious and hard working in school and likely to be teacher's pet. Do not spoil him; the Snake child is all too aware of his charms. He can be sulky, vindictive and temperamental when not given his way.

Although secretive and brooding by nature, this child will be able to discipline himself. He makes up his mind easily about what he wants and will be very practical about setting his goals. You won't find him reaching for somthing he knows is unattainable. Persistent, realistic and unrelenting, he will stick to a task until he masters it.

Besides his natural aptitude for learning and a high I.Q., this child has the ability to keep his own counsel. He will not interfere with others and would prefer others to mind their own business, too. Careful and attentive, he knows how to keep himself out of trouble. He may not be very outgoing, but he makes long and lasting friendships. Observant and calculating, he tends to check out all his options before making any moves.

A capable and meticulous planner, this child excels as a leader, as he will use his powers wisely and fairly. Other children will look up to and support him. However, he could have ulterior motives for some of his actions. He is so intent on being first that he may not care what he has to do in order to remain in control and be No. 1.

His many talents and natural abilities will make him vastly sought after but he will also be the object of jealousy and vicious lies. He must learn to live with criticism and the other risks that come from being among the elite.

His reticent character makes him hide his pain; he is likely to hold grudges for a long time. He is often misunderstood because he refuses or fails to explain himself properly. His lines of communication with others are sometimes poorly connected, especially if he is super secretive and super sensitive to criticism.

Whatever happens, the Snake child will always be able to fend for himself. In life, he will know precisely how to use people and situations to his best advantage. There will be no holding him back; he is destined for fame and fortune.

THE FIVE DIFFERENT SNAKES

METAL SNAKE—1941, 2001

This type of Snake is gifted with a calculating and intelligent mind and enormous willpower. Armed with discriminating tastes and a keen eye for locating opportunity, he can be a scheming loner. He likes to move quickly and quietly. He will establish himself in a solid position before you have a chance to stop or unseat him.

Metal combined with his native sign will make him crave luxury and easy living. Thus, he will devote himself to the pursuit of wealth and power. His vision is clear and farsighted and he will aspire to have the best of everything.

The Metal Snake is by far the most secretive, evasive and overconfident Snake. Consequently, he often suspects others of hidden motives, sometimes to the point of paranoia.

In spite of his ability to gain power and influence, this Snake will have an envious streak and will constantly try to outdo the opposition, either by fair means or foul. He finds it hard to accept defeat or failure. Possessive, domineering and, at times, strangely uncommunicative, he will mark out his path early in life and stick to it with dedication. He can be generous and cooperative with others, but always in a guarded way. Rarely one to gamble all his money in one go, he will keep something in reserve to live and fight another day. Never underestimate him.

WATER SNAKE—1953, 2013

Just as Water seeps through practically any barrier, so a Snake born in its year will wield an all-encompassing influence because of his profound insight. This unassailable Snake is gifted with strong charisma and an inquisitive nature. Shrewd, business-oriented and materialistic, the Water Snake possesses great mental abilities and powers of concentration. He can block out distractions and brush aside unimportant issues to achieve effective overall planning. He never loses sight of his goals nor does he lose touch with reality.

Artistic and well-read, the intellectual Water Snake is also practical. He is as adept at reading and managing people as handling finances. While he may assume a calm and serene demeanor, in actuality this particular personality has a long memory and harbors lifetime grudges. He could have the patience of Job combined with the bite of a King Cobra.

WOOD SNAKE—1905, 1965

An earnest Snake with kindly wisdom and a prophetic understanding of what is going to prevail in the course of events, especially in history.

He has a need for complete intellectual freedom, but in his affections he will be constant and enduring. He seeks emotional stability as well as financial security. This type of Snake will express himself well and could be a forceful, eloquent speaker.

The Wood element in conjunction with his fixed element of positive Fire will make him very magnetic and interesting. He will shine like a beacon light, attracting instead of pursuing the objects and people he desires. Likely to have expensive tastes and habits, he could be vain about his personal appearance. Because he craves admiration and public approval, he will do his utmost to achieve lasting and large-scale success.

The Wood Snake is well-informed but he gathers knowledge not for its own sake but to put such information to everyday use. Don't be surprised if he keeps a file on everyone and cross-references all his data. Good judgment, detective work, discretion and a sharp sense of values will make him a superb investor and an appreciator of the finer things in life. Here is an amiable Snake who will be very close to art, music, the theater and all the beautiful things in life that material success has to offer.

FIRE SNAKE—1917, 1977

An intense and masterful Snake, active in mind and body, the Fire Snake performs energetically. However, Fire added to the already imposing Snake personality can give him too much passion and ambition. Armed with popular appeal and a charisma that could melt down the steeliest resistance, he exudes self-confidence and has an ability to lead. People will vote for this type of person if he chooses to go into politics.

Although he may hold open forums to solicit or assess the views of the majority, the Fire Snake is terribly suspicious by nature and has total faith only in himself. He is too quick to censure and condemn. Sometimes he insulates himself within a closed circle of friends and advisors, thereby isolating himself without knowing it. His strong, almost maniacal desire for fame, money and power will make him insist on concrete results. Persevering and uncompromising, he sets his sights on the highest goals and, once he gets to the top, he will cling to power indefinitely.

The Fire Snake is the most sensual, fervent and jealous kind of Snake. He will display excessive love or hate and can be very preoccupied with himself and his desires. Always in the thick of things, he will make his presence felt wherever he goes.

EARTH SNAKE—1929, 1989

This is a warm and spontaneous variety of Snake, who will form slow but correct opinions of people and situations. More principled, persistent and reliable than the other Snakes, the Earth Snake will be able to communicate with the public and function effectively in group activities.

Armed with his peripheral vision and basic Snake ambition, he can take control and bridge gaps during times of confusion and panic. He or she will not be easy to intimidate and may refuse to be influenced by public opinion. This Snake is constant in his convictions and reserves the right to pass judgment. He will locate and identify new trends and opportunities before others realize their importance.

By and large, this will be the most graceful and enchanting of all the Snakes. Cool, collected and immensely charming, he will be loyal to his friends and will have an army of supporters. Conservative and frugal with money, the hard-working and systematic Earth Snake will succeed in banking, insurance and real estate investments and can learn to reconcile his needs with the resources at hand. Here is a Snake who knows his limits and who will be careful not to overextend himself.

COMPATIBILITY AND CONFLICT CHARTS
FOR THE SNAKE

The Snake is part of the Second Triangle of Affinity, a group made up of the most purposeful and steadfast signs of the lunar twelve. The Ox, Snake and Rooster are the dutiful and dedicated fighters who strive to achieve great heights and conquer by their constancy and unfailing determination. These three are fixed in their views and given to thought and systematic planning. They are the most intellectual signs of the cycle. They depend on their own assessment of facts and figures and give little credence to hearsay evidence. They are the signs most likely to comply with the dictates of their heads than their hearts. Slow and sure in their movements, they like to act independently. They will invariably seek each other out and can intermarry and intermingle most successfully.

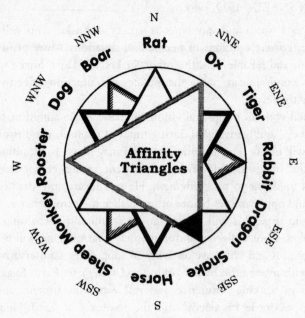

AFFINITY TRIANGLE FOR THE SNAKE

The Snake will encounter his most serious clashes of personality with people born in the year of the Boar. Anyone whose ascendant is the Boar will also come into conflict with the Snake native. In the Circle of Conflict, the Snake and the Boar are 180 degrees apart and thus total opposites. The Snake has Fire as its fixed element while the Boar has Water. In their ways of thinking and philosophical outlook these two lunar signs are worlds apart. Like Fire and Water they do not mix well. They can form relationships only through intermediaries or if they happen to share the same ascendant as in the Boar being born during the Snake's hours or the Snake person being born during the Boar's time.

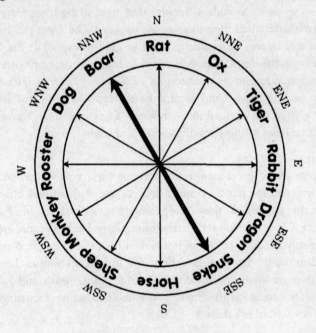

CIRCLE OF CONFLICT

Aside from the most compatible signs for the Snake, the Ox and the Rooster, and the least compatible, the Boar, the other nine lunar signs are compatible with the Snake to varying degrees.

Rat

There is a good degree of attraction and interaction here, and a relationship will be satisfactory provided both Snake and the Rat realize the usefulness of the other. These signs are success-oriented and drawn to power and recognition. The Rat will admire the Snake's wisdom and the Snake will appreciate the Rat's resourcefulness and intelligence. The one danger could come from the fact that they both have a tendency to take big risks. One of them must learn to put on the brakes and draw the line where and when they will stop.

Tiger

A mutually suspicious partnership at best results when the Snake teams up with the Tiger. They do not relate well unless one has the other's sign as an ascendant because they tend to be competitive and unsympathetic when their interests are opposed. The Tiger can be outspoken and openly aggressive in order to get his way, while the Snake will resist to the death. Conflicts and ill feelings also develop when they fail to communicate or misinterpret each other's motives. The Snake usually has the upper hand because he is able to hide his true feelings under a mask of inscrutability while the Tiger can't help throwing a temper tantrum to show his displeasure to the whole world.

Rabbit

There are no great animosities between these two refined and elegant personalities, but they are so self-contained there will only be a lukewarm tie unless they find something special to bind them together. Civil and congenial relationships are likely because neither will openly declare war when it is not to his or her benefit. A mutual ascendant could be very beneficial for long-term unions between these two art-loving personalities. Sharing mutual goals and accomplishments encourage the Snake and Rabbit to realize that they have need for each other's skills.

Dragon

The Snake will find the Dragon's courage and affinity for success very attractive and will have no difficulty teaming up with the Dragon to achieve mutual aims. Sympathetic and compatible relationships can be developed when these powerful signs need each other's talents. The Snake can be practical and ruthlessly focused when he is after something, so he will appreciate the Dragon's philosophy of never giving up. Ambition will be the key word in their partnership. They will reap many rewards if each plays his or her part well.

Snake

Snakes hold little animosity for one another and can usually cohabit amicably if there is no big struggle for power. Because they understand each other so well, they may co-exist even when they have distinctly different goals. Two snakes will intertwine or intermingle when it comes to areas of common interest, then go their separate ways without regret. They could form strong bonds of friendship when they feel unity is needed to achieve their mutual ambition. Otherwise, you won't find them clashing unless there is an object they both desire and their overwhelming jealousy and possessive natures do not permit any resolution.

Horse

The Snake and the Horse will have cool to distant relationships as they are both fixed Fire signs who dance to different drummers. The Horse is quick to sense new vibrations and responds energetically and with passion. The Snake is intuitive and sensuous in a totally different way. Unless they have the same ascendant and share a common perspective, they may selfishly refuse to cooperate and will instead go their separate ways unless the gains far outweigh losses. The Snake could also be too withdrawn and pensive for the hyperactive Horse. The Horse's feelings are always on the surface while the Snake keeps his hidden far beneath his serene exterior.

Sheep

The lovable, compassionate Sheep can sometimes prove frustrating to the intensely intellectual Snake personality. The Sheep has much to offer but often demands too much and can be very unreasonable and sentimental. The Snake will not like to make long-term commitments or give in to whims of the Sheep unless it will benefit him. The Sheep needs the Snake's direction and constancy of purpose while the Snake could benefit from the Sheep's expansive talents and sweet nature. But, then again, the Sheep's best friend, the Boar, will be at odds with the Snake and will point out all his negative traits to the easily influenced and docile Sheep. In such a contest, the Sheep will side with the Boar every time and distance himself from the ambitious and tenacious Serpent.

Monkey

These two resolute and calculating personalities cannot compromise much unless they share a common ascendant and common ambitions. The Monkey finds it hard to trust or like the enigmatic Snake, who tends to keep his thoughts to himself. The Snake sizes up the clever Monkey and is fearful of the masterful Ape's capacity to put one over him when he is not looking. Both will watch each other's moves intently and be unable to relax in each other's company for too long. Sometimes, we could even find them having a contest to see who will blink first. The stakes must be large and the potential gains enormous for these two to cooperate and pool their resources.

Dog

The Dog and the Snake have mutual respect for each other and do not want confrontation if they can avoid it. They will be compatible and amicable to a good degree as the Dog is trustworthy and the Snake's ambitiousness does not disturb the Dog who can be loyal to the steadfast and persevering Snake. The Snake is able to convince the Dog of the validity of his ideas and philosophies and will share the Dog's often idealistic outlook on life, too. The Dog is not prone to jealousy or possessiveness and will understand the Snake's need for dominance and privacy when the Snake tends to become introspective.

THE SNAKE AND HIS ASCENDANTS

We all have a shadow that follows us throughout life. Sometimes it grows bigger than life and at other times it shrinks until it disappears into the soles of our feet. Sometimes it walks tall before us and on other occasions it lags behind like a sulking friend. In Chinese horoscopes, this constant partner, manifested or not, is our ascendant, the animal sign that rules the hour of our birth and becomes a comrade in our journey though life. We may view it as friend or foe or even a little of both. It surfaces when we least expect and shows a better or worse side of our nature. We can often be confounded by the way we listen to our "other self" as well as feel resentful of the significant influence it can exert on us. Actually, a personality has many rings around the centered "self." Each ring can have a different size, texture and aura. When all these factors combine, they bring forth the unique individual that the person truly is. Hence, a Dragon with an ascendant that is not compatible, like the Dog, has perhaps a more difficult inner struggle than say a Snake born during the hours of the Snake. The double intensity of the Snake person will be easily understood by horoscope readers while the more intricate Dragon/Dog may exhibit the contrary Dog and Dragon traits to varying degrees. There are many voices within each person. But, in the end, only the individual determines which course he will follow, which choices he will make.

The time of birth used to determine the ascendant is always the local time in the place of birth.

If you were born between:

11 P.M. and 1 A.M. = The Hours of the Rat

You are an affable, charming Snake who will know how to hustle and cultivate powerful friends who could influence your rise to power. You can be possessive and sentimental about everything, including your money. But you love your family and parents and will be very generous to them. A veritable storehouse of information, you will have informants and confidants all over town and your network of friends will be formidable.

1 A.M. and 3 A.M. = The Hours of the Ox

Your Ox stubbornness is masked by the Snake's elusiveness and charm. You could be twice as difficult to deal with if you have the Ox's stamina and willpower. But the Ox is good for your Snake's love of ease and you will learn to be more self-sacrificing to duty and responsibility even where there is no gain. The Ox is patient but far more rational and less prejudiced than the Snake and will work unfailingly for the good of all. You could be a less selfish Snake who does not feel superior to others.

3 A.M. and 5 A.M. = The Hours of the Tiger

With the Tiger's sizzling personality, you could be a warm and versatile Snake who can dazzle crowds. Both signs being neurotic and suspicious, however, unhappiness will cause you to go on an emotional rollercoaster ride. People feel that you can be temperamental and distrustful when you are in a negative mood. But it would be best for them not to take your outbursts seriously. After all, your colorful personality is basically a generous and giving one. They are bound to benefit greatly by their association with you, whether romantically or commercially.

5 A.M. and 7 A.M. = The Hours of the Rabbit

The Rabbit's ascendant gives you a tranquil, collected and self-confident demeanor, although you may be inclined to narcissism and indulgence. You could be a mellow, noncombative Snake who knows how to wield power through suave political maneuvering and intelligent negotiations. But beneath your outward elegance, your bite could be just as poisonous when your ambitions are stifled or you feel betrayed. An astute judge of situations and people, you rarely make a bad deal in anything.

7 A.M. and 9 A.M. = The Hours of the Dragon

The Dragon's ascendant brings you a touch of egalitarianism and philanthropy. With the combination of the Snake's wisdom and the Dragon's power, you could instigate real and lasting reforms—especially since you tend to espouse mainly noble causes that benefit all humanity. Whatever happens, your commitment is always total—whether it be for good or bad. A natural leader and an inspirational speaker, you will never lack for believers.

9 A.M. and 11 A.M. = The Hours of the Snake

Having the same sign as your ascendant makes you a pure Snake sign with the result that all your good and bad traits are doubled in this combination. Possessive, enigmatic and very, very deep, you will be extremely difficult for others to figure out. You will only show what you want the public to see—nothing else. Your thoughts and ambitions are private and guarded. The only thing one can count on is that once you get a grip of what you are after, you will never let go!

11 A.M. and 1 P.M. = The Hours of the Horse

The Horse's ascendant makes you carefree and freedom loving. You could be a happier Snake personality who sees the brighter side of life and opts for an active, sportive lifestyle with less responsibility than other Snakes who cling to power or wealth. However, since both signs are strongly amorous and sensual, you are very attractive to the opposite sex and your love life is never without excitement or intrigue.

1 P.M. and 3 P.M. = The Hours of the Sheep

Having the Sheep as your ascendant brings true love of humanity and kindness into your soul. From this combination may emerge a very powerful and artistic Snake with impeccable flair and dynamic vision. What's more, the Snake in you will know how to support the Sheep's expensive tastes and love of luxury. But watch out for the Sheep's inclination to spend beyond his means. All in all, however, with the Snake's tenacity, you should have no problems forging ahead.

3 P.M. and 5 P.M. = The Hours of the Monkey

The Monkey ascendant will make you incredibly hard to resist or ignore. The Monkey's genius combined with the Snake's hypnotic charm will break many a heart or defeat many a business opponent. Wisdom, glamour and wit blended to perfection or devious cunning hidden under a veil of elegance—we will never know until after you have struck. With this super combination, you are a person who will never willingly play any game you cannot win. By the way, you are a sore loser, too.

5 P.M. and 7 P.M. = The Hours of the Rooster

The brilliant Rooster brings sunshine into your life. He is very persistent, demanding and fiercely competitive—you will have strong views and be outspoken and critical where your likes and dislikes are concerned. Never contented with second best, you will be an over-achiever and perfectionist. You could also be a community bandleader type with serious designs on absolute power behind your gaily deco-rated front. With your meticulous precision and perseverance, you could outlast us all.

7 P.M. and 9 P.M. = The Hours of the Dog

The loyal Dog blends his equanimity and propensity for self-sacrifice into your Snake personality. As a result, you will be altruistic and won't hesitate to stand up for others. You may even favor militant measures to right wrongs. Less selfish and ambitious than many Snakes, you possess noble convictions and a profound moral sense. As both signs are thinkers and contemplative, you are likely to be very intellectual. But the Dog in you makes you more popular, sociable and involved with people.

9 P.M. and 11 P.M. = The Hours of the Boar

The Boar's large appetites combined with your natural Snake instincts and ambition could be devastating or helpful to others, depending on how you handle them. The Pig is a great partygoer who does everything on a grand scale, but he can also motivate us with his honesty and conscientiousness. With the Boar's natural simplicity and generosity, you could turn out to be a popular leader who really knows how to live it up. This combination makes you more inclined to share your good fortune with others and you will be loved for your big-hearted ways.

HOW THE SNAKE FARES IN THE LUNAR CYCLE

1. The Year of the Rat 1996

This will be a year of activity for the Snake, with much traveling and running around as new outlooks and opportunities present themselves. They may not all be worthwhile but, since the Rat loves to investigate, the Snake will have to check out all options before he can make intelligent choices. The Snake will make some advancement in his career provided he cultivates the right people. This will also be a year of dramatic events, both good and bad. His financial gains will balance out his losses and his problems will be solved through the goodwill of and intervention by powerful friends. He should neither lend nor borrow money during this time.

2. The Year of the Ox 1997

The Buffalo brings a moderate but more predictable year. The Snake can expect people to challenge his decisions. Some obstacles or financial miscalculations will crop up in spite of his inborn caution and intuition. The Ox seems to insist we all work hard during his reign and prove ourselves before any payoff. There will be no exception for the Snake. A time to take things in stride and not complicate matters by being obstinate. The wise and skillful Snake should have little difficulty with authority or with following the Ox's inflexible rules because he knows how to turn the Buffalo into his ally.

3. The Year of the Tiger 1998

This year of small but numerous irritations could really try the Snake's patience. The Snake may be easily drawn into conflicts not of his own making and will find it hard to please those around him at home or work. He must keep his sense of humor and not indulge in senseless acts of revenge. This way he will receive the help he seeks and avoid major upheavals. In the Tiger's reign, there is so much going on that the Snake's equilibrium is threatened by too much stress. The Tiger tends to make a big fuss about every little thing so it would be best for the Snake to go off and meditate until the Tiger has finished with his dramatics.

4. The Year of the Rabbit 1999

Although many commitments keep him very busy, this will be a fairly happy year for the Snake. The year of the Hare may look tranquil, but its currents run deep, and what looks so inviting from the surface may hold some surprises if we take things for granted. The Rabbit is calculating and superficial when in a negative mode and quickly loses interest once he gets what he wants. The Snake usually knows what he wants and will work toward achieving his aims, but this year he'll be unable to spend enough time with those he likes due to all his responsibilities. Money comes and goes easily as the Hare's bounty does not stay in one place for long.

5. The Year of the Dragon 2000

The Snake will experience a difficult but exciting year. No sizable gains can be expected in his business or career because landmark issues and unusual cases crop up to mystify and involve him. He must beware malicious gossip and jealous associates as his ambitions may be challenged by powerful and influential peers. The rule of the Dragon may bring fame, but with it comes responsibility. The worst of his troubles will be over by summer and the cold weather should bring welcome news. A year to avoid extravagances or divulging secrets to newfound friends.

6. The Year of the Snake 2001

This will be a fair year for the Snake, although he may feel that his achievements are not up to his expectations. He should bide his time and not make sudden changes. Patience and a cool head are essential if he is to keep himself out of trouble. However, his basic intensity is magnified and he finds it hard to be casual about anything. Matters could become complicated because of his inflexibility and a misunderstanding on the business front. Romantic problems or a slight injury could be caused by his own erratic behavior. Gains are modest, and so he is going to be more concerned with securing his position or maintaining control of what he already has.

7. The Year of the Horse 2002

The carefree Horse prances in to give the Snake native an energetic time. The Snake must refrain from being emotional and hasty if he wants his hopes to be fulfilled. The Horse's year brings many and varied options. But the Horse usually demands a quick response and rapid decisions. The Snake requires more time to mull over choices and will resent ultimatums. The volatile and hyperactive Horse year could make the Snake nervous and insecure, and his problems and worries could affect his health. However, overall the Snake will succeed admirably. His troubles are temporary and will dissipate like the fog, provided he remains calm and philosophical.

8. The Year of the Sheep 2003

The year of the Sheep is a protected year for the Snake. He will experience no great gains and no sizable losses. Life will be calm and leisurely and he should take advantage of this time to cultivate influential friends who will benefit him greatly later on. A time for the sensuous and ambitious Snake to explore new horizons, develop his talents and enjoy his favorite arts or hobbies. There may be some sad news or minor inconveniences, but these are likely to be beyond his control. Romantically, it will be a busy time as the Snake's love life could be influenced by the passionate but often demanding Sheep.

9. The Year of the Monkey 2004

This will be a good year since the Snake will find help when he needs it most. But because the year of the Monkey is tricky and full of intricate puzzles, he may be involuntarily drawn into disputes. However, things will burn themselves out if he can refrain from adding fuel to the fire. Still, these adverse conditions may cause the Snake undue anxiety. He should keep in mind that this is a year to remain conservative or neutral. The Monkey causes complications just to prove how smart he is and the Snake should not overreact or jump to conclusions. The answers will usually be quite simple and right before him—the Monkey just enjoys a good laugh at the Snake's expense.

10. The Year of the Rooster 2005

The resourceful Chicken brings a very auspicious year. The Snake's achievements could be fantastic as he will receive the recognition or promotion he deserves. He will be rewarded for his patience and past perseverance. The Rooster will provide the Snake with ample opportunity to prove his expertise and the Snake should be able to meet the challenges well. Profits or some big increase in income can be expected. Home life is pleasant, with the Snake reaping the fruits of his efforts. New friends are likely to be helpful and sincere at this time.

11. The Year of the Dog 2006

Good opportunities present themselves to the Snake. This is an excellent time to launch new ideas or start new ventures, although he may have minor health problems or be the victim of fraud if he is not vigilant. Travel and entertainment are also in the cards, although the Dog discourages extravagance and vanity. It would be wise for the Snake to stick to well-trodden paths and work with what and who he knows. The year of the Dog does not generally favor strange new methods or strangers on the whole. If the Snake breaks up any close relationships at this time, he may not be able to effect reconciliation easily as the faithful Dog is unforgiving in matters of rejection or infidelity.

12. The Year of the Boar 2007

The Pig brings feast and famine in the same boat, so this will be a hectic and mixed year. The Snake will have to exert maximum energy for minimum gains. He may suffer financial mishaps caused by poor judgment, a problem with the law or a separation from someone close to him. He should look before he leaps and insulate himself from uncertainty and risks. He will have to hedge his bets or work with a larger team. As a result, he may make less profit but there will be safety in numbers and shared risks. This is definitely a year for the Snake to diversify and refuse to take on more responsibility than he is able to handle.

WHEN MOON SIGNS MEET SUN SIGNS

In my interpretation of Chinese Horoscopes, the Rat is not linked with the first Western astrological sun sign, Aries. Instead, I pair the Rat with its counterpart based on the month and season of the Rat, which are December and winter. This makes the most sense as the lunar month of December (also called the Twelfth Moon or the Twelfth Earth Branch) is supposed to parallel the sun sign, Sagittarius, the Archer. I envision the Eastern and Western horoscope cycles as two large wheels, each with twelve spokes. To correctly juxtapose these cycles, we must find the matching notch that will join them together. Once the Rat and Sagittarius are paired as the first signs, the other eleven fall into place. Please see the Twenty-Four Segments of the Lunar Almanac. All the dates correspond with the twelve Western solar signs.

If you are born in the year of the Snake under the Western sign of

Sagittarius: 22nd November to 21st December
The Sagittarian Snake = Fire + Negative Fire

Here is a Snake who is lighter, freer and more relaxed, endowed with the Sagittarian's cultivated air of nonchalance. Less secretive and fickle, he is fashionable, informed and dashing in a leisurely sort of way. He will also have a somewhat diminished sense of duty because of the Archer's love of freedom. You won't find him or her chained to the workbench. This personality prefers variety, and lots of it. Both solar and lunar signs here are classy, have lofty ideals and love success and recognition—but in different ways. The Snake is tenacious and careful and likes to bide his time. The Archer strikes when the iron is hot and never hesitates to shape his destiny by affirmative action. The outcome of this combination produces a wise but less dutiful Snake.

If you are born in the year of the Snake under the Western sign of

Capricorn: 22nd December to 20th January
The Capricorn Snake = Earth + Negative Fire

Brainy and aloof, staid and pious, expertly elusive while playing his own game—the Capricorn Snake is a veritable Rock of Gibraltar. Since neither solar nor lunar sign is extroverted, this person's thoughts and passions will run very deep and be well concealed. Not one to confide in others or require advice or consolation, he is secure in his beliefs. Possessed of a remarkably high level of endurance, he can wait out his enemies with the patience of Father Time. An avid learner, his grand visions will be realized through careful planning and stern stick-to-it-ness. With the sure-footed Mountain Goat as his other self, the Capricorn Snake is never caught second-guessing anything.

If you are born in the year of the Snake under the Western sign of

Aquarius: 21st January to 19th February
The Aquarian Snake = Air + Negative Fire

With open and airy Aquarius blowing on him, this Snake is not as subtle as other Snakes are. He is more cheerful and bright and rarely broods over circumstances he cannot alter. He shifts his direction as the situation warrants and is generally buoyant in outlook. With this free and easy attitude, the Aquarian Snake is occasionally erratic in his thinking. Because he needs freedom in expressing himself, he is prone to nervous disorders if he cannot release his tensions. With the Snake's influence, he is also susceptible to jealous thoughts and will withdraw to his innermost self when upset. Otherwise, he should find wide acceptance, as his sort of personality has the telepathic ability to convey his wishes without making a deliberate effort to influence others.

If you are born in the year of the Snake under the Western sign of

Pisces: 20th February to 20th March
The Pisces Snake = Water + Negative Fire

With gracious charm and fluid manners, the elegant Pisces Snake conceals his wisdom and psychic powers well. He may look ineffectual and dreamy at times, but he always makes a good public appearance. The Snake is intense, passionate and lucid; the Fish is deep and silent. A person of this nature is easily hurt by callous gestures since he tends to invest all his relationships, whether love or friendship, with deep and unfathomable emotions. The Pisces sign compensates for the Snake's ruthless determination by being compassionate. His warm, watery reserved personality brings forth surrealistic dreams and brilliant observations.

If you are born in the year of the Snake under the Western sign of

Aries: 21st March to 19th April
The Aries Snake = Fire + Negative Fire

This profound personality is deliberate in all he does. He can criticize with finesse and accuracy and cow lesser beings into obedience. The Snake is wise and guarded while the Ram is expansive and confident of his abilities. The result is a capable and intelligent leader, and probably a prolific overachiever as well. Here is a combination in which the plotter and the capable doer are happily joined.

If you are born in the year of the Snake under the Western sign of

Taurus: 20th April to 20th May
The Taurean Snake = Earth + Negative Fire

The Taurean Snake could well surpass us all for tenacity and durability. This is a personality with both feet planted solidly on the ground. Since both signs in this combination subscribe to the belief that a bird in the hand is worth two in the bush, a native of this solar-lunar mixture will be especially careful about money and disinclined to gamble. Although he can be very security conscious, he is never plagued by doubts or fears. He relies on his own abilities and sails assiduously toward his destiny. He will be especially sensitive to music or other arts and stimuli that affect his refined senses. One who rarely has regrets about his course of action, the Taurean Snake is set in his ways and does not look back once he has made a decision.

If you are born in the year of the Snake under the Western sign of

Gemini: 21st May to 21st June
The Gemini Snake = Air + Negative Fire

Distinctively effervescent and poised, the Gemini Snake strikes quickly and accurately. Full of charm and enigmatic reserve, the Gemini Snake never gives away his true motives. He will be especially enchanting to the opposite sex and has a strong, easy appeal that people find irresistible. A person of this combination is easily agitated but strives to maintain control over his or her emotions. Still, the Gemini Snake can be a kind of brinksman, taking things to the very edge as if to test his own judgment and superior reflexes. But if anyone can get away with doing this, he can. The Snake is sensible enough to stabilize the volatile Gemini spirit.

If you are born in the year of the Snake under the Western sign of

Cancer: 22nd June to 21st July
The Cancerian Snake = Water + Negative Fire

This personality might possess a mysterious and highly enchanting nature, like the shimmering reflection of the moon on a placid body of water. He seeks permanence, fame and strong material security, yet is hampered in his pursuit of them by the Snake's philosophical qualities and the Crab's inhibited nature. He loves to have his family and friends around even if they are parasitic and impose on him. The Moon's child is protective of others as well as dependent on love, while the Snake half of this personality is defensive, suspicious and even paranoid about failure. He could well be very successful, but will he be happy and at home with his complicated inner self?

If you are born in the year of the Snake under the Western sign of

Leo: 22nd July to 21st August
The Leo Snake = Fire + Negative Fire

Life is lined with self-made success and tragedy for the Leo Snake because of his or her great intensity and refusal to take second place to anyone. At his best, this person will be a radiant example of grace under pressure, intelligence and understated elegance. He needs a great deal of love and understanding to bring out his virtues and will perform lavishly when admired. However, he is also inclined to be spoiled, selfish and conceited, as a result of getting too much attention poured on him or because of having his own way too often. Beneath his fiery exterior lies a generous lion heart, but his warmth and sincerity will emerge only if he is allowed to lead a quiet life and forget himself by helping others.

If you are born in the year of the Snake under the Western sign of

Virgo: 22nd August to 22nd September
The Virgo Snake = Earth + Negative Fire

Virgo's eye for detail and love of organization plus the Snake's ability to shield his feelings and conduct clandestine maneuvers will surely turn this personality into a secretive and extremely aware and discriminating being. Scholarly, fiercely dedicated and thoroughly goal-oriented, one born with this combination could chain himself to a fixed objective until he succeeds in achieving it. While the rest of humanity is weighed down with the rigors and struggles of daily life, the Virgo Snake can block all that out of his mind once he concentrates. Vices? None, unless you consider being autocratic, unemotional and ruthlessly efficient as such.

If you are born in the year of the Snake under the Western sign of

Libra: 23rd September to 22nd October
The Libran Snake = Air + Negative Fire

This tantalizing combination of warm negative Fire that caresses is easy to relate to. Endowed with impeccable taste, the alluring Libran

Snake is muy simpático indeed! He may be an abstruse thinker, but he takes care to express himself in more conventional ways. With the Snake's steadfastness and patience, a person of this combination wavers little. He will certainly be able to charm people with his wit and sense of humor. Cool as a cucumber and very desirable, he can be pleasure-bent and may rely too much on popular consensus when it is clear he should act independently.

If you are born in the year of the Snake under the Western sign of

Scorpio: 23rd October to 21st November
The Scorpio Snake = Water + Negative Fire

A skeptical, elusive and mystical spellbinder, the Scorpio Snake possesses intense emotions and could be a brilliant tactician. Cloaking his feelings under his powerful aura, he will prove quite inscrutable. Hard to read and understand, this ambitious and performance-oriented person will soak up knowledge like a sponge. Whatever arouses his curiosity will be examined closely with no expense spared. Self-contained and secretive, you won't catch him handing out explanations. Honestly, he cares little about idle gossip since he does not intend to ever explain his motives. Just remember, hell hath no fury like a Scorpio Snake scorned!

THE SEASONS OF THE SNAKE

SPRING

Spring brings out the most dangerous Snakes as they emerge from hibernation with a ravenous appetite. A Snake person born in the spring will likewise be aggressive and adventurous. Awakened from the long sleep of winter, these natives will be more involved in things than other Snakes and will strive to make an impression in all they do. Achievement conscious and careful planners, they will be mentally and physically alert and guarded. Intelligent and creative, they will not shy away from the limelight and may attain the highest positions of power. They also tend to lead perilous existences as they are willing to go where others fear to tread and take fearsome risks when they have set their sights on reaching the pinnacle of success.

SUMMER

Summer Snakes sun themselves endlessly and are slow and deliberate thinkers. They tend to examine every angle of a puzzle before proceeding to take action. But while they may look deceivingly indolent and detached, their razor-sharp minds and keen powers of observation are always working. When they decide to strike, they usually act swiftly and effectively. Snakes born during the heat of summer have exciting lives and are known to be intuitive and extravagant. They are secretive, possessive and jealous when negative, but are also amusing, generous, and loyal to their friends.

AUTUMN

The Snakes of autumn are the quiet, intuitive geniuses of the cycle. Often deeply religious with high moral and intellectual standards, they are soft-spoken and contemplative. Reserved and self-absorbed in their own interests, these persons will pursue a career or profession and seek to be the best in the field. Artistic, elegant and patrons of beauty and the arts, Snakes born in the fall are apt to be loners. They do not like to move with the crowd. Rather, they prefer to stand out as original thinkers and tenaciously follow their ideals with an almost religious zeal. They can be rigid in their views, but most likely will keep their own counsel and will not be openly hostile unless sorely provoked.

WINTER

Winter Snakes are the guardians of wisdom and wealth. They have a protected existence and are usually docile and peaceful. They care about their safety and are guarded in their emotions. Philosophical and patient, the winter Snake is not one to venture out and court trouble. This more retiring Snake stays close to the bosom of Mother Earth and learns to rely on the tried and proven way of doing things. Still, it is never wise to take the Snake for granted and the winter Snake may not be as harmless as he looks. Underneath whatever disguise he may choose to assume, he is still equipped to be a lethal and vindictive foe if attacked.

FAMOUS PERSONS BORN IN THE YEAR OF THE SNAKE

Metal
Pablo Picasso
Carole King
Ann-Margret

Wood
Howard Hughes
Greta Garbo
Seni Pramoj

Earth
Abraham Lincoln
Edgar Allen Poe
King Hassan II of Morocco
Jacqueline Kennedy Onassis
Princess Grace of Monaco

Water
Johannes Brahms
Mao Tse-tung
J. Paul Getty
Mary Pickford

Fire
Franz Peter Schubert
Henry Ford II
Gamal Abdel Nasser
John F. Kennedy
Indira Gandhi

7

The Seventh Sign
of the Lunar Cycle

The Horse

I am the Kaleidoscope of the mind.
I impart light, color and perpetual motion.
I think, I see, I am moved by electric fluidity.
Constant only in my inconstancy,
    I am unshackled by mundane holds,
      unchecked by sturdy, binding goals.
I run unimpeded through virgin paths.
My spirit unconquered—
    my soul forever free.

I AM THE HORSE.

<u>Lunar Years of the Horse in the Western Calendar</u>	<u>Elements</u>
25 January 1906 to 12 February 1907	Fire
11 February 1918 to 31 January 1919	Earth
30 January 1930 to 16 February 1931	Metal
15 February 1942 to 4 February 1943	Water
3 February 1954 to 23 February 1955	Wood
21 January 1966 to 8 February 1967	Fire
7 February 1978 to 27 January 1979	Earth
27 January 1990 to 14 February 1991	Metal
12 February 2002 to 31 January 2003	Water

If you were born on the day before the start of the lunar year of the Horse, e.g., 20th January 1966, your animal sign is the one before the Horse, the Snake, the sixth lunar sign.

If you were born on the day after the last day of the lunar year of the Horse, e.g. 9th February 1967, your sign is the one following that of the Horse, the Sheep, the eighth lunar sign.

The sign of the Horse rules the two-hour segment of the day between 11 A.M. and 1 P.M. Persons born during these midday hours are said to have the Horse sign as their ascendant and will display many of the traits common to this sign and have great affinity for persons born under this sign.

The direction appointed to the Horse is due south; its season is summer and its principle month, June. The Horse corresponds to the Western astrological sign of Gemini which rules summer from the 21st of May to the 21st of June. Fire is the fixed element of the Horse and it is a male or positive yang sign.

THE HORSE PERSONALITY

A person born in the Horse's year will be cheerful, popular and quick-witted although his changeable nature may cause him to be hot-tempered, rash and headstrong at times. The unpredictable Horse native will fall in love easily and may fall out of love just as fast if he follows his capricious heart instead of his head. Earthy and warmly appealing, he is very perceptive, talkative and has raw sex appeal rather than straight good looks. He is noted for his love of sports, outdoor activities and fondness for animals. As agile mentally as he is physically, he is quick to respond to any stimuli and will perform better than most people in difficult situations. A person born under the auspices of the passionate Horse will have a strong, magnetic and commanding personality which could be aggressive and even militant at times.

In many cases, the high-spirited Horse may choose to leave home early. If he does not, his independent nature will goad him to start working young or take up a career at a relatively early age. He is noted for his keen mind and ability to handle money even though he is often an adventurer at heart. Energetic, impetuous and even brash, the Horse is a showy dresser, partial to bright colors and striking designs to the point of occasional gaudiness.

The athletic horse person loves exercise, both mental and physical. You can spot him by his swift but graceful body movements, his animated reflexes and his rapid speech. He is one who will respond quickly and can make snap decisions. His mind works with remarkable speed and whatever he may lack in stability and perseverance, he will certainly make up for with flexibility and open-mindedness. Basically, the Horse is a nonconformist but he will try anything once before making up his mind.

A native of this sign is often called the playboy or playgirl of the cycle. He loves fanfare and being where the action is. But the nimble Horse is just as skillful in business as in love. He appraises situations astutely and is able to manipulate people and events to his advantage, with an above average ability to sense which way the wind is blowing.

On the negative side, the Horse person can be impulsive and stubborn. He is known for his explosive temper and, although he quickly forgets his outbursts, others may not be able to recover or forget. Subsequently, this lack of discretion and self-control may cost him a great deal. This trait also often causes him to lose respect and credibility among his friends and associates. He tends to rush people to do his bidding, is often insensitive to other's needs and is unhappy when they do not perform as quickly and as efficiently as he is able to. Demanding a great deal from others, but himself ill-prepared to surrender an iota of his all-important freedom, he can be childish and petty in satisfying his whims and caprices. Not one to bear a grudge or thirst for vengeance, the Horse has a forgiving heart and can forget grievances once his flaming temper has burned itself out. However, he is often forgetful, absentminded and given to jumping to conclusions. He has to be nudged gently if he is to act with decorum and not appear uncouth, inconsiderate or too impatient to have his own way. He must learn that sometimes a simple "please" or "thank-you" can be more effective than a demanding request that sounds like an order. Most Horse natives know what they want and will have no difficulty identifying their goals—both in the short term and the long term. However, their methods of achieving them may be controversial.

The intelligent Horse will want things done his way. Performance and success oriented, he always has his sights set on some target. Self-centered by nature, the Horse native likes his home and environment to revolve about him. With his remarkable powers of persuasion, he will set out to sway people to his way of thinking. Snapping his fingers and clicking his heels, this trailblazer could talk you into anything once he begins to dish out the charm. People find it hard to resist his positive and self-assured outlook on life.

To be able to really understand the confident Horse, you have to know one thing. He or she firmly believes in "Life, Liberty and the Pursuit of Happiness"—chiefly his or her own! And, if you happen to subscribe to these same things yourself, well, he won't stand in your way. He is not possessive, suspicious or jealous. The Horse only becomes aggressive when he fails to get his way after trying every angle. His selfishness rarely extends to the monetary or material side of life. It would be more accurate to say he is selfish with his time, affection and concern for others, and is unwilling to modify his ways to suit the group. He doesn't always set out to be deliberately inconsiderate or contrary, he just cannot wait for others to catch up with him or match his mental speed and physical activity. For these reasons, unless he develops the virtue of patience, he is likely to be an out-standing performer but a poor teacher.

The Horse's inconsistency stems from his constantly changing moods. He senses nuances that may go unnoticed by everyone else and he modifies his behavior accordingly. In other words, he goes by the feel of things. He often cannot understand why others are not as "in touch" as he is. Don't ask him to explain his hunches and uncanny deductions. He can't. His is the amazing ability to improvise while the game is in progress. Frequently, he will be playing several games at the same time and be more than capable of holding his own. Once he makes a decision, he does not hesitate to act. You will either find him dashing about doing 101 things or flat on his back from sheer exhaustion. More than most signs, the Horse finds it difficult to unwind and may suffer from hypertension and insomnia.

He keeps odd hours. A Horse is unable to stick to a schedule not of his own making and has a lack of respect for standard procedures. When an idea strikes him, he will work around the clock without eating or sleeping. Then, when things are slow in the office, he may take a day off to pursue something more interesting. The Horse always needs a stimulating job in order to display his competence and to provide the challenges he craves.

One who can think up great promotional ideas, the Horse native loves to devise dynamic new approaches, solve tricky problems with amazing practicality, and rapidly master difficult procedures. He is dependable in the sense that he is able to find the quickest, the easiest and the most clever solution no matter what the situation. So, if you have a Horse working for you, give him variety, plenty of rope and send him on missions impossible. He does best given a free hand. But for goodness sakes, keep him busy because his performance will suffer when a job is undemanding.

When you talk to a Horse, emulate him. Be quick and come to the point, otherwise you will lose whatever fragile hold you have on his attention. Even if the answer is No, give it to him directly, without disguise; he is quite able to revise his plans when they meet with opposition. With his hard-to-extinguish optimistic streak, disappoint-ments tend to bounce right off him. Stringing him along just brings out the worst in him. He will not take offense at frankness and will appreciate your being blunt and not wasting his time or trying to deceive him.

It would be unfair to ask a Horse to restrain himself or bottle up his feelings. He has to express himself. If he is forced to hold back his emotions, he may openly revolt—or break out in a rash if he is the silent type. Suspense and strait-jacket procedures frustrate him.

In matters of the heart, the Horse can be a fickle soul. If he cannot be with the one he loves, then why not love the one he is with? Anyhow, there will be little harm in flirtations: long, drawn-out entanglements do not appeal to him. Despite all this, the animated and affable Horse is said to be very susceptible to the perils of love. Consequently, he may have many affairs that end unhappily or several marriages and divorces. Horses should be encouraged to wait until they are more mature before getting married.

The Horse knows which side his bread is buttered on. He won't get caught in a one-sided contract unless it happens to be his side. He has a multitude of friends and makes more and more each day. But he learns never to rely too heavily on any of them. When he is off and running, he likes to travel light—so he may feel that too many commitments will weigh him down.

Quick to warm up and reach top speed, a person born under the Horse sign is equally quick to lose interest. Neither can he sustain a long siege. He certainly won't break down your door like a Dragon or stalk you like a Tiger. He will leave his card and call another day when you are likely to be more receptive. When the winds of change start to blow, the smart Horse will be the first to alter his course.

While he may not have staying powers, you can never be sure when a Horse will resume work on a long-shelved project. His mind is like a jigsaw puzzle; if and when he finds a piece that will fit, he uses it.

Like his best friend, the Tiger, the Horse will sow some pretty wild oats. But reminding him of his blunders will be useless. If there is anything this person dislikes, it's to dwell on his mistakes. With a cheerful though sincere "mea culpa," the Horse will shrug and chalk it up to experience. You can't expect him to win them all! Next time, he promises to proceed more carefully.

The lady Horse is full of spunk. She is tart and saucy, pert and pretty, nimble on her toes and intelligent. She could be a chatterbox, a tennis champion or a Grand Prix driver.

She can do her nails, write a letter, watch TV, talk on the phone and mind the children, all at the same time. Her ideas for relaxing can be taxing. She works off her energy with play that could seem like hard labor to the rest of us. Did someone mention climbing Mount Everest? Give her two minutes to pack—she will join the expedition.

The Horse lady loves to get things done. She would be in ten places at the same time if she could. Sometimes, one could swear that she is competing with herself. There isn't anyone else around who can do so much so fast.

Horse girls may look as soft as whipped cream and will usually smell as fresh as lavender, but, underneath it all, they have brilliant minds to match their agile bodies. She may be the kindly brown-mare type or the firebrand who tosses her hair defiantly, but she'll never lose her talent for assessment. She makes friends easily and will take her romantic involvements lightly. Home is a practical, easy and well-located station where she can refuel and take stock of her situation. But you won't find her parked in one place permanently.

She will love fresh air, greenness and outdoor sights and sounds. She refreshes herself in a thousand ways. The ocean's roar, the rustle of the trees, the magic of the woods, the majesty of the mountains, will all call to her sense of adventure. When she takes off, she isn't being unfaithful or unreliable. It's just her nature to respond to such exciting challenges. If you love her and want to keep her, don't fence her in.

Horses of both sexes will accumulate wealth but not security. They don't care for security so they won't be missing it all that much. They do have an inclination to oversell, stretch the truth, or ad lib with little white lies, none of which, in their eyes, is a fault but more a by-product of their creative imagination. They are not timid about taking the lead, and will run themselves ragged before stopping to listen to advice.

Orientals believe that whatever unbridled passions the Horse possesses, they will be multiplied many times over when he or she is born in the year of the Fire Horse, which comes once in every sixty-year cycle. The last Fire Horse year was 1966 and the next is 2026. In days of old (when liberated and overly assertive women were frowned upon as troublemakers and were difficult to marry off) it was considered unlucky to have a daughter born in this year. Legend has it that the Fire Horse will consume everything in his path and wreak havoc wherever he goes. Many a lady Fire Horse, so they say, has ruined the life of a good man simply because of her passionate nature.

The male Fire Horse is not always considered as unlucky; he may even be fortunate as he can bring distinction on himself and be credited with famous as well as infamous deeds. The Horse, of course, like the Dragon and the Tiger, is identified as a strong masculine sign. However, the fame and fortune of the Fire Horse, as well as of other Horses, seldom benefits their immediate families, especially since they usually leave home early. Leonid Brezhnev, King Faisal of Saudi Arabia and Otto Preminger (all born 1906) are but some examples of modern-day Fire Horses. Aristotle Onassis gave his year of birth as 1905, but some historians put it as 1906, for he is said to have made himself a year older when he left home to get a job. Looking into his biography and phenomenal lifestyle, I am inclined to believe he was a Fire Horse, not a Snake.

A Horse born in the summer will lead a better life than one born in winter. The best part of his life will come during his middle age when he is sufficiently mature enough to grudgingly accept the shackles of responsibility.

The best partners for the Horse will be the Tiger, Dog and Sheep. The next best matches will be with the Dragon, Snake, Monkey, Rabbit, Boar, Rooster or another Horse.

The Horse will not fall for the Rat, who will not care for the independent Horse's shifting ways. He could also come into direct conflict in his dealings with the rigid Ox. The Ox will demand consistency and the Horse cannot, and will not, comply.

In the end, the Horse will follow his own superior instincts and find his own destiny with little or no outside help. Relying on his own abilities, he will be the master of his own fate.

THE HORSE CHILD

A child born in the Horse year will be animated, boisterous and mercurial with a passionate love of life and a buoyant personality. He or she learns easily and acts quickly. While this child will tend to be disobedient, stubborn and willful when held back, he is not the whining, crybaby type. This sprightly little fellow will love the outdoors and should be allowed plenty of excercise and independence—otherwise he will just take them. Being cooped up or asked to sit still could be a punishment for him. Although he may roam the neighborhood and indulge in all sorts of rough games, he will always find his way home at meal time.

He will walk and talk early and will resent parents who restrict him too much. He is also likely to be left-handed. He'll be affectionate, playful and demonstrative, but won't like too much cuddling. A happy-go-lucky daredevil, he does things on the spur of the moment. Constrict him with rules, regulations and tight schedules, and he will bolt. He will be plagued by a restless and searching spirit and needs to be constantly occupied.

It would be well to discipline the Horse child as he should learn to control his volatile temper and impulsive ways. Even though he is self-centered, the Horse is also realistic and will conform and adapt once he sees that there is no other way out.

This adventurous little person will get himself into countless predicaments, but won't need you to bail him out. He is quite capable of getting himself out of trouble. Although he does not deliberately look for trouble, he does not scare easily and prefers to fight his own battles.

All in all, the colorful and lively personality of the Horse child will enliven any household. Parents and family will find this child entertaining and delightful and marvel at his courage, agility and quickwitted intelligence.

THE FIVE DIFFERENT HORSES

METAL HORSE—1930, 1990

This is a popular but unruly type of Horse who is always on the go. Demonstrative, impetuous and bold, he will be a most engaging personality. He is highly amorous and very appealing to the opposite sex. He can be extremely productive when in a positive mode—it will be difficult keeping up with him as he seems to be everywhere at the same time!

Blessed with strong recuperative powers, the Metal Horse is never out of action for long. He is constantly seeking excitement and climbing to breathtaking heights.

Metal will make this Horse more stubborn and self-centered than other types of Horses. He may be a proverbial bubbling stream overflowing with brilliant ideas, but he is not a consistent administrator. If his work provides no satisfaction, no motivation, no rewarding stimulation, he will become irresolute and irresponsible. He cannot exist on a diet of daily routine. Nor can he function with someone glancing over his shoulder. He thirsts constantly for new experiences and challenges. When he is negative, he will have an irrational need for liberty and be unable to establish deep personal involvements for fear they may curtail his freedom or take up all his time. But when he is positive, he will race to the finish, leaving others lagging far behind.

WATER HORSE—1942, 2002

A cheerful, dapper Horse with excellent business acumen, but inordinately concerned with his own well-being, status and comfort. He is very adaptable to change and can make extensive adjustments without batting an eyelash.

This nomadic Horse could be more restless than the others. An inveterate traveler and sports enthusiast, he won't let any grass grow under his feet.

He may also have the habit of frequently changing his mind and may embark on an entirely different course of action without bothering to give his colleagues any notice or explanation. He tends to be guided only by his own bouts of inspiration. Delicately attuned to his environment, he often can discern trends and changes well before anyone else is aware of them.

He will have a delicious sense of humor and can be very amusing when he wants to be. A colorful but fashionable dresser, he can also discourse on any subject with anyone.

When he is negative, he becomes pretentious and inconsistent and can exhibit a deplorable lack of consideration for others. The Water Horse must try to develop a capacity for long-range planning and dedication to his work. His powers of communication and persuasion are above par and, if he can acquire a little patience, he will succeed in rallying people to support him.

WOOD HORSE—1954, 2014

Friendly, cooperative and less impatient, this Horse could be the most reasonable of the lot. But he will still resist being dominated. The Wood element enables him to better discipline his mind and he will be capable of clear and systematic thinking. The Wood Horse will have a happy disposition and be very active socially. Amusing and a good conversationalist, he is not overly egotistical and will not constantly strive to dominate in his interactions with others.

But because he is progressive, modern and unsentimental, he will throw out the old and welcome in the new. Inventions and innovations will always capture his imagination and he will not shrink from trying the unconventional.

He will like to explore many other fields but will try hard to fulfill his responsibilities first. The strong, high-spirited and sanguine Wood Horse does not have a lazy bone in his body, but he would do well to be more cautious and discriminating about what tasks he decides to shoulder.

FIRE HORSE—1966, 2026

A flamboyant and adventurous Horse possessing a superb intellect and great personal magnetism. He tries to bring about the changes he desires through force and sheer willpower. The daredevil of the lunar cycle, he can throw caution to the wind when in hot pursuit of some desired objective.

This is a double Fire sign (Fire also being the Horse's fixed element), and will produce a native who is highly excitable and hot-blooded. The Fire Horse is easily distracted and is too inconsistent to stick to repetitious tasks. He has flair, wit and charm, but his endless stream of bright ideas makes him extremely volatile. His personality is many-faceted and he requires a great deal of spice and variety in his life. He is happiest leading a double or triple life or having several professions to his credit.

He will love to travel, anticipates action and new trends, and will work most efficiently when in charge. He rarely accepts supervision, even from his superiors. More than capable of holding his own, he constantly tries to outperform himself.

The Fire Horse is a competitive thrill-seeker. He can assess and deal with all kinds of people and situations with only a moment's notice. He is skillful at resolving sensitive and complicated situations, but is not above being argumentative and unreasonable. This Horse will have ingenuity and resourcefulness but not perserverance. But with his speed and reflexes, he will never quit without an admirable battle—and we can bet on him to win.

EARTH HORSE—1918, 1978

Happy, congenial but somewhat exact and slow moving, the Earth Horse is apt to be more logical but less decisive than other Horses. He prefers to consider all sides of a question before acting. Once he weighs the pros and cons, he will assess the competition and hedge his bets if possible.

With Earth as his element, he will be less abrupt. He can settle down and learn to toe the line when necessary. He offers less resistance to authority while still holding true to his principles. Finely attuned to his environment, he is gifted with an ability to locate feasible investments. He can revive shaky businesses on the brink and spur lagging industries to achieve greater productivity.

Although he is the look-before-you-leap type, he is, nonetheless, very capricious about little things and will not make up his mind easily. He may vacillate on one occasion and then take on more than he can handle on another. Yet, on the whole, the Earth Horse is able to make serious commitments and will not neglect his responsiblities.

COMPATIBILITY AND CONFLICT CHARTS
FOR THE HORSE

The Horse is part of the Third Triangle of Affinity. This group consists of action-oriented signs who seek to serve humanity, promote universal understanding and facilitate communications. The Tiger, Horse and Dog are good at making personal contact and will develop strong bonds with their fellow human beings. This trio relates well to each other and is basically honest, open and motivated by idealism. Unorthodox at times but always honorable in intent, they act more on impulse and heed their inner conscience rather than the dictates of convention. They keep their own counsel and inspire others to action by their high-spirited and aggressive personalities. Extroverted and energetic, they are always ready to do battle on behalf of the unfortunate and against the unjust. They will get along fabulously together.

TRIANGLE OF AFFINITY FOR THE HORSE

The Horse will encounter the most difficulties with the sign opposite him in the Circle of Conflict. In this case, the Horse's opposite is the Rat. Anyone whose ascendant is the hours of the Horse between 11 A.M. and 1 P.M. (birth time) is also likely to be incompatible with the Rat native. Horses and Rats are on the opposite side of the spectrum. The Horse's season is the summer and his direction is directly south while the Rat is identified with winter and his compass point is north.

The Rat is clannish and possessive, while the Horse is carefree, independent and afraid of being tied down. Both are industrious, but in totally different ways. The Rat opts for constancy and persistence while the Horse prefers independence and will not be as reliable as the Rat would like. Using their wits against each other rather than for a common goal, these two signs do not work well together and should only deal through experienced go-betweens who are respected by both.

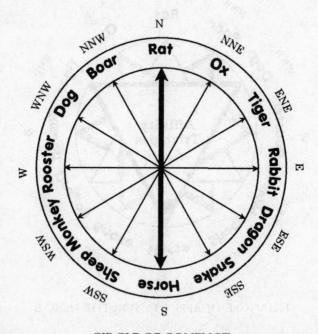

CIRCLE OF CONFLICT

Aside from the most compatible partners, the Tiger and Dog, and the least compatible, the Rat, the other nine signs are compatible with the Horse to varying degrees.

Ox

Relations are moderate between the Horse and the Ox, but there can be no permanent union unless one sign has the other as an ascendant. The Horse is mercurial and independent, while the Ox has his feet squarely planted on the ground. The Horse works by intuition and instinct, the Ox prefers to go by the book. These communication barriers could prevent a close meeting of these two minds. Then, too, the Horse prefers shortcuts while the Ox sticks to the proven path. The Ox could also prove too much of a disciplinarian for the flamboyant Horse.

Rabbit

The Rabbit may not always appreciate the Horse's quick temper and outspoken ways. Discreet and at times inhibited, the passive Hare may not share the Horse's fiery love of action and danger. When the Horse leads the charge, he cannot count on the prudent Rabbit to follow blindly. The Rabbit ultimately trusts only his own judgment and will find the Horse too changeable to rely on. Unless one native has the other's sign as an ascendant, this pair will not be able to truly understand each other's nature.

Dragon

A Horse and Dragon combination means speed and power. There may be some struggle for dominance as the Horse can be impatient and restless under the leadership of the autonomous Dragon. But, since they both usually have good communication skills, they should be able to iron out their differences and map out their respective territories. The intelligent Horse has a keen ability to sense which way the wind blows—and knows exactly when its direction changes. The Dragon could do well to go along with the Horse's superior instincts and ability to steer clear of trouble's way.

Snake

The Snake and the Horse will have a cool-to-distant relationship because they are both fixed Fire signs but dance to different drummers. The Snake could be too withdrawn and pensive to suit the hyperactive Horse. The Horse's feelings are always bubbling on the surface while the Snake keeps his well-concealed deep beneath his impenetrable facade.

The Horse is alert to changes and responds energetically with passion and feeling. The Snake is intuitive and sensuous too, but in another way, and is an introvert to boot. Unless these signs have the same ascendant, it is unlikely they will have a common perspective. More likely, they will selfishly refuse to cooperate and simply go their separate ways.

Horse

Two Horses may find they have a lot in common. To begin with, both are active, outgoing and interested in everything around them. Teamwork can be achieved since they will probably be able to work at the same speed. They will enjoy good to lasting ties if they realize that mutual cooperation is necessary to reach common goals. Because neither expects too much from the other, Horses will have a successful relationship or look for greener pastures. They won't waste time struggling or compromising if they do not belong in the same league. The Horse is a practical and self-confident sign and will not insist on unworkable alliances with anyone.

Sheep

The Sheep will admire the Horse's forthrightness and courage while the Horse may provide the Sheep with the direction and confidence he needs to market his many talents. The Sheep may indulge the Horse's many caprices and the Horse may choose to ignore the Sheep's many complaints. The good-natured and creative Sheep has need of the commanding and quick-witted Horse and will not care to challenge him on any issues. In this relationship, the Horse will provide the leadership and the Sheep will benefit from joining forces with the capable Horse. Compatible and successful business ties could result, too. The Sheep could be the "good guy" while the Horse will defininitely be the "tough" one.

Monkey

The Horse and Monkey will cooperate to a certain degree to achieve common ends. If they share similar interests or a common ascendant, they will have no qualms about using each other's particular talents for their mutual benefit. Whether or not strong ties develop between them will depend on how much each truly requires the skills of the other. You won't find either of these signs holding his breath or pining away. They are both capable of changing course at a moment's notice and will always want to partake in whatever is going on. The only negative aspect to this combination is that each can be selfish or overly calculating.

Rooster

The Horse and the Rooster will have cool to amicable relationships depending on who's the boss. When the Rooster has the upper hand, he could be a dominating and noisy commander. If the Horse is at the helm, he may find the Rooster too critical, eccentric and argumentative to suit his taste. Both signs love adventure—but they have different ways of looking at challenges. The industrious Chicken schemes, researches and won't act before he has all the information, while the Horse will fly by the seat of his pants and astound the Rooster by his speed and unconventional methods.

Boar

The Pig will only be moderately compatible with the Horse because of his inability to match the Horse's quickness. The Horse has need of the Boar's strength and generosity and will seek an alliance with the lucky Pig if there is a bounty to be shared. However, where there are no particular attractions there will be no great clashes either. Special bonds are only possible if they share the same ascendant, and if the freedom loving Horse is able to understand the possessive nature of the amorous Boar. Both signs are highly sociable and will be good friends if they find similar interests.

THE HORSE AND HIS ASCENDANTS

We all have a shadow that follows us throughout life. Sometimes it grows bigger than life and at other times it shrinks until it disappears into the soles of our feet. Sometimes it walks tall before us and on other occasions it lags behind like a sulking friend. In Chinese horoscopes, this constant partner, manifested or not, is our ascendant, the animal sign that rules the hour of our birth and becomes a comrade in our journey though life. We may view it as friend or foe or even a little of both. It surfaces when we least expect and shows a better or worse side of our nature. We can often be confounded by the way we listen to our "other self" as well as feel resentful of the significant influence it can exert on us. Actually, a personality has many rings around the centered "self." Each ring can have a different size, texture and aura. When all these factors combine, they bring forth the unique individual that the person truly is. Hence, a Dragon with an ascendant that is not compatible, like the Dog, has perhaps a more difficult inner struggle than say a Snake born during the hours of the Snake. The double intensity of the Snake person will be easily understood by horoscope readers while the more intricate Dragon/Dog may exhibit the contrary Dog and Dragon traits to varying degrees. There are many voices within each person. But, in the end, only the individual determines which course he will follow, which choices he will make.

The time of birth used to determine the ascendant is always the local time in the place of birth.

If you were born between:

11 P.M. and 1 A.M. = The Hours of the Rat

With the affectionate Rat in him, this will be a merry-making and more companionable Horse. Both signs are good at acquiring and handling money. A Horse with the Rat ascendant tends to be more sentimental, calculating and likely to have strong family ties. Inquisitive and acquisitive, he or she will be able to make commitments and will like things to revolve around his home life.

1 A.M. and 3 A.M. = The Hours of the Ox

After the Ox gets through toning down his restlessness, this may well be a serious and even consistent Horse who can stick to one thing at a time and will not fall madly in love so easily. The stable Buffalo brings order and discipline into the Horse's life and this lends great credibility to his promises and earns him the respect of his peers.

3 A.M. and 5 A.M. = The Hours of the Tiger

This is a good combination of daring and skill. The Tiger provides the daring, the Horse the ability to steer clear of trouble. Now, if only the doubting Tiger would follow the Horse's uncannily accurate hunches. A Horse with this ascendant is colorful, exciting and very adventurous. He or she will never let the grass grow beneath his or her feet. Idealistic, extroverted and passionate, you can count on this person to blaze a path to his dreams.

5 A.M. and 7 A.M. = The Hours of the Rabbit

This Horse will have a touch of moderation in his actions. His extravagant and sometimes outlandish tastes will be muted by the Hare's more discerning preferences. The Rabbit's composed and prudent personality produces a more thoughtful and guarded Horse who can better control both his temper and his tongue. He may also be more passive than other Horses and not as outspoken.

7 A.M. and 9 A.M. = The Hours of the Dragon

Because he can't help winning, or stop running for that matter, this Racehorse is too powerful for inexperienced hands to handle. He also has a tendency to overreact! The powerful Dragon may intensify his ego and need to dominate others. High-spirited and courageous, this Horse cannot help running with the wind and tossing his head defiantly against opposition.

9 A.M. and 11 A.M. = The Hours of the Snake

Let's hope the Snake can distill some of his wisdom into this Horse. If he can, the result will be a slower Horse but one more assured of success. With the Snake as his other self, this Horse is deep, secretive and given to contemplating and thoroughly analyzing his objectives before he acts.

11 A.M. and 1 P.M. = The Hours of the Horse

This pure Horse sign is a thoroughbred who really knows his business. Although he may have a very restless and fidgety nature, he will move with amazing grace. But he can also be conceited and insufferably capricious. A pure Horse sign with all the magnificence and beauty of the Horse's superior reflexes and love of sports, he will opt for a very active lifestyle and it will be hard to keep up with him.

1 P.M. and 3 P.M. = The Hours of the Sheep

With some of the Sheep's harmonious and compassionate ways, this Horse is less boisterous. Still flirtatious and fun-loving, he can be artisitic, sensitive and amorous. With the Sheep ruling his birth time, he may need more security and love than other Horses, but he will be a good listener.

3 P.M. and 5 P.M. = The Hours of the Monkey

This combination will produce a strong alliance of agility and wits. Because both signs are egotistic and swift, this Horse will always strike out for himself. He is also a glib talker who is hard to pin down. Knowledgeable and inventive with the Monkey's brain, this Horse will be a clever tactician with a tendency to be an overachiever. Watch out—he or she will be very competitive.

5 P.M. and 7 P.M. = The Hours of the Rooster

This competent and perceptive Horse will have an ultra-sunny disposition. With the Rooster's fearless and self-confident outlook on life, he will never fall prey to worry. He will be meticulous, industrious and a lover of routine. Always busy, he often has an overwhelming need to both supervise and criticize others. But he is always on time and usually above reproach in his excellent attention to details.

7 P.M. and 9 P.M. = The Hours of the Dog

The Dog makes this Horse more faithful and honest. But both signs here are quick, practical and mentally acute; this may make him condescending, impatient and easily agitated. With the Dog guiding his birth hours, this Horse is likely to be more devoted to his loved ones and kind and protective to those who are less fortunate. One thing is sure, he will not hesitate to speak his mind or fight for his rights.

9 P.M. and 11 P.M. = The Hours of the Boar

A more steadfast and cooperative Horse with some of the Boar's sincerity, he may be less shifty but, at times, he may also be too complacent. The Boar as his ascendant makes him sensuous, boisterous and scrupulous, but it also brings out a kind, obliging nature that makes him a good and true friend who will always lend a helping hand or a shoulder for you to cry on.

HOW THE HORSE FARES IN THE LUNAR CYCLE

1. The Year of the Rat 1996

Problems and unhappy romantic involvements makes this a difficult year for the Horse. He must steer clear of confrontations, especially those not of his own making. In other words, it would be advisable for him to mind his own business and keep his own counsel. There could be some monetary troubles concerning his family as he is unable to balance his finances because of unforeseen expenses. Because this is a time for the Horse to be cautious and persevering, he should not lend or borrow money.

2. The Year of the Ox 1997

Life will be smoother for the Horse in the year of the Ox. He will still have to work hard to achieve his goals but he will be given control over his situation. A few untoward incidents and some monetary gains are in store for him. Problems tend to come from children or subordinates. The Horse should be careful not to shun responsibilities or challenge authority, but should stick to the safe and well-traveled paths in order to achieve his aims.

3. The Year of the Tiger 1998

This will be a moderately happy year for the Horse, with no health problems but a lot of entertainment and additional expenses. Advancement in his studies or the technical side of his profession can be expected. Disputes or broken friendships could result from his losing his temper this year. He will also have a lively and romantic time as he meets new and fascinating people. The Horse should be geared up for excitement and the unexpected this year. With his quick reflexes and agile mind, he should have no trouble adapting.

4. The Year of the Rabbit 1999

The Horse will be lucky this year, especially with his investments. His life will be smooth but still very involved. He can expect happy news or new members in the family. In this protected year, he can venture anywhere and encounter few problems. The more adventurous Horses may get a respite from their hectic life or many travels and be able to take care of matters at home and get a well-deserved rest this year. A blessing in disguise will also make the Horse happy this year.

5. The Year of the Dragon 2000

A mixed year is in store for the Horse. Many unsteady and unsettled situations try the Horse's patience and worries weigh upon his mind, causing health problems. He must not expect the worst because the Dragon tends to blow things out of proportion. The storm will blow itself out and there may not be as much damage as expected. He should look on the bright side of life, cultivate friends and placate enemies. The luck of the Dragon will pull him through and his naturally positive attitude will come in handy.

6. The Year of the Snake 2001

This busy, involved year may bring taxing demands on the Horse's time and energy. Difficulties arise with partners or friends and delays are caused by unforeseen obstacles. His family will be supportive, but he will not be able to achieve very much in spite of his efforts. Above all, the Horse should not be stubborn or hasty in the Snake's year. He must take things in stride and seek good advice before making important decisions. There are hidden dangers lurking this year and the Horse must tread carefully.

7. The Year of the Horse 2002

This will be a good and prosperous year for the Horse, as recognition or a promotion bring him satisfaction and happiness. Plans are realized without much effort and he will be lucky playing his hunches. This is also a year in which the Horse is susceptible to contagious disease, so he must not visit sick people or expose himself unnecessarily. Because he wants to accomplish too much, he may run himself ragged. He should not bite off more than he can chew, nor break off any friendships or partnerships this year.

8. The Year of the Sheep 2003

Changes in residence or a long trip are indicated in this moderate year for the Horse. However, the Horse feels things are moving too slowly or cautiously for his liking. But instead of getting impatient and rebellious, he should take time out to smell the flowers. The good balances out the bad this year and he will encounter no serious problems or worries. Friends and mentors will plead his case, and matters are most likely to turn out to his advantage if he avoids outright confrontations and premature actions.

9. The Year of the Monkey 2004

Sudden gains or unforeseen benefits make this a lucky year for the Horse. He will be able to find whatever he is searching for, but must be careful about taking things for granted. There may be sad news in the family, but the troubles of others will not affect him personally. This is a year for the Horse to learn the value of compromise and collective effort. The Monkey's year will favor the clever Horse if he shares his bounty with the rest of his team. Selfishness will be punished.

10. The Year of the Rooster 2005

The Rooster brings a fair year for the Horse born, with good tidings at home but some slight disturbances in his career. The problems he encounters will not be large ones but they may slow his progress and he will tend to get upset too easily. The Horse hates working with the Rooster looking over his shoulder; hence, his overall performance will suffer from too much supervision and too many restrictions. But if he can weather the storm, the Horse stands to benefit from the harvest the Chicken year brings.

11. The Year of the Dog 2006

This will be a good year for the Horse academically as he could pass exams with honors or be given a job he has sought. Important people will notice him as his hard work pays off. A lawsuit in the family or the departure of a loved one is indicated, but he will encounter no health problems or financial setbacks. The Horse should be vigilant and helpful in order to advance this year. Any rebellious action will be met with harshness.

12. The Year of the Boar 2007

In this not-so-favorable year, some of the Horse's success is destroyed by outside interference; illness or indecision will delay his plans and progress. Investments and projects develop snags and he must deal with many complications. The Boar's year always brings heightened expectations and has a tendency to let people down. However, the Horse's troubles should start to fade with the onset of winter. But he must take care to persevere and work toward more realistic goals.

WHEN MOON SIGNS MEET SUN SIGNS

In my interpretation of Chinese Horoscopes, the Rat is not linked with the first Western astrological sun sign, Aries. Instead, I pair the Rat with its counterpart based on the month and season of the Rat, which are December and winter. This makes the most sense as the lunar month of December (also called the Twelfth Moon or the Twelfth Earth Branch) is supposed to parallel the sun sign, Sagittarius, the Archer. I envision the Eastern and Western horoscope cycles as two large wheels, each with twelve spokes. To correctly juxtapose these cycles, we must find the matching notch that will join them together. Once the Rat and Sagittarius are paired as the first signs, the other eleven fall into place. Please see the Twenty-Four Segments of the Lunar Almanac. All the dates correspond with the twelve Western solar signs.

If you are born in the year of the Horse under the Western sign of

Sagittarius: 22nd November to 21st December
The Sagittarian Horse = Fire + Positive Fire

This personality loves to live life at a feverish pace and there isn't a weary bone in his body. Brilliant and daring, he is forever on the go.

But the Archer's sign could be disruptive to the Horse here: too much speed, spirit and wit without enough perseverance. A person with this combination relies on his intuition a great deal and tends to work himself into a nervous state by taking on more than he can handle or by letting his fertile imagination get the better of him. However, he is very sports-oriented and excercise is the ideal outlet for his accumulated energy. The Sagittarian Horse not only speaks but acts his mind with absolute conviction.

If you are born in the year of the Horse under the Western sign of

Capricorn: 22nd December to 20th January
The Capricorn Horse = Earth + Positive Fire

The Mountain Goat's most welcome gift to this combination is consistency. The Horse should possess more permanent and reliable qualities because of it. Both signs in this match spur the subject toward continuous activity and industry. Responsive, but careful to check the sources of his information, the Capricorn Horse likes to mind his business while tuning in on the wavelengths of others. A less carefree spirit, this Horse will lend speed and grace to Capricorn's solid resolve. He will know how to establish priorities and thus will be able to accomplish much.

If you are born in the year of the Horse under the Western sign of

Aquarius: 21st January to 19th February
The Aquarian Horse = Air + Positive Fire

An enthusiastic personality, full of wanderlust and caprice, he may always have his bags packed for some real or imaginary journey. The Aquarian Horse lives half in the present and half in the colorful future of his magic rainbow. The one thing he never dwells on is the shadowy past and, with his record for surprises, he may very well have one. This optimistic and jaunty Horse's cup runneth over with love of life and involvement. Given to searching for truth, the Horse and Uranus-ruled Aquarius speed on, surrounded by crowds and commitments that keep both mind and body well-occupied.

If you are born in the year of Horse under the Western sign of

Pisces: 20th February to 20th March
The Pisces Horse = Water + Positive Fire

The soul of gallantry and finesse, this Horse is more subtle and receptive to the moods of others. Pisces patience will act as a tranquilizer on the Horse's mobility and tone down his exaggerated mannerisms. Maintaining a steady pace and cautious about resorting to action, this conspicuously conventional creature will not have the Horse's quick sense of urgency nor the Fish's flaw of relying too much on the throb of his tender heart. He is a refined mixture of speed and sensitivity, neither too fast nor too slow, neither too efficient nor too sentimental.

If you are born in the year of the Horse under the Western sign of

Aries: 21st March to 19th April
The Aries Horse = Fire + Positive Fire

As one can see, this sign has too much active fire. The Aries Horse could be perpetually on the go. Yet the Horse could teach the Ram to run with grace and agility and not to use those horns so much. Witty, dashing and spirited, this person tends to overwork. He expresses himself brilliantly but often rashly. Both dauntless and impatient, he will rush to start new ventures but may not persevere in finishing them.

If you are born in the year of the Horse under the Western sign of

Taurus: 20th April to 20th May
The Taurean Horse: Earth + Positive Fire

Here the normal Taurean steadiness and love of regularity may be colored by the rainbow moods of the flamboyant Horse. Still, both are conscientious in attending to their needs and never hindered by overdeveloped scruples or deep self-analysis. A person born with this combination will feel very secure and be able to pursue his interests with quiet determination. He will be a quicker Taurean on one side or a slower Horse on the other, but inevitably he will have a lively personality that will always be receptive to reason and a sound argument.

If you are born in the year of the Horse under the Western sign of

Gemini: 21st May to 21st June
The Gemini Horse = Air + Positive Fire

In this combustible and highly inconsistent combination, the Twin's love of chameleon changes plus the Horse's penchant for constant mobility are combined to the highest degree possible. The Gemini Horse is supremely capable and has lightning-fast reflexes. With this wit around, there will never be a dull moment. He moves at breakneck speed, covering a lot of ground, but never going deeper than the surface. Quickly infatuated and perhaps just as fast to lose interest, this solar-lunar mixture personifies Mercury incarnate.

If you are born in the year of the Horse under the Western sign of

Cancer: 22nd June to 21st July
The Cancerian Horse = Water + Positive Fire

This is an active but calmly collected personality. Although he is refined and in tune with his environment, the Cancerian Horse is still subject to myriad moods and suspicions. This person will not be as self-sacrificing as Cancer is with other lunar signs, but he or she will nevertheless have tasteful preferences and a loving nature. The Horse's presence insures that this person will be more outgoing and less inclined to take life too seriously. The Crab won't be so clinging, as the Horse knows when to let go. The result is a character polished in speech and manners, but with a safety valve to protect himself from getting overinvolved.

If you are born in the year of the Tiger under the Western sign of

Leo: 22nd July to 21st August
The Leo Horse = Fire + Positive Fire

With such a sunny disposition, this personality rarely has shadows of doubt about anything. Idealistic and ambitious, passionate and true, the Leo Horse surges forward in an optimistic but sporadic fashion. He will be impulsive and given to grand gestures. He needs many emotional outlets to release his pent-up energies. A generous and sportive individual, the proud Leonine Horse is expressive and loves physical exercise. A happy-go-lucky innovative leader, he will have droves of friends and fans.

If you are born in the year of the Horse under the Western sign of

Virgo: 22nd August to 22nd September
The Virgo Horse = Earth + Positive Fire

Virgo makes the Horse more predictable and subdued in his passions. His actions are bound to be better calculated and even rehearsed. Although the Virgo Horse's reflexes are slower, he will still be acute and alert, though of a less boisterous nature. The solar Earth sign could put out some of the Horse's flame, but the outcome could be beneficial since the result may be a more responsible, stable personality who will welcome order and stability into his life.

If you are born in the year of the Horse under the Western sign of

Libra: 23rd September to 22nd October
The Libran Horse = Air + Positive Fire

Libra is even more sunny and kind-humored here and will express himself expertly when linked to the quick and ever-youthful Horse. The Libran Horse will be less selfish and more cooperative. But while he is a vacillating diplomat when it comes to the affairs of others, he can be a keen negotiator on his own behalf. And, in spite of his unpredictability and apparent glibness, he will be a capable producer who knows on which side his bread is buttered. This person is forever seeking and finding greener pastures—no one need be too concerned about his welfare.

If you are born in the year of the Horse under the Western sign of

Scorpio: 23rd October to 21st November
The Scorpio Horse = Water + Positive Fire

Scorpio has the fixity that could coax the Horse to apply his strength strategically. Here is a Horse who lacks the casualness and cheerful spontaneity of other stallions; yet, though he may be more serious, he certainly won't be grim. He will still resist being bound to repetitious chores and trivia. Not at all a transparent fellow, he may be moodily handsome and acutely sagacious because of that mysterious and intense Scorpion aura. He could be difficult to reason with when he is hell-bent on going his own way. Never underestimate him.

THE SEASONS OF THE HORSE

SPRING

Spring Horses are loved for their spontaneity and sunny dispositions. Those born during the day tend to be more active, involved and outspoken. They are also likely to be more open, friendly and realistic. In spring, Horses are bound to get more exercise than in winter. And because grass and food are abundant, they will get a good start in life. However, they may tend to be the most impatient of all Horses because they are so active, lively and have a great love for the outdoors and sports. They should be careful not to get distracted and thus lose their focus and commitment. It would be wise for spring Horses to check out every option before making any decisions. They need people to rein in their excitable natures and help them appreciate all aspects of a problem before they rush out to fix it.

SUMMER

The summer Horse is self-assured and will hate to take "no" for an answer; nor will he accept defeat easily. He has few fears in life and will meet challenges head on. Competitive by nature and blessed with tremendous energy, this Horse tends to bite off more than he can chew. Self-indulgent at times, the intelligent summer Horse has trouble keeping a tight hold on his purse strings and tends to overspend without a thought for tomorrow. Usually successful in their understakings, the Horses of summer must learn moderation and caution. Although they tend to be more emotional and headstrong than other Horses, they are also well known for their generosity and uncanny ability to predict new trends.

AUTUMN

A Horse born in the fall will be most concerned with his security. He will mature early, be stable, purposeful and able to take on responsibility. This Horse will strive early in life to show his ability and capacity to take on difficult tasks. Less aggressive than other Horses, he will show dedication to his goals in life. Although he is still a risk taker, the autumnal Horse will always hedge his bets and protect his interests. Serious and, at times demanding, this type of Horse is primarily achievement-conscious and unlikely to go back on his promises.

WINTER

The least outspoken of all the Horses, the winter Horse tends to study a situation thoroughly before giving his opinion. Being also the most unhurried of all Horses, persons of this sign are more conservative in outlook. Winter Horses also have quieter dispositions and will display more pride and love of privacy than Horses of the other seasons. By far the most reliable of the Horses, he or she will be a fast learner and capable manager. Drawing strength from the magnificent calm of winter, this Horse will be able to withstand adversity without complaint. He will be an asset to any team because of his organizational talents and analytical skills.

FAMOUS PERSONS BORN IN THE YEAR
OF THE HORSE

Metal
Neil Armstrong
The Earl of Snowdon
Boris N. Yeltsin
Vladimir Ilyich Lenin

Fire
Rembrandt van Rijn
Leonid Brezhnev
Roberto Rosselini

King Faisal of Saudi Arabia
Otto Preminger
Agnes Moorehead

Earth
Theodore Roosevelt
Kurt Waldheim
Pearl Bailey
Aleksandr Solzhenitsyn
Helmut Schmidt
Leonard Bernstein
Billy Graham
Anwar Sadat
Nelson Mandela

Water
Franklin D. Roosevelt
Ulysses S. Grant
Barbra Streisand
Paul McCartney

Wood
Edward VIII, Duke of Windsor
Nikita Khrushchev
Chris Evert
Patty Hearst

8

The Eighth Sign
of the Lunar Cycle

The Sheep

I am nature's special child.
I trust and am rewarded by trust.
Fortune smiles upon my countenance.
All things blossom
    in the gentleness of my love.
I strive to find beauty in all I behold.
I am fair of face
    and full of grace.

I AM THE SHEEP.

Lunar Years of the Sheep in the Western Calendar	Elements
13 February 1907 to 1 February 1908	Fire
1 February 1919 to 19 February 1920	Earth
17 February 1931 to 5 February 1932	Metal
5 February 1943 to 24 January 1944	Water
24 January 1955 to 11 February 1956	Wood
9 February 1967 to 29 January 1968	Fire
28 January 1979 to 15 February 1980	Earth
15 February 1991 to 3 February 1992	Metal
1 February 2003 to 21 January 2004	Water

If you were born on the day before the start of the lunar year of the Sheep, e.g., 8th February 1967, your sign is the one before the Sheep, the Horse, the seventh lunar sign.

If you were born on the day after the last day of the lunar year of the Sheep, e.g., January 30, 1968, then your sign is the one after the Sheep, the Monkey, the ninth lunar sign.

The sign of the Sheep is the eighth sign of the Chinese Horoscopes and rules the two-hour segment of the day between 1 P.M. and 3 P.M. Persons born during this time are said to have the Sheep as their ascendant and will display many of the traits common to this sign and have great affinity for persons born under this sign.

The direction appointed to the Sheep is south-southwest; its season is summer and its principle month, July. The Sheep corresponds to the Western astrological sign of Cancer which rules summer from June 22nd to July 21st. Fire is the Sheep's fixed element and it has a negative or yin stem.

THE SHEEP PERSONALITY

The Sheep is the most feminine sign of the Chinese zodiac. A native of this year is called the good Samaritan of the cycle. He is righteous, sincere and easily taken in by sob stories. He is likely to be mild-mannered, even shy. At his best, he is artistic, fashionable and a creative worker. At his worst, he tends to be easily overcome by emotions, depressed and withdrawn.

The Sheep is known for his gentle and compassionate ways. He can forgive easily and be understanding of others' faults. He dislikes strict schedules and cannot tolerate too much discipline or criticism. Fond of children and animals, he is close to nature and something of a homebody. The Sheep is apt to mother or even smother the objects of his affection. He is possessed by varying moods and finds it impossible to work under pressure. He also finds it difficult to be objective. His outlook is usually subjective and self-centered.

However, the subdued outer appearance of the Sheep belies his inner determination. When threatened, he can respond passionately and decisively even though he detests fighting. Caught in an argument, he would rather sulk than come right out and tell you what he is upset about. His stony silence and pouting will probably achieve more than angry words and he will eventually have his way. As a child, he will often be spoiled by one or both parents.

The Chinese believe that good fortune smiles on the Sheep because of his peaceful nature and kind heart. He is generous with his time and money. When you have nowhere to go and no money, you can be sure the Sheep will not turn you away. He will always have the three most important things in life: food, shelter and clothing. Wherever he goes, he is bound to meet people who can and will assist him. A person of this sign will make it a point to marry well and will be cherished not only by his mate, but by his in-laws as well.

It is said that a Sheep person born in the winter will have a hard life because in this season there is an absence of grass and Sheep are generally slaughtered for food. However, even in the roughest circumstances, the Sheep will still possess his three basic necessities and people will care deeply for him. His is the eighth sign, and to the Chinese the number 8 symbolizes prosperity and comfort.

The Sheep has fantastic luck; people often leave him money in their wills and even the poorest of these natives will inherit something of value from his parents or relations. Admirers present the Sheep with expensive presents and rich and powerful patrons take him under their wing. Famous personalities adopt him and take him as their protégé. Somehow the fortunate Sheep will always have things made easier for him. His every fall will be cushioned by those looking out for his interests.

Yes, the Sheep can be ingratiating when it comes to currying favors. Consequently, like the Rabbit, he will obtain his desires without force or violence. He will have great passive endurance and will wear you down with pleas and entreaties. You will never know his mettle until you try to break him. He isn't that warm and woolly after all. Basically a survivor, the Sheep will know how to placate or evade his enemies. Failing that, he'll run home crying and get his big brother to beat you to a pulp. The Sheep will always have many powerful allies. Try to remember that before you think about taking advantage of his kind nature.

The Sheep's oblique approach can be infuriating to natives of more direct lunar signs. Admittedly, his roundabout ways can grow quite tiresome, but that is the way he is. The lower type of Sheep can at times be so theatrical he may drive you up the wall. Don't expect him to come right out and say exactly what is troubling him. There is no fun for him in being blunt and brazen. You must be prepared to pry it from him bit by bit. Entice him with rewards. Promise that you won't be angry. Humor him. Give him a wide margin and lots of sympathetic nods. He has little sense of time, so you will probably have to rearrange your other appointments. Finally, if all else fails, go ahead and bully him, bang the table (he will be impressed), stomp around the room, act like an ogre, but never stop showing that you love and care about him. Then he will come up with the secret hurts he has been nursing for weeks and the two of you will be able to clear the air.

At times, it may be advantageous for the kindly Sheep to have bossy, strong associates—managers who will both discipline him and put his talents to use, tough secretaries and tougher chaperones who will turn down those unreasonable demands made on his good nature. In short, the Sheep needs people to insulate him from hassle and the human parasites who want to prey on him.

The Sheep never really cuts his umbilical cord. He will always come home to mother and his favorite apple pie. He never forgets birthdays, anniversaries or other special occasions. He will make it a point to celebrate these days ostentatiously (especially when he is not footing the bill). And he is equally sensitive about his own special dates, too. Woe to you if you forget his birthday or neglect to pay a visit or send a get-well card (at the very least) when he's in the hospital. As far as he is concerned, you practically broke his poor heart in two and he will probably be scarred for the rest of his life.

The Sheep is basically a worrier. He tends to be pessimistic about events and is prone to predict the worst. Of course, he expects you to vehemently dispel his dark thoughts, and he always makes sure someone is around to cheer him up. He knows it's useless to cry alone. He'd rather have an audience, please. Misfortunes touch him deeply and he does not get over hardships easily. Lest others forget, he will also take to recounting his miseries ad infinitum. Another one of his shortcomings is that he has difficulty in denying himself anything. He always overspends and should avoid handling his own finances. An extreme type of Sheep may spread cash around as if he were personally obliged to circulate the currency for the Treasury Department.

The Sheep damsel is inclined to like dainty things, as well as all the frills and trimmings that come with them. She is decidedly coquettish and may spend hours on her toilette. She rarely arrives on time for anything, and acts as fragile as bone china. She'll move like a princess and may have a fresh rose on her desk every morning to remind her (and you) that she enjoys being a girl. The Sheep lady will be spanking clean; she is very concerned with personal hygiene, even though her house may be a mess and she doesn't know where anything is. The more aloof types will be preoccupied by sanitary standards. Her children will be scrubbed clean and always look presentable. She has flawless taste in choosing clothes and exquisite accessories.

She will be good at costume design, window dressing, or stage sets. While she may appear disorganized and scatter-brained, everything will fall perfectly into place at the last minute, totally confounding all her critics.

The Sheep girl will openly show her favoritism and will consort day in and day out with those she dubs her special people, her confidants. If she doesn't love you, well, don't complain. At least she will just ignore you without trying to reform you or come after you with a cudgel like a Dragon or an Ox lady. Hers is the voice of gentle persuasion. She'll twist your arm, but in the most engaging manner. For her, half the fun will be the getting there—the flirting, the cajoling. A Sheep lady's "Yes" could also mean "No" and her "No" could mean "Maybe." If you are a knight in shining armor and want to win this fair maiden, it will be worth the challenge to find out just what her veiled responses mean.

All Sheep people, from nine to ninety, are diehard romantics. Soft music, moonlight and intimate candlelit dinners never fail to work their magic on them.

A person born under this sign will have the beguiling knack of turning his every weakness into a strength. He knows how to get what he wants by insinuation and subtle hints. He is master of the soft-sell technique, so don't ever underestimate him or you will be caught off-guard. His sedate, earnest and sometimes whimpering ways will prove effective in wearing down the strongest defenses. With unfeigned emotion he can plead his case so convincingly he often doesn't even need many words.

The Sheep will come to you with preposterous requests, bordering on blackmail or even highway robbery. And just when you are about to smack him down with a loud, resounding "No," you notice that chaste and innocent look on his face, that tear hanging from the corner of his eye, the slight quivering of his lips, and suddenly you feel like some horrible monster taking a lamb to the slaughter. Needless to say, you reluctantly give your consent to his ludicrous demands, still not clear on why or how such a harmless-looking, vulnerable creature could do you in. Case closed.

Certainly not one to make decisions, the Sheep would rather follow, then complain when things do not turn out right. Yet people love him sincerely because he is so good-natured and kind enough to share whatever he has. He or she will be very close to his or her family and will tend to overindulge them.

Because the Sheep person never likes to deliberately displease those he loves, he may float about doing nothing in order to avoid conflict and will eventually be criticized for failing to take a firm stand on issues. He is difficult to deal with, as he is hypersensitive as well as given to excessive self-pity and emotional ups and downs.

Appreciation of his talents will make the Sheep blossom spectacularly. He craves love, attention and approval—in that order. He should work in a creative field in which he can excel, and be given a free hand to do what pleases him most. Where aesthetics are concerned, don't worry, the Sheep will not disappoint you. He has very discriminating taste and makes discerning choices. Then again, it is only fair to warn you that he also tends to spend a lot and may not be very practical.

Unless he was born at the time of day governed by a strong sign such as a Dragon, Snake or Tiger, he should not take on jobs with too much responsibility or decision-making. Being passive by nature, he shuns confrontation and law enforcement.

On the whole, it can be said that the Sheep will not have to work hard for a living. Good things come to him naturally, which is perfect, as he loves luxury and ease. Like his best friend, the Rabbit, he has the soul of a connoisseur. Anything ugly or lowly depresses him. He is so sensitive to beauty and balance that his moods are largely governed by his surroundings. He functions best in bright, airy and tastefully appointed rooms.

In his life he will need strong and loyal people to lean on. The outgoing and optimistic characteristics of the Horse, Boar and Tiger will complement his personality. He will also find perfect harmony with the Rabbit. The Monkey, Dragon, Rooster, Snake or another Sheep will do very nicely, too.

The Rat will dislike the Sheep's spendthrift ways and lack of self-denial. The Sheep will not find sympathy or happiness with the stern people of the Ox year or the practical Dog persons, who will not have patience enough to listen to the Sheep's petty woes.

THE SHEEP CHILD

The gentle Sheep child will be a treasure to his parents. He will love being cuddled, fussed over, petted and thoroughly spoiled. A sensitive artist and lover of beauty, he will appreciate music, poetry, sweet smelling soap for his bath and all sorts of delicate trimmings that stimulate his fine senses. Ultradependent, he won't like to do anything for himself—if he can help it. Warm, soft, vulnerable and submissive, he likes being catered to.

Like little Linus in the "Peanuts" comic strip, he is most likely to cling to his old woollen blanket or, in the case of a girl, her worn-out rag doll. He hates being teased and if he is strongly criticized or embarrassed in school, he may not want to return for many days. He will seek out more dominant youngsters to take him under their wing. When he is feeling down, he will need loads and loads of sympathy to cheer him up. His fertile imagination and morbid fears can actually make him ill. He can be easily influenced, especially in an adverse way, and will positively drown you with his sorrows when in a melancholy mood.

When ridiculed or rejected, he can withdraw into a magical world of his own and it will be difficult to lure him out. Nor will the Sheep be in any hurry to leave home if he is loved and well cared for. Food and comfort represent love and security to him. When he does decide to set up housekeeping on his own, you can be sure he will do it with exquisite taste. He loves getting dressed up and has a flair for arranging things. Fickle, inconsistent and, at times, petty, he redeems himself by being extremely creative, modest and patient. He has great compassion for the sorrows of others. When he is fond of someone, his love and generosity know no bounds. It will be rewarding to care for him as he will repay your affections a hundred-fold. It will be impossible to remain angry with him for long. He may have his flaws, but he is still a jewel of the highest quality.

Don't be afraid to lead him by the hand or help him make decisions. He will never get enough reassurance and, as a matter of fact, may seek his parents' advice or approval for everything he does.

Don't try to wipe the fairy dust away from his eyes; forget trying to change, mend or rearrange him into sterner stuff. It will be useless—the Sheep will always see life and the world through rose-colored glasses.

THE FIVE DIFFERENT SHEEP

METAL SHEEP—1931, 1991

The Metal Sheep will have great faith in himself and be well aware of the value of his talents. He can camouflage his high degree of sensitivity by putting up a brave front, but beneath it he has a very vulnerable ego and is easily offended by offhanded remarks.

Metal reinforces his abundant artistic inclinations and he will be inspired to search continuously for beauty in all forms. His home could be a masterpiece of interior design, for he is concerned above all with harmony and balance in his daily life. Leaving a familiar environment can be traumatic for him; he will find it hard to adjust to change.

This type of Sheep will also seek security in both his domestic and financial life. His services won't come cheap, although he is not averse to handing out free meal tickets now and then.

His social activities will be limited to those people he cherishes or those who could be of use to his career. The uninitiated will simply have to wait for him to warm up to their advances.

Beneath his calm and helpful exterior, the Metal Sheep has unstable emotions he finds hard to control. As a result, he can be possessive, jealous and overprotective of his loved ones. He should allow the people around him more freedom. Expecting everyone to be at his beck and call will only cause resentment, as well as resistance to the invaluable contributions he could make.

WATER SHEEP—1943, 2003

This type of Sheep will be extremely appealing to others. There may be dozens of people around who will want to mother him, and if he is in need of help, he can summon an army.

Popular but not really knowledgeable, meek but innately opportunistic, the Water Sheep will seek out people he can rely on. When Water is joined with his basic sign, it encourages him to travel the route of the least resistance. He is impressionable and will always go along with the wishes of the majority or those who have a strong influence over him. But while he may readily absorb the ideas of others, he will still cling to what he is accustomed to. He fears changes in his lifestyle and will never be eager to explore the unknown by himself.

Although he has multiple interests and therefore can mix well with almost anyone, he also suffers from a martyr complex and will feel rejected and persecuted whenever he is not allowed to have his way.

WOOD SHEEP—1955

A thoughtful, good-humored Sheep, with leisurely ways, but mindful of other people's wishes. He is sentimental and strives to please; with Wood as his element he will be prevented from being too flippant. His nature will be steadier and more generous and he will have high moral principles.

This loving Sheep will have complete trust in those he believes in. He will put his life in their hands with the simple faith of a child. Even though he is aware of his intrinsic worth, this Sheep allows others to take advantage of him. He capitulates too readily when harassed and makes unwise sacrifices for the sake of keeping the peace.

The Wood Sheep has the tendency to mother others and can be most devoted to those he cares about. He will be overwhelmed by the circumstances of those less fortunate than himself and may have a collection of human as well as animal strays to take care of.

His good deeds and compassion will not go unrewarded. Because he won't mind supporting others, money will always come to him when he is in need. He will receive financial help or inherit money from unlikely sources.

FIRE SHEEP—1907, 1967

The Fire Sheep is sure-footed; therefore, he is more courageous about following his intuitions and he will take the initiative in his work.

His creativity lies in his ability to dramatize rather than invent. He can highlight strong points and play down weaknesses. Even when experimenting with vivid colors, he can produce restful and pleasant compositions.

If possible, he would like to own a stately home. He is indulgent where his personal comforts are concerned and enjoys entertaining lavishly. Consequently, he is likely to overextend himself financially and mismanage his affairs.

Fire makes him very energetic and aggressive. He is outspoken when offended. He will exhibit an enticing personal grace but his emotionalism could, at times, defy logic.

When the Fire Sheep is negative, he is given to wishful thinking without appreciating the benefits of his current situation. He reaches for the proverbial pie in the sky and will be sullen and spiteful when it isn't within his grasp.

EARTH SHEEP—1919, 1979

This type of Sheep is optimistic and more self-reliant than other Sheep. In spite of his strong attachment to the domestic scene and his devotion to family members, he will try to maintain a certain degree of independence.

Earth, as his element, makes him conservative and careful. He won't waste money but he won't be counting pennies, either. But, being a Sheep, he will still find it difficult to deny himself. What may appear as luxuries to others will be bare necessities to him.

However, just as he plays hard, the Earth Sheep will work hard. He can take his responsibilities seriously and will go out of his way to help friends. He is unlikely to ever turn his back on someone in trouble.

Although he may be more adept at concealing his emotions, this particular Sheep is also prone to being neurotic and ultradefensive when criticized.

COMPATIBILITY AND CONFLICT CHARTS
FOR THE SHEEP

The Sheep is part of the Fourth and last Triangle of Affinity, a group consisting of the emotionally- and artistically-guided signs of the Rabbit, Sheep and Boar. These three are mainly concerned with their senses and what they can appreciate with them. They are expressive, intuitive and eloquent in aesthetic and talented ways. Fine arts, architecture, design and fashion, writing, and computer software (and other such innovative fields) are their forte. Diplomatic and compassionate, this trio possesses calmer natures than the other lunar signs. Dependent on others for stimulation and leadership, they are flexible because they are sympathetically attuned to the vibrations of their environment. These three signs are drawn toward beauty and the higher aspects of love. They will extol the virtues of peaceful coexistence with their fellow man. No doubt, these lunar signs will provide each other with excellent company as they share the same basic philosophies.

TRIANGLE OF AFFINITY FOR THE SHEEP

The Sheep will encounter the most difficulties with the sign opposite him in the Circle of Conflict, the Ox. Anyone whose ascendant is the Sheep between 1 P.M. and 3 P.M. (birth time) will most likely also be incompatible with the Ox native. Sheep and Oxen are on the opposite side of the spectrum. The Sheep's season is the summer while the Ox rules in the winter. Fire, the Sheep's fixed element, is in conflict with the Ox's fixed element, Water. The Sheep tends to be emotional, possessive and sensitive; the Ox is stern, practical and disciplined. Both are industrious but in totally different ways. The Ox favors constancy and persistence while the Sheep prefers harmony, creativity and mutual communication. The Sheep will find the Ox cold and calculating; the Ox will lose patience with the Sheep's many fears and insecurities. Since they have a tendency to use their wits against each other rather than for a common goal, these two signs could work well together only when dealing through experienced go-betweens respected by both.

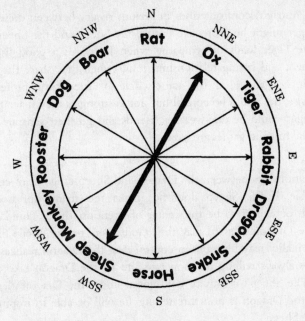

CIRCLE OF CONFLICT

Aside from the most compatible signs, the Rabbit and Boar, and most incompatible partner, the Ox, the other nine signs are compatible with the Sheep to varying degrees.

Rat

The Sheep and the Rat do not have much in common. The Rat is not sympathetic to the frivolous ways of the Sheep. The Rat saves his pennies; the Sheep spends, borrows and indulges every whim. The

Sheep is creative and needs to be on an equal wavelength with others before he or she can be effective; the aggressive Rat enjoys hard work and prefers to handle challenges without needing help from others. Such different outlooks will generate some animosity from both sides. However, a Sheep person born during the hours of the Rat may be the exception. Similarly, if a Rat is born during the hours of the Sheep, he will be able to establish rapport with the Sheep native.

Tiger

No outright confrontations or serious rivalry between these two. The Tiger might be protective toward the Sheep and the Sheep will give the Tiger loads of sympathy when he needs a good listener. Permanent and lasting relationships result when they share the same ascendant or move in the same circle of friends or profession. Otherwise, ties could be cordial but not as strong as they may appear. Both signs could be fair-weather friends and go their separate ways when the fun and games are over.

Dragon

Relationships between the Dragon and Sheep range from cool to acceptable. If the Sheep does not make too many unreasonable demands or expect to be the center of attention, things could work out. The Dragon likes to play the "Godfather" to the docile Sheep, who in reality may be more in control than the Dragon realizes. The Sheep is always willing to cooperate and let the Dragon take command. The Sheep's creativity will bloom under the Dragon's leadership. If the Dragon is non-threatening, he will be able to inspire the sensitive Sheep.

Snake

The lovable and compassionate Sheep can sometimes prove frustrating to the intensely intellectual Snake person. The Sheep has much to offer but often demands too much and can be very unreasonable. The Snake will not like to make long-term commitments or give in to the whims of the Sheep unless it will benefit him. The Sheep needs the Snake's direction and constancy of purpose while the Snake could benefit from the Sheep's expansive talents and kind nature. But, then again, the Sheep's best friend, the Boar, will be at odds with the Snake and will take care to point out all his negative traits to the easily influenced and docile Sheep. In such a contest, the Sheep will side with the Boar every time and distance himself from the ambitious and tenacious Serpent.

Horse

The Sheep admires the Horse's forthrightness and courage while the Horse may provide the Sheep with the direction and confidence he needs to market his many talents. The Sheep may indulge the Horse's many caprices and the Horse may choose to ignore the Sheep's many complaints. The good-natured and creative Sheep has need of the commanding and quick-witted Horse and will not care to challenge him on issues. The Sheep will do well to join forces with the capable Horse—compatible and successful business ties could result.

Sheep

Sheep natives do not have much rivalry when working together. Most of the time the trouble stems from their ascendant signs and their native lack of decisiveness. If they have common interests and similar goals, they will bind together effectively into an unbeatable team. However, Sheep are easily influenced and do have the habit of changing their minds and preferences. In love and business, the Sheep's capriciousness could damage relationships that took a long time to build. Two Sheep could be best friends until they find a third party or something that both want. Then their possessiveness comes to the fore and jealousy could damage their relationship.

Monkey

Sheep and Monkey have no deep understanding of one another. To be mutually attracted, they will have to share an ascendant or have interests and goals in common. The Monkey needs the Sheep's broad influence and diplomatic abilities while the Sheep could make good use of the Monkey's inventive brain. However, the Sheep expects love and gratitude for his largesse but the Monkey would rather have his due in cold, hard cash. Then too, the Monkey tends to be analytical and practical, the Sheep emotional and passive. When things go wrong, the pessimistic Sheep will blame the Monkey. Thankfully, the Monkey is a problem solver and may not take the complaints of the Sheep too seriously.

Rooster

The Sheep will shun the Rooster because Roosters are hard task masters and disciplinarians and the Sheep prefers to be courted in a kindly and loving way. The Rooster is easily exasperated by non-conformists and will have communication problems with the overly sensitive Sheep. Ties between these two signs will be only moderate unless they happen to share a common ascendant. Each has reservations about the other and will tolerate little before going their separate ways. The Rooster will want to show off his expertise, but he will alienate the Sheep by trying to run his life and imposing too many rules. The Sheep cannot abide the Rooster's criticism and regimentation, and they only serve to bring out the worst in the Sheep's personality.

Dog

Dog and Sheep may have few things in common, but they do share a mutual goodwill that keeps each one on his side of the fence. They work at different speeds and have different objectives. The Dog couldn't care less whether anyone likes him so long as he can do his duty and fulfill his responsibilities. The Sheep must have consensus and approval before he can act, and is always so worried about hurting others he can become a fence-sitter. The Dog cannot and will not tolerate disloyalty and can be quite stern when the Sheep fails to make up his mind promptly. The Sheep has difficulty taking sides and may want to please everyone, something the Dog cannot comprehend.

THE SHEEP AND HIS ASCENDANTS

We all have a shadow that follows us throughout life. Sometimes it grows bigger than life and at other times it shrinks until it disappears into the soles of our feet. Sometimes it walks tall before us and on other occasions it lags behind like a sulking friend. In Chinese horoscopes, this constant partner, manifested or not, is our ascendant, the animal sign that rules the hour of our birth and becomes a comrade in our journey through life. We may view it as friend or foe or even a little of both. It surfaces when we least expect and shows a better or worse side of our nature. We can often be confounded by the way we listen to our "other self" as well as feel resentful of the significant influence it can exert on us. Actually, a personality has many rings around the centered "self." Each ring can have a different size, texture and aura. When all these factors combine, they bring forth the unique individual that the person truly is. Hence, a Dragon with an ascendant that is not compatible, like the Dog, has perhaps a more difficult inner struggle than say a Snake born during the hours of the Snake. The double intensity of the Snake person will be easily understood by horoscope readers while the more intricate Dragon/Dog may exhibit the contrary Dog and Dragon traits to varying degrees. There are many voices within each person. But, in the end, only the individual determines which course he will follow, which choices he will make.

The time of birth used to determine the ascendant is always the local time in the place of birth.

If you were born between:

11 P.M. and 1 A.M. = The Hours of the Rat

You are a lovable but opportunistic and crafty Sheep. Both signs are sentimental and close to their families. But the Rat's presence could make you more dependable and less inclined to fall apart during a crisis. The Rat has a more outspoken and spicy disposition than the retiring Sheep, and you could turn out to be an excellent critic, writer or artist who is able to get on the good side of everyone.

1 a.m. and 3 a.m. = The Hours of the Ox

You will be a Sheep who radiates charm mixed with the Buffalo's rugged authority. Punctual, conservative and set in your ways, you are apt to be more patient and determined than Sheep with other ascendants. Studious and reliable, your word is your bond. The Ox's stubborn resolve is mitigated by your innate sympathetic nature, and you will be kind and protective to those you love.

3 a.m. and 5 a.m. = The Hours of the Tiger

The Tiger's feline impetuosity will accentuate your Sheep's exquisite personality in a colorful and attractive way. Creative, innovative and a great success on the stage, you may still have that temperamental side which makes you volatile and indecisive at times. This is a good combination as the Tiger is an optimist while the Sheep tends to worry and complain when matters are not to his liking. The Tiger in you will go out and do something about it. You have the courage and daring other Sheep may lack.

5 a.m. and 7 a.m. = The Hours of the Rabbit

You are a clever but unobtrusive Sheep who is not as charitable as he pretends to be. This is a combination that cannot be counted on to commit readily to anything which involves a great deal of work or sacrifice. The Rabbit ascendant makes you shun too much involvement. You tend to observe from a distance and make astute judgments that win the respect of all. You will make an excellent referee, arbitrator or mediator.

7 a.m. and 9 a.m. = The Hours of the Dragon

With the Dragon as your ally, you will show great determination and an ability to lead. The Dragon ascendant imparts the courage and conviction needed for you to carry out your ideas and plans. But the Sheep in you still has a strong desire for adulation and appreciation although you are less afraid of opposition. You tend to stand by your beliefs and can inspire others with your sterling example and charity.

9 a.m. and 11 a.m. = The Hours of the Snake

You could be a Sheep with great potential and a fine, uncluttered mind. The Snake ascendant makes you more self-assured and competent in whatever field or profession you choose. You can make up your own mind and keep your secrets and emotions to yourself. Patient, calm and ambitious, you will strive to achieve your goals and make your presence felt by all you work with. Your quiet front can be deceiving because both signs here are fiery and subjective.

11 a.m. and 1 p.m. = The Hours of the Horse

You are a happy-go-lucky Sheep who is popular, quick-witted and adventurous. The Horse ascendant make you expressive, expansive and fanciful. The active Horse in you may be in hot pursuit of money while the dominant Sheep side will certainly know how to dole it out. With the Horse as your partner, you do not fear to tread new ground or worry too much about what tomorrow will bring.

1 p.m. and 3 p.m. = The Hours of the Sheep

You have a pure Sheep combination, which makes you very ardent and responsive, but also somewhat of a clinging vine when you become possessive. Actually, you would prefer to rely on others to serve or help you. Still, you are generous to a fault and would want to help everyone if it were possible. Although you have many notable talents to offer, you still feel insecure and need strong associates to guide you and protect your interests.

3 P.M. and 5 P.M. = The Hours of the Monkey

The Monkey could make your Sheep personality more inclined to take action, and give you self-assurance in the bargain. You could also have the Monkey's delightful way of looking at the sunnier side of life. With the Monkey's ascendant, you are not afraid of risks or challenges and will be inventive and innovative in handling your problems. The Monkey's innate self-confidence could also do wonders for your self-esteem, although at times you may tend to have that quirky superiority complex that Monkeys tend to display.

5 P.M. and 7 P.M. = The Hours of the Rooster

You could be that super-efficient Sheep who loves to organize and supervise social functions or charitable events. You are disarmingly charming but may have the Rooster's knack for far-fetched ideas and complicated solutions to simple problems. The Sheep in you is compassionate and giving while the outgoing Rooster side is calculating and opinionated. No doubt, you will be brainy and have many positive qualities, but you need to work as part of a team to bring out your talents.

7 P.M. and 9 P.M. = The Hours of the Dog

With the likeable Dog as your ascendant, you will be a more rational and sensible Sheep. The Dog gives you more strength of character and helps you face reality without complaining or wishing for the impossible. His toughness makes you not so easily susceptible to tears or self-pity. With this combination, you tend to be more cooperative and even amenable to teamwork. As a result, people will value your skills, opinions and level-headed outlook.

9 P.M. and 11 P.M. = The Hours of the Boar

You will be a Sheep who will always lend someone a shoulder to cry on. With the sturdy Boar as your alter ego, you will be able to bear trials and endure hardships with resilience. However, this combination tends to be sensual and indulgent and will enjoy all the creature comforts life has to offer. Self-denial is not one of your strong points and you could go overboard when your passions are aroused. It would be a good idea to have a strong associate to manage your finances and/or control your diet.

HOW THE SHEEP FARES IN THE LUNAR CYCLE

1. The Year of the Rat 1996

The Rat's year brings opportunity and prosperity for the Sheep. However, he or she will also be expected to work hard and meet deadlines. Industriousness and dedication to duty will pay off handsomely. Gifts and gains from unlikely sources such as gambling, lottery, etc. are possible, as are good business opportunities. In general, the Sheep's home life may be placid, but romance and social successes are foreseen if he or she is unattached. No illnesses or major problems should trouble the Sheep. Complaints are minimal and the Sheep would do well to count his blessings instead of grumble.

2. The Year of the Ox 1997

The Sheep will be in for a difficult time as quarrels, misunderstandings and the demands of family and friends keep him occupied and anxious. The Ox year brings more responsibility than the Sheep cares for and he may get into financial troubles as a result of his extravagance and overspending. The Sheep can expect only moderate gains. The more he resists change or authority, the more opposition he will encounter. He would do better to join forces with others or find safety in numbers by working with a group. Once the Sheep is able to solicit support from friends and patrons through peaceful means, his problems should dissipate and his anxiety greatly lessen. This is especially likely to occur in the fall.

3. The Year of the Tiger 1998

This is a year of mixed blessings for the Sheep as the Tiger is unpredictable and temperamental. The Sheep native can retain power but will have to stride hard to keep up with the competition. The year of the Tiger brings many challenges. If he is ready to compete and to develop his many abilities, the Sheep will gain recognition. The rewards the Tiger brings could be in the form of fame, knowledge or happiness instead of pure monetary gain. His immediate family life is calm, but there will be trouble with relatives. He will be busy at work but will still have the opportunity to meet new and beneficial contacts.

4. The Year of the Rabbit 1999

The Rabbit's year will be a fortunate and fairly easy one for the Sheep as he chalks up some gains at work and in his finances. He will benefit from being in the right place at the right time and will meet people who give him information or assistance. However, he should not be too complacent. He could suffer an upheaval at home or some repercussion due to past neglect. Health problems could be caused by accidental injuries or overexertion. But he will emerge from his troubles with more gains than losses.

5. The Year of the Dragon 2000

In this hectic but sober year for the Sheep, gains will be marginal. There may be numerous disputes, but he is fortunate not to face any major calamity. The dramatic Dragon blows things out of proportion and causes people to overestimate and expect too much. The Sheep will find it hard to accumulate money, but he should ride out any financial storms admirably if he takes care not gamble or make drastic changes in his life. In the Dragon's year, it is best to take good news with a grain of salt and be very conservative in assessments.

6. The Year of the Snake 2001

This is a good year for the Sheep as he is able to regain power, position and popularity. The Snake's rule could bring new and influential people to help him and he will travel or receive some additional income. However, bad tidings may delay his progress temporarily, although he will achieve his goals if he can remain patient and persistent. Family life could suffer from the Sheep's many commitments. Romantically, there could be complications due to the Sheep's jealous nature.

7. The Year of the Horse 2002

The Horse brings happy news during a smooth and eventful year for the Sheep native. The Sheep faces no major problems at home or at work although he will wind up doing more than his fair share of work. He can get control behind the scenes and could overcome obstacles by using his influence skillfully. A slight illness or infection is indicated, but in general he will prosper this year in spite of a fast pace which is sometimes not to his liking. A problem that has troubled him in the past will turn out to be a blessing in disguise, so he must not give in to pessimism when things do not work out immediately to his satisfaction.

8. The Year of the Sheep 2003

Generally, the Sheep's year is not very favorable for the Sheep native. Things may start out promising and he could make a lot of plans or receive many invitations. But if he lets his guard down and assumes everything will be taken care of, then problems and complications will pop up and his gains may be greatly diminished. He must take care to check everything twice to make sure there are no loose ends. This is definitely a time during which he must lower his expectations and be as practical as possible. He should not take anything for granted. However, romance and love affairs will blossom as the Sheep seeks comfort and reassurance from others.

9. The Year of the Monkey 2004

The Monkey brings a fairly good year for the Sheep. He could achieve recognition or a promotion at work which will give him a sense of fulfillment. But there could also be many annoying problems or unresolved issues that occupy his mind. The Monkey expects everyone to be on his toes, so competition could be fierce. The Sheep born will enjoy a busy but somewhat controversial year. Opposition and health problems could be upsetting, but they will be minor and short lived. Family and romantic liaisons could hold surprises for the Sheep, and he must keep an open mind and be prepared to adapt to changes rather quickly.

10. The Year of the Rooster 2005

The Rooster's year could be entertaining but expensive for the Sheep. He should cut his expenses and spend carefully. The Sheep should also guard against being too sensitive to criticism as he may be faced with irritating disputes or petty conflicts at home. Problems seem to magnify themselves during the year of the Rooster. The Sheep must keep his wits about him and retain his sense of humor. This is a year in which he should not try to please everyone, but watch his finances very carefully.

11. The Year of the Dog 2006

In this somewhat difficult year for the Sheep, he has to deal with changes, debts and some romantic problems. Family life and work make many demands on his time and he is overstressed from all his responsibilities. The more he tries to take shortcuts or evade duties, the more he will feel caught between a rock and a hard place. This is the time for him to make decisions he has been putting off. But it is not a good time for him to travel extensively or make investments or long-term commitments. He must maintain an optimistic but very conservative outlook.

12. The Year of the Boar 2007

This will be a fair year for the Sheep as he recovers from his past troubles. The generous Boar brings him good news and influential friends. He is able to relax and enjoy himself with the people and sports or activities he loves. His position is still shaky but he feels protected under the auspices of the friendly Pig. He could suddenly have access to funds previously withheld from him or find money given up for lost. The Boar brings luck for the Sheep native. His home and love life will be happy.

WHEN MOON SIGNS MEET SUN SIGNS

In my interpretation of Chinese horoscopes, the Rat is not linked with the first Western astrological sun sign, Aries. Instead, I pair the Rat with its counterpart based on the month and season of the Rat, which are December and winter. This makes the most sense as the lunar month of December (also called the Twelfth Moon or the Twelfth Earth Branch) is supposed to parallel the sun sign, Sagittarius, the Archer. I envision the Eastern and Western horoscope cycles as two large wheels, each with twelve spokes. To correctly juxtapose these cycles, we must find the matching notch that will join them together. Once the Rat and Sagittarius are paired as the first signs, the other eleven fall into place. Please see the Twenty-Four Segments of the Lunar Almanac. All the dates correspond with the twelve Western solar signs.

If you are born in the year of the Sheep under the Western sign of

Sagittarius: 22nd November to 21st December
The Sagittarian Sheep = Fire + Negative Fire

This sun-moon combination produces a well-meaning and philosophical Sheep with a wide-angle view of coming trends. Direct and honest, he is still likely to shun irksome details or dirty work. The Sagittarian Sheep will love to explore new heights and present startling theories. This sort of person is more athletic than emotional. He can laugh off his mistakes and take constructive criticism well. Endowed with a sense of fashion and good taste, he will be able to create innovative new styles with aplomb. Because he is so confident of his powers, he will be more outspoken than other Sheep.

If you are born in the year of the Sheep under the Western sign of

Capricorn: 22nd December to 20th January
The Capricorn Sheep = Earth + Negative Fire

Here the noncommittal and pliable Sheep comes under the steady guidance of the Mountain Goat. Hence, this person is more certain of what he wants and will not hesitate to make his own decisions. Because of the good fortune and benevolence the eighth lunar sign brings him, the Capricorn Sheep will be handsomely rewarded for the hardships and deficiencies he must endure. Less content to stay in the background, this Sheep will take an active role in shaping his own destiny—and we won't be hearing so many complaints either. Don't butt horns with him.

If you were born in the year of the Sheep under the Western sign of

Aquarius: 21st January to 19th February
The Aquarian Sheep = Air + Negative Fire

This sun-moon combination may have too much moderation. Both signs are friendly and tolerant, given to intuitive pursuits and altruistic activities. Freedom-loving Aquarius may refuse to conform and so this mild-seeming person may be inquisitive and unconventional. The good-natured, sensitive Sheep could possess the Water Bearer's deep well of knowledge and the Sheep's ability to bring situations to a peaceful solution. The Aquarian Sheep does not watch his popularity ratings too avidly but will still want to keep everybody happy and contented. Self-denial is quite alien to him, however, and he would rather have his fun now and pay later. But with the Sheep's ability to gather sympathy after the fact, he may not have to pay at all.

If you were born in the year of the Sheep under the Western sign of

Pisces: 20th February to 20th March
The Pisces Sheep = Water + Negative Fire

In spite of his tedious and overly-particular ways, the Pisces Sheep is still delightfully attractive, thoughtful and entertaining. Because of his generosity and kindness, he often ends up with the biggest piece of pie. He can also be sentimental and maudlin where his emotions are concerned. A lover of quiet pastoral scenes, stained-glass windows, organ music and lofty cathedrals, the Pisces Sheep finds the background is a much safer and happier place for him to inhabit. Here he can meditate; solitude brings out the best in his character, enabling him to be a giver of sympathy and good advice.

If you were born in the year of the Sheep under the Western sign of

Aries: 21st March to 19th April
The Aries Sheep = Fire + Negative Fire

This West-East combination may produce a more submissive Ram, but perhaps only in appearances. He keeps his own counsel and, while looking ever so meek and mild, he may be terribly set in his ways. His aggressiveness is muted and buried, but will surface whenever he feels threatened. Hence, the Aries Sheep will be a more controlled and patient personality, free of guile and treachery. Aries will stand his ground and fight for what he believes in, no matter how peace-loving the Sheep half of his nature is. When he leads, he will lead by his fine example and will not be egotistical or despotic.

If you were born in the year of the Sheep under the Western sign of

Taurus: 20th April to 20th May
The Taurean Sheep = Earth + Negative Fire

This team brings forth a strong-willed Sheep who clings too much to the past at times. The Bull is purposeful and blessed with firm ideas about what he wants, which ideally curtails the Sheep's indecisiveness. However, the malleable Sheep is always open to suggestions while the Taurean is not. This combination produces a character full of constructive common sense, calm persuasiveness and an unerring eye for beauty. The Taurean Sheep may be a lover of ease, but he will apply himself diligently to ensuring his personal comfort and security. He has fixed tastes and fixed opinions and does not welcome changes of any kind unless he himself initiates them.

If you were born in the year of the Sheep under the Western sign of

Gemini: 21st May to 21st June
The Gemini Sheep = Air + Negative Fire

A versatile and creative combination emerges when this Sun sign meets this Moon sign. The Sheep's good taste and refined manners coupled with Gemini's wit and humor should strike a congenial balance. With Mercury's influence, the Sheep personality loses some of his sentimentality and acquires some of Gemini's love of action and practical outlook on life. This is an adventurous and many sided personality who loves excitement, new ideas and challenging experiences. It would be hard to keep up with or even just keep track of him when he is out chasing a dozen different things.

If you were born in the year of the Sheep under the Western sign of

Cancer: 22nd June to 21st July
The Cancerian Sheep = Water + Negative Fire

Here we find a character of deep piety, filial devotion and love of children. The Cancerian Sheep is a feminine combination. Consequently, he is easily hurt, quick to retreat and passive in attitude. Timorous and hypersensitive to discomfort and deprivation, this sort of person thrives best in opulent circumstances and conjugal harmony. Appreciation and praise bring out the best in him and with them he can perform miracles. Despite being plagued by frothy inhibitions, the Cancerian Sheep will be largely unselfish and will take great interest in his home and domestic duties. He will also be a patron of the arts. Definitely not a solitary soul, he or she will need a lot of friends and family members around to keep him happy.

If you are born in the year of the Sheep under the Western sign of

Leo: 22nd July to 21st August
The Leo Sheep = Fire + Negative Fire

The assertive Lion will ease the Sheep's shyness and make him bold and high-spirited. The Leo Sheep will be respected and will strive nobly to live up to the confidence placed in him. Less pessimistic and not as easily cajoled by criticism, this Sheep can stand on his own two feet and win the approval he seeks. Fortified by Leo's will and strong character, he is more independent, and will never be lacking in warmth. The Sheep loves to mother others and Leo's generosity is renowned. This sun-moon personality will radiate his kindness to all who come in contact with him.

If you are born in the year of the Sheep under the Western sign of

Virgo: 22nd August to 22nd September
The Virgo Sheep = Earth + Negative Fire

The Sheep is elegant and full of niceties but a bit of a spendthrift. The Virgin is more somber and much more careful with finances. Here, in this combination, we could find the Sheep practicing the virtues of thrift, self-denial and cold resolve. The congenial Sheep will be more resolute if the positive qualities of both are enhanced. Virgo can be a perfectionist and tireless worker. The Sheep is sociable and popular, and he will want to move in the best circles. Here is a more reliable Sheep who values commitment and personal relationships. He is devoted to friends and family and will always have their interests at heart.

If you are born in the year of the Sheep under the Western sign of

Libra: 23rd September to 22nd October
The Libran Sheep = Air + Negative Fire

The Libran Sheep loves and needs attention and sympathy. Approval and friendship are of the utmost importance to him. He or she may look as fragile and exquisite as bone china, but there is a certain restiveness and built-in resilience in this person. An authority on art forms and beauty, he has a superb sense of balance and color. The Libran Sheep is also inclined to be cultured, refined and fastidious in his dress and grooming. His very receptive nature causes him to delay too long and too often, tirelessly tallying up votes and gathering more opinions. If he cannot capitalize on his talents through the forceful management of others, he may end up being a fence-sitter.

If you are born in the year of the Sheep under the Western sign of

Scorpio: 23rd October to 21st November
The Scorpio Sheep = Water + Negative Fire

The sober by-product of this Water and Fire mixture is a person strong of mind and body, graced with a delicacy of expression and creativity that could fool even the most experienced observers. He listens to his intuitions, his loved ones and finally to public opinion—in that order. But whatever Scorpio may have planned, the Sheep puts a limit on the price he will pay for success. He won't like to deliberately hurt others or gloat over his victories. Scorpio is a good co-sign here for the Sheep, as it prevents this subject from wallowing in self-pity and forces him to act on his own more often. Successful and confident, he has innate confidence in his own abilities.

THE SEASONS OF THE SHEEP

SPRING

In the spring, Sheep are bound to get more grass than they do in winter. Consequently, they have a good start in life and will be well-taken care of. However, they may also be the most indulged of the lot as their parents are likely to spoil or pamper them. As a result, they could easily lose interest in various endeavors and avoid commitment as well. They will be popular because of their sweet disposition, but may tend to depend on others to the point of losing their own identity. However, those Sheep born during the day are more sociable, alert and communicative. They also tend to become more involved in things. Overall, the talented spring Sheep will be known for his artistic abilities and impeccable taste. He can contribute much if he is encouraged and directed in the right way.

SUMMER

The summer Sheep is more confident than other Sheep and will be charming and hard to resist. Many people will help look after his interests and he will be well-provided for in life. Intelligent, skillful at projecting his own image and self-indulgent at times, the summer Sheep has trouble keeping a tight rein on his emotions and tends to act on the spur of the moment. Usually successful in his undertakings, the Sheep of summer often expects others to clean up whatever mess he gets himself into. Caution and thrift are foreign to him. He would prefer to buy now and pay later. Fortunately, he always seems to receive bounty from unlikely sources, and people come to his aid whenever he is in need. Important, influential and powerful supporters seem particularly fond of the summer Sheep and will take him under their wing.

AUTUMN

A Sheep born in the fall cherishes his security above all and consequently tends to worry unnecessarily. He has a stable personality and values propriety in his actions. His shyness or reticent nature is a protective shell behind which he takes refuge when his feelings are injured. He can be a die-hard romantic and will worship and woo the object of his affections with great devotion. Definitely not a risk taker, he prefers to go with the majority and not against the flow of popular concensus.

Usually he is dedicated to his goals in life and does not adapt well to abrupt changes. The Sheep born in the fall is not combative and dislikes any discord. He constantly strives for harmony and acceptance. He could find a niche in the arts, where he will be valued for his talents and contributions.

WINTER

The winter Sheep is usually a picture of grace and decorum. Likely to be well-read and elegant, he will have expensive tastes and will be drawn to high society. He or she knows how to cultivate helpful friends and reach influential circles. Quiet, observant and wise in his own way, he will be well-versed in self-preservation. He could be the most calculating and possessive of all Sheep. Clannish and sentimental, he will always maintain close ties to family and friends. People will be attracted by his talent for design; he can magnify the beautiful and artistic traits of even the dullest, most generic project. Diplomacy is his calling card and he will never say the wrong or rude thing if he can help it.

Note: It is said in Chinese folklore that a Sheep person born in the winter will lead a harder life than other Sheep because he is classified, together with the Ox and Boar, as a sacrificial animal, and will be slaughtered for food especially in the cold season when there is no grass. However, this no longer holds true as most domestic animals are always valued and well-taken care of and the long-term storage of food for winter is no longer a problem.

FAMOUS PERSONS BORN IN THE YEAR OF THE SHEEP

Metal
Andy Warhol
Barbara Walters
Catherine Deneuve
Mikhail Gorbachev
Rev. Desmond Tutu

Wood
Andrew Carnegie
Archbishop Fulton J. Sheen
King George IV
Rudolph Valentino
Michelangelo Buonarroti

Fire
Miguel de Cervantes
James Michener
Takeo Miki
Sir Laurence Olivier

Earth
Dino de Laurentiis
Pierre Trudeau
Ian Smith
Mohammad Reza Pahlavi, Shah of Iran
George Wallace

Water
Muhammad Ali
Douglas Fairbanks
Bobby Fischer
Billie Jean King
John Denver

9

The Ninth Sign
of the Lunar Cycle

The Monkey

I am the seasoned traveler
  of the Labyrinth.
The genius of alacrity,
  wizard of the impossible.
My brilliance is yet unmatched
  in its originality.
My heart's filled with potent magic
  that could cast a hundred spells.
I am put together
  for mine own pleasure.

I AM THE MONKEY.

Lunar Years of the Monkey in the Western Calendar   Elements

2 February 1908 to 21 January 1909	Earth
20 February 1920 to 7 February 1921	Metal
6 February 1932 to 25 January 1933	Water
25 January 1944 to 12 February 1945	Wood
12 February 1956 to 30 January 1957	Fire
30 January 1968 to 16 February 1969	Earth
16 February 1980 to 4 February 1981	Metal
4 February 1992 to 22 January 1993	Water
22 January 2004 to 8 February 2005	Wood

If you were born on the day before the start of the lunar year of the Monkey, e.g., 29th January 1968, your animal sign is the one before the Monkey, the Sheep, the eighth lunar sign.

If you were born on the day after the last day of the lunar year of the Monkey, e.g., 17th February 1969, your sign is the one following the Monkey, the Rooster, the tenth lunar sign.

The sign of the Monkey rules the two-hour segment of the day between 3 P.M. and 5 P.M. Persons born during this time are said to have the Monkey as their ascendant and will display many of the characteristics common to this sign and also have a great affinity for persons born under this sign.

The direction appointed to the Monkey is west-southwest; its season is summer and its principle month, August. The Monkey corresponds to the Western astrological sign of Leo, which rules summer from July 22nd to August 21st. The Monkey is considered a male or yang sign and its fixed element is Metal.

THE MONKEY PERSONALITY

Of all the animals in the lunar cycle, the Monkey bears the closest resemblance to the Naked Ape himself, Man. It is therefore no wonder that this sign will inherit most of man's intelligence as well as his capacity for deceit.

In the Chinese zodiac, the Monkey is the sign of the inventor, the improvisor and the motivator, a charlatan capable of drawing everyone to him with his inimitable guile and charm. Being the quick-witted genius of the cycle, he is clever, flexible and innovative. The Monkey can solve intricate problems with ease and will be a very fast learner. He can master anything under the sun and usually has good linguistic aptitude. A person born during this year will be successful at whatever he chooses to do. No challenge will be too great for him.

On the negative side, the Monkey person has an inborn superiority complex. As a result, he doesn't have enough respect for others. Or rather, from his point of view, he has too much respect for himself. He can be extremely selfish, egotistic and vain. There is also a jealous streak in him that surfaces every time someone gets a promotion or something he does not have. He is extremely competitive, but good at concealing his feelings and planning his cunning moves. In the pursuit of money, success or power, the Monkey's prowess is unbeatable.

Because of his innate versatility, the Monkey-born can be a good actor, writer, diplomat, lawyer, sportsman, stockbroker, teacher, etc. He is an immensely sociable character who can get on the good side of everyone. He has the rare gift of making you like him even after he has tricked you.

In the Monkey's many-sided personality, the one quality that isn't missing is confidence, no matter how shy or docile he may look. He has an intense and unshakeable belief in himself. He will also take care to display a proper demeanor, well-rehearsed politeness and a calm dignity. But it would be inaccurate to dub the Monkey as a completely selfish person. No, he is more like a child in his delightful preoccupation with himself. He can be totally oblivious of others if they are not directly involved in what he is doing at the moment. He views himself with the same fascination and ecstatic joy that a baby exhibits the first time he learns how to play with his fingers and toes. Observe how the infant reacts when he discovers how to clap his hands. He will squeal with glee and proceed to do the same thing over and over until he masters the act. Totally occupied with his marvelous discovery, he is unaware of anything else.

So you will find the Monkey evincing the same unabashed joy at his own cleverness and brilliant accomplishments. He won't masquerade his pride but neither will he be coy about it. He honestly believes there isn't anyone else around who can top his act.

If you really know the Monkey well, you will always find it difficult to begrudge his wonderful joie de vivre. It's what makes him so different from others, so enviable at times.

Even in the Bible one can spot a Monkey. Mary Magdalene could well have been a she-Monkey, while the Prodigal Son was definitely a he-Monkey. If you care to recall, they both got to eat their cake and keep it, too. How unfair that they should get to slide back into everyone's good graces like that! But there you have it. The Monkey's not only lucky and clever, but also unsinkable.

Throwing insults, accusations and reprimands at him will prove ineffective—even frustrating. They will just bounce off him harmlessly. It's simply unthinkable for him to believe all those nasty things you call him. It can't be true. He will find your admonitions baseless, maybe even hysterically funny. He has such an accurate picture of himself, his talents and his well-deserved good fortune, that you must be insanely jealous to make such ridiculous statements.

The Monkey does not lack credibility. His main problem lies in yielding to temptation, because he finds it amazingly easy to devise ways to justify his actions or solve dilemmas without too much expense. He relies on brain power, which he has in abundance. As a result, he finds it difficult to get people to trust him. With such an innately clever personality, others are always tempted to suspect his motives. Monkey people are often judged harshly or accused erroneously by those not as able as they are. The Monkey's popularity rating can go up and down like a yoyo. Yet he never seems overly concerned about your opinion of him, no matter how contrite he appears. Perhaps it's because he knows he can always get you to change it.

This does not mean that the Monkey is callous or refuses to accept criticism. Not in the least—when you get to know him, that is. It is just that he realizes before everyone else that nothing is permanent or irreparable. Don't sulk, despair or cry "Doomsday." Let him put his gray matter to work and soon things will be right side up again.

Remember, to him, records were made to be broken, standards to be upgraded to higher specifications, inventions to be rendered obsolete by more sophisticated designs. He is the impresario, the perpetual improver. Rarely discouraged by his failures or impressed by the successes of others, the Monkey strives constantly to do better and often astonishes even himself.

When dealing with a Monkey—be factual. Objectivity is something he lives by. But ultimately, you might as well know, it doesn't matter to him whether or not you approve of his methods. He needs only one sanction—his own.

The Monkey-born can clinch any bargain with a flourish. You will find him conscientious about wheedling the little extras that go along with the deal, too. He may not pounce on you like the Tiger or immobilize you with the power gaze of the Dragon; he will just take one teeny-weeny inch at a time, which may seem quite harmless, but do your arithmetic quickly and you will find that twelve inches makes a foot and three feet a yard. But by the time you finish your calculations you may be surprised by how far he has crept up on you.

His coups de grâce have a lethal whiplash all of their own. But then, after you regain consciousness, you must admit that you have never been kayoed with more charm and ingenuity.

But don't worry, you will live. And just as soon as you have recovered sufficiently from the first shock, he'll be back with an even nicer package, a brand-new failproof scheme, and sure enough you will fall neatly under his spell again. See what I mean? What has he got—witchcraft, sorcery? Never mind, it's too late now; you are a Monkey addict and you are hooked on him or her.

The Monkey is an intellectual. With his superb intelligence, keen memory and mental proficiency, he cannot help but be a winner in just about any area. His genius is fueled by insatiable curiosity. He must try anything at least once. If he is stumped by a problem, he will nonchalantly go on to invent a solution. What else? Besides being bright and crafty, the Monkey is practical; he counts his dollars and cents. You won't find him wasting time or money on losing enterprises.

A realist, adroit in self-preservation, the Monkey will not hesitate to take the easiest way out of a trap. When he is cornered, he can be unscrupulous in his means of escape. But the Monkey does have a conscience, and when it bothers him too much, he will be hit by bouts of charity and may be overwhelmingly generous all of a sudden. Make hay while the sun shines, for these bouts will not last long.

The Monkey girl is Miss Sparkle herself. A natural performer, she creates excitement and stimulation wherever she goes. Few people will be left unstirred by her liveliness and provocative beauty.

She has a good head for figures and will adapt easily to change. She will work with any group, given enough incentive (often monetary) and sound reasons to do so. A great party-goer, entertaining speaker, gracious hostess and tactful confidant, the lady Monkey must never be underestimated. She is ultracompetitive, observant and calculating. Ms. Monkey will also be attracted to the limelight and could be a gifted performer. Cheerful and resourceful, she can take disappointment in stride and will be able to work on her own initiative from the word "Go." This efficient female will not need you to lead her by the hand every step of the way. Independent and self-assured, she knows exactly where she wants to go and may be able to teach you a few handy shortcuts of her own. She may be nosey, but she won't be giving away any of her secrets in exchange for your well-guarded information.

Good at choosing her words, the Monkey girl will say the right thing at the right time. She rarely blunders on important matters or makes silly, unfounded remarks. She's as adept at getting her own way as she is an excellent judge of character, and she will never exceed her limits. You won't find her doling out money either. One has to perform if one expects her to pay something—and perform well, because she can be very critical and snobbish.

The Monkey female is a fashionable but neat dresser; she is especially vain about her hair. Her grooming and coiffure will be as excellent and as fashionable as she can afford. It should be noted that the Monkey native is most prone to skin ailments or allergies. The Monkey girl will have sensitive skin and break out with a rash if she uses too much cosmetics. Although she seems to pamper herself unstintingly, she is not tardy or disorganized. Besides her many activities, she will still find the time and energy to take up several hobbies and investigate every aspect of things that appeal to her. She is one of the most up-to-date women in town. Every Monkey will be an original; they don't make molds of this character and stamp them out by the dozen. Yet in spite of his many flaws, people will rally around him simply because they cannot do without the Monkey's expertise and skills.

He is the top PR man—remarkably original, shrewd with money and, in fact, such a wizard at manipulating everything that industry, politics and trade would be lost without him. The Monkey's guile is famous throughout Chinese history and his name is synonymous with cleverness. He is certainly a big asset to have on your team. But first make sure he is 100 percent on your side. There are bound to be some mercenary Monkeys in the tribe.

It is difficult to be angry with the Monkey for long because he is an expert at making himself likeable and indispensable. He will always maneuver himself into a lucrative position. When he loses, the Monkey is no stubborn fool; he knows how to give in when the odds are stacked against him. Master of the art of survival, the Monkey thrives by the "better to run away and live to fight another day" philosophy.

The Monkey is a born strategist. He never moves without a plan, probably several plans. He'll never turn his back on opportunity (which he will recognize in any disguise) and he'll hitch his wagon to a star, a Cadillac, a jet plane, or anything else that moves. He loves free rides and will travel first-class whenever possible.

The Monkey makes a good critic. He can pinpoint the specific area where something went wrong and suggest workable remedies. Of course, how he goes about it will depend on what type of Monkey he is. Some lower types can be so smug that you would rather die before accepting their help.

But generally speaking, a Monkey is a warm, natural and sponta- neous person who is prepared to work hard—especially if he gets a piece of the action. The bigger the piece, the harder he pitches. Pay him with peanuts and he will turn the tables on you, giving you nothing but peanut shells in return. Take a good piece of advice: Never try to trick a Monkey. Chances are you won't get away with it. Aside from being an expert at taking revenge, the Monkey-born will usually have a wry sense of humor. You catch him chuckling wickedly more often than laughing heartily.

Since the Monkey gets what he wants without too much effort or struggle, he will not treasure his conquests. He loses interest. He should learn to be more constant and more serious. In his life, he will trust only a handful of people and will not have many real or long friendships because of his complicated and suspicious personality. He dislikes confiding in others.

Nonetheless, the Monkey is very much in demand. The Rat will be enchanted by his ingenuity. They will recognize each other by the dollar signs in their eyes. The Dragon will seek him out for his superior wits. Rabbit, Sheep, Dog, Horse and Ox will all benefit from the Monkey's versatility and value his competence. The Boar and Rooster will likewise have need of the Monkey's genius.

Naturally, the Snake with all his wisdom and similarly doubting mind will never be completely comfortable with the Monkey. The Tiger should avoid getting into the Monkey's path, as he will be the prime target of the Monkey's mischief and pranks. The Monkey cannot but show his prowess when challenged, and upon discovering that the Tiger is a bad loser, he will revel in annoying him.

In the final analysis, the Monkey is the supreme innovator and problem solver; the mastermind of the lunar cycle who does not have the word NO in his vocabulary. Like it or not, we will eventually have need of his expertise and superior brain power.

THE MONKEY CHILD

The Monkey child will be captivating. Bright-eyed and bushy-tailed, he won't keep still for a moment. Cheerful, mischievous and very competitive, he will steal his way into your heart. Skillful at flattery and extremely good at playing on your weaknesses, the incorrigible Monkey will always get what he is after.

Unpredictable and ingenious, this curious youngster will usually be found fidgeting with some device. Don't be too upset if he breaks his toys. It is simply because he is not attracted by the exterior; he takes things apart to get inside and see what makes them tick. Intricate or mechanically moving contraptions never fail to amuse or fascinate him. He will be forever trailing after you with brilliant questions about the universe.

One of these days, when you are about to throw out that unreliable clock that never worked well, your Monkey child will pick it up and fix it with a hairpin. Despite all his talents and possessions, however, he is never contented. The grass always looks greener on the other side. The ambitious and conniving little imp is always taking stock of other people's belongings.

He is constantly goaded to improve himself and he prides himself on his vast accumulation of knowledge and skills. He will be involved in myriad activities. Today he will be investigating photography and tomorrow he may be building himself a computer. The Monkey loves electronic gadgetry. Somehow, he knows the right buttons to push. The remarkable thing is that the Monkey can divide his attention among several subjects and still be able to master them all. He can be snobbish and cocky and will like to tease others with his versatile wit. Optimistic and forever hopeful, he will never concede defeat. He will try and try again until he succeeds.

The Monkey child will have a selfish streak and may refuse to share what he has while skillfully helping himself to other children's toys. And, when he does share, he will carefully consider what he can get in return. Even the smallest Monkey is adept at weighing the pros and cons. He will cry foul at the slightest edge others may have over him, but expects you to close both eyes if the scales tip in his favor. Excitable, pretentious and crafty, he will ignore any regulation that restricts him. He should be taught early in life that he cannot always get everything his way—but this does not mean he will not try. The odds are he will probably wear us out before we get him to see things our way.

Then, just when you have reached saturation point and become totally exasperated with him, the Monkey will turn on his sweet saintly smile, apologize from the bottom of his heart, pour flattery all over your wounds and stand on his head to make you laugh. You will immediately forget all the harsh measures you were going to take against him and become his willing captive all over again. Sometimes, Monkey parents have the feeling that they can't live with this child, but that they can't live without him either. But no matter what happens, you can be sure that the Monkey child will bring joy and excitement into your life.

THE FIVE DIFFERENT MONKIES

METAL MONKEY—1920, 1980

This is the fighting Monkey. Strong, sophisticated and independent, he will have an irrepressible urge for financial security. Capable of making wise investments, this type of Monkey will prefer to run his own business or earn extra money from outside work if he has a regular job. He is consistent and will be able to hold on to his savings if he doesn't speculate in any risky ventures.

Metal makes him ardent and demonstrative in his affections. He will have high aspirations and may appear to be status-seeking or overdramatic at times. Still, one can't help but admire how he is always trying to better himself.

Characterized by a lively disposition, the passionate Metal Monkey can be warm, positive and very convincing. He is able to sell you anything conceivable, and his designs, if he is creative, will be both aesthetic and useful. The Metal Monkey can be an excellent trendsetter.

When he is negative, the analytical Metal Monkey can be exceedingly self-conscious and overly proud. His loyalties will be few and limited to people linked only to himself.

Hard-working and practical, he shuns assistance from others and will be more than able to take care of his own interests.

WATER MONKEY—1932, 1992

This is a cooperative but speculative Monkey. The "You scratch my back and I'll scratch yours" sort of person. Yet, in spite of his dignified and worldly demeanor, this type of Monkey is more easily offended than other Monkeys. He will have a secretive but kind nature, and can be deft and patient in the pursuit of his objectives.

Water mated with his native sign imparts to him a greater sense of purpose. But he will not be too direct or obvious in revealing his intentions. He can compromise with grace and work around barriers rather than waste time and energy knocking them down.

The Water Monkey will have flair and originality; he motivates himself as well as others with his pleasant ways, and his ideas meet little resistance because of his ingenious ways of introducing them. He will present things in their best possible light. He has a keen understanding of how human relationships function and will use this knowledge to achieve his ends.

When he decides to be negative, the Water Monkey can suffer from lack of direction. He vacillates and becomes erratic, evasive and meddling. If he can keep the lines of communication open, he should be able to weather all storms with aplomb. Patience is a virtue he must cultivate. After all, everyone cannot be on his wavelength all the time. While people do appreciate his expertise, sometimes they have their own opinions, too.

WOOD MONKEY—1944, 2004

Good rapport with others will be essential to this type of Monkey. But he does not pry into affairs of those around him if possible, and prides himself on keeping his house and accounts in good order.

Although he is basically honorable and desirous of prestige, this Monkey will be restless and have a strong pioneering spirit. He is alert to everything going on around him, and is very curious about new inventions or modes of thinking. The Wood element gives him an intuitive cast of mind, which enables him to predict the probable outcome of events. He searches constantly for answers and will not take setbacks calmly.

While maintaining his own admirable standards, the Wood Monkey will strive constantly to elevate himself above his present station. He is never quite satisfied with what he has and is always on the lookout for greener pastures. As a result, this type of Monkey will leap at new challenges.

This resourceful person will establish order in whatever work he decides to take up. He is rarely given to exaggeration or speculation. Carefully, carefully, he whittles away the opposition bit by bit. Never underestimate him.

FIRE MONKEY—1956,

This active and energetic Monkey will have the traits of a natural leader and innovator. He is self-assured and determined, expressive and truthful, and very interested in the opposite sex.

The Fire element lends him great vitality, and he has a tendency to dominate or teach those less aggressive than himself. He possesses a fertile imagination and should be careful not to let his ideas run away with him. He is inventive but not always cautious about possible consequences.

The Fire Monkey has a powerful and constant drive to reach the top of his professional field. He is competitive to the extreme and capable of great jealousy. His creativity is born of willpower, necessity and initiative, and these enable him to upstage others and keep one step ahead of the game.

The Fire Monkey is the most forceful of all the Monkeys. He relishes being in control and can be opinionated, stubborn and argumentative when he is negative. He is lucky in speculative ventures, especially because he can correctly evaluate risks. But in spite of the bold and collected face he presents to the public, this type of Monkey conceals morbid suspicions of how others may be deceiving him.

EARTH MONKEY—1908, 1968

The placid and reliable Earth Monkey may have a cool and collected nature. He is expansive and given to disinterested acts of charity.

He quietly demands admiration and appreciation of his talents and for his services. If these are not forthcoming, he can sulk and become withdrawn. At times, he appears eccentric because he can be a deep thinker who may have difficulty explaining his novel ideas to others. His genius may go abegging if he refuses to be more conventional.

He is likely to be an intellectual and will be academically studious or very well-read if he is not able to pursue a higher education. Generally, he will be honest and straightforward and will achieve distinction through his thoroughness and devotion to duty.

The Earth Monkey will not be too fond of entertaining, but he will be genuinely kind and loving to those he cares about. Less concerned about his ego than other Monkeys, he can devote himself unselfishly to the good of all. He will value his integrity and can even be overconscientious about operating only within the law.

COMPATIBILITY AND CONFLICT CHARTS
FOR THE MONKEY

The Monkey is part of the First Triangle of Affinity, a group of positive people who are identified as DOERS. The Rat, the Dragon and the Monkey are performance- and progress-oriented signs adept at handling matters with initiative and innovation. Self-starters, they prefer to initiate action, clear their paths of uncertainty and hesitation, and forge ahead. Restless and short-tempered when hindered or forced to be unoccupied, they are full of dynamic energy and ambition. This trio is the melting pot of ideas. They can team up beautifully because they possess a common way of doing things and will appreciate each other's method of thinking.

TRIANGLE OF AFFINITY FOR THE MONKEY

The Monkey will encounter his most serious personality clashes with someone born in the year of the Tiger. Anyone whose ascendant is the Tiger will most likely also come into conflict with the Monkey. In the Circle of Conflict, the Monkey and Tiger are on opposite sides, 180 degrees apart. Metal, the Monkey's fixed element, is detrimental to Wood, the Tiger's fixed element. They will have different opinions and outlooks and difficulty understanding each other or comprehending one another's motives. Unless a Tiger native is born during the hours of the Monkey or vice versa, there is little these two will find in common. Besides trying to upstage each other, the Monkey and Tiger have entirely opposite views and will do things that may be counterproductive to each other, perhaps without even knowing it. Unintentional as these actions may be, they tend to produce friction and suspicions.

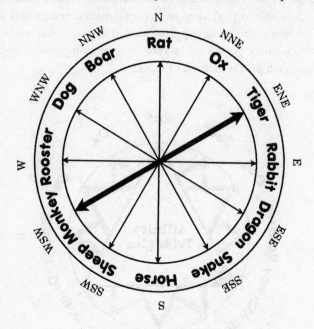

CIRCLE OF CONFLICT

Aside from the most compatible signs, the Dragon and Monkey, and the most incompatible, the Tiger, the other nine signs are compatible with the Monkey to varying degrees.

Ox

The Monkey and the Ox have mutual reservations about each other, and for good reason. The clever Monkey with his intricate thinking process, may sometimes be irritated by the Ox's methodical and stoical ways. The Ox, on the other hand, may find the Monkey's schemes of doubtful merit and cannot comprehend the Monkey's bright but overly-complicated ideas. However, these two signs would actually make a good team if they learn to use the qualities the other has to offer. This way, their differences would be turned into their strengths and they could be a formidable twosome.

Rabbit

The Rabbit may be impressed by the Monkey's superior intelligence and ingenuity, but he may find it hard to trust him unless they share a common ascendant. Then again, the Rabbit never completely trusts anyone and neither does the Monkey. Both are great poker players, but they are also such great sports that they are not sore losers. They could put aside their differences and their subtle rivalry if they find a cause worthy of their combined efforts. The Rabbit knows how to make the Monkey keep his end of the bargain while the Monkey will use his charm to captivate the Rabbit.

Snake

The Snake and the Monkey are two intense and resolute personalities who cannot compromise unless they share a common ascendant and mutual goal. The Monkey finds it hard to trust the Snake completely when this enigmatic creature keeps his thoughts to himself and stares glassy-eyed at the curious Monkey. The Snake, on the other hand, quickly sizes up the clever Monkey and is fearful of the masterful ape's capacity to outwit him when he is not looking. Both will be unable to relax in each other's company for too long and will be looking for each other's shortcomings instead of building a relationship based on their good points.

Horse

The Monkey and the Horse will be able to cooperate to a certain degree and capitalize on each other's talents to achieve common goals. Both signs like getting things done and will not let petty differences get in the way. In this way, they both know the importance of seeing the big picture. Whether or not long-term ties develop depends on how much they enjoy working together. They are both flexible and adaptable to change and may go their separate ways once a mutual benefit no longer exists. The Monkey will appreciate the Horse's lively but practical outlook while the Horse values the Monkey's ingenuity and clever shortcuts.

Sheep

The Monkey will not form strong bonds with the Sheep because he has difficulty understanding the retiring nature of the indulgent Sheep. Their relationship may be cordial to moderately good as the Sheep may have need of the Monkey's skill while the Monkey can benefit from the Sheep's good reputation and popularity. The Monkey may also want to promote the Sheep's many artistic and creative talents and be his manager. The Sheep is too modest to blow his own trumpet, so maybe the Monkey will be his agent—for a healthy share of the Sheep's royalties, of course.

Monkey

Monkey and Monkey make a successful team if they have similar interests or common foes. In love and business, they know how to combine their formidable wits and run circles around the opposition. However, they are also prone to rivalry and jealousy and sometime, somewhere that selfish streak could surface, like when they have to share the spoils. But if both negotiate, compromise or exploit others' weaknesses, they will still end up ahead of the game. The problem is: What if they are not playing the same game? And who says they will follow the rules?

Rooster

Monkeys know how to handle Roosters, but only to a certain degree. They could be immune to Rooster criticism if they want something badly enough, and they are not above flattering the Rooster to put him in a good mood. However, even the Monkey's patience could wear thin if the Rooster insists on examining all the details over and over. Monkeys are easily bored and do not have the long attention spans Roosters do. These two could have very different approaches to a common problem. The Monkey will opt for the shortcut or invent one if possible. The Rooster will take the long and winding path and make simple things difficult by his overanalysis.

Dog

There should be no underlying animosities between the Dog and the Monkey. They have a mutual respect for each other and will try to stay out of each other's way if they have conflicting interests. The Monkey knows better than to step on the Dog's tail since the Dog is unrelenting when aroused. On the whole, the Dog is good-natured when it comes to the Monkey's tricks and will allow the clever Monkey to have his way if he can also benefit. The two signs will enjoy friendly to warm relations if they share mutual friends, goals or interests. However, the Dog is devoted to the Horse and the Tiger, and the Tiger could come between the Dog and the Monkey.

Boar

There will be no large clashes between Monkey and Pig because both are outgoing and can relate easily to each other, especially if they share the same goals. They can establish a fairly good relationship once they realize they need each other's skills. The Monkey can spot opportunity a mile away while the Boar (Mr. Moneybags) will back him up 100 percent. The Monkey will not be as extravagant as the generous Boar and may persuade the Boar not to go overboard entertaining or giving handouts to his family and friends. The Boar also needs the Monkey to curb his optimism and to plan for the unexpected contingencies he may prefer to ignore, but which are sure to crop up in their partnership.

THE MONKEY AND HIS ASCENDANTS

We all have a shadow that follows us throughout life. Sometimes it grows bigger than life and at other times it shrinks until it disappears into the soles of our feet. Sometimes it walks tall before us and on other occasions it lags behind like a sulking friend. In Chinese horoscopes, this constant partner, manifested or not, is our ascendant, the animal sign that rules the hour of our birth and becomes a comrade in our journey through life. We may view it as friend or foe or even a little of both. It surfaces when we least expect and shows a better or worse side of our nature. We can often be confounded by the way we listen to our "other self" as well as feel resentful of the significant influence it can exert on us. Actually, a personality has many rings around the centered "self." Each ring can have a different size, texture and aura. When all these factors combine, they bring forth the unique individual that the person truly is. Hence, a Dragon with an ascendant that is not compatible, like the Dog, has perhaps a more difficult inner struggle than say a Snake born during the hours of the Snake. The double intensity of the Snake person will be easily under-stood by horoscope readers while the more intricate Dragon/Dog may exhibit the contrary Dog and Dragon traits to varying degrees. There are many voices within each person. But, in the end, only the individual determines which course he will follow, which choices he will make.

The time of birth used to determine the ascendant is always the local time in the place of birth.

If you were born between:

11 P.M. and 1 A.M. = The Hours of the Rat

You are blessed with a sparkling personality. Nothing will stop you from savoring everything life has to offer and hanging on to your money at the same time. With the Rat as your ascendant, you will be very enterprising but also sentimental. You will always try to hire your relatives and old classmates and will never like to turn friends away. Frugal, possessive and inquisitive, you are likely to be the life of the party.

1 A.M. and 3 A.M. = The Hours of the Ox

You could be a quiet Monkey, straitlaced but with better creden-tials. With the Ox as your ascendant, you tend to favor the sure and proper way of doing things. Never one to leave things to chance, you tend to plan way, way in advance, and you can be harsh to anyone who does not follow the rules. A good student, hard worker and patient teacher, you put your responsibilities first and believe in caution and devotion to duty.

3 A.M. and 5 A.M. = The Hours of the Tiger

With the colorful Tiger as your ascendant, you could be a forceful and exuberant Monkey. However, both signs here are too self-confident and a bit wary of other people and their motives. You have great vitality and charm, but if you are overly aggressive, you could land in a heap of trouble and still you might be unwilling to take anybody's advice or concede defeat. Nonetheless, it will be impossible to keep you down or ignore your many talents and contributions. Get a handle on your unpredictable temper and half your battles are won.

5 A.M. and 7 A.M. = The Hours of the Rabbit

Since you are fortunate enough to have the Rabbit as your ascendant, you will be a subtle, less mischievous Monkey with more caution and restraint. You could be almost psychic in your assessments and dealings with others. You are discreet and careful, make wise decisions and give excellent advice. The Rabbit provides you with tact and good taste while the Monkey side can still be calculating and ambitious. But, with your savoir faire, no one will ever know unless you let your guard down. And that is most unlikely.

7 A.M. and 9 A.M. = The Hours of the Dragon

The bombastic Dragon ascendant produces an overconscientious and doubly ambitious Monkey. With your phenomenal prowess and the Dragon's high-powered drive, you will prefer to do things on a grand scale and organize vast projects to show off your expertise. Thankfully, you may be the kind of person others rally to and support. With the Dragon in you and your natural Monkey genius, your wildest dreams could come true, if you don't get carried away by your uncontrollable imagination and optimism.

9 A.M. and 11 A.M. = The Hours of the Snake

With the wisdom of the Snake thrown into this combination, you could be a Monkey with great intellect and penetrative powers. You will probably have considerable sex appeal because of that Snake mystique. Tenacious and introverted, you rarely like to explain yourself at length. Formulating your plans in secret, you tend to strike when ready. It will be very difficult for anyone to second-guess you, and they shouldn't even bother to try.

11 A.M. and 1 P.M. = The Hours of the Horse

With the strong and independent Horse as your ascendant, your reflexes will be superior and you are destined to be athletic or sports-loving. Although you tend to make hasty judgements and can be outrageously bold and stubborn, you are liked for your ability to act on your convictions in a commanding way. Your magnetic Monkey personality will opt for quick, easy and unconventional solutions to problems, and you will be very realistic in your outlook. A capable doer, you love to be in the thick of action and are not likely to be a person who shies away from confrontation.

1 P.M. to 3 P.M. = The Hours of the Sheep

You will be a dreamy, romantic and artistic Monkey with many wiles and creative ideas. The Sheep ascendant could make you oversensitive, even melodramatic at times, but the winning Monkey wits should be as sharp as ever. In spite of your peaceful demeanor, you will not miss many opportunities to exploit your talents and resources. Your agreeable and acquiescent nature makes it easy for you to deal with people from all walks of life and get them to trust you. Your success usually comes from working well in a team and you are able to secure considerable influence by networking among your many contacts.

3 P.M. and 5 P.M. = The Hours of the Monkey

Having the same ascendant as your birth sign makes you a "pure" sign, so that you will have whatever positive or negative qualities inherent to your birth sign magnified. Yours could be an extremely adroit and highly evolved personality who will be convivial and supremely optimistic. There isn't anything you cannot do or get away with. Affable, ambitious and always enthusiastic, you will be a problem solver of the highest order. Fascinating and adaptable, you could be an inventor or a master tactician. Your wit and ability to improvise makes you very competitive. If there is an answer to any mystery, you will be the one to find it.

5 P.M. and 7 P.M. = The Hours of the Rooster

The Rooster ascendant makes you an unconventional and adventurous Monkey with very high aspirations. With the Monkey's aptitude, perhaps even the Rooster's daydreams could come true. Calculating, methodical and a tireless investigator you are a veritable storehouse of knowledge and an overachiever with a computer-like brain. Your deductive powers and love of precision and perfection make you an industrious and tenacious worker. However, you should sharpen that Monkey love of humor and zest for life and not be a workaholic like the Rooster.

7 P.M. and 9 P.M. = The Hours of the Dog

With the Dog as your ascendant, you are less materialistic, more loyal and law-abiding, somewhat emotionally detached and less inclined to accept every challenge that comes your way. You don't have to constantly be the best or the brightest. Being loved and accepted for who you are is often satisfying in itself. The Dog may even turn you into a cool satirist who prefers a simple, rustic life. Still, the Dog makes you a realist who prefers to take the middle of the road. Fair-minded, but not apt to hold your tongue, you tend to be protective and honest in your dealings with everyone.

9 P.M. and 11 P.M. = The Hours of the Boar

The Boar that hides in your heart will make you a sporting and less self-conscious Monkey. With the scrupulous Boar's presence, you are not as devious and are easier to deal with. You will strive hard to keep your end of any bargain. A generous heart and larger-than-life need to be appreciated will characterize your personality. Helpful, sincere and amorous, you could be passionate and devoted to both your duty and those you love. You have the ability to overcome great odds with your endurance and tactical mind. Everyone would do well to consult you regarding work or play—you tend to be an expert in whatever field you choose.

HOW THE MONKEY FARES IN THE LUNAR CYCLE

1. The Year of the Rat 1996

The year of the Rat will be a lucky and prosperous one for his friend, the Monkey. Money could come from unlikely sources and he could benefit from ventures he has given up on. This is definitely the time for the Monkey to harvest the many seeds he may have planted in the past. He should also follow up on opportunities and advance his position or ask for loans and favors owed him. On the homefront, he will have a lot of activities—romance, new family members or a big reunion and renewal of old contacts. Problems are easily solved at this time and the Monkey's know-how is sought after by important people.

2. The Year of the Ox 1997

The Ox brings a somewhat moderate year for the aspirations of the Monkey. His profits and enjoyment of life are restricted by the Ox's discipline and regimentation; he must pay more attention to his responsibilities at this time. Although his earnings may increase, he may feel his progress is not up to par. His family life and love life remain calm but he may have to travel and work long hours. This is a year to bide his time, be diligent and curtail his ambition. However, his achievements will be considerable if the Monkey remains consistent and tenacious.

3. The Year of the Tiger 1998

The Tiger brings joy and dissent in the same boat, and the Monkey's affairs of the heart could be turbulent or, at the least, very exciting. Good news and bad news keep the Monkey at both ends of the emotional spectrum, and he must discount whatever profits he's expecting. It is better for the Monkey to be conservative during the Tiger's year. While he has the advantage of being quick and clever, it is not advisable to bait or tease the Tiger this year. Instead, the Monkey should consolidate his resources and think twice before embarking on new ventures. Perseverance and understanding will be the Monkey's best allies this year.

4. The Year of the Rabbit 1999

This will be a good year for the Monkey as the Rabbit brings him better prospects and situations in which the Monkey could capitalize on his wits. Benefits accrue to him from unlikely friends and places. His domestic life and love life will be tranquil, and his career or business will enjoy some upward gains. A safe time for him to make changes in his environment and check out various opportunities. The sensible Rabbit helps the Monkey develop new contacts and ideas. He is able to sell himself and find ways to promote his many abilities. However, the Monkey should watch his tongue and not be over-confident or boastful. People could use his ideas or what he says against him if he is not careful and vigilant.

5. The Year of the Dragon 2000

The Dragon year brings gains for the Monkey more in the form of knowledge or technical know-how than money. The Dragon's year is bright, dynamic and lucky for him. He will make new and influential friends under the auspices of the mighty Dragon and he will be able to market his ideas and find supporters who will invest in him. But the Dragon can blow both hot and cold, so this is not a year to speculate or assume everything will go his way. He must hedge his bets and resist the urge to overspend or be overly optimistic. The Dragon's bounty and promise are never final until the check is cashed.

6. The Year of the Snake 2001

The year of the Snake could prove fortunate for the Monkey if he can avoid confrontation. This is not a time to prove his prowess or engage in any kind of brinksmanship. The Monkey will receive support from his family, superiors and also find romance provided he stays safely within his own boundaries. The Snake reign does not favor too much adventure or speculation for the Monkey, and his happiness could be spoiled by disputes if he sticks his nose where it does not belong. But the practical and capable Monkey is quite likely to come to the obvious conclusion that if he cannot beat the opposition, he should join 'em. That may well be the best policy for this year.

7. The Year of the Horse 2002

This will be a fair year for the Monkey born although he may be faced with extra work and worries that take up a good deal of his time. His frustrations will work themselves out as the Horse tends to be quite efficient at resolving problems, though not always to the Monkey's satisfaction. However, he must be observant and nimble as opportunity does not knock twice during the reign of the Horse. It will be a time to take advantage of the moment and to make hay while the sun shines. The Monkey should expect the best but be prepared for the worst, and should not underestimate the changeable nature of the capricious Horse. In this year, it's best to take whatever he can get as soon as he can get it. Tomorrow, it might not be there.

8. The Year of the Sheep 2003

The Sheep's year brings many involvements for the Monkey and a great proportion of them will be emotional; they could include romance, family ties and marriage. The Monkey may have to meet unexpected expenses, help others out of a jam or entertain and travel more than he likes. But, on the whole, he will be much in demand and sought after by friends and family. He must be discreet and keep his mouth shut, as troubles could be caused by a careless remark or a secret inadvertently revealed. People tend to want something from the Monkey this year; he would be wise to dig beneath the surface and look into their motives before making any long-term commitments. Otherwise, the Monkey should be able to get through the Sheep's reign with little difficulty.

9. The Year of the Monkey 2004

This will be an excellent and fruitful time for the Monkey; his expertise will receive recognition and he finds happiness in his achievements. He will also make progress in his career or further his education. Romance, family and personal affairs will proceed smoothly and enjoyably. Headaches could come mainly from subordinates, debtors or people who finance his bold undertakings and are impatient with his performance. It is also a year to watch out for jealousy and underhanded competitors. The Monkey cannot be expected to please every-one, even in his own year, so it would be advisable not to worry about what people think or about how he could appease them. Sometimes, that is just impossible. Health problems could also arise from overexertion and poor eating habits if the Monkey neglects his own well-being.

10. The Year of the Rooster 2005

The Rooster could usher in a moderate but stable year for the Monkey's undertakings. He will find the extra money he needs and have the right contacts to push his plans through. But the Rooster is critical and demanding. This may be a time for the Monkey to watch his finances and be more frugal and conservative. Friends, family and romantic ties tend to get complicated as the Monkey tries to juggle work and play. He must slow down or he will find himself exhausted and overextended from his many commitments. He should also listen to his superiors and respect their authority, otherwise they could give him trouble. In the Rooster's year one must not underestimate one's opponents or overestimate one's profits.

11. The Year of the Dog 2006

This may be the year in which the Monkey discovers who his true friends are. The Dog year brings reality and responsibility to the Monkey born and he should take stock of what he wants in life. His investments should pay off handsomely and he may be in a position to help others. This is a time for him to mend fences and establish long-term relationships. His family, friends and associates will need his support and understanding. The Monkey would be wise to spend more time with those who matter most to him instead of relentlessly pursuing fame and fortune. His happiness will come from the home-front and his services will not go unrewarded.

12. The Year of the Boar 2007

This could be an active but trying year for the Monkey. Many small misunderstandings could test his patience and things won't move as fast as he expects. The Boar is not the swiftest nor most nimble of animals, but he is capable of selfless devotion and charity. The Monkey tends to be self-involved and may not like the compromises he has to make during the Pig's reign. However, it may be worth the effort to work with what he has or what he can get. Rewards and remuneration should be good and may even exceed his expectations. The one thing to watch out for in the Boar's reign is overindulgence; the Monkey should go on a strict diet and get more exercise. It could be a happy time for his love life, too. Family and friends get together to fête the Monkey for his accomplishments. There will be many reasons for him to celebrate.

WHEN MOON SIGNS MEET SUN SIGNS

In my interpretation of Chinese horoscopes, the Rat is not linked with the first Western astrological sun sign, Aries. Instead, I pair the Rat with its counterpart based on the month and season of the Rat, which are December and winter. This makes the most sense as the lunar month of December (also called the Twelfth Moon or the Twelfth Earth Branch) is supposed to parallel the sun sign, Sagittarius, the Archer. I envision the Eastern and Western horoscope cycles as two large wheels, each with twelve spokes. To correctly juxtapose these cycles, we must find the matching notch that will join them together. Once the Rat and Sagittarius are paired as the first signs, the other eleven fall into place. Please see the Twenty-Four Segments of the Lunar Almanac. All the dates correspond with the twelve Western solar signs.

If you are born in the year of the Monkey under the Western sign of

Sagittarius: 22nd November to 21st December
The Sagittarian Monkey = Fire + Negative Fire

The Monkey provides sustaining fortitude and organizational talent for the high-minded Sagittarian. On his part, the Archer will certainly make sure that the Monkey's objectives are as straight and true as the Archer's aim. This personality will possess both integrity and an impenetrable mind, despite that footloose and fancy-free image he may project to throw us off. A clever and intelligent manipulator, he never reveals his real angle until he is sure of clinching the deal. The native is a lucky and dynamic conjuror produced by the combined forces of the aristocratic Sagittarius and the ingenious Monkey.

If you are born in the year of the Monkey under the Western sign of

Capricorn: 22nd December to 20th January
The Capricorn Monkey = Earth + Positive Metal

Both signs here are coordinated and competent, although the Monkey is delightful where the Goat can be staid and honest. Here, Capricorn has access to the Monkey's mental agility and lively imagination, while the Monkey revels in the unwavering forcefulness the Goat brings. The result is a quiet and diligent personality, still clever but not so audacious. He will keep his feet firmly planted on the ground but his sights will be set on the heavens.

If you are born in the year of the Monkey under the Western sign of

Aquarius: 21st January to 19th February
The Aquarian Monkey = Air + Positive Metal

A spicy character never at a loss for words, the Aquarian Monkey combines the astounding intellect and the agility of the Monkey with the ample generosity of the Water Bearer. Both signs have a streak of willfulness and impertinence, so don't expect this person to fall obediently in line. Cerebral yet playful, sincere yet tricky, direct yet complicated, he is the sum total of Aquarian restlessness and Monkey magic. The Aquarian Monkey is also likely to be ultramodern, flexible and searching due to the eager Monkey's tactics and the Water Carrier's thirst for knowledge.

If you are born in the year of the Monkey under the Western sign of

Pisces: 20th February to 20th March
The Pisces Monkey = Water + Positive Metal

Cool as a cucumber, delicate as the scent of lavender and intricate as a maze, the calculating but innocent-looking Piscean Monkey will be the perfect middleman or woman—benefitting from all the buyers and the sellers of the world with unparalleled ease. The Monkey is naturally charming and Pisces is never outdone when it comes to casting mystic spells. The Monkey's Metal is a vessel here which contains the Fish's mercurial sentimentality, giving his talents more form and substance.

If you are born in the year of the Monkey under the Western sign of

Aries: 21st March to 19th April
Aries Monkey = Fire + Positive Metal

This unique combination sounds off loud and clear like a brass gong. Blessed with an ease of expression, he sells himself and avidly promotes his ideas. The Aries Monkey is full of mental poise and balance. Swinging from one tree to another, he will participate in everything, in every sense of the word. He is unimpressed by restrictions and nothing will deter him from his plotted course. The Ram gives the Monkey an appearance of unabashed honesty; he will look you straight in the eye with sincerity. What goes on in his brain could be a different matter. After he gives you that firm handshake—anything goes.

If you are born in the year of the Monkey under the Western sign of

Taurus: 20th April to 20th May
Taurean Monkey = Earth + Positive Metal

The Taurean Monkey can be composed and businesslike on the surface but bubbling with fertile ideas underneath. The Monkey's presence polishes the Bull's rough edges, making him more appealing. Taurus has an impressively sound character, while the Monkey is famous for his flexible intellect. Together, they will produce an ambitious and communicative person able to master his environment. The Venus child is earthy and faithful, while the Monkey is cooperative despite being preoccupied with his own interests. Consequently, the Taurean Monkey will be shrewd but honest, adaptable but steady. He is everybody's friend, but nobody's fool.

If you are born in the year of the Monkey under the western sign of

Gemini: 21st May to 21st June
The Gemini Monkey = Air + Positive Metal

Although this combination will never produce a deep, soul-searching type of personality, it could be a sign of genius. The Gemini Monkey is the epitome of versatility, as both signs can and will achieve the utterly impossible, and will spout ideas by the dozen. Mercury's Twins are deft and alluring, while the Monkey is the intrepid magician. A person born under this combination is inventive and self-reliant; he probably devised every shortcut in the book. He has the ability to bounce back from defeat ready to accept new challenges all over again. There is no holding him back once he has decided his course.

If you are born in the year of the Monkey under the Western sign of

Cancer: 22nd June to 21st July
The Cancerian Monkey = Water + Positive Metal

This is a home-loving, modest Monkey with unerring fiscal abilities and a good eye for investments. He may have rich tastes and prefer sumptuous and elegant decor for his surroundings. He will like to show off his success with artistic and other expensive possessions. This sort of person will also be found installing multiple gadgets in his home to eliminate irksome everyday chores. Yet behind his demure Cancerian apperance, this Monkey will maintain his indisputable intellectual prowess and enjoy matching wits with the most able opponents.

If you are born in the year of the Monkey under the Western sign of

Leo: 22nd July to 21st August
The Leo Monkey = Fire + Positive Metal

This is a personality fused by two signs of towering ambition and sound intelligence. The Lion is authoritative but never underhanded or mean. This should curtail the Monkey's trickery, although the Monkey could be a splendid alter ego for this stately soul and add the

Midas touch to his undertakings. The Leo Monkey will be aristocratic and self-reliant. He or she can be cheeky or audacious with a tendency to pry into the affairs of others, mostly out of curiosity, not malice. A sparkling, superpositive person to work with or for.

If you are born in the year of the Monkey under the Western sign of

Virgo: 22nd August to 22nd September
The Virgo Monkey = Earth + Positive Metal

The Virgin is a diligent and competent worker while the Monkey's guile will provide the ideal catalyst to put Virgo's administrative talents to work. The Virgo Monkey will be scientific and inventive, knowledgeable but never overconfident. Blessed with an exploring mind and a computerlike memory, he will be a successful and avid businessman, making sure and winning bets. Possessed of excellent critical faculties, he will compare and categorize endlessly to get practical answers of his own whenever necessary. The only problem could be that he takes ages to make up his mind.

If you are born in the year of the Monkey under the Western sign of

Libra: 23rd September to 22nd October
The Libran Monkey = Air + Positive Metal

Artful with words, polite and mindful, the angelic Libran Monkey has a smile that promises paradise. Although what he eventually delivers may or may not be that, the trappings are splendid and no one in his right mind could possibly pass up this delightful package. Yes, he will exploit situations to his advantage, but he is also not adverse to taking in others on a partnership basis. Here, the enterprising Monkey will have Libra's democratic cooperation and therefore will find more acceptance than he normally would.

If you are born in the year of the Monkey under the Western sign of

Scorpio: 23rd October to 21st November
The Scorpio Monkey = Water + Positive Metal

The devious imp combined with Pluto's self-love and intensity will produce a personality who truly exists for his own pleasure. Scorpio's stealth keeps him wedded to an uncompromising way of thinking. Submissiveness and consideration are not his chief virtues. Yet the Scorpio Monkey can be indispensable, efficient, attractive, clever and most aspiring. He will work hard for what he wants but can be pitiless to those looking to take advantage of him. The Monkey is positive and captivating, but also incorrigible when it comes to getting his way. Both signs here are masters of retaliation; he will have to even the score—or die trying.

THE SEASONS OF THE MONKEY

SPRING

Monkeys born in the spring are optimistic and outgoing; they also tend to surround themselves with a large circle of friends and supporters. Exploring their environment, they are astute, sociable and most likely to take the initiative. Springtime is great for Monkeys as vegetation and fruits sprout and they will be well-fed. They are quick studies and can master anything in a short time and, in addition, introduce a few shortcuts of their own. However, they are also nervous and easily agitated due to their superior intelligence and active imagination. Independent and adventurous, they will not like to stay in one place or work at one job for too long. Self-starters and risk takers, they prefer to call the shots and are used to having their way.

SUMMER

Summer brings long, indolent days for the Monkey. They sit around and chatter in the gorge with friends and family. Likewise, Monkeys born in the summer love luxury and are fond of material possessions. They will not have to work hard and tend to be less aggressive. They are confident and quite capable of finding their own niches in life. Actually, they will know how to talk their way into any position they want or manipulate situations to their advantage. Wonderful as friends and reliable as leaders, summer Monkeys love the limelight and are usually commanding speakers or writers. Life could be one long party for them and they do not tend to worry as much as Monkeys of the other seasons.

AUTUMN

Monkeys born in the fall tend to be serious and intellectual. They have more insight than their other Monkey brothers and sisters and tend to be less outspoken or given to taking risks. They have considerable staying power and know how to bide their time when they want something. Not ones to make hurried decisions, they will collect all the facts before acting. Autumn Monkeys are the savers and investors of the lot. They will work diligently for lasting results and are usually less flamboyant than Monkeys of the other seasons. For them, long-term goals and strong relationships are more important than being the life of the party.

WINTER

Winter Monkeys are the thinkers and philosophers of the group. Calculating and hard to predict, they never take things for granted. They love technical matters and can manage intricate tasks with ease. Most likely, they will make good linguists, computer software experts, medical technologists, doctors, engineers and mathematicians. They enjoy intellectual challenges and can be skillful money handlers as well. Monkeys of the winter season will have to work hard to make their mark in the world, but they wouldn't have it any other way. They love to be in control of their own destiny and will strive to excel in whatever area captures their imagination and attention.

FAMOUS PERSONS BORN IN THE YEAR
OF THE MONKEY

Metal
Federico Fellini
Walter Matthau
Milton Berle
Pope John Paul II

Wood

Harry S. Truman
Eleanor Roosevelt
Mick Jagger

Earth

John Milton
Paul Gauguin
Lyndon B. Johnson
Joan Crawford
Bette Davis
John Kenneth Galbraith
Nelson Rockefeller

Fire

Duchess of Windsor (Wallis Simpson)

Water

Leonardo da Vinci
Charles Dickens
Queen Sirikit of Thailand
Edward M. Kennedy

10

The Tenth Sign
of the Lunar Cycle

The Rooster

I am on hand
    to herald in the day,
    and to announce its exit.
I thrive by clockwork and precision.
In my unending quest for perfection
    all things will be restored to
    their rightful place.
I am the exacting taskmaster,
    the ever-watchful administrator.
I seek perfect order in my world.
I represent unfailing dedication.

I AM THE ROOSTER.

Lunar Years of the Rooster in the Western Calendar	Elements
22 January 1909 to 9 February 1910	Earth
8 February 1921 to 27 January 1922	Metal
26 January 1933 to 13 February 1934	Water
13 February 1945 to 1 February 1946	Wood
31 January 1957 to 17 February 1958	Fire
17 February 1969 to 5 February 1970	Earth
5 February 1981 to 24 January 1982	Metal
23 January 1993 to 9 February 1994	Water
9 February 2005 to 28 January 2006	Wood

If you were born on the day before the start of the lunar year of the Rooster, e.g., 30th January 1957, your sign is the one before the Rooster, the Monkey.

If you were born on the day after the lunar year of the Rooster, e.g., 18th February 1958, your sign is the one following the Rooster, the Dog, the eleventh lunar sign.

The Rooster rules the two hour segment of the day between 5 P.M. and 7 P.M. Persons born during this period are said to have the Rooster sign as their ascendant and will display many of the characteristics peculiar to this sign and have great affinity for persons born under the sign. Quite possibly, one parent or grandparent will also have been born in the year of the Rooster.

The appointed compass direction of this lunar sign is directly west; its season is autumn and its principle month, September. This is a yin or feminine sign and its fixed element is Metal. The Rooster corresponds to the Western astrological sign of Virgo, which rules from August 22nd to September 22nd.

THE ROOSTER PERSONALITY

The Rooster, or Chicken as he is also called, is the Don Quixote of the Chinese cycle. The dauntless hero who must look to the earth to survive, he is the most misunderstood and eccentric of all the signs. Outwardly, he is the epitome of self-assurance and aggression, but at heart he can be conservative and old-fashioned.

The Rooster-born, especially the men, will be attractive, even devastatingly handsome. The princely fowl is proud of his fine feathers and has an impeccable carriage. You don't find any roosters slouching; they strut about with dignity. Even the shyest member of the Rooster family will cut a neat, trim figure and maintain a special bearing wherever he goes.

There are two distinct types of Roosters. The rapid-firing, extremely talkative ones and the deadly solemn observers with X-ray vision. Both are equally hard to deal with. The Rooster has many outstanding qualities to crow about. He is acute, neat, meticulous, organized, decisive, upright, alert and direct. He can also be critical to the point of brutality. Don't ever ask him for his frank, candid opinion—you may never recover from his comments. He loves to argue and debate, especially in order to show how knowledgeable and smart he is, but sometimes he has little regard for the feelings of others. And should his feathers be ruffled, he is insufferable. He isn't cut out to be a diplomat. Situations requiring tact, delicacy and discretion will cramp his style. With missionary zeal, he tries to convert everyone to his way of thinking.

An outstanding performer, the Rooster shines when he is the center of attention. Tremendously imposing as a personality, he could well pursue any career that exposes him to the public eye. Gay, witty and amusing, the magnificent Rooster will never pass up an opportunity to recount his adventures and enumerate his accomplishments. He is adroit at expressing himself both in speech and in writing. You will have to concede that he is well-versed and prepared for any subject discussed. If you intend to challenge him on a controversial issue, be ready to fight long and hard—the Rooster has amazing stamina, does his homework, and can wear you out.

When the Rooster is negative, he is egotistic, opinionated and too abrasive for his own good. In his mind, he is 100 percent right. He presides over gatherings to exhibit the excellent opinion he has of himself. However, if you look closely, you will find he puts on this act more to constantly reassure himself of his own worth than to irritate anyone. For all his poise and bravado, the Rooster is not that sure of himself, and is therefore most susceptible to flattery or delusions of grandeur. He is also likely to filibuster until he gets his way.

All members of the Chicken family are good at handling money. They are just fascinated by accounting, sorting out finances and guarding the cash box. The Rooster sets up a budget for everything he can get his hands on, and that includes his time, your time, the mailman's time, company time, the children's schedule, ad infinitum. Even the youngest one is likely to be elected Treasurer of the Little League. He will handle his pennies wisely and before you know it he may be running his own mini-bank, giving loans and charging interest to more spendthrift youngsters.

If you have problems with your finances due to lack of self-control, turn your money over to a Rooster. He'll make you an ironclad budget and slap your wrists every time you touch a penny more than is allowed.

While you may live to lament this move, you can be sure everything he does is for your own good—even if he does seem to be sadistically enjoying it a bit too much. Don't be so ungrateful! You should thank your lucky stars he condescended to help you. After all, he does have your interests at heart.

Now all those bits and pieces of paper you scattered around have been neatly filed by this efficiency expert. Your income is reconciled with your expenditures for the first time in years and your receipts no longer live in a shoebox. You start to see the light of day. And the Internal Revenue wolf has not cast his dark shadow on your doorstep now that the Rooster is here, nor do your creditors haunt you day and night. You would be worse off, you know, if it weren't for this financial savior.

I know, too, you may think you have got more than you bargained for. You will complain bitterly how he jumps on you even for your smallest error. You are now in a state of perfect financial accord, yet totally miserable in this newfound bliss. Your blood pressure shoots up every time you have one of those profound discussions with him. Well, relax. Don't take it so hard. Try to think back. Remember that day you took him on and how he made that sacred vow to help you out of the woods and stick to you "for better or for worse?" It is just that you get to see the worse part first. Stick around, things are bound to get better. His key word is service and he won't disappoint even your loftiest expectations. You many not be able to live with the

Rooster, but you will find that you can't get along without him, either.

Actually, the Chinese character for the Rooster is "Ji," which simply means Chicken. But since this person will do anything but "chicken out" of a situation, I have respectfully chosen to address him as the Rooster. Besides, the Rooster's personality really enhances and dominates that of the entire Chicken family. If there were to be an ad in tomorrow's paper for a "Superman with Fine Fiscal Skills," you can be sure the Rooster would apply, and be more than qualified for the job, too.

His is the sign of the collector, too. Outstanding accounts bug him terribly. And you know what Chickens do with bugs. My, my, you have all these collectable debts due you? Just watch the Rooster roll up his sleeves and take on those culprits who owe you money. You cannot find anyone better to carry out an important directive. He loves difficult assignments. But don't expect him to improvise. He is an explicit person and you have to give him explicit orders. On top of all his other virtues, you cannot ask him to be versatile and inventive too. That would be asking too much.

To truly understand a Rooster, you must accept his predilection for controversy. This may be because of the mental exercise it provides. You must comprehend, difficult as it may seem, that there is nothing personal in his moves. You should have enough sense to keep out of the crossfire since you know his gun is always loaded. And, while he does seem knowledgeable and worldly about everything else, it should be noted that the Rooster can be puritanical regarding sex or affairs of the heart.

For the Rooster to make smooth, unimpeded progress it would be well if he realized that people would not be so reluctant to accept his excellent advice if he could only package it better. A little sugar coating, perhaps? He doesn't have to be like the old-fashioned doctor who prescribes bitter-tasting concoctions with no regard for our delicate taste buds!

When a Rooster spends lavishly, he must be doing it to appease his oversized ego. Or, it may be his way of saying he's sorry. Don't expect long detailed apologies; sometimes, he'd rather bite off his tongue than admit he is wrong. So, take what you can and rest assured he will make it up to you in more ways than one. The Rooster has a good heart, a strong conscience and the best of intentions. It's just that sometimes his noble ideals and oversized self-image get the better of him. Take his criticism lightly and with a sense of humor. There is no point in getting ticked off. No matter what he threatens, he rarely goes through with it and, in the end, he will still roll up his sleeves and come to your aid. He'll never turn his back on someone who needs his help.

The Rooster spends a good deal of money on his clothes. He is a sharp dresser and loves to attract attention. Occasionally, he will have the tendency to overdecorate his home, office or even himself. He is also very impressed with awards of all kinds—medals, trophies and titles (honorary or real). Every Rooster will try to win at least one award, have one professional title to his credit, or get a minimum of one medal per war. With money, he will only be generous with his immediate family or to win the love and admiration of his followers. Otherwise, the only thing one can be assured of getting from him free is advice.

Roosters born at the crack of dawn, during the Tiger's hours, or at sundown (between 5 and 7 P.M., the hours of the Rooster) are definitely going to be the noisiest of the lot. I personally know of one whose family has long been considering using a muzzle to silence his lengthy discourses. Too bad none of them has worked up the courage for the task. Night Roosters tend to be the exact opposite. These quiet Roosters tend to be doubly eccentric, bookwormish, aloof or insulated in their quest for perfection.

All Roosters are perfectionists in one way or another. They will have a sharp eye for details mixed with theoretical flights of fancy. Their ideas sometimes work better on paper than in actual application because the Rooster forgets to allow for human frailties and other varying factors. They have scientific minds and may fail to see why other people cannot exist by fixed formulas as they do.

Yet for all his faults and interfering ways, the Rooster native is usually sincere in his desire to help others and undoubtedly means well in his endeavors. He comes on too strong because he is so sure he is right that he closes his mind to the views of others.

If the Rooster's dreams are too farfetched and overambitious, he will suffer many disappointments in life. He must learn to stop reaching for the sky. Although he can be practical about difficult matters, the Rooster can be very unreasonable over simple things. But it is useless to stand between him and his goals. He is the dauntless knight, who recovers at a moment's notice and goes off to chase another rainbow. Who knows, he may succeed at the next try. The Rooster is brave and chivalrous under stress, but sometimes he carries his heroism far beyond what is required.

The female of this sign is usually more down to earth and less colorful in her aspirations. She is superefficient and will get things done with a minimum of fuss. You can rely on her to have enormous amounts of energy to dedicate to any job she sets her sights on.

One would be hard-pressed to find a more helpful woman than the female Chicken, with the exception of a Boar lady. Although this Hen acts as if she has been press-ganged into her labors, the truth is that she loves to conscript herself to a life of involvement and dedication. What would she do with her vast reserves of energy otherwise? Whereas others are only bored, she can actually be frightened when she finds extra time on her hands.

The Hen is more adaptable than the male Rooster and will interact well with others. She will have no qualms about being a mere worker, one of the group, if it gets her where she is going. Routine appeals to her, and she is always on schedule if not ahead of it. She is as capable and productive as her male counterpart but will go about performing less offensively. Careful, dutiful and less obtrusive, she could excel in precision work, proofreading, preparing long-range studies or compiling statistics and the like. A meticulous worker, she is also likely to make a very thorough and patient teacher, watchful and protective mother, and solicitous wife or nurse. At the helm of things, the female Chicken makes a fine leader and executive. No one can supervise as well as she can; with her love of efficiency and regularity, she gets everything going like clockwork.

She does have the the tendency to harp on things or constantly remind you of what is next on the agenda, but this should be accredited to overzealousness and not because she is out to persecute you. She is much too busy for that. One does, however, get the impression she is out to reform or remake the people she loves. This is simply her way of showing she cares. She cannot bear to see you make mistakes when she is on hand to prevent them. Consequently, she will help you up every time you stumble. Provide you with the right word every time you stammer. Second-guess you on what you may want to eat or wear. Helpful to the extreme, at times, the Hen can drive the objects of her devotion to the limits of their sanity.

She will forgive you for anything, but not before she gets those hurt feelings off her chest with a strong lecture. After that, she won't harbor grudges and is not vindictive by nature.

The lady Chicken is a simple dresser. She will prefer simple, classic and easy-to-wear outfits that are appropriate for numerous occasions and which can be complemented by her large array of colorful accessories. Don't be surprised if she possesses tons of exotic and even atrocious costume jewelry or a vast collection of quaint antique pieces that could be an art exhibit by themselves.

Taking a peek into her handbag could tell you a lot about her character. Besides those little notes she writes herself constantly, she will probably have a tape measure and the clothes and shoe sizes of her entire family. She's armed to the teeth with remedies for every illness and other Do's and Don't's. She is exact and orderly and will enjoy taking charge of distributing or organizing things. It is not beyond her to open the office first thing in the morning and lock up after everyone leaves in the evening. She guards her responsibilities jealously and enjoys the power her authority confers.

Every Rooster is a responsible worker. He will know how to please his superiors, who will be impressed by his sharp intellect and efficiency. But although he has boundless energy and a driving will to succeed, the Rooster is too cocksure when he becomes negative. Then his efforts can be misdirected and he can take on impossible tasks. The irony is that the Rooster will find success and money in the most ordinary, everyday places. Contrary to his own thinking, he will not have to search far and wide for his fortune. As the Chinese put it, "Chickens can find food even in the hardest ground with their sturdy beaks and claws."

That is why, if the vigilant Rooster can come down to earth and apply himself to mundane matters, he can literally dig up gold from his own backyard. He would do well setting up his own business or running the family estate. But, wherever he goes, he will be meticulous and competent enough to have everything operating smoothly in no time at all.

The emotions of the Rooster-born swing from high to low and back again. He is plagued by an active and inquisitive mind. His probing ways keep him chained to his objectives. Once he sets out to prove a point, he will not leave a single stone unturned. He makes an excellent investigator: there is a bit of Sherlock Holmes in every Rooster.

With his many administrative abilities and natural passion for work, the Rooster will start out young and gain success early in life. What he needs most in everything he undertakes is restraint, moderation and a firm hand to direct his irrepressible energies. No matter how competent he is, he must realize that he cannot take the world by storm in a single day and reprogram everyone else to do things his way. In short, the Rooster can perform the most astonishing task with aplomb and then become eccentric and bogged down on the last detail.

The Rooster loves praise, is allergic to criticism of any kind and can be very selfish about sharing the limelight. He will never like to admit he is wrong. He will also go to any length to discredit his enemies. A good provider, the Rooster person is wonderful to his family and will indulge them in anything, provided no one dares usurp his No.1 spot. It would be well for him to have a large family, as he needs a cheering squad to bring out the best in him.

No matter what happens, it will be an advantage that the Rooster is such a tireless worker, for he will have to work his way through life. Things won't just fall into his lap. He is the intrepid dreamer, full of ambition and goodwill, but destined to succeed in ordinary things.

Yet, on the other hand, it doesn't pay to underestimate his powers. Being fiercely competitive, he could peck the formidable Snake to death should he set his mind to it.

To sum up, the colorful but controversial Rooster will never fail to make an impression on you. You will either be enchanted and grow to love him immensely, or you will simply be unable to bear the sight and sound of him.

The Rooster will pair off nicely with the wise and intuitive Snake. The Snake will need the effervescent personality and sunny, dauntless outlook of the Rooster to bring him cheer. The Ox will also welcome the sunshine the Rooster could bring into his regimented existence. Although both will be compulsive workers, the Chicken is not as spartan as the Ox. The Dragon will definitely find the grandiose plans of the Rooster very much to his liking, both of them being outgoing, energetic and ambitious.

The Tiger, Sheep, Monkey and Boar will be the next best partners for the Rooster. But put two Roosters together and you know what you get—a cockfight. With the Hens, there is more likely to be more harmony. The Rooster-born will come into conflict with people born under the sign of the Rat, for while the Rooster lacks a sense of intimacy, the Rat thrives on it. Neither will the Rooster find happiness with the Rabbit. The Rabbit is sensitive and will seek to avoid squabbling or inciting his enemies. The Rooster, on the other hand, is an expert at provoking a fight and can rub people the wrong way by his uncomplimentary remarks. This trait will both scandalize and alienate the Rabbit, who cannot bear such glaring directness. The Dog's relations with the Rooster will range from lukewarm to frosty, depending on how wide the gaps are between their differing points of view. They could work together if necessary but are not fated to be joined together in great harmony.

In his life, the bright and optimistic Rooster will not have to look far and wide to find his destiny; nor fly too high to reach his dreams. All he has to do is work on the ground beneath him and he will discover what he is looking for. His legendary efficiency will serve him well as he establishes himself as an excellent organizer and administrator.

THE ROOSTER CHILD

Even as a child, the Rooster will be a self-starter. A good student, fast learner and industrious little soul, he or she will be forever poking around for answers. You can rely on him to pursue his studies, or anything else that attracts him, with self-generated zeal. It will be a joy to teach him, as he is alert, intelligent and painstakingly precise. He will have all the tendencies of a bookworm.

The Rooster child will be neat and orderly. He will do things in the proper sequence and will be a creature of such meticulous and exacting habits he will sometimes annoy you. He won't be reticent about his opinions either—but rather something of a wise guy around the house. Tough and self-disciplined, he will save the most pocket money among the children. He could be petty about minute discrepancies and will plan the most routine deed with military precision.

This child will be very demanding of his parents, but in return he will be dependable when called upon to do his part. Not one to cry for help, he will detest weakness and dependency in others. If you make some kind of a mistake, he will be the first to notice and call it to your attention. He can't help doing this, it's part of his nature. He tends to be bossy, too, so if you are not careful, your little Chick will soon be running your life.

Fearless, optimistic and dauntless, the Rooster will never change his course of action even if the whole world condemns him. You may have to watch helplessly as he rushes headlong off a cliff, because he won't take any advice once he has made up his mind. Just keep praying that some of his wild, idealistic schemes work. He is never too practical when it comes to his own life. But one day, who knows, his unlikely ventures may hit it big. Many millionaires were born in the year of the Rooster and they all have one thing in common besides money—they were eccentric and opinionated.

What is more tiresome, however, is the fact that he will be completely blind to his own faults. Don't bother to debate with him; it will be a waste of time as he never admits he is wrong. His is the right way and no Buts about it!

In short, the high-powered and resplendent Rooster will have many fine talents (which no doubt he will carefully enumerate to you), but he also carries a big bag of idiosyncrasies. He will never take the middle of the road. With him, you either sink or swim. His simple "love me or leave me" attitude means that if you wish to support him, you must be prepared to go all the way.

THE FIVE DIFFERENT ROOSTERS

METAL ROOSTER—1921, 1981

This practical, exacting and industrious Rooster captivates people with his brilliant powers of deduction. Investigative, optimistic and idealistic, he will have a passionate attitude toward work.

Metal will make him opinionated and headstrong and he will have a strong need to be important and famous. He is a tireless worker who could be so fixated on his own worldview that he finds it hard to even consider the opinions and ideas of other. With his gift for oratory, he may even drown out the voices of his opponents. Although he is factual and reasonable, he finds it hard to be totally impartial when his ego is directly challenged.

If he cannot relate well to others or make any real efforts to compromise, his talents could be wasted and his genius will go a-begging. Overrationalizing and analyzing could be disastrous. When he is negative, he will even subject a blooming romance to a routine clinical examination. He should curb his urge to overdo things and be more open to the views of other people.

Despite his outward bravado, the Metal Rooster can be inhibited with his emotions. He will insist on order in his life and will demand hygienic conditions or even sterile cleanliness in his surroundings.

But while this acquisitive Rooster is attracted to material wealth, he will also be concerned with social reform. He is not above using his expertise on behalf of humanity, as he will find fulfillment in solving social problems or instigating reforms for the advancement of mankind.

WATER ROOSTER—1933, 1993

This is an intellectual Rooster who will enjoy cultural pursuits. Respectable and inspiring, he has tremendous energy and initiative at his disposal and will seek to use his own resources or enlist the help of others to speed up progress.

With Water as his element, he will think clearly and be extremely practical. He can be reasoned with, especially when faced with insurmountable odds. He is not as austere or critical as other Roosters.

A proficient writer as well as a commanding speaker, the Water Rooster can sway the masses and prompt others to action. With his strong scientific leanings, he will be interested in health, medicine and technology. However, since his mind functions with computerlike efficiency, he could lose sight of the main issues should he overemphasize details. Systems and procedures fascinate him and if he becomes obsessed with perfecting them, he could get bogged down in creating a fine bureaucracy—and little else.

WOOD ROOSTER—1945, 2005

This Rooster is an expansive type who can be more considerate of others and has a wider outlook on life. Although he is much less stubborn and opinionated than other Roosters, he still has a tendency to complicate matters and get trapped in a maze of his own making. He should learn to contain his enthusiasm and avoid overexerting himself. In addition, he should not expect everyone to have the same stamina and dedication that he possesses. No matter how well-meaning his intentions, imposing unrelieved rote work and regimentation on his subordinates may totally alienate them.

Wood makes him progress-oriented, and when Wood is matched with his virtuous qualities of honesty and integrity, he will excel in his performance, and his charts and graphs will amaze everyone.

Open-minded, fair and sociable, he can give unselfishly of himself to foster the welfare of others. He will seek to contribute to or improve existing social conditions. Because he always desires to be in a congenial atmosphere, he will seek close association with the people he works with and will have an excellent record of reliability. Still, he is basically a Rooster and will not water down his biting comments when aroused. However, he will always work hard to protect his security. Life will be good for him if he does not take on too many high-flying projects at the same time.

FIRE ROOSTER—1897, 1957

This combination is possibly a shooting star. With Fire as his element, this Rooster will be vigorous, highly motivated and authoritative. He will be able to operate independently and with great precision and skill. On the negative side, he could be temperamental, over-dramatic and nervous.

Strongly principled and single-minded in his pursuit of success, he will display above-average managerial abilities and leadership. The diligent and intense Fire Rooster will stick fanatically to his own views and conduct his own fact-finding tours and feasibility studies. He will be unswayed by the feelings or personal opinions of others, although he will be professional and ethical in his dealings.

At times, he could be too inflexible to effect workable compromises. As a result, he will take to putting people and situations under a microscope for observation. If things do not measure up to his expectations, he could assume the role of an Inquisitor or cause major upheavals.

Yet he does have organizational talents and can project a stimulating and dynamic public image. And, despite his shortcomings, this type of Rooster will have the noblest intentions behind his actions.

EARTH ROOSTER—1909, 1969

This studious and analytical Rooster will dig for the truth, mature early and compile his own data storage banks. Earth ensures that he will be accurate, efficient and careful in carrying out assignments. He will know how to brush aside the gaudy inessentials and view the hard, cold facts for himself. With him, you will get the bottom line first.

Unafraid of shouldering vast responsibilities, he will adhere to the Rooster's reputation for not mincing words. Unpretentious and dogmatic, he will have strong missionary tendencies. He loves conducting sermon-on-the-mount style meetings, exhorting everyone to work harder and follow his shining example. He is satisfied to lead a simple and austere life if he finds his job rewarding. Fanatically systematic, he will keep all his notes, file all his data and record everything he does for posterity.

A hard taskmaster, strict educator and much dreaded critic, the Earth Rooster will sow and reap from sun up to sundown. If he can bring himself to be practical in his aspirations, he will have bushels and bushels of success to show for his efforts.

COMPATIBILITY AND CONFLICT CHARTS FOR THE ROOSTER

The Rooster is part of the Second Triangle of Affinity, which is made up of the most purposeful and steadfast signs. The Ox, Snake and Rooster are the dutiful and dedicated fighters who strive to scale great heights and conquer by their constancy and unfailing determination. These three are fixed in their views and given to thought and systematic planning. They are the most intellectual signs of the cycle. They depend on their own assessment of facts and figures and give little credence to hearsay. They are more likely to comply with the dictates of their heads than those of their hearts. Slow and sure in their movements, they prefer to act independently. They will invariably seek each other out and can intermarry and intermingle most successfully.

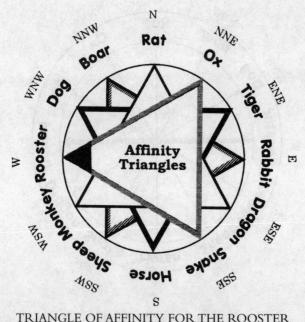

TRIANGLE OF AFFINITY FOR THE ROOSTER

The Rooster will encounter his most serious personality clashes with someone born in the year of the Rabbit. Anyone with his ascendant in hours of the Rabbit will also be likely to come into conflict with the Rooster native. In the Circle of Conflict, the Rooster and Rabbit are on opposite sides, 180 degrees apart. The Rooster's appointed direction is directly west while the Rabbit's is east. Autumn is the season of the Rooster while spring is the time of the Rabbit. Furthermore, the fixed element of the Rooster is Metal, which is destructive to the fixed element of the Rabbit, Wood.

These two will have different opinions and outlooks and have difficulty understanding each other or one another's motives. Unless a Rooster native is born during the hours of the Rabbit or vice versa, there is little these two will find in common. Besides having different personalities and preferences, they will do things that may be counterproductive to each other, perhaps without even being aware of it. Unintentional as these actions may be, they tend to produce friction and disputes.

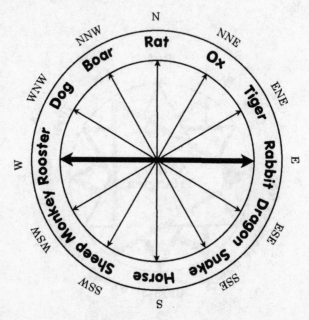

CIRCLE OF CONFLICT

Aside from the most compatible signs, the Ox and the Snake, and the least compatible, the Rabbit, the other nine signs are compatible with the Rooster to varying degrees.

Rat

There will be difficulties in communications. Both like to talk and argue, but these two signs seem to test each other's patience. The Rooster likes to criticize while the Rat can be just as picky and petty. In such a competitive and fault-finding atmosphere, nothing lasting or special can develop. Better for them to work through mutual friends to defuse potential clashes. There will be a better chance for success if they share a common ascendant or if one sign has the other as an ascendant.

Tiger

The Rooster and the Tiger are alike in the sense that they are both attracted to controversy and will take on hot issues. They will either be the best of friends or find each other very irritating. It depends on which day of the week it is. Both tend to blow hot and cold, are drawn to the limelight and may compete for center stage or top billing. The Rooster is the dauntless perfectionist who cannot understand how the feisty Tiger can lead such a charmed life and be so popular. The Tiger, on the other hand, thinks the Rooster makes a mountain out of a molehill and will insist on viewing the whole picture instead of picking on the details as the Rooster is so prone to do.

Dragon

The Dragon is drawn to the Chicken's expertise and competence while the Rooster is in awe of the Dragon's zeal and enthusiasm. They will strive to find prosperity, success and happiness together. In order to achieve a mutual bond and a lasting relationship, both signs must approach a partnership with reduced expectations and muted egos. The Rooster can deal with the Dragon's brashness and the thick-skinned Dragon is not afraid of the Chicken's undiluted criticism and need for accuracy. The Dragon can fight while the Rooster will perch on its shoulder, plan their next move and supervise. We should pity the opposition.

Horse

The Rooster and the Horse will have an amicable to cool relationship depending on who's the boss. When the Rooster has the upper hand and is in control, he can be a domineering commander. If the Horse is at the controls, he may find the Rooster critical, eccentric and a bit too argumentative for his taste. Both love adventure and activity—but have different ways of handling challenges. The industrious Chicken plots and researches and requires all sorts of information before he acts, while the Horse will wing it in a thoroughly unconventional way and confound the Rooster with his speed and progress.

Sheep

The Sheep may shun the Rooster because he is a hard taskmaster and disciplinarian, and the Sheep needs to be courted and praised to bring out his best. The Rooster is easily exasperated by the wiles of the Sheep, and there will be many gaps to be bridged before a good rapport is established between these two. Ties will only be moderate unless they happen to share a common ascendant. The Rooster will try to be helpful but he may alienate the Sheep when he tries to run his life and imposes so many rules. The Sheep cannot abide the Rooster's criticism and regimentation. There will be much unhappiness if they cannot work with the same schedule.

Monkey

Monkeys know how to handle Roosters, but only to a certain degree. They can be immune to Rooster criticism if they want something badly enough, and they are not above flattering the Rooster to put him in a good mood. However, even the Monkey's patience could wear thin if the Rooster insists on examining all the details over and over. Monkeys are easily bored and do not have the long attention spans of Roosters. They could have different approaches to a common problem. The Monkey will opt for the shortcut or invent one if possible. The Rooster will take the long and winding path and make simple things difficult by his overanalysis.

Rooster

Roosters get along with people of their sign only if they belong to the opposite sex. Male Roosters are very selfish about sharing the limelight and it is difficult to have two Cocks as kings of the Chicken coop. They will constantly try to upstage each other and cause a lot of problems for the poor folks who may come between them. Female Chickens may also tend to harp and criticize each other with their sharp tongues, although they may eventually get a lot done. Still, all the discussion could wear out an ordinary person. It's best not to get caught in the Chicken-to-Chicken crossfire, although one doubts they will notice anyone once they are busy trading shots back and forth.

Dog

The Rooster may worry the poor Dog with his high-flying acts of daring and preposterous claims to fame. The Dog would like to be a loyal friend and supporter of the Rooster's high ideals, but he finds it difficult to understand the Chicken's propensity for being controversial. However, the Dog can be patient and understanding if the Rooster proves his motives are aboveboard and he has everyone's interests at heart. Once the Dog is convinced the Rooster's intentions are honorable, he will be protective and accepting of his eccentric ways.

Boar

The Rooster gets along with the Boar because the Pig is such a good sport and also perhaps because he is too thick-skinned to be bothered by the Rooster's criticism. Boars do not take Roosters seriously, which is just as well. Otherwise, they would just make their own lives miserable. The Boar hears what he wants to hear and then makes his own choices. The Rooster can give advice all day long, but thankfully the Boar is a cordial soul who responds to the Rooster's goodwill with his typical kindness and generosity. Both signs are outgoing, but in different ways. Boar and Rooster do not deal with conflict in the same manner. The Boar is not petty and will readily share what he has without much complaint, while the Rooster only calms down once he is able to vent his opinions.

THE ROOSTER AND HIS ASCENDANTS

We all have a shadow that follows us throughout life. Sometimes it grows bigger than life and at other times it shrinks until it disappears into the soles of our feet. Sometimes it walks tall before us and on other occasions it lags behind like a sulking friend. In Chinese horoscopes, this constant partner, manifested or not, is our ascendant, the animal sign that rules the hour of our birth and becomes a comrade in our journey though life. We may view it as friend or foe or even a little of both. It surfaces when we least expect and shows a better or worse side of our nature. We can often be confounded by the way we listen to our "other self" as well as feel resentful of the significant influence it can exert on us. Actually, a personality has many rings around the centered "self." Each ring can have a different size, texture and aura. When all these factors combine, they bring forth the unique individual that the person truly is. Hence, a Dragon with an ascendant that is not compatible, like the Dog, has perhaps a more difficult inner struggle than say a Snake born during the hours of the Snake. The double intensity of the Snake person will be easily understood by horoscope readers while the more intricate Dragon/Dog may exhibit the contrary Dog and Dragon traits to varying degrees. There are many voices within each person. But, in the end, only the individual determines which course he will follow, which choices he will make.

The time of birth used to determine the ascendant is always the local time in the place of birth.

If you were born between

11 P.M. and 1 A.M. = The Hours of the Rat

You possess an endearing mixture of piquant charm and curiosity. The Chicken is more convivial and accepting with the Rat in him. You still argue, but in a more pleasant manner. A hard worker and dedicated soul, you are always ready to help others. However, at times, you stress details too much and can be critical if others disagree with you or disregard your excellent advice.

1 A.M. and 3 A.M. = The Hours of the Ox

The Ox has his hooves firmly planted and could well bring the high flying Chicken down to earth. Both signs may crave authority and can be harsh to those who step out of line. Steadfast and sure of yourself, you are dependable, thrifty and patient. The Ox's influence gives you endurance and purpose although at times you tend to resist change and you do not take advice readily. Remember that you do not have to carry the world on your shoulders; allow others to assist you or learn to share your feelings with them. You could be much the richer for it.

3 A.M. and 5 A.M. = The Hours of the Tiger

This unconventional combination makes you magnetic but a bit incoherent about what you truly want. You can blow hot and cold in the same breath. The Rooster's analytical qualities may be swamped by the Tiger's passionate ways. The result could be great self-confidence and idealism. At your best, you inspire confidence by your courage and eloquence. At your worst, you can be domineering, aggressive and insensitive.

5 A.M. and 7 A.M. = The Hours of the Rabbit

With the Rabbit's ascendant you could be a quiet, efficient Bird who always manages to get his worm. The result will be a Rooster less likely to cause trouble; you are able to refrain from giving your caustically frank opinion and so keep the peace. The Rabbit makes you less combative and gives you a modest amount of humility and decorum; on the other hand, you could also be an expert bluffer. You would do well to heed your Rabbit's intuition before you put on a show of your Rooster bravado.

7 A.M. and 9 A.M. = The Hours of the Dragon

You could be a Rooster who will not let anyone usurp one iota of your power. The Dragon within makes you ultra-assertive, fastidious and fearless. You could mow down the opposition with the finesse of a bulldozer. Straightforward and dynamic, there is not a lazy or deceptive bone in your body. When you are in a position of leadership, you could be awe-inspiring and people will fight to be on your team. The trouble is that you tend to expect too much of others and may push too hard. Life would be much more pleasant if you could tone down your overzealous nature and accept people for what they are.

9 A.M. and 11 A.M. = The Hours of the Snake

The Snake ascendant makes you a wise and wily Fowl, but also aloof and secretive at times. You may resent any interference or prying people. You never give interviews. Studious, intellectual and reserved, you could be a real philosopher. The Snake gives you a decisive and even religious nature. Contemplative and persevering, your endurance is of mythical proportions.

11 A.M. and 1 P.M. = The Hours of the Horse

If you were born during the Horse's time, you could be a practical Rooster with fast and sharp reflexes. Both signs here have colorful and flamboyant tastes.

The Horse can teach the Rooster not to waste time on unfeasible ventures; as a result, your endeavors could bring you higher dividends. You may also have a very engaging personality because the independent Horse will lend you passion and athletic prowess. However, the Horse makes you impatient and temperamental, too. Better watch that tongue of yours.

1 P.M. and 3 P.M. = The Hours of the Sheep

The soft-hearted Sheep as your ascendant makes you an amiable, less assertive and even bashful Rooster. The Sheep's coyness could mellow the Rooster's brash ways, which could be a good thing after all. You will be popular and helpful to your friends. Still your Rooster side could be critical and melodramatic when challenged and downright unreasonable when you are not given your way. Hopefully, the Sheep in you could make you more compassionate and less outspoken. You are a more team-oriented Rooster and obliging when joint efforts are needed.

3 P.M. and 5 P.M. = The Hours of the Monkey

With the Monkey as your ascendant, you might be a crafty but congenial Rooster, more purposeful and adept at making conciliatory deals than most Roosters. One creative, happy, successful and plucky Chicken, you never take "no" for an answer. The world is your oyster and you have the answers to all the problems in the universe. However, there could still be a struggle between your outrageous Monkey self and your controlling Rooster ego. One thing's for sure, you will be resourceful and intelligent and a definite overachiever.

5 P.M. and 7 P.M. = The Hours of the Rooster

Gifted with the same ascendant as your birth sign, you may possess a double dose of meticulous efficiency and a bent for criticism that others may find intimidating. You are likely to be notable, highly eccentric and particular in your tastes. You will be in a class of your own. Didactic, proud and industrious, your intentions are always honest and sincere in your intentions and others will admire your tenacity and industriousness. But when you are negative, you are one tough Bird.

7 P.M. and 9 P.M. = The Hours of the Dog

With the Dog guarding your ascendant, you could be a calculating, erratic but fair-minded Rooster. The likeable Dog makes you less cocky and opinionated. Still, one must expect great color from this combination of two equally idealistic minds and sharp tongues. You are loyal and courageous but difficult to argue with or oppose, once you make up your mind to do something. Respectable, faithful and dutiful, you can be militant in your views and aspirations, but thankfully you have that altruistic and noble Dog conscience.

9 P.M. and 11 P.M. = The Hours of the Boar

With the generous Boar as your other self, you could be a complacent Rooster who will insist on helping others whether they like it or not! Your brilliance and fortitude may place you in great demand, but unfortunately your outgoing nature could turn you into a social butterfly. Unselfish and quite scrupulous, you can also be sensuous and exacting at the same time. The earthy and indulgent Boar characteristics sometimes conflict with the Rooster's love of discipline and order.

HOW THE ROOSTER FARES IN THE LUNAR CYCLE

1. The Year of the Rat 1996

The Rat may bring a busy and challenging year for the Rooster. So many things demand his attention that he feels others are imposing on him. Even though his earnings will be good, he will still be forced to dip into savings because his expenses are larger than expected or other people have wasted his money. Friends and associates cannot be depended upon to be of much help. Only his family and loved ones stick by him and give him comfort and assistance. A year for the

Rooster to practice discretion and much moderation. However, he could encounter success and gains in unlikely places and therefore should not discount opportunities even if they do not appear promising at first glance.

2. The Year of the Ox 1997

In the year of the Ox, the Rooster recovers any losses he may have suffered. He regains lost power too, and will have the ability to conquer adversities or receive outside help. He will have good news at home and do some traveling. Romance may bloom as the Rooster meets new and interesting people whom he can relate easily to. The seeds he planted in previous years may sprout and even bear fruit. However, the Ox year carries a lot of responsibility for the Rooster native and he will have more commitments than he cares for at times. But the Rooster's devotion to duty pays off during the reign of the Buffalo.

3. The Year of the Tiger 1998

The Tiger brings an eventful and exciting year. The Rooster is lucky with money; his business ventures could produce good results. Although he encounters some worries at home and at work, overall plans go according to schedule. Still, in the Tiger's year, he should be careful as things tend to happen too fast for any proper assessment and there may be complications if he is not cautious. The Rooster must not be overoptimistic and neglect to do his homework properly. With so much to do and so many ups and downs, there won't be a dull moment for the involved Rooster.

4. The Year of the Rabbit 1999

This will be a fair time for the Rooster if he remains conservative in outlook. The Rabbit's year could initially look soft and cuddly on the outside but could in reality present some unpleasant surprises. Investments this year are unreliable and the Rooster should not speculate. The Rooster must seek expert advice and be sure to take it or else he will wind up making the wrong choices. He is also prone to miscalculations during this year and his profits may be eaten away by unexpected expenses. It would be advisable for him to join forces with others instead of acting independently. Arguing, criticizing or challenging authority is discouraged. The Rooster does not need any more controversy than he already has. His family and love life may be strained if he is too distracted by his problems at work.

5. The Year of the Dragon 2000

The Dragon brings a very good and prosperous year for the colorful Rooster. Success shines on him as he is able to occupy leading positions or is given the power to shape his own destiny. Home-wise and health-wise, there may be little frustrations that make him tense and tired. He could deal with this by ignoring things that irritate him and giving in on small issues. But he is in the limelight and will find fame or love or both. Birth, marriages and reunions occur in his family, and his circle of friends will be enlarged by the celebrations the Dragon's year bring. However, this will also be a year for the Rooster to tighten his purse strings and watch expenses. The dynamic Dragon tends to be overenthusiastic at times.

6. The Year of the Snake 2001

The Snake ushers in a mostly fortunate year for the Rooster. He will retain his favored position provided he has the support of influential friends. While he will experience no large monetary gains, he will be able to curtail his losses to an admirable degree. However, the Rooster must be on his guard against unfair competition and vicious rumors in this secretive year of the Snake. Nor should he take long or unnecessary journeys. In his home life or affairs of the heart, he must resist making promises that are difficult to keep, especially since his friends and loved ones will pressure him to do more than he is capable of.

7. The Year of the Horse 2002

The temperamental Horse brings a hectic and somewhat unpredictable year for the Rooster. He must watch his step as he could encounter many obstacles in his path. He will pull through if he is not misguided by favorable preliminary results that could turn sour later on. This is a time to play politics or employ diplomacy, as the Rooster will have to make unwelcome compromises. On the work front, he is likely to have both good and bad news. The Horse's year tends to change course without much notice and this catches the Rooster off guard, making him distrust the motives of others. If the Rooster can learn to be adaptable to change and keep his opinions to himself, he should be able to find help from his close friends and loved ones.

8. The Year of the Sheep 2003

The bountiful Sheep brings a good, protected year for the Rooster, with no upheavals. Instead, he receives glad tidings, regains some lost ground and sees some advancement in his career. Troubles may still abound but he will not be directly affected if he can learn to delegate tasks to others. His home life and love life will be quieter and more settled, provided he can avoid controversy. This is not a year to be opinionated or split hairs as the Rooster may need others more than they need him. On the whole, he will be able to relax at home or take a good vacation with his friends, loved ones or family.

9. The Year of the Monkey 2004

The inventive Monkey brings a mixed year for the Rooster. He is faced with some financial problems and must rely on others to help deal with them. The Rooster looks too closely at details and may fail to see the whole picture and thus could be prone to making errors in judgment. The Monkey's year is a time to be ambitious and bold but also flexible and cunning. If the Rooster is not shrewd in the Monkey's reign he could miss out on opportunities. He should be prepared for all contingencies in love and at work because things may look better than they actually are. There is always a hidden catch during the Monkey's year and the Rooster would be wise to look for it.

10. The Year of the Rooster 2005

A moderately happy time is in store for the Rooster. His family, friends and peers gather round and give him the support and praise he needs. He can make a splendid comeback, find love and romance, and prove his adversaries wrong. He will be able to solve his problems with relative ease, and influential or powerful people will support his ideas. Because he is such a magnet for controversy, he may still be involved in petty disputes, but he will emerge from them without too much damage provided he does not carry his bravado to an extreme. A time for him to be practical and not count his Chickens before they are hatched.

11. The Year of the Dog 2006

The Dog brings a good year for the Rooster: order can be restored in his life. Travel, extra work or much entertaining are foreseen on the home front or professionally. His gains will be average but his losses will be minimal due to the aid he receives from people he has helped in the past. He is able to collect favors and debts owed him. While his plans are easily realized, his personal or love life may be clouded by some secret unhappiness or brooding. Others are not as responsive as he would like them to be. But he has little cause for concern. His expectations will be realized, but not according to his timetable or the scenario he has planned. Not everyone goes by his clock. This is a year for the Rooster to be cooperative.

12. The Year of the Boar 2007

The boisterous Pig may provide an expensive or disturbing year for the Rooster, as worries caused by unexpected difficulties plague him and make him somewhat pessimistic. The Boar always gives exaggerated forecasts of benefits but then the Rooster may find the price tag way beyond his means. His family or love life suffers as he spreads himself too thin by trying to please everyone. The Rooster must take temporary setbacks with a grain of salt and see the humorous or lighter side of life. Being angry or vengeful could affect his health as well as his ability to think clearly. Trusted associates may also give him bad advice or encourage him to spend beyond his means. Instead he should discount good news and plan prudently. The Rooster must keep his goals in clear view throughout the year and rely on no one but himself.

WHEN MOON SIGNS MEET SUN SIGNS

In my interpretation of Chinese horoscopes, the Rat is not linked with the first Western astrological sun sign, Aries. Instead, I pair the Rat with its counterpart based on the month and season of the Rat, which are December and winter. This makes the most sense as the lunar month of December (also called the Twelfth Moon or the Twelfth Earth Branch) is supposed to parallel the sun sign, Sagittarius, the Archer. I envision the Eastern and Western horoscope cycles as two large wheels, each with twelve spokes. To correctly juxtapose these cycles, we must find the matching notch that will join them together. Once the Rat and Sagittarius are paired as the first signs, the other eleven fall into place. Please see the Twenty-Four Segments of the Lunar Almanac. All the dates correspond with the twelve Western solar signs.

If you are born in the year of the Rooster under the Western sign of

Sagittarius: 22nd November to 21st November
The Sagittarian Rooster = Fire + Negative Metal

Ambitious, talkative and active, with the decisiveness common to the two signs present here, the Sagittarian Rooster sets his sights very high. Don't argue with him unless your patience is infinite, for he could carry on a debate from here to eternity to prove his point. But since both signs are scrupulously honest, he makes a poor liar. Don't ask him for the truth unless you can stand to hear it. In spite of his unabashed frankness, he can be quite selfless and will not hesitate to volunteer his help if he feels you need it. Sagittarius gives the Rooster more dignity and a surer aim. It's just that you wish he weren't so right and so openly candid most of the time.

If you are born in the year of the Rooster under the Western sign of

Capricorn: 22nd December to 20th January
The Capricorn Rooster = Earth + Negative Metal

A person born with this combination excels in thoroughness, efficiency and a total lack of pretense. Neither sign in this match is known for malleability, so the Capricorn Rooster will resist all attempts to remake him. However, the Rooster is less flamboyant here and perhaps more tight-lipped, though still given to exercising his rhetoric without much forewarning. Rarely ruffled, this person will be a tidy and exact creature who abides no nonsense nor any deviation from the law. Slowly but surely he will climb the ladder of success. He or she will probably like to be in the military, or sports or both.

If you are born in the year of the Rooster under the Western sign of

Aquarius: 21st January to 19th February
The Aquarian Rooster = Air + Negative Metal

This is not at all your run-of-the-mill Rooster. He is not as relentlessly plodding as usual; actually, his clock may be a bit too advanced—he's ahead of his time. But the Aquarian Rooster will still have the Rooster's directness, or genuine honesty as he likes to call it. He says what he wants regardless of the furor he may cause. Actually, he relishes being different and even shocking. Because the Rooster sign helps him persevere and Aquarius has a futuristic outlook, the Aquarian Rooster will be able to draw up far-ranging plans and has a good understanding of people's future needs. He investigates with the candor of a child and the thoroughness of a scientist. Here is a Rooster with a constant axe to grind, who is eternally busy with his fact-finding missions. But he is not as outrageous as he pretends to be, and he has a big, generous heart.

If you are born in the year of the Rooster under the Western sign of

Pisces: 20th February to 20th March
The Pisces Rooster = Water + Negative Metal

The Fish makes the Rooster a peace-loving personality with an exacting but cooperative character. The Chicken's tough moral fiber is all that it should be, but Pisces, with his talent for public relations, always manages to present a prettier picture. A less taciturn Rooster with no dogmatic inclinations, he could put aside his staple diet of routine and methodical plodding and maybe even live a little. The conservative and gentle Pisces Rooster should have no difficulty obeying the rules, but he will see to it that his pattern of life is interwoven with equal amounts of rest and work. Artistic, composed and elegant, he struts around with class.

If you are born in the year of the Rooster under the Western sign of

Aries: 21st March to 19th April
The Aries Rooster = Fire + Positive Metal

Hard to ignore, impossible to dismiss, and difficult to keep up with are three phrases that characterize the Aries Rooster. When he is feeling positive, he can be truly indispensable. When negative, you could have a full-fledged megalomaniac on your hands. Straight as an arrow and thoroughly honorable in intent, this person will make an indelible impression wherever he goes. He tells it like it is, and in the final accounting he remains faithful to his convictions. He has a very clear conscience. He may very well be the kind of a bright and aggressive leader who will never ask anyone to do anything he is not capable of doing himself. A tireless worker, he inspires others with his outgoing personality and infectious idealism.

If you are born in the year of the Rooster under the Western sign of

Taurus: 20th April to 20th May
The Taurean Rooster = Earth + Negative Metal

This combination of two such hard-working signs could give us a person who staunchly believes in Spartan denial (it's good for the soul, you know) or similar tests of endurance only he can think up. He will win hands down, of course, while you droop with exhaustion; he does not know the meaning of the word fatigue. While both signs here are serious in outlook, the Bull will certainly have better control over his tongue than the Rooster. The end product may be a bit on the dry side, as both Bull and Rooster have a similar brand of laconic humor. But it would be wise to take him seriously; he is always on target and ahead of schedule.

If you are born in the year of the Rooster under the Western sign of

Gemini: 21st May to 21st June
The Gemini Rooster = Air + Negative Metal

Here Gemini's inconsistency will be ameliorated by Rooster efficiency and love of precision. This is a sporty fellow who candidly speaks his mind and gets to the point without much ado or any fear of reprisals. But the Gemini Rooster is still touchy about criticism and will swerve at the slightest blow to his ego or opposition to his ideas. The personality produced in this combination is bound to be more colorful than usual: a finger-snapping, hustle-bustle soul full of life, good intentions, organizational talent and practical aspirations. Never boring to be around, he has a delicious sense of humor and can be witty even in the most desperate situations. His sunny disposition and ability to see every dark cloud's silver lining makes him invaluable in a crisis.

If you are born in the year of the Rooster under the Western sign of

Cancer: 22nd June to 21st July
The Cancerian Rooster = Water + Negative Metal

Here is a careful, motherly and efficient person with a warm, demonstrative manner. The Cancerian Rooster is always genuinely helpful, though you will note the aggressiveness of the Chicken still shines through. But for once, the orderly Rooster's good intentions will be expressed and carried out with Cancerian kindness and good taste, winning him support and endorsement on all fronts. In this combination, Cancer's passive tenaciousness is linked to the Rooster's active perseverance. This person will be difficult to defeat, as he will allow nothing to hinder him from achieving his goals. Less direct and more intuitive, he tends to cover up his critical nature by being more diplomatic in his comments.

If you are born in the year of the Rooster under the Western sign of

Leo: 22nd July to 21st August
The Leo Rooster = Fire + Negative Metal

Let's hope that the Lion's generosity will subdue the Rooster's penchant for hair-splitting. But since both signs are strong and masterful, the Leo Rooster could be hell-bent on success or simply having his way. The Rooster can apply himself to mundane matters with devotion and steadiness, while the Lion has his heart set on glory. A person of this mixture wants or rather demands to be heard. He could have all the necessary assets to reach the pinnacle of power, but one cannot help feeling that he is a little too commanding to have around. However, his colorful personality and magnanimous charm could make up for his natural bossiness. And others may really want or even need him to take charge and bring some excitement into their lives.

If you are born in the year of the Rooster under the Western sign of

Virgo: 22nd August to 22nd September
The Virgo Rooster = Earth + Negative Metal

This is an incredibly secure Fowl who has both feet firmly planted on the ground. Because both signs here are virtuously eccentric, he could puzzle us with his unusual preferences as well as his perfectionism. A clear and logical thinker, he excels in mental tasks. He is the perpetual student: you can put your encyclopedia away and trust him to be an absolute authority in his field or fields. He is a walking library of facts, and is seldom wrong. He will meticulously register every bit of information for the benefit of posterity. A lover of charts and graphs, he is incurably performance-oriented. On the negative end, both signs are given to the peculiar pastime of faultfinding. Please keep in mind that his critique is never personal and may be just a recitation of facts. He has nothing against you. Believe it or not, he is trying to help.

If you are born in the year of the Rooster under the Western sign of

Libra: 23rd September to 22nd October
The Libran Rooster = Air + Negative Metal

The Scales of Libra gives the Chicken's exacting nature great equilibrium. This Rooster will take to feathering his nest with eiderdown and expensive perfume. He is an intellectual who loves comfort and is so smooth in delivering his lines that there may be little if any room for argument. Although he is likely to be particular and observant as all Roosters are, Libra will enable him to better comprehend the views of others, thus resulting in a person less critical over trifles and much more animated and happy. He will enjoy a higher popularity rating than other Chickens. This is a Fowl with a sweet nature who may also be indecisive because he is forever weighing the pros and cons.

If you are born in the year of the Rooster under the Western sign of

Scorpio: 23nd October to 21st November

The Scorpio Rooster = Water + Negative Water

Such fortitude and stamina! This combination is made up of two strong, individualistic and high-minded signs. Curt and to the point, the quiet Scorpio Rooster abhors compromise. Don't even hint at it. It means defeat to him and he is never ever going down as a quitter. Since this personality sets out to win, he usually does, although his methods won't win him hordes of friends. Never mind, he may prefer proud isolation to yielding even a single inch of ground. Scorpio's watery currents bring out the sleuth in the Rooster and little if anything escapes this commanding investigator. Sensuous and intensely devoted, here is passion and daring in the same boat.

THE SEASONS OF THE ROOSTER

SPRING

Roosters born in the spring are inquisitive and outspoken. If they are born during the day, especially around dawn, they can really sound off like a church bell or even a booming canon. Life for them will be full of predicaments and missions impossible, but they wouldn't want it any other way. Eloquent, meticulous and very tenacious, they will not give up their perches on the wall. You have to find some other spot to make your announcements, these spring Roosters will hog the microphone. Extremely good students and teachers, they have long attention spans and can excel at detailed work or intricate tasks. They are not easily discouraged and will stick to something until they master it. Their didactic powers can be amazing and they will track something to its source even if they have to move a mountain.

Roosters born during the evening, after the sun sets, will be just as methodical, contemplative and pedantic, but they will be more quiet. They will diligently do their homework before they give an opinion. You can always rely on them to be thorough and well-informed.

SUMMER

Summer Roosters enjoy a good life and have more than their fair share of excitement. They always gravitate to where the action is and are never at a loss for words. These Roosters have a bird's eye view of what is going on around them and are in a superior position to assess how things should be done. They are deliberate and intelligent in their outlook and fearless in their quest for information or perfection. Although they will be extremely dedicated and resourceful people, they also tend to be controlling and will take life too seriously. They will never shirk their duties or be found wanting on their jobs. Pursuing their objectives with an almost military precision, these proud Fowls will have a lot to crow about.

AUTUMN

The Roosters of fall are a mixed bunch of inquisitive and industrious souls. They tend to be intellectual and guarded. They do not like to take anything for granted and are always checking and rechecking their information. Authoritative and proud of their skills, they will be very critical if anyone slips up. With their eagle eyes, they do not miss a trick and are highly resistant to doing things that are unconventional or experimental. Autumn's Roosters are conservative and old-fashioned and prefer not to stray from the proven path. They operate like clockwork and prefer fixed schedules. The Roosters of dawn and dusk are more outspoken and noisy while their evening brothers and sisters are less aggressive and ambitious. However, all of them make their presence known in one way or another.

WINTER

Winter brings forth the most analytical Roosters who love to plan and investigate. Gifted with scientific minds and a love of finding the truth, they are the geniuses of the mathematical and computer worlds. Wizards are such complex and intricate beings, however, that they can be helpless when it comes to doing practical chores. Eccentric and proud, they do not like to reveal their true feelings except to the few people they feel they can trust. When they are negative, they can nit-pick to exasperation. They are often misunderstood because of their love of controversy and their pompous know-it-all attitude. Winter Roosters are also tight-fisted and frugal but given to bouts of overspending for overrated items or things they feel will enhance their importance or knowledge. But, on the whole, these natives will do more than their fair share and take on responsibilities without complaints. As a matter of fact, they will fight for more commitment than others feel they can handle.

FAMOUS PERSONS BORN IN THE YEAR OF THE ROOSTER

Metal
Prince Philip
Peter Ustinov
Alex Haley
Deborah Kerr

Wood
King Birendra of Nepal
Elton John

Earth
Edwin Land
Baron Guy de Rothschild
Queen Juliana of the Netherlands
Peter Drucker
Elia Kazan
Katharine Hepburn

Fire
Daniel K. Ludwig
Pope Paul VI
Grover Cleveland
Paul Gallico

Water
Emperor Akihito of Japan

11

The Eleventh Sign
of the Lunar Cycle

The Dog

The martial strains have summoned me
    to hear your sorrows,
    still your pain.
I am the protector of Justice.
Equality—my sole friend.
My vision is never blurred by cowardice,
    my soul never chained.
Life without honor
    is life in vain.

I AM THE DOG.

Lunar Years of the Dog in the Western Calendar	Elements
10 February 1910 to 29 January 1911	Metal
28 January 1922 to 15 February 1923	Water
14 February 1934 to 3 February 1935	Wood
2 February 1946 to 21 January 1947	Fire
18 February 1958 to 7 February 1959	Earth
6 February 1970 to 26 January 1971	Metal
25 January 1982 to 12 February 1983	Water
10 February 1994 to 30 January 1995	Wood
29 January 2006 to 17 February 2007	Fire

If you were born on the day before the start of the lunar year of the Dog, e.g., 17th February 1958, your animal sign is the one before the Dog, the Rooster, the tenth lunar sign.

If you were born on the day after the last day of the lunar year of the Dog, e.g., 8th February 1959, your sign is the one following the Dog, the Boar, the twelfth lunar sign.

The Dog rules the two hour segment of the day between 7 P.M. and 9 P.M. Persons born during this period are said to have the Dog sign as their ascendant and will display many of the characteristics common to this sign and have great affinity for persons born under this sign. Quite possibly, one parent or grandparent will also have been born in the year of the Dog.

The Dog's appointed direction is west-northwest; its season is autumn and its principal month, October. The Dog sign is the eleventh in the Chinese cycle and corresponds to the Western astrological sign of Libra, which rules autumn from September 23rd to October 22nd. The Dog's fixed element is Metal and its sign is denoted a masculine or yang sign.

THE DOG PERSONALITY

The Dog may be the most likeable sign in the Chinese horoscope. A person born in the year of the Dog is honest, intelligent and straightforward. He has a deep sense of loyalty and a passion for justice and fair play. A Dog native is usually animated and attractive and will exude sex appeal. Generally amiable and unpretentious, he will know how to get along with others and is not too demanding. The egalitarian Dog likes to meet others halfway, is always willing to listen to reason and can be counted on to do his share.

If you have a forthright Dog for a friend, you know that when you are in trouble, all you have to do is dial D-O-G. No matter how much he or she complains, scolds or feigns indifference, the Dog person cannot ignore a real call for help. At times, the Dog protects the interests of others more avidly than his own. If anyone will bail you out ten times out of ten, he must be a Dog. The Dog-born sometimes sticks to the object of his affection no matter how unworthy the person may be. You don't find a Dog leaving home just because he discovers that his master or mistress has the proverbial feet of clay. He makes allowances for such frailties and will probably remain loyal through thick and thin. And if he does leave home, well, don't blame him; it must be a truly dismal place indeed! The Dog does not desert easily.

Like his equally humanitarian friend, the Tiger, the Dog seldom directs his wrath at someone personally. He will take you to task over a specific act or offense without hating you entirely or forever. His anger is more of a bright flash. It could come without warning and may die as quickly, too. But it will always be a justifiable kind of anger—without malice, without rancor and without jealousy. When all is said and done and proper reparations have been made, he can bury the hatchet.

Not all Dogs look for fights. It would be more apt to say the Dog person is a clear-eyed and open-minded observer who aims to preserve the social fabric and guard the interests of the general public.

Once in a while, when the Dog decides to take up a cause he thinks is right, he will emerge victorious. Fortunately, he is not one to champion bad causes because his ideals and morals are of the highest order. As the symbol of justice, the Dog is very serious about his self-imposed responsibilities.

Collectively speaking, the Dog is not materialistic. Nor is he cer-

emonious; he prefers plain talk. He usually sees right through people's motives anyway, so fancy language merely affects him the
wrong way. He is a natural lawyer and will listen to your case objectively. But don't pry into his affairs or he will become secretive and
withdrawn. The Dog was born with his defense shields up. You will
have to gain his confidence gradually and wait for him to warm up
to you.

The Dog is reputed to be cynical, but this is a callous generaliza-
tion. Actually, it is more fitting to say that puppies are universally love-
able and irresistible, young dogs are frisky and full of life and only
mature or old dogs earn the right to be the diehard cynics of the
Oriental zodiac. Staunch public defenders and members of the Old
Guard must indeed belong to the elite Dog unit, getting bleary-eyed
with disillusionment as the years go by but remaining ever faithful in
rallying to the bugle's call. Ranting in disgust about how low our
morals have sunk, the Dog will still be found pitting his strength
against the forces of evil and answering every S.O.S. that comes his
way.

Even as a young pup, the Dog will be able to spot the good guys
and the bad guys. He'll want to be the one of the good guys, of
course. While the lady Dog will be Joan of Arc, he will be the knight
in shining armor.

The Dog, whether he admits it or not, will have an inborn need to
divide people into fixed categories. To him, you are either a friend or
foe; a supporter or an opponent. He doesn't allow any mousey grays
or other shades of in-between. He has to know how to classify you
before he can relax in your company. His decision to trust or not trust
you is often a final one. And if he does suspect you, well, he may not
be rude enough to come right out and accuse you without evidence,
but you can be sure he will be watching you. However, even snarling,
barking, mad dogs have a good idea of how the legal system works
and won't come after you without a warrant. But when he's onto
your scent and picks up your tracks, it will be difficult to shake him
off.

On the whole, the Dog is only violent when he is attacked on his home territory. He will work hard when he has to or wants to; otherwise, he has a certain "lie by the fire" kind of laziness. Yet, while he is tolerant and forgiving of his friends, he can be critical of and emotionally cold to people he dislikes. Practical, fearless and the owner of one very sharp tongue, the Dog person is ultrarealistic and outspoken. He will make a good judge because he favors no one, not even himself, in the final analysis.

But while the Dog will be respected for his integrity, he will be loved for his warmth, charisma and superb understanding of human nature. With his astute intelligence and noble character, he makes a good but sometimes reluctant leader. People trust him and hold him in high esteem because of his sense of duty. The Dog is an unemotional, although altruistic leader. But he is also prone to bouts of erratic and cantankerous behavior. This may be because he is really an introvert at heart and hates having to function in a social and political arena.

The Dog does not care much about money, but should he have desperate need for it, no one is better equipped to find it. In many cases, he will be born into a good family; if not, he will elevate himself without shunning his family or hiding his humble origins.

While he puts on a bright and cheerful appearance, the Dog is by nature a pessimist. He tends to worry unnecessarily and will expect trouble to be lurking in every corner. But there are times when his predictions come true. Anyway, it would be wise to note that both Orientals and Westerners believe that everyone needs a Dog at home to distinguish friend from foe, and to warn of when danger approaches.

You can trust the Dog to hand you the bad news with the good. With his matter-of-fact way, he may even be quite good at breaking sad tidings, especially to theatrical and overemotional people. It is not that he enjoys informing people of disaster, but it is against his nature to hedge or delay the inevitable. He is a definite person and he has a need to give you a definite answer. As for himself, he can face the hard facts of life even if he is young and untried.

When he is in the right, the Dog can be obstinate and unbending.

It is hard to influence the unprejudiced Dog once he makes up his mind. He will cut the opposition's arguments to ribbons with his flawless logic and acid wit. His bad temper and hot criticism can do a lot of damage but he only resorts to them when he is getting nowhere with diplomacy and formal protests. The Dog may be pugnacious and quarrelsome but he will take his fights into the open and rarely stoops to underhanded methods in order to win. He excels as a military man, lawyer, teacher, judge, doctor, captain of industry, or missionary. He is one person who can carry on revolutionary activities while holding pacifist views. Ethical and moralistic by nature, he will never want to change sides once he has made his choice and will go down with the ship rather than abandon it.

The lady Dog will be a thoughtful and capable person who will be a simple dresser, preferring casual, serviceable clothing. She will opt for a loose and flowing hair style that will frame her expressive face quite dramatically. Dog girls have a warm enduring beauty. Ava Gardner, Sophia Loren, Brigitte Bardot, Jane Fonda, Connie Chung and Cher are but a few of the glamorous examples of fabulous females born under this sign.

She can become curt, impertinent and impatient when she is crossed, but on the whole she is unaffected and attentive to the needs of others. Cooperative, unprejudiced and a very good sport, she will enjoy dancing, swimming, tennis or any other lively outdoor activity. A real friend to her husband and children, she will allow them enough freedom to express themselves and choose their own futures without being possessive or interfering.

Although she exhibits a fairly amiable disposition and has a ready smile for everyone, the Dog lady likes to form friendships slowly. You will have to come over to her house for tea (a good sign of acceptance) and discover each other's qualities leisurely. Compare likes and dislikes. Exchange mutual oaths of loyalty. When her sense of equilibrium is satisfied, you will get the royal stamp of approval. Henceforth, your name is engraved in gold in her little black book under the heading "Friend" (she has another section for enemies), and when you call upon her she will come to your rescue wherever she may be.

The Dog person is never without resources, and even when he does not have direct power, he will wield influence with important or decision-making people through his sound advice and remarkable insight. People lend him their ears, and he champions moderation in all things. Yet the Dog-born is the first to see and try to avoid the perils of being at the top of the power game; as a result, he is often criticized for his lack of desire for fame and authority. He keeps his aspirations to himself and is modestly prepared to serve others, if that is his duty, or else be left alone to do whatever pleases him most. Moreover, he is not renowned for his patience and has the tendency to snap at others when irked.

It will never be easy for the Dog to trust everyone profoundly, as the Boar does, but he does his best to bring out the good in his fellow men. Once you have gained his allegiance, he will have complete faith in you and give you his undivided support. Try criticizing someone who is dear to the Dog, and you will be in for a very strong rebuttal. And while he will not go out and fall madly in love like the Horse or Tiger, he will be deeply attached to and affectionate with those he loves. If you are looking for true companionship and fidelity throughout life, you can't go wrong loving a Dog.

Most people born under this sign are tough—they can endure a good deal of stress without cracking up. The Dog's stable mind makes him a good counselor, priest or psychologist. During times of crisis, he can suffer great hardships and deprivation without complaining. He earnestly wishes that the world were a better place to live in, and he will not be afraid to go out and do something about it. Many saints and martyrs were born under the idealistic sign of the Dog.

A Dog who is born at night is reputed to be more aggressive and high-strung than one born during the day. Dogs of all seasons will be well-provided for throughout their lives and have need of little.

The Dog will be most compatible with the Horse, the Rabbit and the Tiger. He will have no conflict with the Rat, Snake, Monkey, Boar or another Dog. The Rooster he will have difficulty understanding but will strive to stake out boundaries and co-exist with. The one he will never really get himself to believe in is the overconfident Dragon.

Neither can he find it pleasant to tolerate the constant complaints of the indulgent Sheep. Likewise, the Dragon will be enraged when the Dog pours cold water over his grand designs, and the Sheep will call the Dog insensitive.

In his life, paradoxically, the Dog's happiness may come from worrying about and protecting those he loves. Often putting his own wishes on hold, he is always ready to sacrifice himself for the good of others; the Dog is a humanitarian deserving of the respect and love of those who know him.

THE DOG CHILD

This child will be friendly, happy and well-balanced. Cheerful and even-tempered, he expects little of others and can accept his parents and friends as they are. Open, confident and loyal, he will perceive other people's viewpoints with amazing clarity while still maintaining his own convictions and dignity. He will never allow himself to be bullied and in all probability will put up a hefty fight with the neighborhood tyrant and win the respect of his peers.

Sensible and fairly consistent, the young Dog will get his schoolwork done without much trouble. He will be reasonable when asked to help around the house and will be protective toward younger family members.

Playful and outgoing, he will insist on having a certain degree of independence. But the faithful Dog will never stray too far from home. This child will be known and liked for his sense of humor, warmth and candid ways. When offended, the Dog child can turn rebellious, mean and hypercritical. But his anger flares and subsides relatively quickly and he returns to his normal equilibrium. He will not keep a grudge for long and can forgive and forget readily once he feels you have listened to his grievance.

When he is negative, the Dog is pugnacious, argumentative, caustic and unbendingly opinionated. He is only liberal and fair-minded if not pushed too far. When he feels he has been taken undue advantage of, the Dog will retaliate bitterly and without any compassion. Once he starts to fight, the Dog will not be open to discussion or negotiations anymore. It is better never to challenge this tolerant child to the point of no return. The unassuming Dog can erupt like a volcano.

If the Dog child is rejected or unappreciated, he could be lethargic, insensitive, cynical or plain indifferent to the wishes of his parents. Compliment and encourage him and this child will flourish and reciprocate lavishly. Basically, he is cooperative, so there should be no need to cajole or threaten him in any way. Efficient and diplomatic, the Dog will exhibit a lack of prejudice, or at least make a point never to show it. He is inclined to avoid scenes rather than create them. But, with his conscience as his guide, you can be sure he will speak up if his rights are trampled. He hates to be taken advantage of or treated unfairly.

It will be safe to give him responsibilities or take him into your confidence even at an early age. The trustworthy Dog will not like to be accused of having a loose tongue. He will guard a secret like a sacred trust.

To sum it up, the Dog will always defend what is his. He will have a high sense of values and to him home, and family will come first.

THE FIVE DIFFERENT DOGS

METAL DOG—1910, 1970

This type of Dog can be unwavering in his convictions and highly critical of every infraction of the law, according to his interpretation. However, his principles are of the highest, and fundamentally he is noble and charitable. He will give himself to a lifetime of selfless dedication if he finds an object or cause worthy of his devotion. Yet he can be ruthless when aroused and will pursue his enemies until they are annihilated. However, at home he is loving and gentle and, at times, overprotective.

The Metal element combined with his lunar sign, which is also governed by Metal, produces a double Metal sign, which is extremely formidable. Tibetans call this combination the "Iron Dog" and look upon its year with considerable apprehension as it could be either very good or very bad, depending on whether it takes on a negative or positive course.

The stern and principled Metal Dog will exercise strong mental discipline over himself and take things very seriously—especially when they concern the affairs of his heart or country.

His loyalty is unquestionable and he has strong political views. Never one to be labeled as indecisive, he will pick a side and never desert his affiliation. Consequently, even though he hates injustice and foul play, this type of Dog can resort to extreme measures when he insists that others subscribe to his views.

WATER DOG—1922, 1982

This intuitive type of Dog will be difficult to lead astray. He could be very attractive or a striking beauty if a female.

Water gives him more reflective qualities and he will be sympathetic even to the views of the opposition. However, despite his pleasant personality and democratic stance, he does not always establish strong personal bonds with those close to him and is often too liberal when he should be more firm.

More easygoing than other Dogs, he will tend to be lenient with himself as well as with others, often indulging in self-gratification and adventurous sprees. But because his strong temperament will be toned down by the Water element, this Dog is able to contain his emotions to an admirable degree and will present a calm and charming exterior. He projects an impressive public image.

A good counselor, fair judge and legal-minded operator, the Water Dog will be fluid in expressing himself, using psychological approaches that are hard to reject or refute. He is also fated to have a large circle of friends and his company will be much sought after.

WOOD DOG—1934, 1994

This is an enchanting, warm-hearted and even-tempered sort of Dog who, in spite of his candor and wariness of strangers, will form close and lasting relationships with those he chooses to befriend and love. Honest, considerate and well-liked, this Dog seeks intellectual stimulation and will work hard to develop himself.

Wood gives him a more stable and generous nature and he will seek growth, balance and beauty in his environment. He will also be attracted to money and success but will preserve himself from too much materialism. With an aptitude for dealing with vast numbers of people from all walks of life, he or she will act with maturity and common sense.

The popular Wood Dog will gravitate toward refinement and social grace despite his hidden assertive qualities. Energetic and cooperative, he will like to deal in partnerships or ally himself with the powerful.

He is basically group-oriented and will be eager to please as many of his associates as possible. Thus, this type of Dog can sometimes be held back because he refuses to move without the sanction and backing of others. He must learn independence even if it means rocking the boat on occasion.

FIRE DOG—1946, 2006

This is a highly dramatic and attractive Dog that will be thrown into the limelight by his alluring yet friendly personality. He will be defiant and rebellious when forced to do something against his will, but he will be very popular with the opposite sex. Although he may be a life-of-the-party type, he is careful to practice what he preaches and will not be spoiled by success and fortune. Fire makes him very fierce when attacked, and he will only make threats he can carry out. This Dog's bite is just as strong as his bark.

The buoyant and self-assured Fire Dog has great magnetic charm and can convince others to follow his lead. His independent spirit and courage prevents him from being afraid of getting involved with others. He will constantly thrill to new experiences and adventures. But he needs a strong shining example to pattern himself after. He will relate better to people older than himself, those from whom he can learn a great deal, or can depend on to bring stability into his life.

Fire makes him or her more creative and pure in expression. He will be charged with super willpower and a natural honesty that people find hard to resist. His outgoing character combined with the

Dog's basic faith and idealism will help him to succeed in ambitious endeavors and overcome great barriers.

EARTH DOG—1898, 1958

This Dog will be an impartial dispenser of sound advice and justice. An efficient and constructive thinker, he moves slowly and to good purpose. He is faithful to his beliefs but will bow to majority rule. Vigilant and careful, he will appreciate the proper use of money and power, and have a fixed scale of values from which he seldom deviates.

Quiet, kind-hearted but secretive, he will understand how to inspire others and instruct them wisely. Yet because of his high moral standards and unfailing idealism, he tends to overperform and may demand excessive dedication and loyalty from others.

A good fighter and an equally good survivor, this Dog is practical and less sentimental. The realistic Earth Dog will value his individualism and self-respect, and will speak without reserve straight from his heart. He will not abuse powers bestowed on him and will delegate duties with a keen eye as to other people's potentials. He is never totally crushed by defeat nor overconfident in victory.

COMPATIBILITY AND CONFLICT CHARTS FOR THE DOG

The Dog is part of the Third Triangle of Affinity, a group consisting of action-oriented signs who seek to serve humanity, promote universal understanding and heighten communications. The Tiger, Horse and Dog are good at establishing personal contacts and developing strong bonds with their fellow human beings. This trio relates well to each other and is basically honest, open and motivated by idealism. Unorthodox at times but always honorable in intent, they act more on impulse and tend to heed their inner conscience rather than the dictates of convention. They provide their own counsel and inspire others to action by their high-spirited and aggressive personalities. Extroverted, energetic and united against adversity and injustice, they will get along fabulously together.

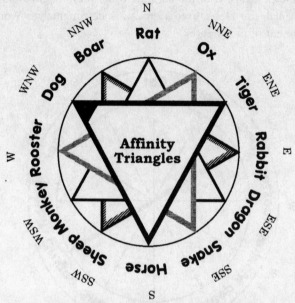

TRIANGLE OF AFFINITY FOR THE DOG

The Dog will encounter his greatest personality clashes with someone born in the year of the Dragon. Anyone whose ascendant is the Dragon (born between 7 A.M. and 9 A.M.) will most likely also come into conflict with the Dog native. In the Circle of Conflict, the Dog and Dragon are on opposite sides, 180 degrees apart. They will have different opinions and outlooks and have difficulty understanding each other. Unless a Dog native is born during the hours of the Dragon or vice versa, there is little these two will have in common. Besides having different personalities and preferences, they will do things that may be counterproductive to each other, perhaps without meaning to. Unintentional as these actions may be, they tend to produce friction and disputes. They find it hard to relax in each other's company and tend to doubt or question each other's loyalties. It would be advisable for them to work through experienced mediators who are respected by both of them.

The Dog's season is in the autumn while the Dragon rules in the spring. Metal, the Dog's fixed element, is detrimental to Wood, the fixed element of the Dragon.

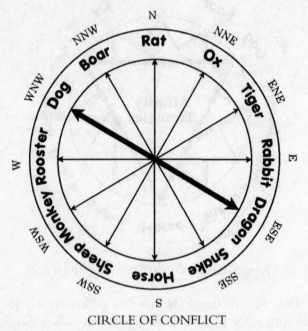

CIRCLE OF CONFLICT

Aside from the most compatible signs, the Tiger and Horse, and the least compatible, the Dragon, the other nine lunar signs are compatible or incompatible with the Tiger to varying degrees.

Rat

The Dog is friendly but pragmatic. The Rat has great respect for the Dog who, because he has a different set of priorities, does not contest the Rat in a struggle for dominance. Both know their limits and territories. They do not have any serious differences in outlook, and will work together as a team when necessary. However, should the Rat clash with the Horse, the Dog will not take the Rat's side since most Dogs will vote for the Horse (or Tiger) every time.

Ox

Dog and Ox could do well together if they move in the same circles and have the same goals. Trouble is that they may not have great sympathy or attraction for one another. The Dog is warm, likeable and idealistic at the same time. The Ox is stern, determined and loyal only to his ideals. He can be uncompromising. These two could go their separate ways if the chemistry is not right. The congenial Dog may find the Ox too rigid and uncooperative unless they both champion the same cause. In a fight for justice or freedom, this could be a great duo. Otherwise, they move at different speeds.

Rabbit

The Dog and the Rabbit will have a compatible and rewarding union since they can establish trust and understanding with little effort. Both will do their share to make the relationship workable or else peacefully call a truce and make a graceful exit. When these two join forces, they will find harmony and happiness if neither is overly aggressive or demanding. The Rabbit is not combative but is a bit more selfish than the Dog. The Dog will rely on the Rabbit's intelligent advice and his ability to take the middle of the road and avoid stress or conflict.

Snake

The Snake and the Dog have mutual respect for each other and do not want confrontation if they can avoid it. They will be compatible and amicable to a degree, as the Dog is trustworthy and the Snake's ambitiousness could do the Dog some good. The Dog will be loyal so long as the Snake is persevering, steadfast and faithful. The Snake is able to imbue the Dog with his ideas and philosophies and will share the Dog's idealistic outlook on life. The Dog is not overly possessive and will understand the Snake's need for privacy when the Snake becomes introspective or secretive.

Sheep

The Sheep and the Dog may have few things in common, but they do share a mutual goodwill that keeps each on his side of the fence. They work at different speeds and have different objectives. If he is able to do his duty and fulfill his responsibilities, the Dog could-n't care less whether anyone likes him. The Sheep needs consensus and approval before he can act; he is always so worried about hurting others that sometimes he becomes a fence-sitter. The Dog cannot and will not tolerate disloyalty and can be quite stern when the Sheep fails to promptly decide whom to support. The Sheep has difficulty taking sides and may want to please everyone, an attitude the Dog cannot comprehend.

Monkey

There should be no large challenges for dominance between the Monkey and Dog. They are guided by different priorities and values but tend to stay out of each other's way if they have conflicting inter-ests. The Monkey knows better than to pull the Dog's tail since the Dog is unrelenting once he is aroused. The Dog can be good-natured when it comes to the Monkey's tricks and may not take the Monkey too seriously if he can benefit from the Monkey's expertise. They will enjoy friendly to warm relations if they share mutual goals and inter-ests. However, the Dog is devoted to the Tiger and could be defensive and protective should the Monkey try to provoke the Tiger.

Rooster

The Rooster may worry the poor Dog with his high-flying acts of daring and nonsensical ideas. The Dog would like to be a loyal friend and supporter of the Rooster's splendid ideals, but, at times, he finds it hard to understand the Chicken's propensity for controversy. However, the Dog can be patient and understanding if the Rooster proves his motives are aboveboard and he has everyone's interests at heart. Once the Dog is convinced the Rooster's intentions are honor-able, he will be accepting of his eccentric but exacting ways.

Dog

Dogs are quite compatible unless they have strongly conflicting ascendants. They have congenial, reasonable outlooks, and do not tend to look for fights once they have established their positions. Dogs can work together in a spirit of cooperation once they are aware of their respective responsibilities. No doubt, they will snap at each other and

be argumentative if they feel threatened, but common goals or enemies could keep them vigilant and united. However, if one has a
dominant Dragon ascendant or an incompatible Sheep ascendant,
there could be trouble.

Boar

The Boar is sincere and helpful by nature and will have no serious
personality clashes with the Dog. Relationships will be acceptable and
agreeable if the Pig displays moderation and modesty and does not
impose on the Dog's sense of propriety. The Dog could be critical of
the Boar's lifestyle and values, and tend to lecture the Pig or try to
make him less indulgent. The thick-skinned Boar will not readily take
the Dog's well-meaning advice but, on the other hand, he will not be
offended or discouraged either. These two will get along moderately
well, especially if they share the same loyalties.

THE DOG AND HIS ASCENDANTS

We all have a shadow that follows us throughout life. Sometimes it
grows bigger than life and at other times it shrinks until it disappears
into the soles of our feet. Sometimes it walks tall before us and on
other occasions it lags behind like a sulking friend. In Chinese horoscopes, this constant partner, manifested or not, is our ascendant, the
animal sign that rules the hour of our birth and becomes a comrade
on our journey though life. We may view it as friend or foe or even a
little of both. It surfaces when we least expect and shows a better or
worse side of our nature. We can often be confounded by the way we
listen to our "other self" as well as feel resentful of the significant
influence it can exert on us. Actually, a personality has many rings
around the centered "self." Each ring can have a different size, texture
and aura. When all these factors combine, they bring forth the unique
individual that the person truly is. Hence, a Dragon with an ascendant
that is not compatible, like the Dog, has perhaps a more difficult inner
struggle than say a Snake born during the hours of the Snake. The
double intensity of the Snake person will be easily understood by
horoscope readers while the more intricate Dragon/Dog may exhibit
the contrary Dog and Dragon traits to varying degrees. There are
many voices within each person. But, in the end, only the individual

determines which course he will follow, which choices he will make.

The time of birth used to determine the ascendant is always the local time in the place of birth.

If you were born between:

11 P.M. and 1 A.M. = The Hours of the Rat

You can be so loving but not always so giving. That Rat ascendant is figuring out a monetary angle even as the Dog self is moralizing. You are considerate but inquisitive and careful about money— mainly your own. A rather crafty Dog with a charming disposition and many interests, you always put your loved ones first, and you dote on your family. However, you can be combative, critical and very self-protective when your interests are threatened. Your shrewd assessment of people should be valued, for you have an intuitive sense of friend and foe.

1 A.M. and 3 A.M. = The Hours of the Ox

With the Ox ruling the time of your birth, you may have a brusque personality but will possess unquestionable veracity. Although you have a spotless reputation, you could be too conservative and dour in many ways. You are a staunch defender of what you believe in, and you do not like to change your opinions or learn new tricks. But you are completely relaxed in the company of loved ones and can be a devoted friend to people you trust. Everyone can rely on your word and you try never to let anyone down or break your solemn promises.

3 A.M. and 5 A.M. = The Hours of the Tiger

Both signs here are tirelessly active and courageous, and your Tiger ascendant gives you extra sparkle and a great appetite for life. However, the Tiger could make the Dog in you more impatient and critical than he already is. This combination could produce a more motivated and passionate Dog with a keen sense of adventure and love of risk. With your noble heart, you will always come to the rescue of anyone less fortunate or bravely defend an unpopular cause you believe in.

5 A.M. and 7 A.M. = The Hours of the Rabbit

The Rabbit ascendant may create a Dog who is all for détente. You tend to weigh the pros and cons carefully before taking sides. The gentle Hare is apt to be lighthearted and will not like baring fangs. You will just hop your way out of trouble and be more concerned with your creature comforts and bank account. Instead of chasing down the opposition and challenging them to a duel, you may organize a class action lawsuit and seek huge punitive damages. All the while, you will maintain that Rabbit reserve and soft-spoken sophistication.

7 A.M. and 9 A.M. = The Hours of the Dragon

The Dragon in you could produce a very idealistic Dog who will be a miracle worker or a missionary. You would perhaps qualify for sainthood if you can only accept other religions beside your own. Dragon and Dog are opposite signs but they can create a dogmatic combination. You like things done your way and are not averse to using all the power you have to enforce the rules.

9 A.M. and 11 A.M. = The Hours of the Snake

As a Dog with a Snake ascendant, you could be a quiet, religious person who guards his secrets well. Competent and mentally superior, you are an intellectual and a philosopher who rarely seeks or takes advice. Now and then, the Snake in you will bend the Dog's sense of justice a little, so you will not be averse to taking shortcuts in order to achieve your goals. You have an air of mystery that others may find attractive or sexually appealing. When angry you are fierce and unforgiving. Others would be unwise to tangle with you, especially where your ambitions are concerned. The Snake in you is vindictive.

11 A.M. and 1 P.M. = The Hours of the Horse

The happy Horse ascendant could make you a sharp, sunny Dog with stunningly quick responses. You never miss a cue and could be everyone's best friend—but they shouldn't ask you to prove it. You will go merrily on your way if imposed upon too often. Yet you are sportive, extremely intelligent and astute, a pleasure to know and be with. The Horse makes the Dog less argumentative but more temperamental. You might have bursts of anger, but once they pass, you forget about them. You don't carry grudges. Your lightning-swift reflexes and keen powers of observation combined with your sense of fair play will be your main assets.

1 P.M. and 3 P.M. = The Hours of the Sheep

The soft-hearted and creative Sheep ascendant blesses your birth sign with a warm, sensitive nature that will be sympathetic to the woes of friends and strangers alike. You won't lose the Dog's keen sense of responsibility, but the Dog may keep one eye closed now and then to make allowances for the weaknesses of those you love. People will open their hearts and purses to you and seek your advice and assistance. You attract them with your understanding nature and your ability to relate or at least listen to their problems. Because of your generosity and helpful nature, you will never be found without friends and supporters.

3 P.M. and 5 P.M. = The Hours of the Monkey

The Monkey's ascendant produces a Dog with a stretchable conscience and unfailing wit. Nothing is impossible for you. You can be amusing, diverse and versatile. With this splendid interlacing of character and ingenuity, you are never without an answer or a question. The Dog is less guarded because of the Monkey's curiosity and enthusiasm. You will always have that positive mental attitude that winners are made of. And you are less likely to stay in one job or in one place for long, for the Monkey leads the Dog away from familiar grounds in search of adventure and knowledge.

5 P.M. and 7 P.M. = The Hours of the Rooster

With the Rooster ruling your birth time, you could be a preachy Dog who always has the "right" point of view. Sometimes you tend to preach more than practice. You are very analytical and capable of achieving your goals, but you tend to investigate and contemplate too long before you act. Conservative and cautious, you can be domineering but people are still sufficiently impressed with your credentials to believe in your ideas. Industrious, devoted and extremely supportive, you have no qualms about fighting for what you believe in and defending your territory.

7 P.M. and 9 P.M. = The Hours of the Dog

Having both your ascendant and birth sign under the auspices of the faithful Dog could make you ultra-defensive and ever alert. You are on the lookout for causes to fight for, wrongs to right and lost lambs to save. This in addition to all your other self-appointed duties in life, such as guarding hearth and home. You have a big heart and an honest nature. But, let's face it, at times you can be a totally committed revolutionary. You will always stand your ground, you never leave your post or surrender anything that is yours. No matter how docile or harmless you may appear, people should be warned that you will bite as well as bark.

9 P.M. and 11 P.M. = The Hours of the Boar

With the passionate Pig ruling your birth hours, you could be one burly, sensuous and emotionally charged Dog. The Boar is sociable and capable of excess while the Dog is fearless in censoring others who step out of line. You tend to worry more about the welfare of others than your own. But then, as the Chinese proverb goes: "One who secures the good of others, has already secured his own." You will never be without people who love you and will care for you in good times and bad.

HOW THE DOG FARES IN THE LUNAR CYCLE

1. The Year of the Rat 1996

The Rat brings forth a very fortunate year. The Dog could be successful in business or may receive additional income from investments. The seeds he planted in the past will finally bear fruit. His health is good but there will be some problems in his home life or with young children. He should avoid lending money to friends and relatives alike. The Rat's year also brings good news mixed with gossip and rumor, so the Dog must learn to discount what he hears and only believe in proven facts. Overall, this will be a busy and exciting time for the Dog.

2. The Year of the Ox 1997

The coming of the Ox ushers in a year of uncertainties for the Dog. He may suffer from hasty decisions or may have to make difficult concessions. The Ox's reign is rigid but may be sympathetic to the Dog's objectives if the Dog can remain patient and pragmatic. He must avoid confrontation at all costs and be conciliatory toward his

foes. If the dog manages to keep the peace with a spirit of cooperation and understanding, he could end the year with a bonus. His
tenacity, loyalty and hard work will pay dividends as people who have
doubted or tried to obstruct him will finally realize his worth.

3. The Year of the Tiger 1998

The optimistic Tiger gives the Dog a moderately happy year. There will
be no serious disputes at home or at work. Instead the Dog will meet
new friends, rediscover old contacts and find new loves in his life. Some
romantic squabbles are predicted, but they will do no permanent damage as the Dog is honest and noble in his affections. However, the Dog's
net results this year could be mixed unless he is careful about spending
and overrated reports that should not be taken at face value. Friends
and family will make too many demands on his time—the Dog should
be cautious and not allow others to take advantage of his generosity.

4. The Year of the Rabbit 1999

The virtuous Hare brings a favorable year for the aspirations of the
Dog. He can start his own business or go into a partnership. He will be
able to advance his position and can reorganize matters to the benefit
of others. Difficulties are resolved with a minimum of complications
because it is so easy for him to gain the people's cooperation. In his love
and home lives, the Dog will find harmony or solve problems without
much difficulty. The Dog will find few obstacles in his path. He is able
to concentrate on doing what he likes and pursuing his hobbies.
Because the Rabbit gives the Dog a lot of room to maneuver in, the
Dog will be able to relax and, as a result, become more productive.

5. The Year of the Dragon 2000

The Dragon's year puts the Dog on guard. The Dog will have to strive
very hard to maintain his former status and may have to constantly fight
off the competition. The Dog cannot believe the Dragon's outrageous
predictions and grandiose schemes. They are too good to be true and
the Dog may stir up conflict to prove his point or poke holes in the
Dragon's plan. But people may not listen to the Dog's pessimistic warn-
ings, and he will not be able to find support or get others to agree with
him. A time for him to lie low and join forces with others instead of

acting independently. He will receive good news in the winter. Protective measures should be taken for himself and his loved ones no matter what others say, even if they ridicule his concerns.

6. The Year of the Snake 2001

The wise and powerful Snake brings a good and productive year. The Dog will have to work hard but he will receive due recognition for his efforts. He will be lucky in love and in his business investments, and will secure the support of the right people. He should take things easy and enjoy his personal life more. He will also benefit immensely from good advice or tips given him if he follows through with them decisively. Like the Snake, he must "wait long and strike fast" in order to take advantage of these rare windows of opportunity. He should deal calmly with setbacks and refuse to be drawn into controversy or lose sight of his goals.

7. The Year of the Horse 2002

The Horse's fast-paced year is a time of expansion and progress for the Dog. Promotions and real financial gains are indicated; he will be at the peak of his power and luck. There may be unhappy news at home or misunderstandings in affairs of the heart as the Dog tries to please everyone and stretches his time and resources. He may incur the loss of a small belonging or investment due to speculation. The Dog will entertain or travel a lot this year, chasing good opportunities. He will have to use his wits a great deal, but new friends and contacts will provide him with assistance and open doors for him. Healthwise, he must guard against overexhaustion and learn to pace himself.

8. The Year of the Sheep 2003

This may only be a moderate year for the Dog because the Sheep's year is too capricious for the strong-minded Dog. Anxiety and petty worries beset him and consume his time and energy. This will be a year for him to take long-range views and do future planning instead of being discouraged by the current slow state of affairs. The Dog can prevent losses and resolve differences provided he holds his tongue and refuses to lose his temper. If he remains patient and conservative, matters will work out well in the end, but only after much scolding and flexing of muscles. However, all's well that ends well, and the Dog must not be too harsh on himself or on others during the year of the complacent Sheep.

9. The Year of the Monkey 2004

The unsinkable Monkey brings the Dog a fairly workable year. It will be hectic and not as fruitful as he expects, but there will be good news or celebrations at home. The Monkey year provides activity and involvement for the Dog, including a time of extra expenses, more traveling than usual or a change in residence. New friends and important people will fête the Dog and ask him to join their ventures. He should investigate before making commitments since the Monkey is clever and quick but also scheming in his motives. If the Dog can get a free ride, he should go for it. Every person is out for himself this year, so the Dog should not hesitate to take advantage of the situations offered him or else he will be left out.

10. The Year of the Rooster 2005

The over-achieving Rooster year brings a mixture of good and bad for the Dog native. He could encounter problems with health, romance, government or superiors that, while petty, are still very irritating. The Rooster will reward the hardworking Dog, but not without criticism and unwanted advice. Friends are not too helpful or understanding this year and the Dog finds he cannot get things done without interference. Still, he must persevere and overlook the faults of others in order to maintain harmony. Progress is slow but sure, and the Dog will be able to achieve his goals only after some struggle.

11. The Year of the Dog 2006

The Dog ensures a protected year for his own sign. Monetary and health problems are few and the Dog will be able to increase his knowledge, spend time in study and meditation, or regain lost credibility. He will have some career achievements but will have no large profits or return on investment. However, this is an opportune time for him to make new contacts and gain influential friends and supporters as well as plot his course and find new alliances. His family or love life will prosper because he is able to take time out for personal affairs. People or projects that he had given up on will present him with new possibilities.

12. The Year of the Boar 2007

The earthy Pig brings a calm and prosperous year for the Dog. The Dog person could make some gains through speculations or reap unexpected benefits because of past efforts and investments. There may be some small delays and additional expenses, but he should take things in stride and not make too many demands on his friends and family. On the home front and in his social life, he will be much sought after. His popularity rating is up, and people will seek his advice and cooperation in a congenial atmosphere. The year of the Boar brings the Dog the goodwill of others as well as workable possibilities.

WHEN MOON SIGNS MEET SUN SIGNS

In my interpretation of Chinese horoscopes, the Rat is not linked with the first Western astrological sun sign, Aries. Instead, I pair the Rat with its counterpart based on the month and season of the Rat, which are December and winter. This makes the most sense as the lunar month of December (also called the Twelfth Moon or the Twelfth Earth Branch) is supposed to parallel the sun sign, Sagittarius, the Archer. I envision the Eastern and Western horoscope cycles as two large wheels, each with twelve spokes. To correctly juxtapose these cycles, we must find the matching notch that will join them together. Once the Rat and Sagittarius are paired as the first signs, the other eleven fall into place. Please see the Twenty-Four Segments of the Lunar Almanac. All the dates correspond with the twelve Western solar signs.

If you are born in the year of the Dog under the Western sign of

Sagittarius: 22nd November to 21st December
The Sagittarian Dog = Fire + Positive Metal

This combination produces a playful, adventurous, yet respectable Dog. Swift, open and sincere, he will be well-liked for his considerate ways and sensible outlook. He is informal, warmly personal, and is always ready with a helping hand and a kind word. Although he is well-spoken and well-mannered, he is also realistic, responds quickly to situations and will show his feelings without pretense. A notable keeper of confidences, he rarely squirms or falters under pressure. This solar-lunar union produces an expansive and thoughtful personality.

If you are born in the year of the Dog under the Western sign of

Capricorn: 22nd December to 20th January
The Capricorn Dog = Earth + Positive Metal

The Capricorn Dog is likely to be generous and benevolent but also given to careful and systematic rituals. Things must be done in the correct sequence and with the right priorities. He attaches a great deal of importance to the welfare of his family, is neighborly and a lover of all humanity. However, the Mountain Goat should be able to help him watch out for himself, so that this Dog will be a moderate who looks after his own interests without appearing selfish or greedy. With the Dog's reason and fairness, Capricorn is less stubborn. But this person will remain true to himself above all. When faced with having to make a stand on a controversial issue, you can be sure he will be more accurate than kind.

If you are born in the year of the Dog under the Western sign of

Aquarius: 21st January to 19th February
The Aquarian Dog = Air + Positive Metal

The strongly individualistic Dog is made more changeable, adaptable and daring by the Water Carrier's sign. Invariably rich in humor, he never refuses to give others help or good advice. When dark clouds gather, this person is a crusader in the truest sense of the word. Blessed with a generous heart, he is a giver. Yet he never stays long enough in one place for the grass to grow under his feet, and although he is never intolerant, he does not have many intimate relationships either. He may become rather absent-minded when he wraps himself up in his ideas and causes. Because he is always ready to be involved in a new issue, he tends to neglect the old camp for the new. An expert at instigating reforms, he is very broad-minded and will never condemn anything without trying it first.

If you are born in the year of the Dog under the Western sign of

Pisces: 20th February to 20th March
The Piscean Dog = Water + Positive Metal

This East and West combination produces a brave and astute personality. Because the Fish makes the Dog much less defensive and vigilant, the Piscean Dog will not be combative or too aggressive. He prefers security, serenity and comfort, and although he remains attentive to the needs of others, his own interests may come first. Lovely and disconcertingly attractive in his retiring way, this restive Dog is quite happy with the Fish's deep understanding of the inner self. He is therefore less interested in external conflict. He faithfully does his duty, but prides himself on minding his own business. Gifted with foresight and the ability to put things in their proper perspective, the Piscean Dog knows himself or herself well.

If you are born in the year of the Dog under the Western sign of

Aries: 21st March to 19th April
The Aries Dog = Fire + Positive Metal

A poised, determined and dedicated personality, the Aries Dog walks with confidence and his head held high. This warm-hearted and vivacious person will be noted for his refreshing frankness and will be sincere but never offensive. The Aries Dog could be a real trooper when called upon to make sacrifices, as he will seek emotional and spiritual fulfillment over material benefits. He will also excel as a leader because of his noble and selfless ways. The Ram is full of drive and initiative, so the cynical Dog will bounce back quickly after disappointments. The Aries Dog will be a driving force in matters that need his brand of realism and focus.

If you are born in the year of the Dog under the Western sign of

Taurus: 20th April to 20th May
The Taurean Dog = Earth + Positive Metal

The Taurean Dog is a cautious and stable character. Subscribing to the notion of "live and let live," he will not trample on your rights if you do not trample on his. He is easy to be with, and will do his best to make you relax in his company. The Bull is more physical than mental, while the Dog is loyal and generous to others. Together, they form a frank and honest person blessed with endurance and warmth who is never so committed to his own ideas that he won't stop and consider another's point of view. Positive, active and cheerful, he will try his best to please, while sensibly looking out for his interests as well. Realistic and traditional, he will not take to changes in his routine or anything unconventional.

If you are born in the year of the Dog under the Western sign of

Gemini: 21st May to 21st June
The Gemini Dog = Air + Positive Metal

This East-West combination produces a Dog of rapid movement and a multitude of talents. Blessed with star quality, this personality could be an excellent entertainer, as he or she will project a natural and likeable image to the public. Gemini's mercurial spirit quickly adapts to changes and is easily sparked by enthusiasm and excitement. At times, this native seems to have a dual personality: the Dog is appealing in his honesty and kindheartedness, while the Twins tend to be super-optimistic daredevils who won't mind burning the candle at both ends. In the end, this person may suffer because he or she tries to live up to expectations beyond his or her capacity. Yet, it is hard not to envy the Dog for his or her exciting and productive life.

If you are born in the year of the Dog under the Western sign of

Cancer: 22nd June to 21st July
The Cancerian Dog = Water + Positive Metal

The acute sensitivity of the Crab is intertwined here with the internal balance of the Dog. This rational personality will not be too rash or emotional and will be able to maintain his equilibrium and fair-mindedness. However, he may suffer bouts of emotionalism, and become introspective and sulky now and then. But don't let the crabbiness fool you. He does know what he wants in life. In spite of the Dog's sharp and critical tongue, this sign will be an avid appreciator of beauty. The Cancerian Dog may have discriminating taste. He may also be possessive and over-protective. In general, a person of this combination will display a natural affection for others and enjoy serving his home and community while living in refined and comfortable circumstances.

If you are born in the year of the Dog under the Western sign of

Leo: 22nd July to 21st August
The Leo Dog = Fire + Positive Metal

The Lion's august appearance could brighten the warm yet pensive outlook of the Dog and instill in him more ambition and confidence. This native will possess a strong moral fiber and could be domineering and outspoken. Endowed with a safer and saner judgment than most, he can make decisions which are usually above reproach. He hates injustice and will never betray any trust placed in him. Unlikely to humor any fence sitters in his camp, he will insist you support him wholeheartedly or get out of his life. The Lion is captivating and forceful while the Dog is realistic. The result is a person who is not naive about the high cost of success and has the stamina for the large-scale campaigns he must wage in order to win his battles.

If you are born in the year of the Dog under the Western sign of

Virgo: 22nd August to 22nd September
The Virgo Dog = Earth + Positive Metal

This East-West duo produces an academic and responsible soul. Two such fretfully caring signs could combine to produce a worrier, overly concerned with the woes of humanity and with fulfilling a myriad of self-imposed obligations. The sum of their admirable qualities could be much reduced when it comes to total appeal. For although the Dog is more even in temperament, he will be inhibited by the industrious and straitlaced Virgo. Reliable, fair-minded and spiritual, the Virgo Dog is always working for a higher order and a better system. He is also always cleaning up the messes other people make. Virgo's excellent mental powers and the Dog's neutrality may also produce an able legal executor, lawyer or judge.

If you are born in the year of the Dog under the Western sign of

Libra: 23rd September to 22nd October
The Libran Dog = Air + Positive Metal

The Dog is not one to weave underhanded or intricate plots, while Venus's child is not a troublemaker and prefers to remain in everyone's good graces. The result is a Dog who can demonstrate grace under fire with an angelic smile. This kind of person will receive good reviews by being a just and able arbitrator, even if he occasionally seems a touch overgenerous. However, sometimes he has trouble making up his mind or attending to his own needs because he puts off decisions on difficult issues. Libra's peaceful disposition and the Dog's charitable nature will make this subject the sort of social worker who not only genuinely sympathizes with you but also feels obligated to come up with a solution to your problems.

If you are born in the year of the Dog under the Western sign of

Scorpio: 23rd October to 21st November
The Scorpio Dog = Water + Positive Metal

This combination is powerful, dedicated and energetic; a person who will display the Dog's righteous spirit and Pluto's deep insight into human nature. The Scorpio Dog likes to honor his promises but Scorpio here could be detrimental to the liberal Dog's nature. He or she will approach problems with the kind of singlemindedness that is not amenable to compromise. Pugnacious when aroused and unsparing with words, this person can be fierce and unyielding even in the face of defeat. Because he believes in absolute commitment, the Scorpio Dog will serve God or the Devil with equal fervor. But he will never have two masters. In the end, he will be true only to himself. His passion and loyalty never waver as he heads resolutely toward his goal.

THE SEASONS OF THE DOG

SPRING

Dogs born in the spring are carefree and happy by nature and will love teamwork and group action. However, they do need to be relied upon and given responsibility. Helpful and sociable, the noble spring Dogs will keep abreast of what is going on around them and have much to contribute to their families and community. Fated to have a large circle of friends as well as a busy life, these dogs are noted for their bright and optimistic outlooks and ability to devote themselves to unselfish pursuits. However, if they are born into families that do not or cannot take good care of them early in life, they could become cynical, averse to trying anything new or mistrustful of others. Dogs who have been deprived or treated cruelly will have a pessimistic view of life and be unable to relate to or trust others.

SUMMER

Summer nurtures Dogs with its long, warm and sunny days. They will have more confidence in themselves and be at ease with their world. Of course, the Dogs born in the evening of any season tend to be more restless and anxious than their brothers and sisters born during the day. Summer Dogs are noisy and inquisitive. They like to have a large territory and will fight to establish their dominance. Although they have above average communications skills, they are often argumentative, overprotective and at times even militant. Not as cautious or restrained as their siblings of other seasons, they tend to be independent and strong-willed and may not like to retreat once they have started a battle. However, summer Dogs make the most loyal and best friends you can find. They will always totally support whatever or whoever they believe in.

AUTUMN

Autumn breeds idealistic and reflective Dogs who take their duties seriously and care deeply about serving others. They are very dependable and faithful and expect others to be the same way. The

Dogs of the fall season are the most patient of the lot and not as out-spoken. They will investigate before sounding an alarm. However, they can be tenacious and hostile when challenged. Again, the night Dogs are more watchful and protective and do not tolerate even the slightest invasion into their rights or territory. Their defensive nature is heightened by any unhappy experience in life; they never forget injuries. At home, they are selfless and attentive to their loved ones and family, and will be able to bond closely with those they trust and rely upon.

WINTER

The Dogs born in the cold of winter are the most affectionate and protective of all. They obey without question and give of themselves without reserve. However, if they are disappointed or rejected early in life, they can turn into paranoid and reclusive cynics. Their outlook is established early in childhood and their beliefs will not change with time. As a matter of fact, these Dogs tend to reinforce their positions by employing their own code of ethics to determine what they view as fair or unfair. These caring, warm and honorable Dogs can become pugnacious and militant toward those they feel treated them unjustly. They cannot abide discrimination of any kind. The Dogs of winter can be the best of friends or the worst of enemies. There is little in between for them.

FAMOUS PERSONS BORN IN THE YEAR
OF THE DOG

Metal
David Niven
Chiang Ching-kuo
Mother Theresa

Wood
Voltaire
Sir Winston Churchill
Herbert Hoover

Elvis Presley
Ralph Nader
Brigitte Bardot
Sophia Loren
Carol Burnett

Fire
King Carl Gustav of Sweden
Ilie Nastase
Cher
Liza Minelli
William J. Clinton
Donald Trump

Water
Itzhak Rabin
Charles Bronson
Pierre Cardin
Zsa Zsa Gabor
Ava Gardner
Norman Mailer
Prince William of Great Britain

Earth
Golda Meir
Chou En-lai

12

The Twelfth Sign
of the Lunar Cycle

The Boar

Of all God's children
   I have the purest heart.
With innocence and faith,
   I walk in Love's protective light.
By giving of myself freely
   I am richer and twice blest.
Bonded to all mankind by
   common fellowship,
   my goodwill is universal
   and knows no bounds.

I AM THE BOAR.

Lunar Years of the Boar in the Western Calendar	Elements
30 January 1911 to 17 February 1912	Metal
16 February 1923 to 4 February 1924	Water
4 February 1935 to 23 January 1936	Wood
22 January 1947 to 9 February 1948	Fire
8 February 1959 to 27 January 1960	Earth
27 January 1971 to 15 January 1972	Metal
13 February 1983 to 1 February 1984	Water
31 January 1995 to 18 February 1996	Wood
18 February 2007 to 6 February 2008	Fire

If you were born on the day before the start of the lunar year of the Boar, e.g., 26th January 1971, your animal sign is the one before the Boar, the Dog, the eleventh lunar sign.

If you were born on the day after the last day of the lunar year of the Boar, e.g., 16th January 1972, your sign is the one following the Boar, the Rat, the first lunar sign.

The Boar rules the two hour segment of the day between 9 P.M. and 11 P.M. Persons born during this period are said to have the Boar sign as their ascendant and will display many of the characteristics common to the Boar and have great affinity for persons born under its sign. Quite possibly, one parent or grandparent will also have been born in the year of the Boar.

This lunar sign's appointed direction is north-northwest; its season is autumn, its principal month, November. This is a yin or feminine sign and its fixed element is Water. The Boar or Pig sign is the twelfth and last in the Chinese cycle and corresponds to the Western astrological sign of Scorpio which rules from October 23rd to November 21st.

THE BOAR PERSONALITY

This is the sign of honesty, simplicity and great fortitude. Gallant, sturdy and courageous, a person born in this year will apply himself to an allotted task with all his strength. You can rely on him to see it through. Outwardly, he may appear rough-hewn and jovial, but scratch the surface and you will find pure gold.

The Boar is one of the most natural people you could ever meet. The original nice guy, winner of the "Charlie Brown" award, he will never hit you below the belt. The Boar person is popular and sought after because, like the Sheep and the Rabbit, he seeks universal harmony. No doubt he will have fights and differences with others, but he will not carry grudges unless you give him no choice. He doesn't like to add fuel to the fire in a confrontation and will usually let bygones be bygones. The lenient Boar will always take the first step forward to establish an excellent rapport with others. If he fails, it certainly won't be for lack of trying. He will be blessed with great endurance. He can work steadily on one thing at a time with incredible patience and will make an excellent and inspiring teacher.

However, the Boar is equally known for his wanton pursuit of pleasure—and even depravity, when he gives in to his negative traits. Often, the saint and sinner in him are intertwined as he zealously pursues his objectives. Perhaps this is because he has a trusting heart and will rely on those he believes in to the point of being blind to their faults. When the awful truth that he has been duped eventually surfaces, complete with irrefutable evidence, the Boar could be in denial for years before admitting the object of his trust betrayed him.

On the plus side, the loyal and thoughtful Boar will make lasting and beneficial friendships. He enjoys gatherings of all kinds, gives parties and hosts fêtes, joins clubs and every sort of association. A capable organizer who hates arguments and bickering, he knows how to bring people on different sides together. His credibility and sincerity are his best assets. Yet, he can be a bit too affable and condescending at times, and he expects others to tolerate his weaknesses.

The Boar will not dazzle you like the Dragon, nor bewitch you like the Monkey or Tiger, nor mesmerize you like the hypnotic Snake. He will simply grow on you until you cannot do without him. The solicitous Boar is synonymous with diligence and old-fashioned chivalry. He won't mind taking up the burdens of others; he won't

rebel at staying in the background or even supporting the whole cast
with his incredible strength. He is the kind of person we tend to take
for granted until he leaves us to fend for ourselves—totally stunned
by the realization of our dependency on him.

It will be easy to trust the kindly Boar. He rarely has ulterior
motives. In fact, he is too innocent and naive, and, as a result, the
favorite victim of swindlers. Still, the guileless Boar is fortunate in that
he will always find people to help him even though he does not go
begging for favors. He would prefer to be on the giving end, and
when he is in a position to help you, you can be sure he will extend
his hand. Fortune will favor him because of his all-round goodness
and faith in his fellow man. The Boar believes in miracles and miracles
will happen to him.

Calm and understanding, the Boar is a genial fellow who can and
will tolerate a lot of nonsense from his friends. He is quick-tempered
too, but since he hates quarreling, he will end up giving his opponents the benefit of the doubt. All told, he or she is one of the most
accommodating people you could ever find.

A person born in this year will be a great fund-raiser. He will have
a penchant for social work and charity because he seeks to identify
with as many people as possible.

When the world is cruel to you and fate has dealt you a stinging
blow, run to a Boar. The author of the Good Neighbor policy, he will
welcome you and your troubles with open arms. He is a good listener, and even when you are definitely in the wrong, he will never
have the heart to tell you so. He will do what he can without rubbing
any salt into your wounds. His sympathy is limitless. He'll get others
involved. He'll call upon his Masonic brothers or hold a fund-raising
dinner to help pay your debts. The Boar doesn't mind commitments.
He's made for them. He has a good strong back and the biggest heart
to be found. These hard-to-come-by virtues are no mean asset by any
standard. With a Boar, it is simply, "Ask and you shall receive."

Now, to be perfectly fair, we must look at the other side of the
coin. While the Boar may be generosity itself, he also adheres to the
"What's mine is yours and what's yours is mine" maxim.

When your Boar friend comes calling, he will help himself to your

food, your wine, your clothes, your new golf set, your expensive cam-
era, your car, etc., with an easy and childlike simplicity. Telling him off
could be a problem. He will react with great disbelief and hurt. He
won't understand or accept your one-way street mentality.

Ms. Boar will be either spotlessly clean or terribly untidy. All Boars
tend to come in these two categories and there are only rare cases of
in-betweens. Whichever she is, she will be very personable and modest. She will devote her every ounce of energy to the objects of her
affection and ask very little in return. You can identify her by her
remarkable purity of expression and trusting ways. Yet, although she
loves with total abandon, she will show a preference for anonymity or
even secrecy. She can worship someone at a distance for years or serve
him with passionate devotion without his knowing. She could play
the perfect hostess to her husband's cronies and spoil the children by
constantly answering to their beck and call—not to mention picking
up after them all the time. But she won't mind, and when she makes a
complaint, it will be but a mild one. Actually, she loves tending to her
family and looks upon them not as burdens but as her pride and joy.
With her, it will be a labor of love. Wherever she presides, people will
congregate in an atmosphere of happiness and contentment.

Defenseless against deception, the Boar person likes to trust everyone and will believe almost anything told him, even by strangers or
people he knows only superficially. Needless to say, the Boar and his
money are easily parted. The unsophisticated Boar should avoid handling finances. With him, it could be, "easy come, easy go." He is soft-
hearted and too sympathetic to hold the purse strings.

By nature, the Boar is a materialist, yet he loves to share whatever
he has. The more he gives, the more he seems to have. Unselfish and
unassuming, he is surrounded by an ever-widening circle of friends
who he will allow to take advantage of him. He has equal need of
them, too, as the sociable Boar must always feel part of the gang and
enjoys footing the bills and being looked up to. The worst thing that
could happen to him is not being on the team.

On the other hand, he is also thick-skinned and can dismiss insults
and unpleasantries with a shrug. He does not like to look too far
beyond tomorrow. It may be these traits that help him recover quickly

from the misfortunes that befall him. The gregarious Boar just does not take calamity all that seriously. It is very difficult to keep a Boar down for long. Chances are he will come back stronger than before.

Behind the sweet and reasonable facade of the Boar, there hides a remarkable resoluteness. He can ascend to the seat of authority any time he pleases, but the Boar is his own worst enemy. His scruples always get the better of him and serve more as a hindrance to his progress than anything else. On the other hand, when he is pushed to the limit, he can respond savagely and turn into a raging foe. He can summon up tremendous energy and perform Herculean feats.

While the Boar may appear gullible at times, he may be smarter than you think. Actually, he does know how to take care of his interests, but in an inoffensive manner. By allowing you to take him for a ride, he may just be giving you enough rope to hang yourself. The Chinese saying "What is yours will always find a way to come back to you" applies to the Boar's policy with double force.

Anyway, being of such a scrupulous nature, the Boar will rarely become a trickster or thief. He is uncomfortable with ill-gotten gains and will be haunted by severe guilt over the slightest transgression.

Once the Boar is driven to litigation, everyone loses. He may be surrounded by an army of lawyers or even held incommunicado by those familiar with his forgiving nature. He doesn't really hate you and personally regrets being the instrument of bitterness and strife, but once his legal advisors have set the wheels into motion, he is forced to go along with the suit. Even when he does win, he may be plagued by remorse for the rest of his life. Lawsuits will drag the Boar deep into the mud of the legal pit. His involvements in legal cases are often doomed to be long and complicated.

The Boar has strong passions. Endowed with extraordinary vigor and stamina, he is admired for putting his heart and soul into his work. Then again, his very strength could turn out to be his undoing. Because his virility and vitality are above average, the Boar will love to savor the good things in life without restriction. If he is unable to practice self-control and rein in his enormous appetites, the Boar will be corrupted or debased by those who know how to exploit his frailties.

In matters of the heart, the honest Boar loves without reservation. As a rule, he is very considerate and does not camouflage his emotions. In a love affair, he or she is likely to end up the injured party. Furthermore, the grieved Boar could carry the torch for years to come.

His main fault will be his inability to say "No" firmly to himself, his family and his friends. In some cases, he will oblige others by making concessions it would have been wise to avoid, and end up in a heap of trouble. However, when difficulties result, he will assume the burden without complaint. He will become bankrupt at least once in his life, but will always manage to make a comeback, brighter and bolder than before. The secret of his success lies in his good faith, generosity and incredible resilience.

The Boar will elect to work hard in life, and he will play just as hard, too, drawing on his bountiful supply of energy. With his basic aptitude and conscientiousness, he will triumph and provide well for those about him. His life is fated to be blessed with all needs, and the money, power and success he garners he will share unselfishly with one and all. With his robust and free-spending ways, the burly Boar will always be found living it up. He is the perfect friend, forever willing to do you another favor, or lend you another dollar. Maybe this explains why he is so lucky! At times, it seems he owns the Horn of Plenty.

Although intelligent and well-informed (somehow everyone tells the Boar their secrets), he is not deep. He accepts things at face value and would rather conceal the misgivings he has about others in order to keep the peace.

It is also said that the Boar has a fatalistic streak, and, when he has nothing further to lose, he can turn into the most negative and debauched of creatures, throwing himself into an abyss of self-gratification and eventual destruction.

Most of the Boar's problems stem from his overgenerous and overoptimistic nature. If he could contain his basic urge to do too much for others or to promise more than he can deliver, he should have few major upsets.

The Boar will have a happy life when he shares it with the quiet and sagacious Rabbit or the gentle Sheep. He will also get along well with the Tiger. The Rat, Ox, Dragon Horse, Rooster and Dog will make good secondary teammates and have no serious conflicts with the Boar. He may not find the company of other Boars too stimulating, but will be able to take it in stride. Most of his problems will arise from the Snake and the Monkey, for he will be no match for their cunning and wit.

All in all, the chivalrous Boar represents fortitude and goodwill. He will have his greatest triumphs unselfishly working for the benefit of the majority and his rewards will be as lavish as his generous heart deserves.

THE BOAR CHILD

The Boar child will be self-reliant, sociable and easy to deal with. Dependable and determined, he will take the lead in school activities and acquire prestige by his perseverance and dedication. This youngster will be courageous in the face of great odds; he will not whimper or complain. As a matter of fact, because he will be endowed with a remarkably strong body, he can withstand a good deal of pain and suffering without crying.

The Boar, like the Rat, will have a hefty appetite and you won't have to force him to eat or pamper him like the Sheep child. He will cheerfully work hard and will not be easily depressed or discouraged. But his placid exterior masks a passionate nature. The Boar finds it difficult to be casual or detached in his affections. If he loves his parents, he will worship the very ground they walk on; if not, he will be full of remorse and guilt instead of blaming anyone else. He will not need as much of your attention as other children but he must be assured that he will have your support when he seeks it.

The Boar child has a certain individualism of his own. He will allow you to be the boss so long as you do not expect him to be your slave. His give-and-take attitude will make him popular around the neighborhood. He competes more for the fun of playing than to win. Often, he may not treasure his belongings and may give things away easily. The only things he seems to accumulate are friends.

In spite of his excellent ability for organizing group efforts, mediating potentially stormy situations, and calming fiery natures, the Boar will have trouble coming out in favor of a particular side. He will also find it difficult to question other people's motives or restrain himself from indulging in his rich tastes and love of comfort on the sly. He needs to learn judgment and self-control from his elders.

Therefore you should not fear to discipline him. This is one child who can take reproach with a positive frame of mind. Setbacks can even imbue him with renewed vigor. Whenever he instigates change, he will be able to convince everyone of their necessity. The Boar child will put all his strength, conviction and dedication behind anything he undertakes.

With his soft approach and artless persuasiveness, the Boar can and will inspire others to do his bidding. It is he who needs more discipline if his talents are not to go to waste. He may excel at planning functions, projects and other people's activities, but he is lax about applying the same rules to his own daily life.

Whatever you do for him, the Boar will pay you back double. This goes for the bad as well as the good. He is totally blind to the faults of his loved ones and is filled with immense loyalty to his friends. His instinctive understanding of another person's emotions or needs will at times make him seem wise beyond his years.

This child will constantly be looking for more ways to work off his huge supply of energy. He will unabashedly display his affection with lots of hugs and kisses. Wherever he is, you will find a lot of togetherness. He loves to seal relationships with a special glue of his own. In him, you will see unselfishness and a truly great passion for living. The Boar child is a special gift to any parent.

THE FIVE DIFFERENT BOARS

METAL BOAR—1911, 1971

This is a proud, passionate Boar with overpowering sentiments, who values his reputation. Intense and more dominating than other

Boars, he often possesses excessive appetites and may lack refinement or tact.

He exerts less control over his personal life than his brother Boars, and can't help being very sociable, extroverted and openly demonstrative with his affections. He is not likely to be secretive but will be direct and trusting, even credulous. As a result, he underestimates his enemies and overestimates his friends. Ambitious and forceful, but not always objective, the Metal Boar could be a dangerous opponent, as he can be violent in expressing his anger or resentment.

This Boar will not concede defeat graciously. He will never be a quitter and be relied on to have immense powers of endurance. An active doer blessed with great positive strength, the staunch Metal Boar will have enough vigor for ten.

WATER BOAR—1923, 1983

Persevering and diplomatic, this Boar is blessed with all the qualifications of an outstanding emissary. Perceptive at discovering people's hidden desires, he will be resourceful when bargaining with his opponents. Still, Water makes him look for the best in others and he often refuses to believe their evil intents until the last minute. This type of Boar has a touching faith in his causes and loved ones. A believer in miracles, he can be used by others if he is not careful.

The cordial, peaceful and earnest Water Boar will be a great party-goer. He loves to be around people and will stick scrupulously to the rules of the game, showing his goodwill by meeting others more than halfway.

True to his Boar nature, he will have his share of passion and out-pourings of love. When he is negative, he can be preoccupied with sex, enjoyment of rich foods, excessive drinking, or will indulge in expensive luxuries at the expense of others.

WOOD BOAR—1935, 1995

The Wood Boar can unwittingly manipulate others with remarkable facility. Although he is concerned with his personal gains and ambitions, he will also be inclined to devote a good deal of time to charitable organizations and is an excellent manager of social functions and club activities. He loves to help all who come in touch with him, and will try his best to get along with everyone. Since he is a splendid promoter, he will also be adept at securing financing for his business deals.

Extremely good-hearted, he will recommend clemency even for the most unworthy people, and is often not selective about whom he associates with. Consequently, his boisterous, unworthy friends may dupe or drag him into the mud with them if he spends too much time in their company.

On the other hand, he will be rewarded for the confidence he places in people and will assume important positions because of his gift for bringing people together.

Wood makes him expansive but scrupulous enough to operate by accepted methods. He will seek to be connected with the right people and will undertake ambitious corporate ventures.

A persuasive talker, the Wood Boar will love to entertain; he also has the ability to create a congenial atmosphere wherever he goes. His positive and cheerful ways will encourage people to support both his vices and virtues.

FIRE BOAR—1947, 2007

Fire will conduct powerful and intense emotions right to this courageous Boar. As a result, he will display stouthearted heroism in his endeavors and can follow through with his plans in a pigheadedly determined manner.

He could attain the highest levels of achievement or plunge to the lowest depths of degradation, depending on which path he chooses and how tight a rein he has over his immense energy and sensuality.

The Fire Boar will never fear the unknown. Intrepid, optimistic, and trusting his innate ability, he will try his luck at anything and succeed against vast odds. He is motivated by love and will try to accumulate wealth in order to provide a gracious lifestyle for his all-important family. He doesn't mind doing favors for anyone, even strangers, and will be famous for his generous handouts to friends.

When in a negative state, this Boar can be willful, bullying and guilt-ridden. Generally, though, he is characterized by his largesse and lack of prejudice. He favors manufacturing or other labor-oriented enterprises because he enjoys employing a large number of people, given the opportunity.

EARTH BOAR—1899, 1959

This peaceful, sensible and happy Boar may have enough sense to be charitable to himself and others. This is one native who may understand the meaning of the phrase "Charity begins at home." The Earth element makes him productive and he will readily take on financial responsibilities or related activities as well as plan for his own future.

Renowned for his steadiness and patience, he will relentlessly apply himself to an objective until he attains it. His willpower enables him to endure stress and shoulder burdens well beyond the capacity of others.

Devoted both to his work and his family, the Earth Boar demonstrates a diligence and drive that are hard to surpass. But he will not be authoritarian; rather, by pushing himself he will serve as a motivation for others.

Although this person may be portly because of a fondness for food and drink, he tends not to worry too much over his problems. His ambitions are reasonable and not beyond the scope of his health. Therefore, he will easily obtain the security and material success he craves.

A kind, thoughtful friend, reliable associate and helpful employer, the Earth Boar will steer clear of troubled areas and concentrate on finding and maintaining tranquility and domestic harmony in his life.

COMPATIBILITY AND CONFLICT CHARTS
FOR THE BOAR

The Boar is part of the Fourth and last Triangle of Affinity, a group made up of the emotionally- and artistically-guided signs of the Rabbit, Sheep and Boar. These three signs are mainly concerned with their senses and what they can appreciate with them. They are expressive, intuitive and eloquent in aesthetic and talented ways. Fine arts, architecture, design and fashion, computer software and other innovative fields are their forte. Diplomatic and compassionate, this trio has calmer dispositions than other lunar signs. Dependent on others for stimulation and leadership, they are flexible because they are sympathetically attuned to the vibrations of their environment. These signs are drawn toward beauty and the higher aspects of love. They will extol the virtues of peaceful coexistence with their fellow man. These lunar signs will provide each other with excellent company since they share the same basic philosophies.

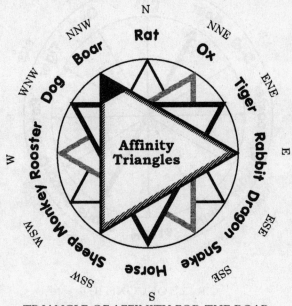

TRIANGLE OF AFFINITY FOR THE BOAR

The Boar will encounter his most serious personality clashes with someone born in the year of the Snake. Anyone whose ascendant is the Snake will most likely also come into conflict with the Boar native. And vice versa, someone with a strong Boar ascendant will not find harmony in the company of Snakes. In the Circle of Conflict,

Boar and Snake just will not see eye to eye—after all, they occupy opposite positions on this wheel of conflict, 180 degrees away. The Boar's fixed element, Water, is detrimental to the Snake's fixed element, Fire. They are both yang or negative signs. The Boar faces north-northwest, the Snake has south-southeast as its appointed direction. Intentionally or not, they will not seek each other out, and in their relationships with one another they will encounter distrust, unhappiness and complications. It would be best for them to deal through intermediaries and mutual friends they respect.

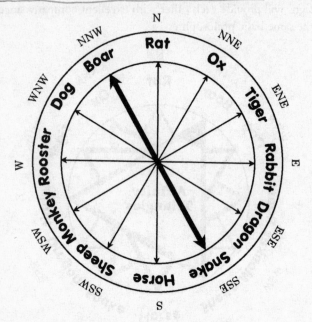

CIRCLE OF CONFLICT

Aside from the most compatible signs, the Sheep and the Rabbit, and the most incompatible sign, the Snake, the other nine signs are compatible with the Boar to varying degrees.

Rat

This could be a moderately happy and workable partnership. The generous Boar will respond to the Rat's need for commitments and affection. The crafty Rat brings intuition and self-preservation into the union, which the Boar will find invaluable in any venture. The Rat will also discover that luck always favors the good-hearted Pig. Both will benefit from their association and come out feeling like winners.

Ox

The Ox will be compatible with the Boar to only a moderate degree. There will be no great personality clashes between these two unless the Boar's best friends, the Sheep and the Rabbit, are at odds with the Ox. There is also the possibility that the Boar may encounter trouble with the Ox's strongest ally, the Snake. The relationship will also be cool if the Ox enforces the rules too rigidly and dominates the Boar. Otherwise, the social Boar will get along with the Ox and do his best to keep the peace. There may be no big struggles here, but there may be no lasting bonds either.

Tiger

The Tiger and Boar could be an enthusiastic team. Both are outgoing and generous and secure in each other's company. The honest Boar is forgiving of the Big Cat's outbursts, and the Tiger is as passionate and as dynamic as the strong Boar could desire. They will find a rapport in love and business—the Tiger will provide the ideas, the Boar will find them captivating and offer his wholehearted support. One concern, however, is that both have large appetites and tend to be impulsive. They could live it up and defer fulfilling their responsibilities indefinitely. Someone needs to put the brakes on and inform them when enough is enough.

Dragon

The honest and obliging Boar will happily be the Dragon's friend and join his fabulous group of faithful followers. There should be no large differences or serious conflicts in such a partnership. Both signs value sincerity and commitment, and will work passionately for what they believe in. On the negative side, the Boar may be more scrupulous and, at the same time, more self-indulgent than the Dragon cares for, and the Dragon may be too egotistic and pompous for the Boar. After all, the Boar prefers to make friends, not vanquish enemies, as the Dragon is more fond of doing.

Horse

The Horse and Pig will be moderately compatible because of the Boar's inability to match the Horse's quick reflexes and occasional temperamental bouts. The Horse needs the Boar's strength and generosity and will seek an alliance with the lucky Pig because he knows the Pig will share his bounty. However, while there are no long-term attractions due to differences in chemistry, there are no large clashes either. Special bonds are possible between these two only if they share the same ascendant, and if the independent Horse can understand the possessive nature of the amorous Boar. Both are outgoing and will be good friends if they find similar interests.

Monkey

There will no large clashes between the Monkey and the Boar if the Monkey can refrain from playing tricks on the unsuspecting Pig. The Monkey might find that hard to do, but once he realizes the two need each other, he will sing a different tune. Thankfully, the Pig is a good sport and will admire the Monkey's ingenuity and ability to spot opportunity a mile away. However, they may not appreciate each other's shortcomings. The Monkey will not admire the Boar's extravagances and freewheeling generosity to friends and family, while the Boar will find the Monkey's all-too flexible conscience deplorable. If there is trouble, the Monkey could leave the Boar holding the bag.

Rooster

Roosters get along with Boars because Pig natives are honest and giving and perhaps because they do not take offense easily at Rooster criticism. Boars won't take Roosters too seriously, which is just as well; if they did, they would make themselves miserable. The Boar hears what he wants to hear and then makes his decision. The Rooster can spout advice and admonitions all day long and the Boar will be cordial, patient and unaffected. The Boar will let the Rooster do the books and guard the cashbox so long as the Rooster allows him to have his fun. Since they have need of each other's skills, their relationship will prosper if they can identify their areas of expertise and stick to them.

Dog

The Boar is sincere and helpful by nature and will have no serious personality clashes with the loyal Dog. Relationships will be acceptable and agreeable to a certain extent provided the Pig displays moderation and modesty and does not challenge the Dog's sense of propriety. The Dog might be critical of the Boar's lifestyle and values, and try to remake the Pig into something less unruly and emotional. If they share the same loyalties, the Boar will not be unwilling to listen to the Dog, but that does not mean he will change. The Boar enjoys the pursuit of pleasure while the Dog tends to find pleasure attending to his duties. They will be compatible only to a certain degree, after which their paths could diverge.

Boar

A Boar and another Boar tend to rub each other the wrong way. They clash because they are so alike they find it hard to resolve their problems. Often, they want the same things or are interested in the same person, and find it difficult to control their desires and possessiveness. They both tend to mirror the other's unflattering traits, a circumstance which can prompt some mutually contentious behavior. Yet, if each has a real need for the cooperation of the other, they will be able to set aside their differences and work together for the common good. Still, there had better be a referee nearby at all times.

THE BOAR AND HIS ASCENDANTS

We all have a shadow that follows us throughout life. Sometimes it grows bigger than life and at other times it shrinks until it disappears into the soles of our feet. Sometimes it walks tall before us and on other occasions it lags behind like a sulking friend. In Chinese horoscopes, this constant partner, manifested or not, is our ascendant, the animal sign that rules the hour of our birth and becomes a comrade in our journey though life. We may view it as friend or foe or even a little of both. It surfaces when we least expect and shows a better or worse side of our nature. We can often be confounded by the way we listen to our "other self" as well as feel resentful of the significant influence it can exert on us. Actually, a personality has many rings around the centered "self." Each ring can have a different size, texture and aura. When all these factors combine, they bring forth the unique individual that the person truly is. Hence, a Dragon with an ascendant that is not compatible, like the Dog, has perhaps a more difficult inner struggle than say a Snake born during the hours of the Snake. The double intensity of the Snake person will be easily understood by horoscope readers while the more intricate Dragon/Dog may exhibit the contrary Dog and Dragon traits to varying degrees. There are many voices within each person. But, in the end, only the individual determines which course he will follow, which choices he will make.

The time of birth used to determine the ascendant is always the local time in the place of birth.

If you were born between:

11 P.M. and 1 A.M. = The Hours of the Rat

The crafty Rat ascendant makes you a shrewd Boar, one who is well-equipped to make investments and judgments and will never be left high and dry. You love with all your heart and can be devoted and indulgent to your family and loved ones. Tough but generous and caring, you will know how to stand up for your rights. Both signs here are very sociable and know how to make the most of their carefully cultivated friendships. The Rat in you is cautious while your Boar self would be carefree. You could have the best of both.

1 A.M. and 3 A.M. = The Hours of the Ox

You could be a strong-tempered Boar with regular habits and opinionated views. You take life seriously and therefore will be reliable and purposeful. The Ox will see to it that you do not get too carried away by sensuality and generous commitments that are hard to fulfill. You can also be relied upon to watch your waistline. The Ox ascendant makes the Boar in you realistic and very down to earth. You will be more reserved and not as outspoken as other Boars. Capable of self-sacrifice and hard work, you will be valued and respected by your family and friends.

3 A.M. and 5 A.M. = The Hours of the Tiger

You are likely to be a daring, bighearted and athletic Boar, a fine performer and an organizer. The dynamic and colorful Tiger makes you more lusty and passionate than most mortals. Both signs here are basically led by emotion and this makes you easily influenced by others. The Boar may have huge appetites while the Tiger ascendant loves to be in the center of things. You could be a commanding speaker or entertainer. Whatever you do, you tend to give to it your whole impressive self.

5 A.M. and 7 A.M. = The Hours of the Rabbit

With the Rabbit as your ascendant, you are an easygoing but sagacious Boar who will not like to carry any more burdens than he has to. You are a great party man, too—but you also never forget to collect what is due you. The prudent and practical Hare teaches your Boar self to be less trusting of others. Hence, you will not be easily led nor as as obliging as others may want you to be. Artistic, diplomatic and intuitive, you will always read the fine print before signing a document.

7 A.M. and 9 A.M. = The Hours of the Dragon

You are a strong, dutiful Boar with an immense devotion to those you love. Your Dragon ascendant makes you think big and you like to do things on a large scale and get everyone you know involved. Whether you sink or swim, you will have no lack of supporters. Both signs here are strong but innocent. You may carry things to the extreme and rely too much on your ability to rally people on behalf of worthy causes. If you have good advisers to guide you, you will be able to achieve many successes. If not, you may get carried away with your super optimism and enthusiasm.

9 A.M. and 11 A.M. = The Hours of the Snake

With the intellectual Snake as your ascendant you may be a calmer and more meditative Boar who will pursue your goals with more consistency. Here the ambitious Snake could relax your Boar's scruples and make you go after what you want without so much self-imposed guilt. A more reserved and secretive Boar, you have an unshakeable self-confidence. But at times you could be very possessive and extravagant.

11 A.M. and 1 P.M. = The Hours of the Horse

You are a Boar with more mettle for doing things that stir your imagination. With the spontaneous and self-assured Horse as your ascendant, you will be more outgoing and strong willed. For once, the Horse should be commended for making your Boar nature more self-ish and inconsiderate in order to achieve personal profit and recognition. The Horse will want you to put yourself first, and the naive and good-hearted Boar will become a little more self-centered with the Horse directing the action.

1 P.M. and 3 P.M. = The Hours of the Sheep

You may be a compassionate and sentimental Boar with the kindly Sheep in charge of your ascendant. Tremendously sociable and popular, you have a gift for relating to people and making them love and trust you. However, you may present an image that is too conciliatory, and allow people to take advantage of you. You will work hard for others or be overly generous with your money and talent in other ways. If you view the world through rose-colored glasses, you could be disappointed. Your particular combination will attract parasites as well as influential supporters.

3 P.M. and 5 P.M. = The Hours of the Monkey

You will be clever and conniving with the mischievous Monkey as your other self. Not likely to be tricked or taken advantage of, you will easily differentiate your friends from your foes. A Boar who conceals his ambitions under a friendly and sociable exterior, you know how to influence people with your inventive mind. The Monkey here will be able to manuever and manipulate situations to your advantage. However, you may not be as generous and affectionate as you could be with the wily and calculating Monkey pulling your strings.

5 P.M. and 7 p.m = The Hours of the Rooster

With the Rooster as your ascendant, you are an unorthodox and studious Boar who has a definite opinion on everything under the sun, and is full of good intentions and helpful advice. You perform splendid tasks for free and are absurdly tenacious and hardworking, even in unrewarding circumstances. The Rooster is efficient, though at times detached from the real purpose of many activities, while the Boar in you may be oblivious to your true worth. If the Rooster can be more resourceful and less competitive, your Boar half will be able to exploit his many positive qualities and bring people together to work as a team. You could be a tireless volunteer.

7 P.M. to 9 P.M. = The Hours of the Dog

With the practical Dog as your ascendant, you could be a direct, logical and less sensuous Boar, guided by the Dog's sound judgment. Unable to tolerate deceit, you are not as good-natured and forgiving as most Boars. With your innate strength of character, you are loyal, reliable and giving—but always guarded. Tough and uncomplaining, you do your job without much fuss. You will find that people keep turning to you for help because of your common sense and altruism. Bold and passionate when challenged, you will love to champion unselfish causes that benefit the lives of others.

9 P.M. and 11 P.M. = The Hours of the Boar

Having the same ascendant sign as your birth sign, you are a true Boar—a diamond in the rough. Once you have been cut and polished, you will blaze forth with the magnificence that is in you. The task is to uncover the real you. Despite your naturally boisterous and outgoing nature, you tend to hide your light under a basket and come across as someone who is obliging and modest. All your fine qualities are intact and waiting to be discovered. But you are often too intent on pleasing other people and may shortchange yourself by putting aside your desires to attend to their wishes, which you regard as more important or urgent.

HOW THE BOAR FARES IN THE LUNAR CYCLE

1. The Year of the Rat 1996

The Rat's year will bring uncertainties and some self-denial for the Boar. Things could be unsettled at work, and at home the Boar may find his hands full with more than he can handle. He cannot be presumptuous this year as things do not always go as planned. The opportunity the Rat year brings could also carry a great deal of commitment and responsibility for the Pig and, in the end, may prove to be more expensive than anticipated. However, he will find friends to help him or he will pool his resources with others to achieve his goals. But the difficulties and worries tend to annoy him and make it hard for him to relax and enjoy life as he usually does.

2. The Year of the Ox 1997

The hardworking Ox could bring a fruitful year for the Boar. Because of this year's good prospects, the Boar is able to tap hidden resources or start his own business. His gambles or hunches could pay off handsomely, and he finds new friends who are reliable and trustworthy. However, he may have trouble with authority figures who try to control or discipline him. But on the whole he will be well-rewarded for his labors. He will encounter no large or troublesome problems, although there may be complications in romantic or family affairs since the Boar could be distracted and neglectful of his personal life.

3. The Year of the Tiger 1998

The arrival of the Tiger year appears more promising to the Boar than it really is. As a result, the Boar gets his expectations up and he may be disappointed if things don't pan out. This could be a difficult time for him to borrow or get back money that is due him. He may focus on the promises of people who are out to deceive or give him false hopes. A host of unexpected expenses, fines, legal fees or extra taxes could materialize. He must be very careful about trusting his associates and take the precaution of attending to important matters himself. This is a year for the Boar to be careful and conservative in outlook.

4. The Year of the Rabbit 1999

The reign of the Rabbit brings a fair year for the Boar with some modest results. Obstacles may still crop up but there will be no major upheavals as the Boar recaptures lost ground and makes good progress. His love life and family environment will be tranquil and there will be reunions and other happy gatherings. The Boar will enjoy entertaining and making new contacts. He also makes some financial gains and is able to consolidate his position to a good degree. This year brings new social ties and romantic involvement for the Boar person.

5. The Year of the Dragon 2000

The Boar experiences a smooth year during the Dragon's reign. He will win the support of powerful people and will please his superiors. Because he is devoted, generous and supportive, he will also gain the recognition and respect of coworkers. His family and love life are uneventful. However, he could suffer health upsets when he must work harder than usual, pushing himself to the limit of his strength, and the loss of some personal property is a possibility. However, he is proud of his accomplishments and gratified to know that people depend on him. He will not let them down. And he is too busy to complain or spend time on self-pity.

6. The Year of the Snake 2001

The Year of the Snake brings a hectic and uneasy time for the Boar, although he can expect moderate success. He will be occupied with travel, aggressive speculation and joint ventures. Situations could become complicated and confusing if he is unable to discover his competitors' hidden motives until the last moment when he cannot do much to influence the outcome. This is a time for him to look closely at everything and shy away from any proposal that looks too good to be true. The Boar may also have problems with the opposite sex. His family or loved ones will make such unreasonable demands on his time and energy that he feels cornered by his obligations. Setbacks could result mainly from overspending or extravagance.

7. The Year of the Horse 2002

This will be a good year for the Boar provided he avoids speculation or entrusting his money to newfound friends. The Horse brings the Boar benefits formerly withheld from him but which now appear from all directions, turning past problems into blessings in disguise. The year will prove fortunate and prosperous for the Pig's family, love life and career. However, the Horse sets a fast pace and the Boar must keep up or he will lag behind and miss out on some of the action. Hopefully, the strong Boar has the stamina and willpower to ride out this year with more gains than losses.

8. The Year of the Sheep 2003

The Sheep brings harmony and happiness for the Pig born and ensures him a fair though event-filled year. Although financially the Boar may not make great strides, he can count on the goodwill of others to help him out of any difficult situations. One way or another, he will be repaid for past favors and sacrifices. There will be no serious health problems nor any big upheavals, although romantically he could find excitement and new loves. His gains will be in the form of knowledge, professional training or career development. He should plan for the future, spend time with his family or friends, and explore new opportunities.

9. The Year of the Monkey 2004

This is a moderately satisfying time for the Boar with the Monkey bringing both good and bad news. The Boar could be vulnerable this year because others will seek to take advantage of his kindness and generosity. As a result, he may suffer a lack of money or support, and be afflicted by various domestic and personal problems. Although results are not entirely favorable, he will be able to borrow money or join up with others and solve his difficulties. He should rely on the advice of the more informed and take a more passive role in decision making. This is not a time for him to go it alone. There is safety in numbers; it's a good idea to check he has ample insurance, too.

10. The Year of the Rooster 2005

The colorful Rooster brings a busy and possibly controversial year for the Pig. The Boar's domestic scene is calm but his advancement will be curtailed or interrupted by little problems that are magnified and blown out of proportion by the interference of others. The workaholic Rooster can be demanding and critical, and his year will be tough on any Boar who is sensuous or indulgent, or who chafes under regimentation and tight-fisted supervision. The Boar likes to work hard and play hard but prefers to do so according to his own schedule. Unfortunately, the Rooster brings him a very full and varied timetable. Family members and lovers will not be as understanding or as helpful as the Boar would wish. He spends a great deal of time and effort overcoming obstacles, and must patiently deal with negotiations that are complicated and prolonged. Thankfully, the Chicken will give credit where credit is due, and the Boar will be rewarded for his gallant efforts if he perseveres.

11. The Year of the Dog 2006

The year of the Dog could bring mixed benefits for the stouthearted Pig. Although there could be frustrating times for the aspirations of the Boar, he will be able to overcome his problems by gathering support from his huge circle of supporters. Still, he should not expect too much during the reign of the unmaterialistic Dog. Forced to attend to his responsibilities, the Boar will not be able to put off making hard choices. But if he can face the music squarely and deal with sticky situations, he could save himself a lot of problems later on. Difficulties this year arise from his past neglect, miscalculations, or errors in judgment. He must be careful in whom he places his confidence and must take criticism constructively. His family and loved ones will stand loyally by his side and help him face any hardships he may encounter.

12. The Year of the Boar 2007

The Boar's life will stabilize this year as he enjoys gains and some progress. He may still experience some friction at work or at home, but no serious setbacks are indicated. A lot of entertaining and travel awaits the gregarious Boar and his loved ones. His popularity and social life will be happy and fulfilling as he finds new friends and opportunities along the way. However, he must also exercise some control over his spending and tighten his belt financially if he is not to go into the red. The Boar tends to go overboard in his projections and may make overoptimistic promises that are hard to keep. This is a time for him to step back and quit while he is ahead of the game.

WHEN MOON SIGNS MEET SUN SIGNS

In my interpretation of Chinese horoscopes, the Rat is not linked with the first Western astrological sun sign, Aries. Instead, I pair the Rat with its counterpart based on the month and season of the Rat, which are December and winter. This makes the most sense as the lunar month of December (also called the Twelfth Moon or the Twelfth Earth Branch) is supposed to parallel the sun sign, Sagittarius, the Archer. I envision the Eastern and Western horoscope cycles as two large wheels, each with twelve spokes. To correctly juxtapose these cycles, we must find the matching notch that will join them together. Once the Rat and Sagittarius are paired as the first signs, the other eleven fall into place. Please see the Twenty-Four Segments of the Lunar Almanac. All the dates correspond with the twelve Western solar signs.

If you are born in the year of the Boar under the Western sign of

Sagittarius: 22nd November to 21st December

The Sagittarian Boar = Fire + Negative Water

This combination produces a candidate for the good citizen award, a person with considerable humor and large appetites. Both signs here are noble but naive, although the Archer can be the more blunt when declaring his wishes. Jupiter's bounty and the Boar's luck are heaped together on this subject because of his trusting and uncalculating nature. One can count on the Sagittarian Boar to share his last cent with a friend. Neither sign succumbs to despair easily, so this person will be made of sturdy stuff, perhaps even a bit thick-skinned. Yet when he achieves success, he won't hoard his money. He will dole it out and somehow everyone will benefit from his good fortune.

If you are born in the year of the Boar under the Western sign of

Capricorn: 22nd December to 20th January

The Capricorn Boar = Earth + Negative Water

This is a tough but cautious Boar with towering ambitions who makes a slow but steady climb all the way to the top of the mountain.

Both solar and lunar signs here do not fear facing obstacles, although this conservative person has great respect for the wishes of others. Punctilious and hardworking, the Capricorn Boar will have the Pig's good faith and the Goat's "better safe than sorry" mentality—no pie-in-the-sky dreams for this conscientious worker. The Capricorn Boar upholds tradition with pride and does not skirt his responsibility when rules have to be enforced.

If you are born in the year of the Boar under the Western sign of

Aquarius: 21st January to 19th February
The Aquarian Boar = Air + Negative Water

The Boar is amorous by nature and has considerable strength of character. Joined with an Aquarian, this native can be candid, reckless, defiant, and definitely a personality who will stir one's imagination. His didactic qualities could be well-masked behind that boisterous exterior. A trend-setter, he is never content to play a fixed role. This sign either makes delightful ripples or strong, splashing waves, but he will certainly like to keep on the move and be progressive and ambitious. When the Water Bearer's broad outlook is joined to the Boar's spirit of cooperation and brotherhood, the result is a person who is happy, prosperous and popular in spite of any shortcomings.

If you are born in the year of the Boar under the Western sign of

Pisces: 20th February to 20th March
The Pisces Boar = Water + Negative Water

The Fish has the essential instincts for survival and a quiet confidence in his ability to comprehend the human mind. The Boar has vast reserves of energy and a positive mental attitude that makes everything possible. A combination of these two signs could produce effective and harmonious results if each plays his part well. Both Boar and Fish seem always able to find support when they need it, and somehow this person will muddle through with unbelievable success. He is totally devoted to his loved ones and lavishes affection upon them, but, along with his worthy friends, there will be the unworthy who take advantage of his goodness. However, confrontation is not the Boar's cup of tea. He treasures his personal relationships and, should matters come to a head, he prefers to settle out of court.

If you are born in the year of the Boar under the Western sign of

Aries: 21st March to 19th April
The Aries Boar = Fire + Negative Water

Sunny optimism and passion are the key words for this energetic combination. Here the Boar's easygoing nature could override that famous Aries temper and directness. Naturally, he will be concerned with everyone's welfare and have the interests of the majority at heart. Both signs are robust, rowdy, and given to free and generous displays of affection. The result is an unselfish but strong-minded personality, rich in raw sex appeal and expendable energy. Sturdy and magnanimous, the Aries Boar is a veritable pillar of strength.

If you are born in the year of the Boar under the Western sign of

Taurus: 20th April to 20th May
The Taurean Boar = Earth + Negative Water

Solidly reliable, the Taurean Boar can be as impregnable as a fortress when he wants to be. But most of the time, he is an affable fellow with large and lusty appetites. A person of this combination will do everything with mucho gusto, as both solar and lunar signs here are remarkably sensual and healthy. Patient and conscientious, the Taurean Boar will be a genuine friend and confidant. This combination produces a Bull who is more cooperative and a Boar who is favored with people skills and perseverance.

If you are born in the year of the Boar under the Western sign of

Gemini: 21st May to 21st June
The Gemini Boar = Air + Negative Water

The Twins' whirlwind activities will sometimes leave the poor Boar somewhat lightheaded. But while the generous Boar invests goodwill and honesty in this bargain, Mercury will provide initiative, stimuli and quick thinking. The Gemini Boar will be a sociable and very popular problem solver. He sees the whole picture with scientific clarity, yet never ignores humane aspects in his final consideration. He will want life to be varied and is at his best where there is a frequent change of scenery. A good sport and an athletic person, he won't let any grass grow under his feet.

If you are born in the year of the Boar under the Western sign of

Cancer: 22nd June to 21st July
The Cancerian Boar = Water + Negative Water

The two signs in this combination are emotional and given to the pursuit of physical pleasure and luxury. The Boar is highly sexed and easily dissipated by overindulgence; the Crab, while more aesthetic in outlook, is constructive only when he can relinquish his hold on things no longer essential to him—and, unfortunately he tends to be possessive and at times, melodramatic. Both Crab and Boar have lovingly generous natures and are very impressionable. But then, while the Moonchild votes for quality and stability, the Boar is in favor of quantity and rapid progress. If the positive qualities of both solar and lunar signs can be joined together here, this personality will no doubt find love, wealth and contentment.

If you are born in the year of the Boar under the Western sign of

Leo: 22nd July to 21st August
The Leo Boar = Fire + Negative Water

A gregarious Boar with refreshingly natural humor and some excesses to boot. Gifted with irrepressible vitality, the Leo Boar will do everything with zest and relish hard work compounded by equally hard play. He will lead the crowd when it comes to partying and looking for adventure. Because his emotions are usually expressed in red-hot tones, he is dramatic and could claim the theater as his favorite habitat. This personality is most unselfish, never hypocritical and will have a childlike faith that brings out the best in the people he deals with. But, watch out, he could also be a big spender who does not believe in saving for that rainy day.

If you are born in the year of the Boar under the Western sign of

Virgo: 22nd August to 22nd September
The Virgo Boar = Earth + Negative Water

The sensual and generous Boar should redeem the Virgo personality from too much intense or monotonous work. Yet the cautious Virgin's deep intellectual qualities could assist the trusting Boar in making sound decisions. The Virgo Boar commits himself less willingly despite his modest and kind appearance. He examines all the pros and cons before making any decision and is a hard person to fool or mislead as he is very prudent. This Boar is astute and knowledgeable, a reliable soul who is able to identify with the group while remaining sensibly honest to his convictions. Here Virgo's fine fiscal aptitude is joined to the Boar's incredible luck.

If you are born in the year of the Boar under the Western sign of

Libra: 23rd September to 22nd October
The Libran Boar = Air + Negative Water

Two agreeable signs unite here to form a very magnanimous and unselfish person. Sensitive and artistic Libra is given the Boar's sustaining stamina and noble character. The Libran Boar will not only be gentle and tolerant but very much alive when it comes to sensuality. However, his patient and faithful exterior may conceal inner ambitions and secret aspirations that are difficult to guess. Libra always wants to take the middle of the road while the Boar is a social animal with an immense capacity to help others. Rich and mellow like good red wine, this is a loving, sentimental and constant native. Who could ask for more?

If you are born in the year of the Boar under the Western sign of

Scorpio: 23rd October to 21st November
The Scorpio Boar = Water + Negative Water

Lavish with his affections but very much set on gratifying his own wishes first, this hefty Boar is his own man—or woman. Aggressive and power-conscious, he will pursue his ambitions unabashedly. Still, this crafty and intuitive Boar knows how and when to compromise, though often it turns out to be at the expense of others. Despite his outward generosity, the intense and passionate Boar can be relentless when it comes to getting his rights. As a result, he is capable of great endurance and sacrifice when called upon to do so. He also sees no lack of admirers queueing up for the pleasure of his company. But do watch for that vengeful streak.

THE SEASONS OF THE BOAR

SPRING

Boars born during the spring are active, outgoing and highly communicative. They are gifted with childlike innocence and will radiate goodwill, refusing to believe the bad in people even when they have to suffer injustice and persecution. Their faith is often rewarded, however, and these Boar people are well regarded and cared for by those they love. Confident of their own abilities, they gravitate toward teamwork and community service. They are traditional in outlook although they may have extravagant tastes and they tend to indulge given the opportunity. Sincere, honest and scrupulous in their dealings, they must protect themselves against exploitation by linking up with powerful people who will shield them.

SUMMER

The boisterous Boars of summer are quite a crowd to reckon with. Amorous, aggressive and sometimes given to excess, they can overwhelm the ordinary person with their immense zest for life and love. Their rich earthy personalities and inclinations ensure they will be uninhibited about getting involved in things. Summer Boars wear their hearts on their sleeves and will fly their flags high when they support some cause or team. They can always be found in the center of a crowd, promoting something with a passion. The rowdy summer Boars will not like to do things by half measures, and will therefore follow their dreams with an awesome devotion. On the domestic and romantic fronts, they will be generous to, but possessive of, their loved ones.

AUTUMN

Boars born in the fall will value their security and tend to worry and feel guilty about a great number of things. They have long wish lists but shun risks and danger, so consequently they may hesitate or wait too long to take positive action. However, they are sturdy, reliable and sincere; they do not like to mislead or take advantage of others. Boars of this season born during the day are bound to be more outgoing and outspoken than their brethren born in the quiet of the night. The evening boars of autumn will have a life of ease while daytime boars must fight and assert themselves. They prefer to go with the majority instead of striking out on their own. Fall Boars dedicate themselves to fixed goals and do not like too much adventure or sudden changes in their lifestyles.

WINTER

The winter Boars are gracious and thoughtful. They tend to have extravagant and expensive tastes and appetites. These Pigs could be the most fatalistic and scrupulous of all Boars. However, they are obliging and honest and quite naive in both love and business. Gifted with strength of character and a larger-than-life heart, they can be generous to the extreme. Unless they learn to use their talents wisely, they will be exploited by others because of their innocent and trusting natures. However, when winter Boars feel they have nothing left to lose, they could turn into unruly and destructive foes—bringing down the house with them as they rampage through it. Their kindly exterior hides an intelligent and ambitious mind. They must learn to curb their emotions and work with disciplined and innovative people who can help them properly direct their efforts.

FAMOUS PERSONS BORN IN THE YEAR OF THE BOAR

Metal
Hubert Humphrey
Ronald Reagan
Lucille Ball
Merle Oberon
Rosalind Russell
Prince Bernhard of the Netherlands

Water
Prince Rainier III of Monaco
Lee Kuan Yew
Maria Callas
Henry Kissinger

Fire
Field Marshal Bernard Montgomery
Chiang Kai-shek
Andrew Jackson
Hillary Rodham Clinton

Wood ✓
Françoise Sagan
King Hussein
Julie Andrews

Earth
Ernest Hemingway
Humphrey Bogart
Alfred Hitchcock
John D. Rockefeller

13

The 144 Marriage Combinations

RAT HUSBAND + RAT WIFE

There is a bit too much togetherness here. Each may be too conscientious and domesticated. If they are too alike, they could suffer from overexposure to each other's personality. Mr. Rat could be more easygoing than Mrs. Rat, who may have an inclination to be fussy and bossy. These worldly and calculating persons may watch each other rather intently and not like the close-up picture they see.

RAT HUSBAND + OX WIFE

In this happy combination, the affectionate Rat husband will be very attractive to his security-conscious wife because he is a good provider—the chief requisite in her book. She, on the other hand, is more than dutiful, competent and reliable. She will love attending to his needs and will keep his house in order. Each will admire each other's qualities and do more than his or her fair share. The ardently demonstrative Rat could even make the Ox lady more responsive and less obstinate.

RAT HUSBAND + TIGER WIFE

He is success-oriented and a home and family man. She is affectionate and generous but very unconventional. They will have a lot in common as they are both sociable, active and have many interests. He will seek power and riches and she loves the prestige and recognition these provide. However, he could be resentful of her unpredictable ways and she may criticize him for being niggardly at times. But both are basically optimists and will try to work out their differences or call it quits.

RAT HUSBAND + RABBIT WIFE

This match may not bring out the best in either party. These two individuals are charming and pleasant but hardly selfless and dedicated. Even with the best of intentions, constant coexistence may strain both of them. He is possessive and romantic, and she tends to be too passive in her response to him. Expectations of both sides may be greatly reduced in the final accounting.

RAT HUSBAND + DRAGON WIFE

These two share courage and determination and will find a bright and rewarding future together. They will not try to restrict each other unduly, and the Rat will find his Dragon wife an admirable companion provided she takes care not to be overbearing. Both are very competent and have enough self-assurance to trust the other. They will look at the brighter side of life and enjoy a very gratifying relationship.

RAT HUSBAND + SNAKE WIFE

These two possessive partners are realistic enough to make the necessary adjustments in their marriage if they admire each other sufficiently. The Rat will value the Snake's brilliance and tenacity while she finds him ambitious and clever enough to set up house with. Of these two materialistic and performance-conscious parties, he may be the more adaptable and easygoing. She is cautious, and he can count on her excellent ability to sniff out traps. The Snake finds the Rat's devotion very touching and will respond passionately.

RAT HUSBAND + HORSE WIFE

Both parties have independent and active spirits, but he will be very irked by her restlessness and inconsistency. She, on the other hand, will be unhappy and nervous because of his bickering. They cannot appreciate each other's way of thinking and may not try very hard to make the relationship work.

RAT HUSBAND + SHEEP WIFE

The Rat may not like setting up house with an oversensitive and impractical Sheep lady. She will respond only when pampered and indulged. The prudent Rat may conclude she is too expensive to maintain, and she may find him too calculating and greedy to suit her tastes. Neither is openly combative but they could harbor deep resentments and as a result be very frustrated and dissatisfied.

RAT HUSBAND + MONKEY WIFE

This is a strongly compatible match: he will fall for her charm and ingenuity and she will find his go-getter attitude very admirable. Both are achievement-conscious and will push each other up the ladder of success. Neither is hypersensitive and both are able to accept the other's faults with understanding. As a result they will manage to smooth out any rough spots in their relationship. Likewise, they could work together or choose separate paths or careers without creating any problems.

RAT HUSBAND + ROOSTER WIFE

These two will not blend together well. She appraises him critically, finds him wanting, and feels obligated to call his attention to all his shortcomings. He feels resentful and hurt, and, what's more, finds her eccentric and overly analytical ways very annoying. He wants a doting wife, not a psychiatrist. She is surprised at his attitude and labels him ungrateful.

RAT HUSBAND + DOG WIFE

Both are peace-loving and independent. He can be hard-working and energetic and she will be loyal and tactful. The Dog wife is warm and responsive and the Rat husband is charming and equally affectionate. The danger in this match is that they may both do too much compromising and end up with a bland relationship that makes each uninterested in the other.

RAT HUSBAND + BOAR WIFE

Both have a great zest for life. They will find each other attractive physically as well as mentally. But both signs are overly optimistic and imprudent and may just push their luck too far. Neither has enough willpower to apply the brakes and provide a stabilizing force to the union. They need something concrete to seal the marriage.

OX HUSBAND + RAT WIFE

He is always dependable enough to bring home the bacon and she is loving and doting enough to cook it just the way he likes it. Theirs will be a very satisfying and rewarding union. He is strong and silent and loves being fussed over and admired by his outgoing wife, and she is content with the security and stability he provides. Both will have few complaints.

OX HUSBAND + OX WIFE

Both members of this team are serious and industrious to a dismal extent. Neither is lively enough to think of providing some respite from all the work they have planned. The result is an extremely reserved and civil union of two security-conscious subjects who are both pessimistic and strong-willed. They may end up showing each other too much of their negative sides.

OX HUSBAND + TIGER WIFE

He is interested in personal success and achievement; she is interested in herself. He is practical, well-organized and stable; she finds him too predictable and dour. The Tiger wife can be very temperamental if she feels neglected, while the Ox cannot abide tantrums and will not tolerate her fussing over nothing. They are on different wavelengths. The reserved Buffalo will be shocked by the Tiger's unrestrained and passionate display of emotion. She, on the other hand, will be frustrated by his coldness and may need a more warm-blooded and responsive partner.

OX HUSBAND + RABBIT WIFE

The Rabbit finds the Ox steady, realistic and dependable while the Ox sees her as sociable, sympathetic and feminine. However, he can be very exacting and will criticize her lack of discipline, and she will respond by becoming withdrawn and oversensitive. But getting to know each other may be well worth an effort in this marriage, as both of them could sustain a satisfying relationship if they can adjust a little.

OX HUSBAND + DRAGON WIFE

This will not be an entirely harmonious union. He is slow and deliberate, much too methodical for the pioneering and dynamic likes of the fiery and excitable Dragon woman. He could make her more persevering, but she will still be imprudent and daring at times. It's possible she can liven him up with her optimism—or drive him farther away. He can be a cold and unemotional loner, while she needs fun, friends and variety. Both these strong personalities will have to respect and admire each other a great deal before they will agree to make any adjustments in their relationship.

OX HUSBAND + SNAKE WIFE

This is a very enduring and happy combination. The Ox has high standards of achievement and the Snake wife is equally ambitious and materialistic. She will be appreciative of the luxury and comforts the Ox can provide. He finds her very well-mannered and presentable—and astute in financial matters as well. Both will be happy fulfilling their part of the relationship. He will be a source of strength for her and she will be his pride and joy.

OX HUSBAND + HORSE WIFE

There are not many favorable aspects to this match. She is carefree and uninhibited and he is industrious and down-to-earth. He wants a well-organized and pleasant home and she is too restless and busy to settle down. She needs freedom and diversion. He cannot comprehend this nor her lack of devotion to him. It will be difficult for either sign to find harmony in this relationship.

OX HUSBAND + SHEEP WIFE

She can organize an artistic and comfortable nest for him while he acts as her defender. He is prudent and persevering while she is sentimental and capricious. That is to say, he accumulates and she spends. The Ox is strong and decisive; the Sheep is weak and insecure. Therefore, she loves being sheltered and reassured. But Mr. Ox may not be so obliging because he expects a great deal from others. His Sheep wife may become depressed when he insists she practice discipline and self-denial. Actually, both parties may find the going rough at times.

OX HUSBAND + MONKEY WIFE

Both are self-assured and know what they want. And what they want may not be each other. He is simple, serious and down to earth. She is attractive, complicated and self-centered. They both love success and money but have entirely different ideas on how to attain the former and spend the latter. Mrs. Monkey is quite accomplished and independent and not as security-minded as Mr. Ox. She could find him becoming tyrannical when she takes his orders lightly. On his part, he cannot quite get her to pay him the respect and admiration he craves. If he flaunts his authority, she will enrage him—by laughing in his face. Neither will ever succeed in subordinating the other.

OX HUSBAND + ROOSTER WIFE

Both parties are hard-working and industrious. He values self-respect and devotion to duty, which is why his competent and conscientious Rooster wife will win his admiration. They both love analyzing and organizing, and neither is easily hurt by criticism. These two can be objective and methodical when managing the office as well as the household. Both love simple pleasures and intellectual pursuits and will excel in specialized fields. She doesn't mind his exacting nature as she is very attentive to detail; he, on the other hand, will take her criticism constructively and not feel reproached. They will be a happy and contented pair.

OX HUSBAND + DOG WIFE

He looks for money and prestige, and abhors dependency. She is generous, open-minded and a loyal ally. But he could be too Spartan and domineering for his friendly and communicative wife. She will be tough, outspoken and antagonistic should he push her too hard. He could be too rigid and aloof for her tastes; he may find her questioning mind and cynical logic hard to swallow. Otherwise, they might enjoy each other's company.

OX HUSBAND + BOAR WIFE

They will make the best of each other's outstanding qualities. He is serious, well-mannered and success-oriented while she is patient, self-sacrificing and devoted. He is hard working and she is trusting enough to support and encourage him every step of the way. Her tastes may be more extravagant than his, and she is more sensual and demonstrative. However, she will be understanding of his needs and help make him less reticent and stubborn.

TIGER HUSBAND + RAT WIFE

There will not be much togetherness in this marriage. The Tiger is too hot-headed and imperious for the domesticated and sentimental Rat. She can be considerate and thoughtful only when properly appreciated, but he is too impatient and involved with himself. He finds her petty, possessive and demanding. Each party will be dissatisfied with the other's performance.

TIGER HUSBAND + OX WIFE

A clash of temperaments imperils this match from the start. He is the nonconformist, the activist and the defiant rebel. She loves tradition, respects authority and behaves conservatively. These two stubborn individuals are miles apart in their thinking. It will be difficult for them to find a common ground on which to tolerate each other's outlook on life.

TIGER HUSBAND + TIGER WIFE

Both parties are attractive, vibrant and charming and may have a great deal in common. However, both are equally rebellious, stubborn and quick on the draw when displeased, and their easily-bruised egos could easily place a strain on the relationship. Each needs a good deal of personal freedom. They both have an excellent sense of humor which gives them some perspective and may enable them to patch up their differences, but the family budget could have a perpetual hole in it—these Tigers are big spenders.

TIGER HUSBAND + RABBIT WIFE

The demure Rabbit may be attracted to the rugged and appealing Tiger man, but when she takes a closer look she may be put off by his impulsiveness and daring. He, on the other hand, can barely tolerate her moody and worrying nature. She is rational and opportunistic; he is led by his feelings and has little need for diplomacy or tact. She is polite and sensitive; he is loud and spontaneous. Both will have to make a major effort to put up with the other's idiosyncrasies if the relationship is to work.

TIGER HUSBAND + DRAGON WIFE

Both spouses are energetic, ambitious and brave. However, they could overstimulate each other. With both of them being so innovative and daring, there may be no one left to finish the job once their mutual initial enthusiasm fades away. The Dragon wife aspires to leadership and will fight the Tiger for dominance. He will let her get away with some things so long as she does not restrict his actions or expect him to be docile. This overly dynamic duo cooperate successfully only after a good deal of adjustment on both sides.

TIGER HUSBAND + SNAKE WIFE

Each will question the other's motives and notice only their negative traits. The Tiger husband will oppose the wise and practical Snake's sensible course of action. He finds her jealous, overly possessive and too philosophical. She cannot comprehend his love for courting disaster. It doesn't help that she may be financially shrewd since he is overgenerous and a spendthrift. This couple cannot accomplish very much together.

TIGER HUSBAND + HORSE WIFE

These two make a well-balanced and harmonious pair, as they are both outgoing, fiery and spirited. But while the Tiger fights for a cause, the Horse prefers to direct both their energies to more practical and rewarding pursuits. He will appreciate her quick and intelligent mind, especially since she can steer him toward worthwhile objectives. Neither one is domesticated enough to be too possessive. He is thoughtful and affectionate when humored, and she is flexible enough to put up with his unpredictability. They will have a passionate relationship and will greatly enjoy each other's company.

TIGER HUSBAND + SHEEP WIFE

He is outgoing, involved and vivacious. She is domesticated, sensitive and clinging. Although he will be companionable, he cannot devote himself exclusively to her needs; indeed, he finds her too dependent and indecisive. She is basically understanding but could wallow in self-pity if she considers him curt, impatient or unconcerned about her trivial complaints. Each will have to adjust to the other's ways before they can make this marriage work.

TIGER HUSBAND + MONKEY WIFE

They live in different worlds. Although both are sociable, energetic and outgoing, the temperamental Tiger will dislike the competitive Monkey because she is too intelligent and sure of herself to be intimidated by his loud dramatics. Unfortunately, he is productive and forceful only when given center stage. If the Monkey lady demands equal billing, he could feel hemmed in and very resentful. Both are lavish spenders, but the Monkey is more prudent and clever about finances. This mixture of two inconstant and self-possessed personalities will prove too overwhelming to do either of them any good.

TIGER HUSBAND + ROOSTER WIFE

She is too smart, well-informed and critical to put up with the dynamic but overreacting Tiger. He is upset by her nagging, faultfinding ways and love of detail. And while he is openhanded, generous and outspoken, she is efficient, thrifty and methodical. He is idealistic; she is a keen intellectual. The Tiger is unconventional and ruled by his heart; the Chicken is eccentric but ruled by her head. Each is very self-absorbed and will be unhappy with and irritated by the other.

TIGER HUSBAND + DOG WIFE

This is an ideal marriage of two charming, attractive and humanitarian signs. He is passionate and animated. She is loyal, understanding and helpful. The Tiger is impulsive and impatient; the Dog is logical and clear-headed enough to advise him without getting personal. He admires and respects her loyalty and good sense and she will not try to monopolize his affections. The fact that each is warm and responsive to the other's needs without invading his or her privacy guarantees a very satisfactory relationship.

TIGER HUSBAND + BOAR WIFE

These two dedicated and inspired individuals will work more energetically for the goals of others than for their own. They will make a happy team: the Boar will be tirelessly devoted to the idealistic pursuits of the Tiger, and he will admire her courage and stamina. Although she can be trusting and congenial, she will make him more materialistic because of her taste for luxury. They are both sensual, uninhibited and passionate in love. Both can brush aside little differences and will enjoy journeying through life hand in hand.

RABBIT HUSBAND + RAT WIFE

The Rat is sociable, active and crafty. The Rabbit has a mild disposition and is not inclined to the strenuous activity and involvement favored by his gregarious and entertaining wife. But both love home life and are realistic about their goals. Because she can be devoted and outgoing enough to brighten up his moods, this will be a responsible and good match.

RABBIT HUSBAND + OX WIFE

The Rabbit is gentle, sagacious, and receptive to ideas and the feelings of others. The Ox wife may be lacking the emotion and sensitivity to understand his refined personality. On the other hand, he can be acquisitive, indulgent and selfish. She can be pragmatic, but virtuous and well-disciplined. Each could supply the other with missing attributes if they care enough to make their union work.

RABBIT HUSBAND + TIGER WIFE

The imaginative and docile Rabbit is inclined toward mental and creative endeavors. The lady Tiger is dramatic, sensuous and electric. She may be too strong and colorful for the quiet and impeccable Rabbit. For her part, she finds him impersonal and lacking in emotion. He could help solve her problems but she may be too inattentive to listen. She could build up his confidence and assertiveness but he is not too keen on her method of teaching. These two tend not to mix well together as, in the final analysis, what one likes, the other doesn't.

RABBIT HUSBAND + RABBIT WIFE

This duo will cohabit peacefully. Both are calm and intelligent enough to do whatever is practical and necessary to make their relationship work. However, they can gratify each other only to a certain point, as each does what is essential and not much more. This is because the Rabbit is basically selfish and self-serving. Matrimony will have to be a well-thought-out affair with equal sharing of responsibilities. There will be trouble if one thinks he is bearing a little more of the weight than the other. Both are gifted and intuitive but may neglect to encourage each other.

RABBIT HUSBAND + DRAGON WIFE

She is independent, vivacious and cheerful. He is capable but introverted and calculating. She could lift his spirits and make him more ambitious in his objectives. He could teach her a thing or two about diplomacy and fine manners. He doesn't mind her assuming the dominant role because he knows she will seek his excellent advice in the end. He is competent and kind and she has a backbone strong enough for both of them. This is a realistic and positive marriage combination.

RABBIT HUSBAND + SNAKE WIFE

These two are compatible to a good degree if they can enhance each other's stronger points. He has great potential, vision and tact. She is determined to succeed and approves of his materialistic aims. But though both will have the same refined tastes and inherent love for ease and beauty, the Snake could be too ardent and demanding for the Rabbit's superficial style of involvement. On the dark side, both signs are philosophical and meditative, and the lines of communication could be severed should they decide to be negative.

RABBIT HUSBAND + HORSE WIFE

They may find their relationship difficult, but should consider matters carefully before passing judgment. Because she is governed by her emotions and intuitions, she is bored by his deliberation and sensitivity. He finds her thoughtless, inconstant and mercenary. The Rabbit prefers rest and solitude; the Horse is constantly on the go. Each is too preoccupied or self-absorbed to make any great effort to adjust to the other, but this union will never work unless they do.

RABBIT HUSBAND + SHEEP WIFE

Each is receptive to the vibrations of the other partner. The Rabbit appreciates the Sheep's compassionate and sensitive ways, and she finds him kind, astute and sagacious enough to make their decisions. Her dependence could make him feel more important and purposeful. He is a good listener and she needs sympathy and advice more than action. Both are romantic and affectionate and will enjoy domestic bliss.

RABBIT HUSBAND + MONKEY WIFE

Some hostilities may develop here. She is so self-assured and proud of her accomplished wit that he may feel humbled by her. For her part, she will hate his anxiety and brooding. Both have the ability to see through others, and consequently when they look into one another, they may not find anything so fascinating. These two realistic individuals will not cooperate unless each has something substantial to gain from the commitment.

RABBIT HUSBAND + ROOSTER WIFE

He would prefer to be catered to and served. She is too straightforward, meticulous and efficient to put up with his whimsical requests. Both are knowledgeable but eccentric. While he broods in dark silence, she will compose a long list of his faults and make it public. They could make life very uncomfortable for each other.

RABBIT HUSBAND + DOG WIFE

In this beneficial and very agreeable combination, each party will make only reasonable demands on the other. As a result, both will be satisfied and fulfilled. The Dog will be loyal and affectionate to the Rabbit even when he feels indifferent and moody. She admires his suave and diplomatic ways and he can rely on her support and logical assessment of situations. She is the more positive of the two and will encourage him when he is depressed. On the other hand, he is always considerate and sensitive enough to know what is bothering her.

RABBIT HUSBAND + BOAR WIFE

These two will find each other interesting and sympathetic. He is talented and astute and can negotiate his way out of trouble. Because she admires his poise and refined ways, she will meet him more than halfway. She is dependable, generous and obedient; he will be touched by her devotion and unselfishness. Neither of them is given to fault-finding; rather, they will be content to count their blessings, especially in such a rewarding union.

DRAGON HUSBAND + RAT WIFE

The Dragon will find his Rat wife's loyalty and optimism endearing. She will follow her hero to the ends of the earth. He is magnanimous while she is thrifty and resourceful. Therefore, while he could make a lot of money and then lose it, she will likely have stored some of it away for a rainy day. She is talkative and lively but always amenable to letting him play the boss. This will be a fruitful and lasting union.

DRAGON HUSBAND + OX WIFE

Both signs are dutiful but stubborn. The latter factor could make or break the marriage. He works for glory and recognition while she wants to see material benefits. If his ventures do not result in hard cash, she can be harsh and unsympathetic. He is dynamic and extroverted while she may be too conforming and conservative. He needs love and admiration; she can be cold and undemonstrative. A good deal of compromise is needed here. But if both parties try hard and succeed, they will be immensely proud of and dedicated to each other.

DRAGON HUSBAND + TIGER WIFE

This is not a quiet, conventional and uneventful marriage. Both partners are progressive, pioneering and active. They could provide each other stimulating company provided they understand their basic individual need for freedom and expression. The Tiger wife may respect and adore her Dragon spouse but will never give up her identity. He will be in trouble if he tries to give her obedience training. Both are quick-tempered and will resist being dominated. If they can maintain a workable balance, they will enjoy an adventurous marriage.

DRAGON HUSBAND + RABBIT WIFE

She needs his strength and daring while he relies on her competence and companionship. The Dragon is forceful and outspoken; the Rabbit is indulgent but tactful. She will arrange an artistic and restful home for him. She is adaptable but moody and defenseless; he serves as her warrior and protector. This will be a good marriage if they strive for their common welfare, and do not allow petty or calculating concerns to interfere.

DRAGON HUSBAND + DRAGON WIFE

This will not be a very peaceful arrangement unless these two first agree on their goals. Both are individualistic, strong-willed and aggressive. Mrs. Dragon will not like to be overshadowed; in fact, she may be more assertive than he is. The masterful Mr. Dragon expects to be in control, but in this situation he may have to surrender some of his rights. Both partners would be wise to maintain their own careers to avoid suppressing the other.

DRAGON HUSBAND + SNAKE WIFE

A fulfilling and stimulating relationship will result if these two diverse personalities can adjust to each other. He is active, impulsive and domineering. She is sensual, unhurried and a lover of ease. As he is always geared to work and success, she can impart to him some of her tenacity and common sense. She may have a finer business acumen than he does; at the very least, she will handle the family finances well. They can both build a sound foundation for their life together.

DRAGON HUSBAND + HORSE WIFE

The Horse lady will be clever and resourceful enough to stretch whatever income Mr. Dragon brings home. But the serious-minded Dragon may find her too restless and downright indifferent about a steady diet of housework. Life will be more fruitful and delightful for both if they live in the city and Mrs. Horse keeps a job as well as manages the home. Actually, both parties perform better when provided with variety and freedom. The constantly aspiring Dragon will find his wife's practicality very profitable, while she depends on him to be strong and reliable.

DRAGON HUSBAND + SHEEP WIFE

This may not turn out to be such an appealing match, as they will live harmoniously only after much effort. He is adventurous and independent while she is ruled by her emotions and moods. She loves home and family but he may not care to be so domesticated. She cries easily and he finds it hard to express the sympathy and gentleness she craves. He is ambitious and decisive where she is artistic and intuitive. He is the knight in shining armor who will love helping a lady in distress—but not if she is going to make a habit of it.

DRAGON HUSBAND + MONKEY WIFE

This is an ideal match romantically and mentally. He is drawn to her magnetism and she admires his leadership. They are both ambitious and above-average performers. They will shine together beautifully. Combined, these two will look for new worlds to explore and conquer. Both are socially inclined and will probably maintain a beautiful home and entertain a good deal.

DRAGON HUSBAND + ROOSTER WIFE

This combination could achieve a great deal of togetherness but they will have to smooth out some rough edges first. Her discriminating but at times callous remarks could often deflate his towering ego. He is dynamic and full of energy while she is efficient, economical and critical. Both will be happier if they agree on what areas each should control. Intellectually, they are on equal levels, but they should not try to overpower one another with their accomplishments.

DRAGON HUSBAND + DOG WIFE

Many disputes will ensue because of the wide gap in this duo's basic temperaments. Both are aggressive and forceful but in different ways. He loves freedom and will act independently while she demands cooperation and unflagging loyalty. Subconsciously, each may be trying to attain the attributes of the other that he or she lacks. However, they don't have the first idea of how to go about it. Both signs are proud and willful when challenged. Neither will want to give in easily or lose face. A great many adjustments are needed in order for this marriage to work, perhaps too many.

DRAGON HUSBAND + BOAR WIFE

In this successful and stable union, the Boar wife will always encourage and support her ambitious Dragon mate. He is impulsive while she is patient and enduring. He is a fighter and she loves to be the peacemaker. They will have no trouble cooperating on the same goals. She will devote all her energy to whatever he undertakes. He can have the limelight so long as he makes her feel needed. He is the daredevil and she will uncomplainingly help him up every time he falls. Both will be intensely romantic.

SNAKE HUSBAND + RAT WIFE

This aspiring and covetous pair will never stop moving upward. Theirs could be a successful and profitable union provided they have the right attitude and agree on their priorities. The sociable and charming Rat wife will dote on her ambitious but introverted spouse, even though she craves more togetherness than he is prepared to give. However, both of these shrewd and resourceful parties should take care not to let petty jealousies impede their progress. Nor should they keep secrets from each other.

SNAKE HUSBAND + OX WIFE

Both parties here are cautious and selective and will find that they made a good decision in choosing the other. Both are down-to-earth, dignified, and share the same beliefs and driving ambition. He is tenacious and scheming; she is disciplined, orderly and protective of family and home. They can rely on each other in a crisis. In such a marriage as this one, the Snake will learn to confide in the tight-lipped Ox and she will stand by him against all adversities. They can look forward to a happy life together.

SNAKE HUSBAND + TIGER WIFE

This will be a difficult and upsetting relationship. Neither can understand nor overlook the other's frailties. Both signs are passionate and deeply suspicious. They cannot ever really trust each other. The Snake is refined, intellectual and constant. The Tiger wife is altruistic, lively and idealistic. The self-contained Snake finds her too unconventional, stimulating and outspoken. She, on the other hand, is resentful of his secretiveness, aloof behavior and intense ambition. They speak entirely different languages and cannot communicate.

SNAKE HUSBAND + RABBIT WIFE

The Snake is forceful and dominant and the well-bred Rabbit will be receptive to his way of thinking. Since they share the same exclusive and refined preferences, these two can achieve harmony both mentally and romantically. However, these signs are basically not very obliging. They may neglect each other in their search for self-expression and gratification of their desires. But the Rabbit is not as possessive as the Snake and will not be too upset if he gets wrapped up in his work and does not pay her much attention. She will be content so long as he provides her with a lovely home and pays all the bills. The result is a relatively peaceful combination.

SNAKE HUSBAND + DRAGON WIFE

He is loving but possessive and complicated. She is generous, open and excitable. He is careful and deliberate in his actions. She may have to struggle with him to put across her views. Some friction is bound to develop in the marriage, but secretly the Dragon female longs for someone wiser and more dominating than herself. The Snake will not only provide a stabilizing force for the union, he will also admire the ambition and enthusiasm of his Dragon wife. Together, they could surge forward with greater determination. This is a mutually helpful and constructive alliance.

SNAKE HUSBAND + SNAKE WIFE

Both will be on the same wavelength and communicate well, especially when involved with the same project. They won't cling to each other too much, as both are independent thinkers. In their search for power and success, they can be relentless and enduring. Their mutual ambitions usually bind them together. If jealousy does not get in the way, they could accomplish a great deal.

SNAKE HUSBAND + HORSE WIFE

Each has a different approach to life. He is cautious, tenacious and strong-willed—his goals are long-term. She is adventurous, mercurial and impatient—she cares more for the joys of the moment. He is consistent in his endeavors; she is impulsive, quick-witted and inconsistent. He finds her irresponsible and hard to keep up with, while she dislikes his serious, calm and deliberate mental deductions. This will not be a very satisfying union for either.

SNAKE HUSBAND + SHEEP WIFE

These two are companionable only to a certain extent. The lusty Snake may like to get wrapped around the object of his affections but won't like it when the Sheep clings to him indefinitely. He will feel trapped. The realistic and efficient Snake is basically an achiever. The Sheep is sensitive, sentimental and docile. He will sacrifice a great deal to realize his ambitions. She is self-indulgent and may be easily discouraged when the going gets rough. He is highly intelligent and she is highly emotional. They may find it hard to bridge the gaps in their relationship in times of difficulty.

SNAKE HUSBAND + MONKEY WIFE

These two will not get on well together at all. Their relationship will be a battle of wills and wits, as both are scheming and competitive. The Monkey could easily incite the Snake to anger, and since he is not forgiving he will retaliate swiftly. She is opportunistic, insensitive and competent enough to challenge him; he is equally ambitious, conniving and set on having his way. A tug-of-war might occur to determine who is smarter. Each seems to bring out the worst in the other. In this alliance, neither may reap any benefits in the end.

SNAKE HUSBAND + ROOSTER WIFE

These are two brainy, calculating and very performance-oriented signs who will prefer power and money in the bank to holding hands romantically in rags and poverty. She is the efficient and perfect housekeeper. He is the brains behind each financial deal. They will share the same dreams of prestige and material security. The Snake is philosophical enough to put up with the Rooster's rambling and eccentric ways. In the end, he will still rely on his innate wisdom to make a decision. On the other hand, she is happy that he understands her and allows her to let off steam and run his life to a certain extent. In this combination each will be able to expend energy productively; they will have a strong spiritual and mental affinity for each other.

SNAKE HUSBAND + DOG WIFE

The Snake is power-hungry, cool and deliberate in his actions. The Dog is affectionate, loyal and fair. They may have a mutual admiration for each other, but she will support him only to the extent her principles allow. He expects total commitment and adheres to the belief that the end justifies the means. Both have strong convictions. They may clash if she finds him straying from the righteous path. He feels he must make hay while the sun shines and cannot understand why her conscience is so easily offended. She is not materialistic and cannot comprehend his fascination with wealth and power. Their disapproval of some of each other's ways may prevent a close relationship.

SNAKE HUSBAND + BOAR WIFE

The Snake possesses unfailing determination and willpower. The Boar is easygoing and community-spirited. He feels she will not be able to understand him nor further his career because of her indulgent and compromising attitude toward others. He is mystical, sophisticated and deep. She is simple, trusting and naive. He finds her scruples unappealing and has no use for her goodwill unless there is a calculated motive behind it. She is incapable of deciphering his complex and doubting mind. The Snake can be aloof and does not care for the Boar's sweetness and sincerity, and the Boar's feelings will be hurt. Their diametrically opposed personalities cannot provide either with much happiness.

HORSE HUSBAND + RAT WIFE

He requires physical as well as mental freedom. She is levelheaded, industrious and affectionate. She will be content to stay in a close-knit family; he must constantly explore uncharted seas. She is resourceful and thrifty. He is adventurous, flirtatious and changeable. They will not see eye to eye on how things should be done because of the differences in their temperaments. The Rat views the Horse as selfish and inconsiderate. He finds her too bossy and possessive. After careful appraisal, neither may find the other appealing enough to join forces with permanently.

HORSE HUSBAND + OX WIFE

There is little prospect for a happy cohabitation here. He is too versatile, high-strung and outgoing for the organized, proper and dedicated Ox woman. He is always giddy with excitement and she is too sober to share his zest. He finds her very respectable but too undemonstrative and rigid. She feels she cannot depend on him because of his lighthearted and unpredictable moods. He finds her humorless and difficult to work or play with. Her man must be more disciplined and responsible. These two have very little in common.

HORSE HUSBAND + TIGER WIFE

There will be a unity of spirit between these two signs. They are bound to each other by the same animated, lively and passionate outlook on life. He is captivated by her vivacious personality and she is greatly attracted to his colorful, vibrant and self-assured demeanor. Both are active, affable and appealing. The Horse can manage to keep the money coming in and the Tiger is at her best as his radiant and charming hostess. Since they share the same philosophy, they will gravitate toward the same goals. Much togetherness can be achieved in this marriage.

HORSE HUSBAND + RABBIT WIFE

These two parties may not find accord because of the differences in their personalities. He is annoyed by her detached, cautious and impeccable ways. She can be affectionate, inspired and very personable once he can reassure her that he is a dedicated and capable provider and family man. But he does not care to have her or anyone else anchor all their hopes on him, so off he goes in whatever direction he pleases. No doubt he will perform well, but the tender Rabbit cannot tolerate uncertainty or insecurity. As a result, both will be discontented and unhappy.

HORSE HUSBAND + DRAGON WIFE

This will be a moderately rewarding partnership. He is versatile and ingenious while she is always enthusiastic about taking on new and exciting projects. If she is not engrossed in her own profession, the Dragon lady may want to apply her idealistic views and objectives to the ventures of her high-spirited, adventurous and equally outgoing spouse. He is perceptive enough to accurately assess their chances for success, while she is persuasive and powerful enough to deal with his inconsistencies. They will both lead a busy, roving life as neither is domestic enough to stay meekly at home.

HORSE HUSBAND + SNAKE WIFE

This is an unlikely match although both are mentally agile and realistic. But while he is mercurial and needs freedom and variety, she can be resistant to change and resentful of his rash and self-centered ways. She may be too determined, private and refined for his tastes, and in turn the Snake woman may not find the Horse's strong appetites consistent enough to be worth her while. Both have to be very unselfish to make this marriage work.

HORSE HUSBAND + HORSE WIFE

Teamwork and cooperation are possible because they work at similar speeds. It would be better if they were born in different seasons so as to provide more variety in their relationship. Both are passionate but independent and restless. Their witty, lively, materialistic and adventurous personalities may make life very hectic, but there is no guarantee they will get anywhere unless one is skillful enough to control the other. They may not be able to build a solid foundation for a home, as both are bored by routine and restrictions.

HORSE HUSBAND + SHEEP WIFE

She is delicate, sensitive and kind-hearted. He is cheerful and his practical nature will inject humor and purpose into her life. The Horse can be easygoing with the gentle Sheep, who is compassionate enough to overlook his selfishness if he can liven up her moods and teach her the quickest route around her self-magnified problems. He will be grateful for a pleasant and warm home and will find the Sheep cares enough for him to adjust her way of life to his needs. Each will complement the other and this could be a very happy marriage indeed.

HORSE HUSBAND + MONKEY WIFE

Both are adaptable and intelligent enough to leap over obstacles to their progress. But their very similarities may breed mutual contempt. Just as he is practical and opportunistic, she can be unscrupulous. She is versatile and adroit and he may irritate her with his shrewd and mercurial movements. The Monkey is bright and beguiling while the Horse is equally witty and persuasive. They may end up trying to con each other into submission.

HORSE HUSBAND + ROOSTER WIFE

This is an incongruous but sometimes workable arrangement. He is witty and skillful while she may be frank, knowledgeable and zealous. He could start something magnificent and then dash off when he gets bored. The efficient Rooster will complain and no doubt criticize his lack of dedication, but she will sort out the details and finish the job. He is too high-spirited and detached to be really annoyed by her outspoken and faultfinding ways. He may not even stay around long enough for her to finish the lecture. He is the colorful and vigorous performer and she is the most capable of administrators. Neither will be greatly disturbed by the faults of the other if they find their union productive enough.

HORSE HUSBAND + DOG WIFE

This can be a lasting and cooperative match. Both are animated and demonstrative persons who may find real joy in their union. The Dog is loyal, honest and sincere, and will pay attention to the Horse's excellent intuitions. She will be impressed by his intelligent, high-spirited and perceptive ways, while he loves her sense of humor, reason and logic. The Dog is realistic enough to understand and accept the Horse's shortcomings. As a result, he will not take offense at her curt but observant and straightforward manner.

HORSE HUSBAND + BOAR WIFE

He is persuasive, magnetic and appealing and will be able to convince the compromising and good-natured Boar to accede to his wishes. She is kind-hearted and, being sociably inclined, enjoys activities with the sportive Horse. Then again, being a devoted soul, she craves for more togetherness and affection than the self-centered Horse can provide. He, on the other hand, is not amused when she is too conforming and so considerate she pleases everyone else besides him. Each may have some difficulty coming to terms with the other's weaknesses.

SHEEP HUSBAND + RAT WIFE

Both are charming and capable of great warmth and tenderness but that is where the similarities end. The Rat wife is resourceful, inquisitive and hard-working. The Sheep husband is likely to take life too easy for his industrious spouse. She saves and treasures money, while he splurges and indulges his whims. She is alert, practical and levelheaded. He is creative but emotional and sometimes indolent. She can be fussy and faultfinding when irked. He finds her too shrewd and conniving to deal with. There may not be a great deal of give-and-take in this union since the partners have difficulty understanding each other.

SHEEP HUSBAND + OX WIFE

The Sheep is artistic and leisurely. He must savor and enjoy life as he pleases. Although the Ox lady is dutiful enough to keep house and take good care of her family, she will not relish his indulgent and impractical demands. But he must be loved and appreciated to bring out the best in him. Her emphasis on order and discipline will be too constricting for the Sheep. She is resolute and uncompromising and feels she must make optimum use of her time and energy. He is artistic and must wait for the right mood to strike him. She is impatient and scornful of his soft ways and he is thoroughly averse to regimentation and being pushed around. Drastic compromises are needed for this pair to cohabit peacefully.

SHEEP HUSBAND + TIGER WIFE

The Sheep is a domestic soul and needs affection and understanding. The Tiger lady is temperamental and unconventional. He is easily hurt by her sudden bursts of fury and dramatic scenes. A genteel soul, he needs a quiet and comfortable home. She prefers a fast life and cannot tolerate his unhurried and worrying ways. She is too strong for his liking; he is too weak to handle her effectively. Both may end up dissatisfied in this combination.

SHEEP HUSBAND + RABBIT WIFE

These two personalities may be compatible to a high degree. If the astute and inscrutably suave Rabbit wife takes the lead, she can help the Sheep achieve great things with his inherent talents. The Rabbit is suitably gentle for the sentimental and, at times, passive Sheep; but she is also decisive and shrewd where he tends to be too generous or compassionate. She will provide him with the right environment to work in, and he will be grateful for her guidance and subtle way of steering him onto the right path. Both are sensitive to and solicitous of each other's moods. In this marriage, they could accumulate more than just love and happiness.

SHEEP HUSBAND + DRAGON WIFE

This will be a moderately workable arrangement. The Sheep might be fascinated by the Dragon's brilliance and dominant ways. She, on the other hand, could be drawn to his kindness, devotion and sincerity. On the darker side, the Sheep may be too timid to go along with the Dragon's super-ambitious undertakings, and she may find him too reserved and unadventurous to suit her. He will be able to depend on her for encouragement, but she could push him beyond his level of endurance. Each will have a trying time in this union.

SHEEP HUSBAND + SNAKE WIFE

Things will not be completely idyllic in this marriage, but it could work out if each party makes a sincere effort. Both are materialistic and receptive to beauty and refinement; these characteristics could seal their union. However, the Sheep lacks the perseverance of the scheming Snake. She, on the other hand, could be too secretive and distrustful for the sensitive Sheep to tolerate. She is calculating and guided by her wisdom while he is emotional and led by his artistic inclinations. They will occasionally disapprove of each other's behavior but still find much they can agree upon. The Snake's unfaltering determination could be a valuable asset for the Sheep to cling to.

SHEEP HUSBAND + HORSE WIFE

He is domesticated and home-loving and will provide a secure base for the freedom-loving Horse lady. And her happy and affable nature will counterbalance his depressed moods. He may be jealous and possessive while she is independent and impulsive. But the Horse will not take the Sheep's self-pitying ways too seriously. She is capable, delightful and quick at sensing delicate signals. He could curb her restless ways by providing her with enough variety and attractive options to stay and spice up his life. This could be a strong and possibly enduring marriage.

SHEEP HUSBAND + SHEEP WIFE

The Sheep cares deeply for the welfare of his family, but in this combination the Sheep wife may turn out to be the stronger of the two. Both love luxury and dependency too much, but they could succeed as a unit if they combine their strengths. He will assume responsibility when there is no one else around to do so, and she loves to be the power behind the scene. Both are good homemakers and compassionate enough to put up with each other's weak points. They should be careful about being too protective or indulgent with their children.

SHEEP HUSBAND + MONKEY WIFE

There is no deep or permanent attraction here, as the Monkey is too complicated and egotistical for the Sheep. Because he is so much more subdued in taste and action, all her expertise and craftiness will only upset and annoy him. He cannot keep up with her inconsiderate demands no matter how good-natured and obliging he may be. She is clever and appealing and will use his weak points to manipulate him.

He is creative, pure-minded and compassionate, but these qualities will go unappreciated since the Monkey prefers someone who is more shrewd and conniving.

SHEEP HUSBAND + ROOSTER WIFE

He is kind-hearted and considerate enough to make a sincere effort at anything. She loves to investigate, analyze and administer other people's lives. He is pessimistic and subjective; she is optimistic and objective. Her energetic and fearless attitude could intimidate the sensitive and unobtrusive Sheep. He finds her too meticulous, argumentative and sharp for his taste. She, on the other hand, will say it is difficult to deal with someone so sentimental and self-indulgent. They have vast dissimilarities in their basic outlooks, which may prevent them from enduring each other's peculiarities easily.

SHEEP HUSBAND + DOG WIFE

This relationship will probably not work because the realistic Dog will naturally criticize the Sheep's indulgence and enumerate his weaknesses, making him more pessimistic than ever. While she is reasonable and affectionate, she is not always willing to tell the little white lies necessary to placate the Sheep's touchy feelings. He needs a lot of compassion and support to be able to put his best foot forward. But the unsympathetic and hardy Dog can be irked by his complaints and self-gratification. There is not much congeniality to go around as each tends to bring out the other's negative traits.

SHEEP HUSBAND + BOAR WIFE

A sound marriage will result because of the obvious lack of friction. Neither minds making concessions and both prefer activities centered around the home. The Boar is gregarious and not as sensitive as the Sheep, who may take offense easily because of his reticent nature. She is less extravagant too, and could be more sociable and outgoing, thereby reducing his shyness. On the other hand, he can make up for her lack of refinement and is responsive to her ardent need for warmth and togetherness.

MONKEY HUSBAND + RAT WIFE

These two partners will work most constructively together. She is a happy and competent homemaker, while he is the great strategist she will be immensely proud of. The Rat could get the enchanting Monkey to settle down nicely and he will adore her industry and thrift. They will be constantly discovering desirable qualities in each other, and their marriage will be rewarding, fulfilling and financially auspicious.

MONKEY HUSBAND + OX WIFE

These natives are too egotistical and forceful to coexist happily. He is an extrovert, a natural showman. She is an introvert and reticent. No doubt both parties have excellent positive sides, but they may not have a chance to display them. He has an innate superiority complex and considers her dull and unimaginative. But the blunt and proud Ox will not mince words when it comes to pointing out his flaws. Both will have to exercise great control to achieve any kind of rapport.

MONKEY HUSBAND + TIGER WIFE

This is not a very harmonious combination and these two may not find much happiness in their union. Both are allergic to restraints of any kind and do not like playing second fiddle to anyone. They are both apt to think only in terms of "I" and are goaded by strong ambition and self-esteem. The Tiger can be arrogant when not given her way and the Monkey is naturally smooth and cunning in his undertakings. Each could have doubts and secret reservations about the other. One has to be more masterful in order to control the other. As a result, there may always be a struggle between them.

MONKEY HUSBAND + RABBIT WIFE

He is a positive and innovative thinker and a captivating performer. She is personable and well-mannered, although somewhat superficial. Both can be diplomatic and secretive when it comes to gaining their objectives. The Monkey needs a lot of attention and compliments to keep him charming and companionable. The Rabbit is drawn toward quiet surroundings rather than active pursuits. He delights in controversy; she abhors dissent. They have totally different approaches toward life. However, both are realistic and will either make adjustments in their relationship or seek another solution.

MONKEY HUSBAND + DRAGON WIFE

This is one of the best matches, as both will be able to harness their positive forces and achieve lasting unity and success together. Each is aware, aggressive and very ambitious. The Monkey is practical and crafty, while the Dragon possesses more than enough willpower and energy for two. He will plan while she will set their goals higher each time. He loves challenges and she reassures him by backing him through thick and thin. Both will indulge the other, exchange ideas and work in harmony.

MONKEY HUSBAND + SNAKE WIFE

Each may tend to magnify the frailties of the other. He is lively, outgoing and enterprising while she is persevering, ambitious and sophisticated. No doubt they are in the same big league but they cannot help challenging, and at times opposing, each other because of their natural jealousy and innate suspicious inclinations. Both may have to make an effort to be sincere and straightforward before they can feel comfortable with the other.

MONKEY HUSBAND + HORSE WIFE

Both partners in this union are versatile, flexible and outgoing. Whether they can coexist in a spirit of goodwill will depend largely on their ability to control their self-centered personalities. Neither is long on endurance, and they will not persevere in working out their differences if one finds the other lagging behind. They are both independent and practical individuals who can cooperate if they want to, as they possess the same quick mind and keen faculties.

MONKEY HUSBAND + SHEEP WIFE

The Sheep lady loves to play house, but she may make too many demands on the wily Monkey. He may be flattered by her attentiveness but still finds her flaws outweighing her virtues. She, on the other hand, is no match for the calculating and evasive Monkey, who may not always take her seriously. The Sheep stands to lose more in this relationship, as the Monkey will exploit her kind and generous nature. Unfortunately, each of them is on a different wavelength.

MONKEY HUSBAND + MONKEY WIFE

This combination could be binding as long as envy does not get in the way. If these two can think in terms of "we" instead of "I," they can achieve much together. No problem will be too great when met in the spirit of true cooperation. Monkeys can rise above pettiness and jealousy by learning to share the good with the bad. These two could live in harmony provided they remain loyal and do not blame each other in the face of adversity.

MONKEY HUSBAND + ROOSTER WIFE

These two ambitious, materialistic and similarly powerful personalities may clash more often than they cooperate. Both crave acclaim and recognition. The Monkey man likes to get things done with a minimum of fuss and supervision. He prides himself on his ingenuity and innate capabilities. The Rooster girl is efficient and fastidious. She's prone to second-guessing him and picking up on his imperfections. They try each other's patience and endurance. He cannot abide her questioning and love for argument. She finds him too cocksure and conceited to pay her much attention, let alone heed the advice she dishes out. Both will find the ride pretty rough unless they can admit to some of their inherent shortcomings and meet each other halfway.

MONKEY HUSBAND + DOG WIFE

These two can enjoy a good marriage since the partners are usually favorably disposed to each other. The Monkey is productive and generally intelligent and sociable. The Dog wife will be cooperative and congenial if he expresses a genuine desire to work together. He is apt to be more materialistic and ambitious than she and will be pleased if she does not try to overtake or outperform him. She, on the other hand, is captivated by the Monkey's many-sided personality. He finds her a strong and refreshingly unpretentious ally and advisor. But while the Dog loves the Monkey's talents, she could take a dim view of his negative traits and he may find her inspiring and fair-minded practices restricting at times. Overall, however, both are well-balanced enough to make the necessary compromises in this relationship.

MONKEY HUSBAND + BOAR WIFE

There may be a strong attraction in this combination, but the trials of everyday married life could wear it away. The Boar lady is prodding, energetic and staunchly devoted to her loved ones and her goals, but she often operates on blind faith, and in this case the Monkey cannot resist the urge to take advantage of her. She, on the other hand, benefits from his financial acumen and guile but is not impressed by his unscrupulous and opportunistic ways. He finds her overconscientious about spreading good will around. He could also resent her extravagant generosity at his expense. Both may need to make extra efforts to put up with each other's frailties.

ROOSTER HUSBAND + RAT WIFE

He is analytical and a perfectionist; she is stimulating, practical and quite brainy in her own right. He is bossy, dogmatic and prone to giving lectures. Her own resourcefulness and competence make her unwilling to follow his orders blindly and reluctant to accept criticism, and, when offended, she can be sharp and petty. It's clear to her that he lacks the sensitivity and warmth she seeks in a mate. This is not a promising match for either party—they tend to agitate each other unnecessarily.

ROOSTER HUSBAND + OX WIFE

These two will enjoy an excellent and lasting union. The Rooster is open, frank and brave and more than compensates for the Ox's reserve and restraint. He is also hard-working and serious enough to suit her love of dignity and prestige. His security-consciousness will also appeal to the steadfast and resolute Ox lady. In response to his sunny and optimistic ways, the Ox may become more demonstrative and productive. However, she is likely to be the prudent and down-to-earth one in this partnership, and in spite of his noisy and competent discourse, the Rooster will love to lean on his strong and noble Ox wife. They will find each other responsible and dedicated.

ROOSTER HUSBAND + TIGER WIFE

A turbulent and spicy marriage will result from this pairing. Both are active and progressive souls but they have wide differences in their personalities. He is too egotistical and eccentric for the colorful Tiger lady, and she is too much of a fighter to ever concede to his relentless and detailed criticisms. Under different circumstances these two may have an energetic and diligent partnership, but in this combination they are likely to be stubborn and petty.

ROOSTER HUSBAND + RABBIT WIFE

They are unlikely to find their ideal love with each other. Their personalities may clash strongly because both are vexed by each other's negative traits. He is outspoken, exacting and overzealous in his cutting criticism. She is an artistic and reticent intellectual who may be a bit self-indulgent and unwilling to work hard. When the industrious and ruthlessly efficient Rooster gets through with her, she may feel like a victim of the Inquisition. Needless to say, the Rabbit will be defiant and uncommunicative. The Rooster's lack of tact and indelicate ways are not intentional, but he cannot avoid hurting the Rabbit, who thrives on sympathy and consideration.

ROOSTER HUSBAND + DRAGON WIFE

In this excellent and productive marriage combination, the analytical and brainy Rooster will be drawn to the bold, bright personality of the purposeful Dragon lady. She will immediately recognize his inherent worth and intellectual prowess. Together they can succeed in all their aspirations. She is not one to be intimidated by his bossy aggressiveness. She can and will dismiss his loquaciousness with a shrug, as she is bound to have a few peculiarities of her own that he will have to bear. However, overall he finds her enthusiasm and energy boundless and exhilarating. And she will not resent his running her affairs provided he treats her as an equal and respects her opinions.

ROOSTER HUSBAND + SNAKE WIFE

This combination will be a prosperous one. The exuberant and intrepid Rooster man could brighten up the Snake's solemn outlook and bolster her spirits as well. Both are intellectuals but in different ways. She is serene, reflective and deliberate; he is overcharged with zeal and dauntless optimism. This union provides them with the opportunity to balance the scales by offsetting each other's excesses.

ROOSTER HUSBAND + HORSE WIFE

A smooth marriage is not likely because these two strong-minded individuals are so easily irritated by each other. The provocative and undiplomatic Rooster will castigate the Horse for her high living and flightiness. But she is too sophisticated, witty and flamboyant to settle for the simple and hard-working life he has planned. The Rooster may have grandiose ideas, but his methods are dependable and precise. The Horse may be more practical and realistic about her goals, but she is unpredictable and inconsistent in her methods. He cannot comprehend her changeable ways and she cannot abide his strict routine and obsession with facts and figures.

ROOSTER HUSBAND + SHEEP WIFE

The tough-minded Rooster has the stamina to match his taste for work and achieving perfection. The Sheep is kind-hearted, emotional and dependent. He may patronize her need to cling, but won't put up with her self-pitying and indulgent ways. He can deal more easily with facts than with her tender feelings. She can understand his optimistic drive and ambition, but may find him too cold, calculating and particular. Genteel and easily hurt, she could pack up and go home to Mama if he censures her too much or too often. The tolerance factor in this combination is very low.

ROOSTER HUSBAND + MONKEY WIFE

This pairing is likely to result in a cool and defensive union unless both partners can alter their behavior. The Monkey could have the annoying habit of grabbing what she wants and hanging on to it, oblivious of how others may feel. The Rooster is too rigorous and exacting to let her get away with this. She is not amused by his skillful and parsimonious ways, nor impressed with his gift for oratory and debate. She possesses equal powers of rhetoric and will use them to provoke him. These two definitely tend to rub each other the wrong way, and will only cooperate when the inducement to do so is irresistible.

ROOSTER HUSBAND + ROOSTER WIFE

This match could provoke an unhealthy "holier than thou" competition between these two aggressively virtuous personalities. Both are peevish and often obsessed with their own views and will not pay much heed to the other's opinions. However, they are duty-oriented and have conscientious and responsible natures. Who knows, they may be able to relinquish some of their demanding ways to achieve common goals. Then again, both are argumentative and opinionated, and there may be endless discussions before they sign a peace treaty or agree to call a truce.

ROOSTER HUSBAND + DOG WIFE

Both parties here have fine minds, value their integrity and are self-assured. However, both are also very outspoken. If the Rooster starts to nag and grumble about the Dog's frailties, she could respond by throwing all attempts at harmony out the window and giving him some scalding rhetoric in return. Both have sharp tongues and could hurt the other quite painfully. A workable relationship is possible only if one of them is unselfish and sensible enough to induce the other to lay down his arms.

ROOSTER HUSBAND + BOAR WIFE

The trusting and easygoing Boar accepts things at face value and prefers to politely skim the surface rather than offend others. The Rooster makes pointed accusations; he is the unrelenting private eye who has to get to the root of the problem even if it means upsetting everyone's apple cart. The Boar is an independent thinker but is always receptive to suggestions; the Rooster is keenly observant of every detail. She would love to take his advice if only he could put a little sugar on it! However, she is also prone to being naive and easily imposed on by others, and therefore may have need of his sharp faculties. This could be the one steady common denominator of their marriage.

DOG HUSBAND + RAT WIFE

This union could develop fairly well if the parties have strong mutual interests. Both are sensible and outgoing and could find contentment because of the lack of friction in this marriage. She may be more affectionate and thrifty, but the Dog is reasonably easygoing and tactful enough to avoid bickering with her about unimportant issues. Both will try to give each other enough breathing space to ensure freedom of expression and movement.

DOG HUSBAND + OX WIFE

Both are faithful and loyal and will take their conjugal duties seriously. However, difficulties could arise from the Ox's overbearing attitude and rigid opinions. The Dog prefers free speech and equality and may not humor the narrow-minded Ox for too long. The Ox, on the other hand, may resent the Dog's overdirect and outspoken ways; she can nurse grievances for a long time. They both denounce pettiness and injustice, but are sometimes guilty of these faults themselves. To work, this relationship needs a lot of understanding and compromise from the partners.

DOG HUSBAND + TIGER WIFE

Both are idealistic by nature and have the same humanitarian interests. The Dog can be more objective and logical than the animated but hotheaded Tigress. He is thus able to advise her when she gets too emotional or impulsive. He is diplomatic and unbiased and will persuade her to see reason without touching any of her sensitive spots. The Tiger, on the other hand, is demonstrative, affectionate and honest, which the Dog likes, and her sanguine disposition could liven up any relationship. As a result, these two will feel completely at ease with each other. This admirably well-suited match should enhance this couple's unpretentious and generous personalities, and bring out the best in both of them.

DOG HUSBAND + RABBIT WIFE

This will be a good and enduring match. The Rabbit is imaginative, charming and diplomatic. The Dog is straightforward and agreeable in manner. Both enjoy honest fun and entertainment, but will prefer activities that have a useful purpose. They have innately cooperative spirits and will allow each other a fair degree of independence and assertiveness. She has a strong need for comfort and luxury, while he is less materialistic and more understanding. Both will have little difficulty in putting up with each other's peculiarities. This union should bring out the best in each partner.

DOG HUSBAND + DRAGON WIFE

They may have the wrong chemistry for each other as their basic dispositions are uncomplimentary. Both possess leadership abilities but in totally different directions. The Dog thrives on cooperation and may resent the Dragon's audacious, high-handed and overpowering tactics. She may find him taciturn and erratic if she pushes him too much; the Dog has a reputation for being pugnacious and acidly sharp when hurt. Neither can conform easily to the other's wishes and, at its best, this could only be a love-hate relationship.

DOG HUSBAND + SNAKE WIFE

He is level-headed and open-minded but may still be puzzled by her mystique. She has a fair respect for his intelligence but is inclined toward more sophistication and luxury than the unmaterialistic Dog can endure. Both lack the proper understanding to ever be totally enchanted with each other's personality, but they may be realistic enough to have an amicable life together if each can accept the other for what he or she is.

DOG HUSBAND + HORSE WIFE

This will be a happy and fruitful match, as these two people have a sound understanding of each other's needs and deficiencies. The Dog is honorable and intelligent enough to work well with the capable Horse. He also admires her keen sense of timing and strategy, while she finds him reasonable, practical and dependable. They will both get the cooperation they seek and still be able to enjoy the degree of individualism and independence they require.

DOG HUSBAND + SHEEP WIFE

Because they may have either strong or weak conflicts of interest, this union will make both partners less amiable than they normally are. The wistful ways of the sentimental Sheep will only irritate the logical Dog, who will be more curt and impatient than sympathetic. She is tolerant and unselfish when handled correctly, but in this case she may become withdrawn and dejected by the Dog's hardy and direct manner. In the final analysis, both may find that they have too little in common to bear the strain of their very different personalities.

DOG HUSBAND + MONKEY WIFE

This can be a workable and fairly positive match if these partners are generous and forgiving enough to discount each other's frailties. The Monkey wife will admire the Dog for his sensible approach and logical outlook; no one appreciates the value of intelligence more than she. He, on the other hand, sees her as a capable go-getter and will bask in her witty and charming personality. She is the more materialistic of the two, he the more idealistic. She values tangible wealth; he puts his principles first. Nevertheless, together they could contentedly travel right down the middle of the road.

DOG HUSBAND + ROOSTER WIFE

A cool to moderate coexistence is in store for this couple. Both are discriminating and forthright souls who may be easily displeased with each other's faults. Normally, they strive hard to be agreeable, but this match could bring out their most offensive traits, making them willful and uncompromising. Both are too quick to retaliate when challenged and can be fierce fighters. The Dog is pleasant and easygoing only as long as you keep out of his hair. The Rooster is virtuous and equally sincere in her efforts, but she has much too rigid an outlook to suit the Dog. She will make him feel like she is out to reform him and he will never tolerate that.

DOG HUSBAND + DOG WIFE

These two are reasonably compatible. After all, they have the same warm and stable nature, although the female of the species may be the more outspoken and critical one. This idealistic and conscientious couple will seek and value each other's opinions. Dogs are conformists when it comes to marital relationships and will perform well when they desire harmony and equality at home. There should be no major problems in this union provided they consult and respect each other. This couple should always make joint decisions as neither can tolerate being left out.

DOG HUSBAND + BOAR WIFE

This couple may have quite dissimilar personalities but could still maintain a fairly agreeable relationship. He is dependable and sharp enough for her to rely on, while she is loving, uncomplaining and affectionate enough for him to enjoy a comfortable feeling of togetherness. They are not averse to mutual concessions and will share whatever they have with each other. Their union will be happy because neither will need to harp on the other's weaknesses.

BOAR HUSBAND + RAT WIFE

There is a good measure of attraction between these two and they will strive to have a companionable and peaceful relationship. Both are outgoing, sociable and energetic and will probably center their life around their home, friends and mutual interests, all of which will include a good deal of entertaining. This couple will be drawn to active pursuits and have definite ideas about their involvements. She could be the more sensitive and prudent of the two, while he is positive but too conciliatory at times for his own good. He may have need of her wise counsel.

BOAR HUSBAND + OX WIFE

This is an acceptable union, but unlikely to be a strong one. The different outlook and behavioral patterns of these two partners will engender underlying friction. As a rule the Boar is warm, generous and understanding, but the Ox lady may only notice his sensuality and love of extravagance and find him too immoderate for her needs. On the other side, the Ox's predilection for hard work and constant security and self-discipline may unnerve the Boar. He is jovial, gregarious and open, and he works only to ensure his leisure. She is serious, systematic and rigid and finds contentment in her labors.

BOAR HUSBAND + TIGER WIFE

This will be a warm and gratifying union, as each side has a strong desire to please the other. Both are affectionate, dynamic and progressive in their basic attitude and will nicely complement each other. The Boar is kind and understanding enough to cope with the unpredictable moods of the Tiger, while she finds him devoted, courageous and unselfish. The Tiger is usually repentant for her outbursts when she meets no opposition, and the Boar's good humor and compassionate ways will bring out the best in her and make her more compliant to his wishes.

BOAR HUSBAND + RABBIT WIFE   *Ken & Nat*

The Boar's courage and dedication please the quiet and well-mannered Rabbit. She is sagacious, resilient and subtle, and will impart some of her astuteness to him without his noticing. He finds her kind and cautious and will lavish on her both his affections and the luxuries she likes. The Boar is selfless enough not to seek more than the Rabbit can give and she will be happy to be the object of his attentions and generosity. Both could feel enriched by this union.

BOAR HUSBAND + DRAGON WIFE

In this fairly successful relationship, the gains will probably outweigh the losses. Both signs are ardent and forceful, although in different ways. The powerful Dragon wife could stimulate any spouse into action or break him in the process. The Boar is not averse to bending to the desires of his loved one and will be tireless in his efforts to achieve success and win her approval. They are evenly matched in energy and love of physical exertion. Their mutual flaw is that they are both too responsive to stimuli and could be easily carried away by their enthusiasm and excesses. There may be no one to apply the brakes.

BOAR HUSBAND + SNAKE WIFE

The aesthetic Snake cannot abide the Boar's sincere but mundane and simple ways. He finds her too complex and secretive. The Snake is too highly evolved, ambitious and profound for the overindulgent and trusting Boar. She will not approve of his open and easygoing ways and will be aloof and unsympathetic to him. The Boar, in turn, will find the Snake's uncommunicative and coldly calculating attitude very disconcerting. Both will suffer from unfulfilled expectations and will lack appreciation of each other's positive traits.

BOAR HUSBAND + HORSE WIFE

Both signs are pleasure seekers with very sociable personalities; they could benefit each other to a certain extent. She is imaginative and resourceful while he is dependable and good-natured. The Boar admires the Horse's animated and cheerful ways, and she finds his devotion and honest fortitude very pleasing. Because both understand the value of compromise, they will have an active and involved marriage, but without stepping on each other's toes. They will, however, opt to live their lives to the fullest. On the darker side, neither party will worry too much about tomorrow.

BOAR HUSBAND + SHEEP WIFE

In this warm, intimate marriage, both will give their best to the union and have a deep love and genuine concern for the other. The Boar is sturdy, gallant and thoughtful enough to please the gentle and compassionate Sheep lady. She, on the other hand, will mother him as well as make him the object of her worship. The sensual and simple Boar will interpret her possessiveness as true love and devotion. He is generous and protective too, so the Sheep will be able to perform at her best, something she can do only when she knows she is loved and appreciated, as she will be in this union.

BOAR HUSBAND + MONKEY WIFE

This will be a fairly civil union, but the partners may not be very fascinated by each other. The Boar is too straightforward and scrupulous for the complicated Monkey. She has more pungent tastes and the Boar will definitely be too bland. On the other hand, while the Monkey is deviously charming, her complexity and pretentiousness may prove too much for him. Both are bound to be irritated and bruised by the incapacities of the other. Still, they could make a go of this match if they can figure each other out and concentrate on their positive qualities.

BOAR HUSBAND + ROOSTER WIFE

If both parties make the proper concessions, this could turn out to be a feasible match. There will be areas of disagreement, but both have the capacity to work out differences if they admire the other enough. The Boar may be too passionate and warm for the analytical and mentally inclined Rooster; she is too argumentative and knowledge-able to follow or love him blindly. However, on the positive side, nei-ther is too thin-skinned and criticism will affect them like water run-ning off a duck's back. The honest and accommodating Boar has a true need for the Rooster's diligent and critical mind, and, although she is capable and self-confident, she will need the affable Boar's diplomacy and reliability.

BOAR HUSBAND + DOG WIFE

These two will enjoy a kind and agreeable relationship despite their differing attitudes toward life. Both are robust, open and honest and like doing their best whenever possible. However, the Dog can be aggressive and will not withhold her criticism if the Boar is too self-indulgent or lax in his duties. She is not as passionate as he, and may lack understanding of his large appetites and sensuality. Still, they may be able to find a common ground for cooperation. The Dog has more insight than the Boar and will be loyal to him. And the Boar is toler-ant and generous enough to forgive the Dog's peculiarities and see her as the trustworthy and noble ally she is.

BOAR HUSBAND + BOAR WIFE

This combination could work out well if the partners are able to take the good with the bad. Being born under the sign of the Boar, both of them will be strong, courageous and modest, but they may lack direction and tenacity and may not be able to shore up each other's weak points. Sincerity and goodwill without resolute and sys-tematic organization could wreak havoc for two such well-meaning people. One of them will have to be unemotional and disciplined to cope with reality as well as adversity, otherwise their mutual love and loyalty will not be much protection for them.

Index